AN INDEX TO THE
WILL BOOKS AND INTESTATE RECORDS OF
LANCASTER COUNTY, PENNSYLVANIA

1729–1850

SECOND COURT HOUSE IN PENN SQUARE, LANCASTER

Erected 1784–87; taken down in May, 1853

Pennsylvania State House from 1799 to 1812. Occupied site of earlier Court House in which important treaties with the Indians were made; also where Continental Congress met in September, 1777, and the Supreme Executive Council, from October 1, 1777, to June 28, 1778.

AN INDEX

TO THE

Will Books and Intestate Records

OF

Lancaster County, Pennsylvania

1729 - 1850

WITH AN

HISTORICAL SKETCH

AND

CLASSIFIED BIBLIOGRAPHY

PREPARED BY

ELEANORE JANE FULTON AND BARBARA KENDIG MYLIN

CLEARFIELD

Reprinted for
Clearfield Company, Inc. by
Genealogical Publishing Co., Inc.
Baltimore, Maryland
2005

Originally Published: Lancaster, Pennsylvania, 1936
Reprinted: Genealogical Publishing Co., Inc.
Baltimore, 1973, 1974, 1981, 1987, 1994
Library of Congress Catalogue Card Number 72-10550
International Standard Book Number 0-8063-0535-5
Made in the United States of America

THE PUBLISHERS

Eleanore Jane Fulton, born in Lancaster, Pennsylvania, daughter of Hugh Ramsey Fulton, Esq., and Sarah Thompson Kerr. Graduate Lancaster High School 1899, and Millersville State Normal School, 1901 and '02. Majored in Anthropology at the University of New Mexico, summer 1929; Univ. of Arizona, 1929 and '30; Univ. of Colorado, 2d term, summer session of 1930; Denver University, A.B., 1931, and election to Delta Epsilon, honorary scientific fraternity; graduate student at Univ. of California, 1931 and '32.

Member N.S.D.A.R., N.S.U.S.D. of 1812, Huguenot Society of Pennsylvania, Lancaster County Historical Society, American Association of Univ. Women, American Association for the Advancement of Science.

Barbara Kendig Mylin, born in Lancaster County, Pennsylvania, daughter of Hon. Amos Herr Mylin and Caroline Emily Hepburn Powell. Graduate of Millersville State Normal School, 1904; formerly Assistant Principal Lititz (Penna.) High School, 1909; Girls' Grammar School, Camden, N.J., 1909-19; private secretary since 1924.

Member Institute of American Genealogy, Lancaster County Historical Society, Pennsylvania German Society.

CONESTOGA WAGON

Invented in Lancaster County, Pennsylvania

"The Prairie Schooner"   "The Ship of Inland Commerce"

FOREWORD

The original Register of Wills(1729-1826)given to us by "Uncle Dan" Kachel, was the inspiration for this publication. Later, after genealogical committees of Donegal Chapter, N.S.D.A.R., had copied the Index to both Will Books and Intestate Records down to 1850, we obtained permission from the Board of Management, for a consideration, to put this valuable material into print. We found it necessary to check up with the Court House records, to correct errors and supply omissions. Certain omissions in the Court House records were learned to be due to the fact that some of the Wills could not be copied until deciphered or translated from the German. When later some of these were done, they were entered in Vol.II of Will Books X and Y.

The Wills of those persons who died in this region prior to the erection of Lancaster County (May 10, 1729) are registered in the Chester County Court House at West Chester, the County Seat since September 25, 1786, when they were removed from old Chester. There are no Orphans Court records prior to 1740.

Typed or photostatic copies of Wills may be obtained by writing to the Office of the Register of Wills.

We have thought to make this volume more interesting and far more valuable by putting "flesh on the bones" - in other words, precede the Index with a brief review of these early inhabitants and their settlements. Their attainments and accomplishments, varied and notable, are suggested in the extensive though by no means exhaustive bibliography.

We wish here to express our appreciation for the advice and suggestions given us by Dr. G. M. Brumbaugh of the National Genealogical Society, and Dr. Jean Stephenson, National Chairman of the Committee on Genealogical Records of the Daughters of the American Revolution, both of Washington, D.C. And we wish to thank Mrs. Charles M. Coldren, genealogist, of Lancaster, Penna., for her valuable assistance in solving some of the mysteries in the Court House records and in the selection of a comprehensive bibliography; also Mr. M. Luther Heisey, librarian of the Lancaster County Historical Society, for his graciousness in permitting us the use of the library and lending us plates for the illustrations.

The Publishers

LANCASTER COUNTY, PENNSYLVANIA

This was a long-time home of the Indian. Here in the forest primeval he hunted wild game, and in the productive valley lands of many streams he grew corn and tobacco; while along the great waterway of the picturesque Susquehanna, restless nomads ceaselessly moved northward and southward. Inhabiting this region were the Susquehannocks, the Shawanese, the Ganawese or Conoys, the Nanticokes, and the Lenni Lenapes or Delaware Indians[1]. They called this, their home, "Chanastocka," or Conestogoe, said to signify "the great magic land,"[2] expressing the same rapture over its beauty and fertility as did their white successors who named portions of it "Paradise" and "Eden." It was natural for Penn's followers to refer to the Indians of Conestogoe as "Conestogoes," though the term was locally applied to a small group, remnants of several tribes who lived on the Conestoga flats below Lancaster. It was this group which concluded with William Penn a treaty[3] "to endure as long as the sun should shine or the waters run into the rivers."

Throughout the seventeenth century there came into this region explorers, adventurers and traders -- French[4], English[5], Dutch[6], Swedes[7], and Finns[8] -- most of whom passed on.

In 1681 William Penn was granted by King Charles II all this area of land now known as Pennsylvania, in payment of a 16,000 pounds debt owing to his father, Admiral Penn, and immediately he began plans for its colonization[9]. Documents show that he was greatly attracted to the region of the Susquehanna at the mouth of the Conestoga, and considered it a suitable place for a great Capital City. Later the site of Philadelphia on the Delaware was chosen, but Penn, still retaining his interest in the Susquehanna-Conestoga tract, gave orders that 16,000 acres be reserved for him, his heirs and assigns forever[10]. Conditions changed in the years that followed, and "Conestoga Manor" which might have been the great landed estate of the Proprietary and Governor-in-Chief of the Province, was divided into farms and gardens and is one of the most productive areas of the "Garden Spot".

Before the end of the seventeenth century Penn's Land was beckoning to the oppressed of the Old World, and ships were bringing into the port of Philadelphia passengers bent on founding for themselves new homes in this land of religious and political freedom. They soon spread over the three original counties of Philadelphia, Bucks and Chester, and then reached out into the Conestoga country -- English and Welsh Quakers, Swiss Mennonites, French Huguenots, Scotch-Irish Presbyterians, Germans from the Palatinate, and English and Welsh Episcopalians. [11]

---

1. Eshleman, Lancaster County Indians.
2. Dubbs, The Names of the Townships. L.C.H.S.Pub., Vol.I, p.6
3. Colonial Records, Vol.II, pp.15-18; Penna.Archives, Vol.I, p.144
4. Jesuit Relations, Vol.V, p.291, note.
5. Captaine John Smith, Generall Historie of Virginia, Vol.I, p.114
6. Watson's Annals, Vol.I, pp. 3,4,6.
7. Acrelius' New Sweden, pp. 23,43,47.
8. Hazard's Register, Vol.V, p.130.
9. Proud, History of Pennsylvania, Vol.I, p.170 et seq.
10. Diffenderffer, Early Local History Revealed by an Old Document. L.C.H.S. Pub., Vol.II, p.3 et seq. Sachse, Penn's City on the Susquehanna, L.C.H.S. Pub., Vol.II, p.223.
11. Klein, Lancaster County, Pennsylvania, pp.15,16.

For the Quaker, first of all, Penn's "Holy Experiment" was a haven of refuge[12]. From England and Wales they came, settling in great numbers in Chester County, then over into the wilds beyond. The records show that the first deed to land in what is now Lancaster County was granted to John Kennerley in 1691. This "William Penn Deed" was for 375 acres in what is now Sadsbury Township, near Christiana[13].

It is also known that Quakers came from the Nottinghams into Little Britain Township at a very early date. Within a few years they were firmly established throughout the Octorara and Conowingo valleys[14]. Some continued up the Susquehanna under the leadership of John Wright, who in 1730 procured a patent for a ferry, and soon "Wright's Ferry", at the site of Columbia, became the great gateway to the West[15]. The Quakers, or Friends, were especially prominent in the political affairs of the county during provincial times. They have been characterized by their "plain living and high thinking", their vigorous intellectuality and a well developed sense of moral responsibility. They were bitterly opposed to slavery and gave protection to runaway slaves[16]. For years they were leaders in the temperance movement.

It is to the Swiss Mennonites, followers of Menno Simon from the cantons of Berne and Zurick, however, to whom is given the credit for making the first permanent white settlement in what is now Lancaster County. Several families of these hardy pioneers took up a tract of 10,000 acres north of Pequea creek in what is now West Lampeter Township, on a warrant dated October 10,1710[17]. Here they settled under the pastoral care of their Bishop, Rev. Hans Herr, and soon one of their number, Martin Kendig, was sent back to the Rhineland for other kinsmen. Here they put into practise the German methods of farming they had learned during their sojourn in the Rhine Valley, and it is to these Swiss and Germans from the Palatinate that Lancaster County is largely indebted for making of it the richest agricultural county in the United States. Though the Mennonites have never participated in any of the wars in which this country has been engaged, they have willingly and generously contributed at their Nation's call in times of distress in war, flood or famine. These early settlers have been well characterized by Lloyd Mifflin in his sonnet[18]:

THE PIONEER OF PEACE: THE MENNONITE FARMER

Like some great patriarch of old he stands
    Among the sheaves - far from the town's embroil -
    Bearded and grey, true sovereign of the soil;
    A later Boaz, at whose wise commands
The harvest turns to gold. Lord of wide lands,
    Mellowed by cycles of unending moil,
    He typifies the dignity of toil,
    As earth attests the power of his hands.

Driven by persecution to our shore,
    A man of peace and Christian tolerance rare,
    With tranquil faith he thro' life's tumult goes,
Nor ever turns the needy from his door;
    While thro' the years of patient work and prayer
    He makes the valleys blossom as the rose.

12. Proud, History of Penna., Introduction - Rise, Principles, Religious System and Practice, or Manners, of the Quakers who first Settled the Province, Under His Government.
13. Hensel, A William Penn Deed. L.C.H.S.Pub., Vol.I, p.117.
14. Magee, Early Settlement and History of Little Britain Township, Including Fulton Township. L.C.H.S. Pub., Vol. XVII, p.138.
15. Beck, H. H., Address at Unveiling of Bronze Tablet to John Wright,Pioneer Ferryman. L.C.H.S. Pub., Vol.XXXV, p.200.
16. Brubaker, The Underground Railroad. L.C.H.S. Pub., Vol.XV, p.95.
17. Eshleman, Annals of the Swiss and German Pioneers of S.E. Penna.
18. Mifflin, L.C.H.S. Pub., Vol. XIV, p.236.

ROBERT FULTON

Artist and Inventor—1765–1815

(From the painting by Benjamin West)

Born in Little Britain (now Fulton) Township,
Lancaster County, Pennsylvania

In 1791 he exhibited portraits in the Royal Academy, London
In 1807 he first successfully applied steam to navigation

A child of Lancaster, upon this land,
  Here was he born, by Conowingo's shade;
  Along these banks our youthful Fulton strayed,
Dreaming of Art. Then Science touched his hand,
  Leading him onward, when, beneath her wand,
  Wonders appeared that now shall never fade:
  He triumphed o'er the Winds, and swiftly made
The giant, Steam, subservient to command."
          Sonnet by Lloyd Mifflin

After the revocation of the Edict of Nantes by Louis XIV in
1685, half a million French Huguenots left the country. Penn's
colony not only welcomed them but encouraged their coming. In the
first group to reach this section were Maria Warenbauer, widow of
Daniel Ferree, or Fiere, and her three sons and three daughters,
one the wife of Isaac LeFevre. It was in 1711-12 that they came
into the Pequea Valley in what is now Paradise Township. Soon
after settling here, Philip Ferree married Leah DuBois of New
Paltz, New York - another important Huguenot community[19]. Since
then many more have come, contributing much to the happiness and
prosperity of our people because of such traits as gaiety and an
optimistic outlook on life, ingenuity and adaptability,tolerance,
unlimited energy, and efficiency at the handicrafts[20].

Scotch-Irish Presbyterians soon followed. Simultaneously with
the building of their homes they arranged for a place of worship.
There is tradition of a Presbyterian Society at Chestnut Level in
Drumore Township, in 1711, and evidence of an organization there
in 1717. Donegal Church was in existence in 1720, possibly even
as early as 1714; Pequea in 1724; and Middle Octorara in Bart
Township in 1727[21]. In connection with their church they established a school, and as most of the ministers were graduates of
Edinburgh, Glasgow or Dublin, they were well qualified to develop
these into classical schools of a high order, such as the Latin
school at Pequea, founded by Dr. Robert Smith in 1750, the Chestnut Level Academy, established by Dr. James Latta in 1771[22], and
the classical school at Donegal conducted by Rev.Colin McFarquhar
in 1776[22]. Such schools as these, taught by such learned men in
our neighboring counties, developed into Princeton and the University of Pennsylvania[23]. Because of a scholarly ministry and an
educated laity, Presbyterianism cultivated "an intellectual freedom which meant spiritual and political freedom[24]." Thus were
developed men and women of indomitable courage, ever ready to es-
pouse a cause which had for its purpose the removal of shackles
from body, mind or spirit. Of restless energy, the Scotch-Irish
guarded the frontier and pushed it farther and farther westward[25].
With a genius for organization, they took a peculiar interest in
"the construction of a country and the formation of a government"[26].

Germans from Hesse-Darmstadt settled in Martic Township about
1710[27], and Germans from the Palatinate came into the Townships
of Earl, West Earl and East Earl in 1717[28]. They were men and
women of a hardy type and the possessors of many virtues. Most of
them were of the Lutheran and Reformed persuasions, and they began early to establish churches and schools. One of the finest
contributions the Germans have made to this community and to the
country at large is Franklin and Marshall College, together with

19. Landis, Madam Mary Ferree and the Huguenots of Lancaster County. L.C.H.S.
        Pub., Vol.XXI, p.101 et seq.
20. Strassburger, The Huguenots: Their Rise and Their Settlement in America.
        (1927)
21. Clark, Rev. R.L., History of Westminster Presbytery, pp.253,277,410,380.
22. Risk, R.B., The Founding of Chestnut Level Academy.
23. Houston, Dr.J.W., Early Schools in the Valley of the Octorara. L.C.H.S.
        Pub., Vol.II, p.31 et seq.
24. Snowden, Hon. A.L., Address Before Penna. Scotch-Irish Society, 1903.
25. Hensel, The "Scotch-Irish" in Lancaster County, Pennsylvania. L.C.H.S.
        Pub., Vol.IX, p.246 et seq.
26. Magee, The Whitesides of Colerain. L.C.H.S. Pub., Vol.XVII, p.228.
27. Klein, Lancaster County, Penna., p.129.
28. Diffenderffer. The Three Earls, p.22.

the Academy and the Reformed Theological Seminary. From the time
when Franklin College was founded at the suggestion of Benjamin
Franklin, in 1787, - the third institution of higher learning
in the State - it has had a succession of learned men on its
faculty. Its first president, Dr. Henry E. Muhlenberg, the past-
or of Trinity Lutheran Church, was a profound scholar, an able
theologian, and excelled in the natural sciences, especially bot-
any, because of which he has been called the "American Linnaeus".
On the faculty at the same time was Dr. Melsheimer, professor of
Greek, Latin and German, who also acquired distinction as the
"Father of American Entomology". His collection is now a part of
the Agassiz museum of Harvard University[29].

A group of Germans settled on the Cocalico in 1732 under the
leadership of Conrad Beissel, a Lutheran who was influenced by
the Pietists of Heidelberg and initiated into the Rosicrucian Fraternity, and here formed the Ephratah Community, a mystical, semi-
monastic society[30]. These "Solitary Brethern" and "Spiritual
Virgins" observed the seventh day as their Sabbath and practiced
the rites of an occult philosophy. After a time their Cloisters
became centers of industry. Here was made much of the paper used
during the Revolution, and oil was pressed for printer's ink. By
1742-43 their book-bindery "was the largest and best equipped in
the colonies", and on their hand-press "some of the earliest and
most important American printing was done". Here the "Martyr
Book" was translated from the Dutch into German, and printed and
bound with leather and brass mountings. Wagon loads of unbound
copies were later requisitioned by Washington's armies and used
for wads in cannon[30].

In 1754 a Moravian settlement was made in Warwick Township and
named by Count Zinzendorf[31], its founder, Lititz, after a barony
in Bohemia. Here members lived under close "spiritual supervis-
ion" and "all the industrial and civic agencies were undertaken
by the church authorities or with their sanction." There was a
"tenacious clinging to early customs and regulations" until 1855,
when the lease system was abolished and "Lititz ceased to be an
enclusive settlement".[32] Lititz early became a musical center.
Here, in 1765, David Tanneberger began making organs, some of
which were described as "the best and largest in America." Here
was established a school for girls, which in 1794 became Linden
Hall Seminary, famed for the cultivation of "lady-like grace and
high moral purpose." Here also was the Lititz Academy for Boys,
conducted by John Beck for fifty years. In 1865 another private
school for boys was established by A. R. Beck, son of John Beck,
which was conducted for thirty years[33]. Here during Revolutionary days the Moravians cared for sick and wounded soldiers --
Continental, British and Hessian. Here in the Moravian Cemetery
is buried General Sutter, the discoverer of gold in California.

The Germans have given us many interesting customs, one being
known as the "Feast of Roses." Wilhelm Heinrich Stiegel, manager
of the Elizabeth iron works from about 1760, and the manufacturer
of the famous "Stiegel glass", gave to the Lutheran congregation
in Manheim a plot of ground on which he erected a church, in consideration of five shillings and a yearly rental of one red rose,

29. Klein, Lancaster County, Penna., p.1020 et seq.
30. Williams, E.M., The Monastic Orders of Provincial Ephrata.
       In Dr. Klein's History, pp.384-476.
31. Rupp, History of Lancaster County, p.283.
32. Klein, Lancaster County, Penna., p.242 et seq.
33. Ibid. pp.1008-1013.

WHEATLAND, LANCASTER, PA.— HOME OF JAMES BUCHANAN

Born April 23, 1791; died June 1, 1868

Congressman and Senator. Minister to Russia under President Jackson. Secretary of State under President Polk, Minister to England under President Pierce, and Fifteenth President of the United States

"if the same shall be lawfully demanded." This annual payment has developed into a beautiful ceremony at which not one rose but many are brought into the church each year.34

The English of the Established Church settled first in Pequea and Salisbury townships, where in 1729 they built "St.John's Pequay".35 Though the English have been greatly outnumbered by other nationalities, they have from very early days held prominent places in the political, legal and medical annals of the county. The second Episcopal Church of the county was built in 1733 at Bangor in Caernarvon Township by Welsh who had come over from the townships of Radnor and Haverford, in Chester County, about 1718 36. It is said of Churchtown that "in the days of the forges, it was a busy hive of industry. Tailors, hatmakers, cabinet and chairmakers, harness shops, blacksmiths, Conestoga wagon builders, and nearby fulling mills, gave employment to many persons, and an air of prosperity was evident to the traveller."37

As early as 1720 there were Jews in this vicinity trading with the Indians. In 1735 Joseph Simon came to Lancaster and soon was extending his enterprises as far as the Mississippi38. He was a broad-minded, public-spirited man who took part in the affairs of the town, county and province. He was frequently visited by his granddaughter, Rebecca Gratz, said to have been the inspiration of Sir Walter Scott's heroine Rebecca in "Ivanhoe".39

The foregoing gives an idea of the many distinct groups that first came into the region now known as Lancaster County. So rapidly did they come into this Conestoga region that in 1718 the section of Chester County west of the Octorara creek was erected into Conestoga Township. In 1720 the township was divided, and West Conestoga was made to include all the territory west of the Pequea creek. In 1721 Pequea Township was formed, which included the settlements along the Pequea. By 1722 West Conestoga Township became Donegal, named for that county in Ireland from which many of its settlers had come.40

Increasing population, the great distance from the County Seat at Chester, poor roads, lawlessness in Conestoga, and difficulty in collecting taxes, all made it imperative that a new county be formed. So it came about that on May 10, 1729, the "Upper Parts of the Province of Pennsylvania, lying towards Susquehanna, Conestogoe, Dunnegal, etc.," were erected into a new county and named LANCASTER by John Wright who had come from the shire of that name in England. Whereupon Lieutenant-Governor Gordon appointed the following as justices of the peace to constitute the first court: John Wright, Tobias Hendricks, Samuel Blunston, Andrew Cornish, Thomas Edwards, Caleb Pierce, Thomas Reed, and Samuel Jones. These magistrates sat at the tavern of John Postlethwaite on the "Great Conestoga Road" to confer "withthe most prominent inhabitants" on the names of the townships and their respective boundaries.41

34. Ibid., pp.259-262
35. "Vestry Book of St.John's Pequay"
36. Klein, Lancaster County, Penna., pp.122 et seq; pp.827,828
37. Lincoln, Dr.J.B., The Story of Caernarvon. L.C.H.S. Pub., Vol.XVIII, p.79
38. Hirsh, Early Jewish Colony in Lancaster County. L.C.H.S. Pub., Vol.V, p.91
39. Klein, Lancaster County, Penna., pp.860-864
40. Ibid., pp.16,17,54,55
41. Ibid., pp.17-21; 526, 527.

Here the Court sat during the August and November terms, 1729 and February, May and August of 1730[42], after which it was removed to Gibson's Tavern at Hickory Town, a favorite rendezvous of the Indians, and at this time a small community where Governor Hamilton owned considerable land, laid out a town site and offered a plot for the erection of public buildings. His offer was accepted, and Hickory Town became Lancaster the County Seat.[43]

The building of a Court House was commenced in 1731. It was described as a two-story brick structure. On or about June 9, 1784, it was destroyed by fire while undergoing repairs. In this first Court House, located in the center of Penn Square, many important scenes were enacted[44]. Here was held, in 1744, a council between the deputies from the "Six Nations" of the Iroquois Confederacy and Lieutenant-Governor George Thomas and Commissioners from Maryland and Virginia, with Conrad Weiser as interpreter and more than five hundred Indians attending. It was the most important council yet held in Pennsylvania, for by the terms of the treaty, "England secured the right to the Valley of the Ohio" and the English colonies were guarded against surprise by the French and their Indian allies.[45]

This first Court House was the "Capitol" of Pennsylvania at two different times[46] - first, for a few days beginning August 11, 1762[47], then from October 1, 1777, to June 28, 1778, when the Supreme Executive Council fled to Lancaster[48] at the approach of Howe's army into Philadelphia. Here during this time the first President of the Council, Thomas Wharton, Jr., died while in office, May 23, 1778, and lies interred in Trinity Lutheran Church.[49] At the same time, and for the same reason, the Continental Congress left Philadelphia and came to Lancaster[50]. On Saturday, September 27, 1777, they held a session here[51]. Many of the members were in Lancaster several days, gradually moving over the Susquehanna to York for greater safety.

After the burning of the first Court House in 1784, another one was erected and completed in 1787. It was a two-story brick structure, larger than the first and trimmed with cut stone. It was used until 1853, when the present one on East King Street was completed. This second building in Penn Square was also used as a State House for Pennsylvania - at this time from 1799 to 1812.[52] Thus Lancaster was three times the Capital of Pennsylvania, and for one day the Capital of the Nation. It was while the Legislature was meeting here that Thomas Mifflin, the first State Governor of Pennsylvania, died, and on January 22, 1800, was buried just outside the west wall of Trinity Lutheran Church. He was a signer of the Declaration of Independence and a Trustee of Franklin College.[53]

42. Landis, Postlethwaite's and Our First Courts. L.C.H.S., Vol.XIX, p.224 et seq.
43. Klein, Lancaster County, Penna., pp.55-57; 318,319; 867-870.
44. Eshleman, H.F., Great Historical Scenes Enacted in Lancaster's First Court House, 1739-1784. L.C.H.S. Pub., Vol.VII, p.177 et seq.
45. Mombert, History of Lancaster County. (App.), pp.58,67,68,78,81. Col.Rec. Vol.IV, p.698; Vol.V, p.307; Vol.VI, p.776.
46. Eshleman, H.F., Great Historical Scenes Enacted in Lancaster's First Court House, 1739-1784. L.C.H.S. Pub., Vol.VII, p.177 et seq.
47. Col.Rec., Vol.VIII, pp.721,730,734,749; Pa. Archives, 1760-1776, p.90.
48. Klein, Dr.H.M.J., Lancaster County, Penna., p.325.
49. Worner, W.F., Old Lancaster, pp.8-17.
50. Christopher Marshall's Diary, p.130.
51. Journal of Congress, Vol.II, pp.265,270,272,273.
52. Klein, Lancaster County, Penna., p.870.
53. Ibid., p.706.

LLOYD MIFFLIN, Artist and Poet —"America's Greatest Sonneteer"
Born in Columbia, Lancaster County, Pennsylvania, September 15, 1846
Died at "Norwood," Columbia, July 16, 1921

For a period of many years preceding 1800, Lancaster was the largest inland town in the country. Through the efforts of James Hamilton it was incorporated as a borough, May 1, 1742[54]. It was chartered as a city, March 20, 1818.[55]

When originally erected, Lancaster County included a very large area, its western limits being undefined. It has since been reduced to its present size by the establishment of many counties which trace their parentage to Lancaster County. These, according to a Genealogical Map of the Counties of Pennsylvania, compiled and prepared in the Bureau of Land Records of the Department of Internal Affairs in 1933[56], are as follows:

York, August 19, 1749; Cumberland, January 27, 1750; Berks, March 11, 1752; Bedford, March 9, 1771; Northumberland, March 21, 1772; Westmoreland, February 26, 1773; Washington, March 28, 1781; Fayette, September 26, 1783; Franklin, September 9, 1784; Dauphin, March 4, 1785; Huntington, September 20, 1787; Allegheny, September 24, 1788; Mifflin, September 19, 1789; Lycoming, April 13, 1795; Somerset, April 17, 1795; Greene, February 9, 1796; Adams, January 22, 1800; Center, February 13, 1800; Beaver, March 12, 1800; Indiana, March 30, 1803; Cambria, March 26, 1804; Schuylkill, March 1, 1811; Lebanon, February 16, 1813; Union, March 22, 1813; Perry, March 22, 1820; Juniata, March 2, 1831; Blair, February 26, 1846; Fulton, April 19, 1850; Montour, May 3, 1850; Snyder, March 2, 1855.

Eleanor J. Fulton.

54. Ellis & Evans, History of Lancaster County, p.372
55. Ibid., p.373
56. Genealogical Map of the Counties of Penna., Compiled and Prepared in the Bureau of Land Records, of the Department of Internal Affairs, 1933

GEORGE ROSS—1730–1779

A Member of the First Continental Congress
and
A Signer of the Declaration of Independence

INDEX
to the
WILL BOOKS OF LANCASTER COUNTY, PENNSYLVANIA

Abt   1729 - 1850   Axer

Name	Year	Bk.	Vol	Page	Name	Year	Bk.	Vol	Page
Abt, John Henry	1812	Y	2	11	Anderson, George	1770	A	1	224
Acclas, Samuel	1845	T	1	530	Anderson, Hannah	1825	O	1	335
Achenbach, John	1772	C	1	107	Anderson, James	1740	A	1	48
Achey, George	1802	H	1	223	Anderson, James	1790	F	1	231
Ackenbach, Mattias	1795	Y	2	14	Anderson, John	1775	C	1	325
Acker, Ann	1800	H	1	42	Anderson, John	1818	M	1	193
Acker, Casper	1764	Y	2	19	Anderson, Margaret	1759	B	1	319
Acker, Esther	1801	H	1	43	Anderson, Margaret	1802	H	1	152
Acker, Peter	1793	Y	2	15	Anderson, Richard	1748	I	1	1
Ackerman, Wendel	1764	A	1	206	Anderson, Robert	1779	D	1	1
Acord, Leonard	1765	B	1	426	Anderson, Samuel	1764	B	1	556
Adam, Jacob	1840	S	1	288	Anderson, William	1767	A	1	212
Adams, George	1751	-	-	-	Andrew, Arthur	1799	G	1	475
Adams, James	1777	C	1	418	Andrew, Christian	1799	G	1	474
Adams, William	1773	C	1	110	Andrew, John	1783	D	1	281
Adams, William	1774	C	1	111	Andrew, John, Sr	1832	Q	1	288
Addams, Richard	1816	L	1	537	Andrews, Jane	1815	L	1	536
Addams, Samuel	1798	G	1	323	Andrews, John	1775	C	1	323
Aiken, Thomas	1765	B	1	423	Andrews, John	1830	P	1	456
Albert, Elizabeth	1816	L	1	535	Andrews, John	1845	U	1	39
Albert, John	1849	U	1	711	Andrews, Joseph	1842	T	1	33
Albert, Michael	1754	B	1	64	Andrews, Michael	1769	B	1	561
Albert, Philip	1780	C	1	599	Andrews, Peter	1841	S	1	390
Albrecht, Andrew	1802	H	1	179	Andrews, Robert	1762	B	1	415
Albright, Andrew	1833	Q	1	169	Ankrim, Samuel	1772	B	1	642
Albright, Elias	1813	K	1	430	Ankrum, Samuel	1790	F	1	218
Albright, Frederick	1831	Q	1	106	Anne, Conrad	1848	U	1	479
Albright, George	1839	S	1	143	Annon, Robert	1820	M	1	382
Albright, George	1843	T	1	322	Anthony, Philip	1820	M	1	454
Albright, Herman	1819	M	1	356	Antrican, Samuel	1798	G	1	409
Albright, John	1806	J	1	5	Anzel, Martin	1841	S	1	551
Aldeberger, John	1770	A	1	224	Apple, Christian	1824	P	1	267
Alexander, David	1741	A	1	51	Apple, Elizabeth	1846	U	1	126
Alexander, James	1802	H	1	164	Apple, John	1826	O	1	480
Alexander, James	1807	J	1	7	Archer, Archibald	1823	N	1	324
Alexander, Jane	1822	N	1	233	Armor, Robert	1784	E	1	88
Alexander, John	1763	B	1	418	Armstrong, James	1747	J	1	3
Algayer, Michael	1785	E	1	283	Armstrong, James	1759	B	1	278
Allen, William	1741	J	1	1	Armstrong, John	1835	R	1	142
Allen, William	1744	J	1	1	Armstrong, Reuben	1808	I	1	4
Allen, William	1782	D	1	40	Armstrong, William	1811	K	1	190
Allison, James, Sr	1742	A	1	74	Arndt, Charles	1784	D	1	410
Allison, James	1749	A	1	179	Arndt, John	1849	U	1	809
Allison, James	1762	B	1	417	Arnold, Frederick	1826	O	1	587
Allison, James	1776	C	1	324	Arnold, George	1783	D	1	279
Allison, John	1747	J	1	4	Artzt, Philip	1790	F	1	285
Allison, John	1767	B	1	431	Ashbach, Andrew	1772	C	1	108
Allison, John	1784	E	1	34	Ashmore, Richard	1747	J	1	2
Allison, Rebecca	1764	B	1	420	Ashton, Elizabeth	1845	T	1	528
Allison, Rebecca	1818	-	-	-	Ashton, Samuel	1841	S	1	562
Allison, Richard	1758	B	1	228	Aston, Alexander	1743	A	1	84
Allison, Robert	1760	I	1	2	Aston, Peter	1769	B	1	574
Allison, Robert	1766	B	1	429	Atchison, John	1778	C	1	487
Allison, William	1739	A	1	36	Atkinson, Ezekiel	1842	T	1	155
Alter, Anna	1822	N	1	166	Atkinson, John, Sr	1767	B	1	433
Alter, John	1799	-	-	-	Atkinson, John	1846	U	1	217
Altig, John	1771	-	-	-	Atkinson, Margaret	1803	H	1	345
Altig, John	1774	Y	2	16	Atkinson, Mathew	1756	B	1	148
Altz, Michael	1796	G	1	5	Atkinson, Michael	1758	B	1	216
Amend, John	1798	G	1	321	Atkinson, Stephen	1742	A	1	72
Ament, Henry	1835	R	1	112	Atkinson, Stephen	1765	B	1	424
Amweg, Jacob	1790	Y	2	12	Auer, Melchior	1773	Y	2	17
Amweg, John Martin	1768	Y	2	18	Aux, John	1808	I	1	3
Amweg, Michael	1779	C	1	523	Axer, Jacob	1843	T	1	210
Ancrim, Mary	1800	A	1	185	Axer, Mary Barbara	1797	G	1	290
Anderson, Elizabeth	1776	C	1	326	Axer, Michael, Jr.	1817	M	1	111

Name	Year	Bk.	Vol	Page	Name	Year	Bk.	Vol	Page
B					Barcley, John	1765	B	1	445
Bachert, George	1804	Y	2	79	Bard, George	1769	B	1	562
Bachman, Christian	1811	L	1	39	Bard, George	1805	H	1	591
Bachman, Christian	1849	U	1	807	Bard, George Phillip	1793	I	1	25
Bachman, Elizabeth	1841	S	1	557	Bard, John, Sr.	1850	U	1	827
Bachman, John	1849	U	1	799	Bard, Martin	1758	B	1	253
Bachman, Mary	1805	H	1	595	Bard, Martin	1817	M	1	19
Bachman, Michael	1756	B	1	141	Bard, Mary	1837	R	1	310
Bachman, Peter	1823	O	1	9	Bard, Michael	1832	Q	1	155
Bachman, Philip	1839	S	1	180	Bare, Anna	1759	B	1	292
Backenstross, Jacob	1807	J	1	15	Bare, George	1811	L	1	46
Baeder, Peter	1778	Y	2	37	Bare, Henry	1750	I	1	12
Baer, Anna	1850	U	1	953	Bare, Jacob	1736	I	1	6
Baer, Benjamin	1799	G	1	477	Bare, John	1767	B	1	451
Baer, Christian	1831	Q	1	24	Bare, John	1847	U	1	276
Baer, Christian	1840	S	1	264	Bare, Martin	1758	B	1	207
Baer, David	1848	U	1	523	Bare, Martin	1784	D	1	441
Baer, Henry	1794	F	1	580	Barge, Baltzer	1794	F	1	566
Baer, Henry	1843	T	1	315	Barkheffer, Conrad	1746	-	-	-
Bahm, Peter	1799	G	1	416	Barkley, Martha	1795	G	1	379
Bahm, Philip	1825	O	1	278	Barkley, William	1816	M	1	2
Bahmiller, Conrad(German)	1831	Y	2	132	Barnes, Barney	1849	U	1	776
Bailey, James	1813	K	1	434	Barnes, James, Sr.	1827	P	1	108
Bailey, Mary	1759	B	1	288	Barnes, Robert	1823	O	1	98
Bailey, Robert	1798	G	1	311	Barnet, Henry	1828	P	1	254
Bair, Abraham, Sr.	1828	P	1	174	Barnet, John	1734	A	1	15
Baird, David	1804	H	1	430	Barnet, John, Sr.	1785	E	1	168
Baird, James	1758	B	1	242	Barnet, Samuel	1758	B	1	249
Baird, Thomas	1767	B	1	460	Barnet, William	1762	I	1	17
Baishore, Baltzer	1791	F	-	332	Barnet, William	1764	A	1	215
Baker, Abraham	1845	T	1	576	Barnitz, Joseph	1844	T	1	386
Baker, Andrew	1843	T	1	234	Barnitz, Michael	1815	L	1	442
Baker, Bernard	1770	A	1	228	Barr, Adam	1770	A	1	229
Baker, Henry	1816	L	1	549	Barr, Christian	1816	M	1	12
Baker, John	1798	G	1	317	Barr, George	1814	K	1	456
Baker, John, Sr.	1804	H	1	489	Barr, Henry	1771	I	1	20
Baker, John	1825	O	1	325	Barr, Henry	1843	T	1	182
Baker, Joshua	1754	B	1	57	Barr, Jacob	1768	A	1	223
Baker, Margaret	1832	Q	1	161	Barr, Jacob (Bart)	1803	H	1	393
Baker, Peter	1783	D	1	283	Barr, Jacob (Drumore)	1803	H	1	272
Baker, Peter	1785	E	1	197	Barr, Jacob	1834	R	-	-
Baker, Philip	1777	C	1	422	Barr, John (Strasburg)	1813	K	1	423
Baker, Sarah	1823	O	1	51	Barr, John (Conestoga)	1827	P	1	114
Balance, Joseph	1840	S	1	274	Barr, John (Strasburg)	1828	P	1	250
Balance, Robert	1794	I	1	35	Barr, John	1843	T	1	230
Baldridge, John	1766	B	1	448	Barr, John	1845	U	1	42
Baldridge, William	1775	C	1	124	Barr, John	1844	T	1	453
Baldwin, Maria	1840	S	1	357	Barr, Martin	1827	P	1	23
Baley, James, Esq.	1793	F	1	507	Barr, Samuel	1827	P	1	23
Baley, John	1793	F	1	546	Bartel, George	1846	U	1	120
Ball, William	1847	U	1	264	Bartges, Michael	1791	F	1	283
Balmer, Christian	1785	Y	2	54	Bartholemew, Benard	1835	R	1	176
Balmer, George Michael	1772	C	1	120	Bartlet, Rebecca	1767	B	1	456
Balmer, Michael(Mt.Joy)	1815	L	1	458	Bartlett, Sarah	1810	K	1	188
Balmer, Michael(Warwick)	1817	L	1	548	Barton, Mathias W	1838	S	1	74
Balmer, Samuel, Sr.	1843	T	1	261	Bartruff, Andrew	1795	G	1	387
Balsbach, George	1773	Y	2	30	Bartruff, John	1849	U	1	796
Balspack, Peter	1748	A	1	155	Barwick, John	1742	J	1	8
Bamberger, Jacob	1811	L	1	47	Basehore, Daniel	1820	M	1	378
Bander, Florin	1822	N	1	231	Basehore, Mary	1833	Q	1	443
Barber, Eleanor	1825	O	1	38	Bassler, Abraham	1759	B	-	-
Barber, Hannah	1771	C	1	117	Bassler, Esther	1809	K	1	81
Barber, John	1849	U	1	700	Bassler, Jacob	1817	M	1	113
Barber, Rhoda	1849	U	1	792	Bassler, John	1843	P	1	190
Barber, Robert	1782	D	1	49	Bateman, George W	1830	P	1	492
Barber, Sarah	1841	S	1	490	Batten, Elizabeth	1840	S	1	337
Barber, Susanna	1827	P	1	4	Batten, Hiram	1838	R	1	497
Barclay, Hugh	1764	A	-	214	Bauder, John	1845	P	1	549
Barclay, John	1778	C	1	490	Bauer, Andrew	1777	C	1	419
Barclay, Robert	1849	U	1	772	Bauer, Elizabeth	1813	K	1	414
Barclay, Sarah	1841	S	1	425	Bauer, Elizabeth	1846	U	1	175
Barclay, William	1836	R	1	254	Bauer, Jacob	1845	T	1	540
					Bauer, Peter	1761	B	1	370

Name	Year	Bk.	Vol	Page	Name	Year	Bk.	Vol	Page
Bauer, Peter	1829	P	1	407	Becker, Ludwick	1774	Y	2	29
Baughman, John	1829	P	1	341	Becker, Ludwig	1825	O	1	273
Baum, Eve	1844	P	1	378	Becker, Martin	1844	T	1	363
Baum, Philip	1793	Y	2	48	Becker, Nicholas(German)	1831	Y	2	132
Bauman, Christian	1815	L	1	451	Becker, Peter	1802	Y	2	75
Bauman, John	1813	K	1	425	Becker, Peter	1804	H	1	498
Bauman, John	1837	R	1	305	Becker, Peter	1833	Q	1	417
Bauman, Soloman	1838	R	1	470	Becker, Peter	1837	R	1	355
Baumgardner, John	1826	O	1	569	Becker, Saloam	1844	T	1	341
Bausman, Andrew	1814	K	1	639	Beckley, John	1763	A	-	-
Bausman, William	1784	E	1	16	Beeble, Daniel	1773	C	1	125
Baxter, John	1768	A	1	216	Beehler, David	1784	Y	2	61
Baxter, William	1750	A	1	189	Beer, Peter	1801	H	1	86
Bayer, Adam	1777	Y	2	34	Begholt, Philip	1788	F	1	19
Bayley, Henry	1744	A	1	94	Behm, Christopher	1782	D	1	51
Bayley, Thomas	1737	A	1	28	Behm, Rudolph	1773	B	1	645
Beale, Thomas	1789	F	1	117	Beidler, Christian	1767	B	1	438
Beam, Jacob	1781	D	1	6	Beigler, George, Jr	1821	N	1	100
Beam, Jacob	1836	R	1	261	Beiler, Christian	1804	I	1	43
Beam, John, Jr	1842	P	1	80	Beimensderfer, John	1794	F	1	579
Beam, Margaret	1846	U	1	141	Beistel, Andrew	1777	C	1	420
Beam, Martin	1812	L	1	64	Beitler, John	1836	R	1	199
Beam, Peter	1785	E	1	253	Bell, Cathrine	1822	N	1	229
Beam, Rudolph	1819	M	1	324	Bell, Walter	1796	G	1	222
Beamy, Peter	1784	D	1	420	Bell, William	1783	D	1	391
Bear, Andrew	1815	L	1	539	Bender, Adam	1745	A	1	95
Bear, Andrew	1817	M	1	14	Bender, Benjamin	1777	C	1	424
Bear, Ann	1795	I	1	40	Bender, David	1824	O	1	171
Bear, Barbara	1812	K	1	375	Bender, Henry	1825	Y	2	137
Bear, Barbara	1844	T	1	419	Bender, John	1782	Y	2	43
Bear, Benjamin	1802	Y	2	86	Bender, John	1809	K	1	137
Bear, Christian	1775	C	1	329	Bender, John	1838	R	1	466
Bear, David	1819	M	1	257	Bender, John.George	1783	Y	2	43
Bear, Elizabeth	1798	G	1	169	Bender, Leonard	1782	D	1	55
Bear, Elizabeth	1847	U	1	442	Bender, Leonard	1807	I	1	21
Bear, Ephriam	1824	O	1	189	Bender, Michael	1816	M	1	5
Bear, Henry	1821	M	1	476	Bender, William	1847	U	1	339
Bear, Henry	1836	R	1	290	Benedict, Leonard	1837	R	1	307
Bear, Isaac	1774	B	1	647	Bennet, Henry	1807	J	1	19
Bear, Jacob	1769	I	1	18	Bensing, John	1847	U	1	375
Bear, Jacob	1834	R	1	8	Bentz, Jacob	1847	U	1	402
Bear, John(Leacock)	1812	L	1	66	Bentz, Peter	1814	K	1	459
Bear, John(Leacock)	1817	M	1	16	Berg, Andrew	1796	Y	2	73
Bear, Margaret	1814	K	1	649	Berg, David	1819	Y	2	136
Bear, Martin	1793	F	1	444	Berg, Feronica	1808	I	1	62
Bear, Martin	1800	G	1	604	Berg, Frederick	1794	Y	2	46
Bear, Martin	1814	K	1	457	Berg, Frederick	1804	Y	2	79
Bear, Martin	1838	S	1	75	Berg, Jacob	1811	L	1	35
Bear, Michael	1770	A	1	226	Berg, Maria	1804	Y	2	79
Bear, Michael	1821	N	1	49	Bergdolt, Daniel	1831	Q	1	85
Bear, Samuel	1743	A	1	83	Berger, Anthony	1841	S	1	409
Beard, James	1847	U	1	401	Berger, John	1768	Y	2	22
Beatty, James	1823	O	1	8	Bergman, Baltzer	1811	L	1	52
Bechard, Philip	1824	O	1	182	Berkinpine, George	1841	S	1	503
Becher, John	1847	U	1	275	Bernhard, Leonard	1749	I	1	10
Becher, Peter, Sr	1835	R	1	114	Berringer, Michael	1803	Y	2	81
Bechtold, William	1815	L	1	445	Bersinger, Andrew	1774	B	1	648
Bechtolt, John	1810	L	1	31	Best, David	1842	P	1	11
Beck, Christianna	1826	O	1	443	Betey, Abraham	1784	E	1	157
Beck, Jacob	1829	P	1	398	Bethel, Ann	1823	M	1	271
Beck, Mary Ann	1828	P	1	230	Bethel, Elizabeth	1842	P	1	34
Beck, Peter	1811	L	1	54	Bethel, Mary	1846	U	1	177
Beck, Peter	1837	R	1	379	Bettle, Lydia	1764	A	1	215
Beck, Samuel	1771	C	1	116	Betz, Elizabeth	1844	P	1	517
Beck, Susanna	1844	T	1	367	Betz, George	1781	D	1	165
Becker, Christian	1749	A	1	171	Beyer, Casimer	1784	Y	2	63
Becker, Christian	1837	R	1	391	Beyer, David F	1841	S	1	439
Becker, Henry	1807	Y	2	68	Beyerle, John Michael	1766	B	1	441
Becker, Jacob	1772	C	1	119	Bichter, Jacob	1757	B	1	177
Becker, John	1819	M	1	223	Bieler, Dietrich	1824	O	1	150
Becker, John	1842	P	1	62	Bier, Elizabeth	1836	R	1	217
Becker, John	1844	T	1	426	Bier, Peter	1846	U	1	1C?

Name	Year	Bk.	Vol	Page	Name	Year	Bk.	Vol	Page
Bierly, Ann Maria	1788	F	1	80	Boggs, Alexander	1839	S	1	146
Bigard, James	1749	A	-	180	Boggs, Andrew	1765	B	1	437
Bigler, Morris	1814	K	1	455	Boggs, Ann	1790	F	1	253
Bilheimer, John	1770	A	1	229	Boggs, Ann	1848	U	1	500
Billman, Christian	1766	B	1	447	Boggs, James	1753	B	1	19
Billmayer, Leonard	1772	C	1	121	Boggs, Margaret	1796	F	1	640
Binckley, Henry	1816	L	1	550	Bohre, Mathew	1782	D	1	46
Bingeman, Paul	1837	R	1	354	Boilston, Sophia	1795	F	1	651
Bingham, David	1759	I	1	15	Boilstone, Jacob	1791	F	1	323
Bingham, James	1804	H	1	426	Bollinger, Cathrine	1797	G	1	21
Bingle, Felix	1781	D	1	38	Bollinger, Christian	1796	J	1	12
Binkley, David	1840	S	1	271	Bollinger, David	1762	-	-	-
Binkley, Elizabeth	1832	I	1	211	Bollinger, David	1819	M	1	308
Binkley, Henry	1776	C	1	413	Bollinger, Elizabeth	1800	G	1	612
Binkley, Henry	1805	H	1	588	Bollinger, Henry	1773	C	1	127
Binkley, John	1749	A	-	173	Bollinger, Jacob	1762	Y	2	99
Binkley, John	1797	G	1	41	Bollinger, Maria Esther	1786	E	1	354
Birglebach, Cathrine	1819	M	1	346	Bollinger, Mary	1833	Q	1	460
Birney, William	1810	K	1	194	Bollinger, Peter	1839	S	1	227
Bishop, John	1828	P	1	205	Bollinger, Rudolph	1772	J	1	9
Bishop, Peter	1815	L	1	303	Bolt, Barbara	1846	U	1	230
Bishop, Peter	1843	T	1	200	Boltz, Michael	1784	E	1	112
Bishop, William	1783	Y	2	45	Bomberger, Christian	1742	A	1	68
Bitner, Abraham, Sr	1841	S	1	564	Bomberger, Christian	1815	L	1	297
Bitting, Ann Maria	1815	L	1	447	Bomberger, Christian	1828	P	1	149
Bitzer, John	1810	K	1	147	Bomberger, John	1758	B	1	200
Bitzer, Martin	1834	R	1	46	Bomberger, John	1818	Y	2	127
Bitzman, John Michael	1791	F	1	298	Bomberger, Martin	1794	F	1	541
Bixler, Abraham	1819	M	1	240	Bomberger, Moses	1841	S	1	509
Bixler, Abraham	1847	U	1	265	Bomberger, Peter	1846	U	1	131
Bixler, Christian	1762	Y	2	25	Bomgartner, Christian	1761	B	1	370
Black, David	1753	B	1	27	Bontnig, William	1796	G	1	148
Black, George	1812	L	1	68	Booch, John Peter	1750	I	1	11
Black, Hugh	1759	B	1	297	Boorman, Stephen	1782	D	1	170
Black, James	1806	I	1	57	Booth, David	1840	S	1	261
Black, Robert	1847	U	1	365	Borger, George	1817	M	1	19
Blackburn, David	1837	R	1	302	Borgner, Peter	1768	Y	2	33
Blackburn, Joseph	1839	S	1	145	Borgner, Peter	1784	Y	2	63
Blair, Jennet	1775	B	1	649	Borkholder, John	1837	R	1	348
Blanck, John, Sr	1835	R	1	139	Borland, John	1848	U	1	589
Blanck, Nicholas	1809	K	1	14	Born, Daniel	1776	Y	2	26
Blandford, Joseph	1835	Y	2	135	Borrel, John	1806	I	1	55
Blank, John	1790	Y	2	51	Borry, Ludwig	1796	G	1	60
Blank, John	1794	I	1	36	Borst, Lydia	1839	S	1	200
Blank, John	1846	U	1	128	Bortsfield, Jacob, Sr	1842	P	1	90
Blantz, Michael	1774	C	1	245	Boss, Jacob	1798	G	1	412
Blasser, Abraham	1759	Y	2	96	Bossard, Henry	1749	I	-	-
Blasser, Mathias	1800	H	1	44	Bossler, John	1812	K	1	392
Blattenberger, John	1793	I	1	34	Bossler, Joseph	1808	I	1	69
Blattenberger, Peter	1823	O	1	95	Bott, Elizabeth	1823	N	1	287
Blauck, John	1806	I	1	52	Bott, John	1808	I	1	63
Blaugh, John	1763	-	-	-	Bott, Ulrich	1820	M	1	456
Blazer, Christian	1747	A	1	142	Bourk, Richard	1748	A	1	162
Bleacher, Michael	1845	T	1	582	Bower, John	1748	I	-	8
Bletcher, Henry	1747	I	1	6	Bower, Ann	1806	I	-	51
Bletz, Andrew	1802	H	1	207	Bower, Elizabeth(Ephrata)	1846	U	1	164
Bletz, Frederick	1784	Y	2	521	Bower, Frederick	1815	L	1	306
Bletz, John	1784	E	1	78	Bower, Nicholas	1784	Y	2	64
Bletz, John Adam	1784	Y	2	522	Bowermaster, Andrew	1845	T	1	630
Blickenderfer, Christian	1800	G	1	608	Bowermaster, Sarah	1849	U	1	710
Blickensderfer, Mathias	1809	Y	2	66	Bowman, Ann	1803	H	1	269
Blontz, George	1807	I	1	385	Bowman, Daniel	1816	L	1	544
Blum, John	1759	Y	2	23	Bowman, Feronica	1826	O	1	487
Blumenshein, Cathrine	1821	N	1	74	Bowman, George	1804	Y	2	80
Blumenshine, Henry	1792	Y	2	50	Bowman, Henry	1841	S	1	547
Boeshore, Jacob	1779	Y	2	37	Bowman, Jacob	1753	B	1	12
Boetner, Adam	1819	M	1	354	Bowman, Jacob	1784	D	1	447
Boettner, George	1796	G	1	218	Bowman, John	1738	A	1	34
Boffenmeyer, Margaret	1825	Y	2	131	Bowman, John	1785	E	1	245
Boffenmyer, Margaret	1828	P	1	234	Bowman, John	1795	F	1	618
Boger, Mathias, Sr	1784	E	1	237	Bowman, Joseph, Sr	1811	L	1	50
Bogge, William	1782	D	1	42	Bowman, Mary	1804	Y	2	84

Name	Year	Bk.	Vol	Page	Name	Year	Bk.	Vol	Page
Bowman, Mary	1845	T	1	618	Breneman, Isaac	1804	I	1	45
Bowman, Peter	1805	Y	2	83	Breneman, Jacob	1808	Y	2	72
Bowman, Peter	1844	T	1	424	Breneman, Jacob	1838	R	1	537
Bowman, Samuel	1782	D	1	50	Breneman, John	1805	H	1	599
Bowman, Thomas	1763	A	1	214	Breneman, John	1806	I	1	48
Bowman, Valentine	1778	Y	2	36	Breneman, John	1818	M	1	171
Bowser, Leonard	1767	B	1	443	Breneman, Melchior	1737	Y	2	28
Boyd, Elizabeth	1839	S	1	188	Breneman, Melchoir	1794	I	1	38
Boyd, George	1800	H	1	46	Breneman, Melchoir	1810	K	1	160
Boyd, James	1805	H	1	607	Brenisen, Rudolph	1764	B	1	433
Boyd, James	1823	O	1	1	Brennaman, Henry	1813	K	1	418
Boyd, Jane	1772	I	1	21	Brenneman, Abraham	1815	L	1	449
Boyd, Jennette	1761	B	1	399	Brenneman, Christian	1820	M	1	396
Boyd, John	1759	B	1	262	Brenneman, Feronica	1805	H	1	582
Boyd, John	1799	G	1	492	Brenneman, Jacob	1845	U	1	33
Boyd, John	1807	J	1	18	Brenneman, John	1843	P	1	320
Boyd, Robert	1755	I	1	14	Brenneman, John(Manor)	1843	P	1	285
Boyd, Samuel	1770	A	1	225	Brenneman, Mary	1842	T	1	8
Boyd, Samuel	1840	S	1	229	Brenneman, Melchoir, Jr.	1817	M	1	114
Boyd, Thomas	1777	C	1	423	Brenneman, Michael, Jr.	1824	O	1	215
Boyd, Thomas	1790	F	1	223	Brenner, Adam	1813	K	1	400
Boyd, William	1847	U	1	428	Brenner, George	1795	Y	2	74
Boyer, Jacob	1753	B	1	21	Brenner, Gerhart	1774	C	1	127
Boyer, Jacob	1775	C	1	326	Brenner, Jacob	1825	O	1	323
Boyer, Jacob	1848	U	1	543	Brenner, John	1826	O	1	513
Boyer, John	1750	B	1	127	Brenner, Louise	1784	E	1	126
Boyer, John Nicholas	1784	Y	2	59	Brenner, Michael	1840	S	1	354
Boyer, Mary	1823	N	1	310	Brenner, Philip	1788	F	1	37
Boyer, Peter	1811	L	1	44	Brenner, Philip(E.Donegal)	1836	R	1	241
Boyer, Philip	1781	D	1	4	Brenner, Philip(Hempfield)	1836	R	1	271
Boyes, Elizabeth	1818	M	1	145	Brenner, Philip Adam	1782	D	1	53
Boys, William	1843	T	1	322	Bresnehen, Dennis	1840	S	1	295
Brabson, Thomas	1791	I	1	23	Bressler, George	1806	I	1	59
Brackbill, Benjamin	1823	N	1	315	Bressler, Peter	1843	T	1	301
Brackbill, John	1813	K	1	432	Breton, Ann Lee	1834	Q	1	527
Brackbill, John	1849	U	1	763	Bretz, Martin	1782	D	1	44
Bradley, Alexander	1832	Q	1	294	Bretz, Philip	1815	L	1	538
Bradley, Bernard	1838	S	1	67	Brice, George	1821	N	1	61
Bradley, Francis	1738	A	1	31	Brice, James	1777	C	1	483
Bradley, Patrick	1811	L	1	49	Bricen, William	1846	U	1	198
Brand, Jacob	1789	F	1	171	Bricker, Christian	1782	Y	2	41
Brand, John	1783	D	1	393	Bricker, John	1807	J	1	23
Brand, Samuel	1784	Y	2	66	Bricker, Peter	1761	Y	2	23
Brandon, William	1753	B	1	7	Bricker, Peter	1837	R	1	341
Brandt, Ann	1837	R	1	372	Brickham, James	1789	F	1	188
Brandt, Christian	1841	S	1	418	Brien, Edward	1816	L	1	555
Brandt, Esther	1826	O	1	422	Brien, Edward H.	1837	R	1	375
Brandt, Frederick	1794	Y	2	47	Brightbill, Dorst	1771	I	1	19
Brandt, John, Sr.	1842	P	1	174	Brindle, Henry	1833	Q	1	350
Brandt, John	1849	U	1	728	Brinisholtz, Christian	1771	C	1	118
Brandt, Joseph	1845	P	1	542	Brinton, Moses	1789	F	1	96
Brannon, John	1798	G	1	326	Brinton, Susanna	1826	O	1	541
Brannon, Margaret	1811	L	1	56	Brinton, William	1842	T	1	93
Brantigan, Samuel	1846	U	1	119	Brintzel, George	1799	G	1	544
Breadback, Nicholas	1749	I	1	11	Brisben, William	1811	L	1	61
Breadhurst, Henry	1810	L	1	1	Bristoll, Sarah	1831	Q	1	88
Breckbill, Henry	1837	R	1	388	Britch, Peter	1759	B	1	275
Breckle, John George	1846	U	1	91	Britz, George	1821	N	1	18
Brecklebach, John	1761	B	1	381	Britznis, Adam	1820	M	1	442
Breds, Martin	1782	Y	2	39	Britznis, Isaac	1819	M	1	228
Brehm, Henry	1823	N	1	313	Brodhead, Daniel	1809	K	1	11
Brehm, John	1844	T	1	492	Bromberger, Elizabeth	1799	G	1	490
Brehm, Philip	1816	M	1	6	Brookens, James	1846	U	1	127
Breidenhart, Christopher	1787	F	1	126	Brooks, Samuel	1840	S	1	235
Bremer, Christian, Sr.	1829	P	1	343	Brooks, Washington	1838	R	1	500
Breneisen, Valentine	1786	E	1	329	Brooks, William	1784	E	1	65
Breneman, Adam	1760	B	1	298	Broom, Philip	1842	T	1	41
Breneman, Christian	1757	Y	2	21	Brosey, John	1806	I	1	48
Breneman, Christian	1771	C	-	113	Brosius, Abraham	1776	C	1	327
Breneman, Christian	1834	Q	1	512	Brosius, Joseph	1830	P	1	513
Breneman, Henry	1808	Y	2	72	Brotzman, Peter	1833	Q	1	442
Breneman, Henry	1815	L	1	454	Brown, Abraham	1819	M	1	201

Name	Year	Bk.	Vol	Page	Name	Year	Bk.	Vol	Page
Brown, Adam	1828	P	1	240	Brubaker, Francis	1850	U	1	978
Brown, Adam	1845	U	1	30	Brubaker, Hans Jacob	1802	Y	2	85
Brown, Archibald	1802	H	1	203	Brubaker, Henry	1820	M	1	365
Brown, Benjamin	1826	O	1	526	Brubaker, Jacob	1774	Y	2	27
Brown, Cathrine	1784	E	1	158	Brubaker, Jacob	1803	Y	2	87
Brown, Charles	1746	I	1	6	Brubaker, Jacob, Jr	1804	Y	2	77
Brown, Christian	1812	L	1	63	Brubaker, Jacob	1819	M	1	397
Brown, Collin	1770	A	1	227	Brubaker, Jacob	1820	M	1	397
Brown, Conrad	1773	B	1	644	Brubaker, Jacob	1840	S	1	259
Brown, Daniel	1777	C	1	420	Brubaker, John	1748	Y	2	21
Brown, Daniel	1782	D	1	47	Brubaker, John	1809	L	1	439
Brown, David	1766	B	1	450	Brubaker, John Jacob	1755	B	1	89
Brown, David	1808	I	1	67	Brubaker, John Jacob	1802	H	1	219
Brown, David	1843	P	1	225	Brubaker, John S	1850	U	1	832
Brown, George	1756	B	1	147	Brubaker, Maria	1805	H	1	586
Brown, Jacob	1767	B	1	459	Brubaker, Mary	1839	S	1	118
Brown, Jacob	1843	P	1	176	Brubaker, Michael	1747	I	1	7
Brown, James	1768	B	1	559	Brubaker, Peter	1820	M	1	439
Brown, James	1838	R	1	465	Brunkhart, Martin	1792	F	1	348
Brown, Jeremiah	1799	G	1	488	Brunner, Barbara	1847	U	1	326
Brown, Jeremiah, Sr	1831	Q	1	68	Brunner, Casper	1783	D	1	285
Brown, John	1768	Y	2	32	Brunner, Casper, Sr	1832	Q	1	305
Brown, John	1786	E	1	362	Brunner, George	1823	O	1	32
Brown, John	1816	L	1	541	Brunner, George Michael	1788	Y	2	52
Brown, John	1834	R	1	20	Brunner, John	1784	Y	2	58
Brown, Joshua	1799	G	1	485	Bryan, Ann Maria	1844	T	1	453
Brown, Joshua	1823	N	1	337	Bryan, Christopher	1809	K	1	109
Brown, Levi	1846	U	1	181	Buch, Christian	1789	F	1	113
Brown, Margaret	1748	A	1	154	Buch, Henry	1811	L	1	42
Brown, Martin	1760	B	1	339	Buch, John George	1769	A	1	223
Brown, Mary	1842	T	1	39	Buch, William	1833	Q	1	464
Brown, Patrick	1840	S	1	241	Buchanan, Arthur	1767	B	1	457
Brown, Robert	1828	P	1	200	Buchanan, Arthur	1806	I	1	56
Brown, Sarah	1839	S	1	165	Buchanan, Dorcas	1810	L	1	33
Brown, William	1771	C	1	115	Buchanan, James	1746	I	1	5
Brown, William	1797	G	1	147	Buchanan, James	1798	G	1	137
Brown, William	1801	H	1	57	Buchanan, Walter	1787	E	1	446
Brown, William	1818	M	1	195	Buchanan, William	1778	C	1	503
Brown, William	1831	Q	1	127	Buchannan, Margaret	1845	T	1	559
Brua, Dewalt	1755	Y	2	30	Bucher, Benedict	1787	E	1	435
Brua, Jacob	1800	G	1	602	Bucher, Engle	1778	Y	2	35
Brua, Jacob	1837	R	1	409	Bucher, John, Sr	1762	-	-	-
Brubach, Ann Mary	1834	R	1	10	Bucher, John	1793	I	1	24
Brubach, Gerhart	1816	M	1	7	Buchwalter, Durst	1782	Y	2	42
Brubacher, Daniel	1762	-	-	-	Buckius, Samuel	1849	U	1	717
Brubacher, David	1824	O	1	193	Buckley, Daniel	1827	P	1	50
Brubacher, Elizabeth	1825	O	1	330	Bucksritter, Isreal	1792	P	1	398
Brubacher, Elizabeth	1843	P	1	192	Buckwalter, Abraham	1819	M	1	220
Brubacher, Jacob	1764	Y	2	31	Buckwalter, Abraham	1820	M	1	394
Brubacher, Jacob, Sr	1804	H	1	413	Buckwalter, Abraham	1831	Q	1	72
Brubacher, Jacob	1819	M	1	208	Buckwalter, Abraham	1832	Q	1	317
Brubacher, Jacob(German)	1831	Y	2	134	Buckwalter, Anna	1834	Q	1	510
Brubacher, Jacob	1846	U	1	65	Buckwalter, Christian	1848	U	1	527
Brubacher, John	1785	E	1	312	Buckwalter, Daniel	1845	P	1	631
Brubacher, John	1803	H	1	313	Buckwalter, Francis	1816	L	1	545
Brubacher, John, Sr	1804	H	1	432	Buckwalter, Henry	1805	H	1	602
Brubacher, John, Sr	1828	Y	2	128	Buckwalter, Henry	1844	T	1	464
Brubacher, John	1842	P	1	72	Buckwalter, John	1808	I	1	65
Brubacher, John	1843	P	1	263	Buckwalter, John	1832	Q	1	241
Brubacher, John Jacob	1752	-	-	-	Buckwalter, John	1841	P	1	1
Brubacher, Magdalena	1844	T	1	539	Buckwalter, John	1844	T	1	510
Brubacher, Peter	1796	J	1	11	Buckwalter, Joseph	1748	A	1	142
Brubaker,Abraham(German)	1809	Y	2	71	Buey, James	1737	A	1	29
Brubaker, Abraham	1811	L	1	38	Buffenmyer, Mathias	1806	Y	2	76
Brubaker, Abraham	1840	S	1	277	Buffenmyer, Rosina	1817	M	1	112
Brubaker, Abraham	1847	U	1	356	Buffenmyer, William	1846	U	1	218
Brubaker, Abraham	1850	U	1	950	Buffington, Lydia Ann	1837	R	1	428
Brubaker, Ann	1787	E	1	599	Bugh, George	1785	E	1	265
Brubaker, Ann	1825	O	1	374	Buhrman, Henry	1844	T	1	516
Brubaker, Daniel	1848	U	1	498	Bulla, William	1805	H	1	600
Brubaker, Elias	1847	U	1	350	Bundel, Jacob	1827	P	1	69
Brubaker, Elizabeth	1837	R	1	296	Bunting, Walter	1821	N	1	75

Name	Year	Bk.	Vol	Page
Burg, John	1834	R	1	58
Burg, Mary	1843	T	1	283
Burgard, William	1814	K	1	643
Burhman, Billy	1811	L	1	57
Burket, Cathrine	1849	U	1	666
Burkhart, George	1783	D	1	288
Burkhart, Jacob	1821	M	1	519
Burkholder, Abraham	1776	C	1	329
Burkholder, Anna	1823	M	1	329
Burkholder, Christian	1785	Y	2	57
Burkholder, Christian	1809	K	1	59
Burkholder, Christian	1839	S	1	196
Burkholder, Isaac	1833	Q	1	405
Burkholder, Jacob	1839	S	1	95
Burkholder, John	1781	D	1	2
Burkholder, John	1801	H	1	52
Burkholder, Martin	1811	L	1	59
Burkholder, Ulrich	1804	H	1	593
Burkman, William	1816	M	1	3
Burkwalter, Durst	1782	D	1	44
Burns, Samuel	1841	S	1	478
Bury, Jacob	1824	O	1	249
Buser, John	1849	U	1	685
Bush, Barbara	1791	F	1	299
Bush, John	1821	M	1	492
Bush, William	1786	E	1	379
Bushong, John	1749	Y	2	20
Bushong, John, Sr.	1831	Q	1	127
Busser, Jacob, Sr.	1831	Q	1	109
Butler, Thomas	1758	B	1	248
Buyers, Robert	1801	H	1	48
Byer, Ann	1832	Q	1	191
Byer, Elizabeth	1760	I	1	16
Byers, Jacob	1755	Y	2	22
Byers, Samuel	1785	E	1	301
Byler, Christian	1812	K	1	195
Byrod, Frederick	1840	S	1	287
C				
Cahey, Francis	1811	L	1	71
Cain, Cornelius	1750	-	-	-
Cain, Daniel	1849	U	1	650
Cairns, William	1773	J	1	30
Caldwell, Andrew	1752	J	1	25
Caldwell, Andrew	1758	B	1	209
Caldwell, Andrew	1771	B	1	650
Caldwell, Andrew	1825	O	1	357
Caldwell, David	1782	D	1	292
Caldwell, James	1785	E	1	207
Caldwell, John	1782	D	1	57
Caldwell, Mary	1800	G	1	613
Caldwell, Robert	1755	B	1	82
Caldwell, Samuel	1836	R	1	192
Calhoun, James	1772	C	1	137
Calhoun, James	1822	N	1	178
Calhoun, John	1750	B	1	84
Calhoun, John	1754	B	1	68
Calhoun, William	1823	N	1	266
Camber, Joseph	1834	Q	1	522
Camera, Mathias(Kamera)	1823	O	1	16
Cameron, John	1841	S	1	447
Camers, John George	1734	A	1	16
Campbell, Adams	1840	S	1	239
Campbell, Andrew	1754	B	1	33
Campbell, Andrew	1797	G	1	150
Campbell, Barbara	1836	R	1	229
Campbell, Cathrine	1832	Q	1	231
Campbell, Daniel	1809	K	1	34
Campbell, George	1759	B	1	273
Campbell, James	1771	J	1	26
Campbell, James	1771	B	1	651
Campbell, James	1781	D	1	14
Campbell, John(Gamble)	1748	I	1	73
Campbell, John	1799	G	1	495
Campbell, John	1841	S	1	411
Campbell, Martha	1826	O	1	492
Campbell, Patrick	1772	B	1	656
Campbell, Patrick	1817	M	1	22
Campbell, Robert	1810	L	1	285
Campbell, Robert	1813	K	1	436
Campbell, Samuel	1747	A	1	136
Campbell, William	1748	I	1	74
Campbell, William S	1849	U	1	724
Canady, David(Kennedy)	1775	C	1	348
Canady, Frances(Kennedy)	1790	F	1	266
Canady, James(Kennedy)	1776	-	-	-
Canady, James	1799	G	1	525
Canady, John(Kennedy)	1752	B	1	168
Canady, Mary(Kennedy)	1777	D	-	-
Cann, Adam	1818	M	1	119
Cann, Henry	1824	O	1	184
Cann, John(see Kann)	1812	L	1	167
Capp, Anna Maria	1832	Q	1	326
Capp, Daniel	1829	P	1	295
Capp, Martin	1832	Q	1	303
Caragan, Michael	1802	H	1	233
Carbaugh, Simon	1789	P	1	115
Care, Michael	1748	A	1	161
Carithers, Robert	1772	B	1	655
Carmichael, Thomas	1785	E	1	274
Carmichail, Daniel	1753	I	1	79
Carmony, John	1781	D	1	12
Carolus, John	1807	J	1	33
Carothers, Robert	1770	A	1	232
Carpenter, Abraham	1815	L	1	310
Carpenter, Abraham, Sr.	1829	P	1	319
Carpenter, Catherine	1785	Y	2	88
Carpenter, Christian	1800	H	1	58
Carpenter, Emanuel	1780	D	1	8
Carpenter, Esther	1847	U	1	420
Carpenter, Gabriel	1767	B	1	469
Carpenter, George	1792	F	1	377
Carpenter, Henry	1773	C	1	139
Carpenter, Henry	1797	G	1	113
Carpenter, Henry	1820	M	1	417
Carpenter, Henry	1849	U	1	755
Carpenter, Isaac	1838	R	1	474
Carpenter, Jacob	1772	C	1	135
Carpenter, Jacob, Sr.	1797	G	1	119
Carpenter, Jacob, Esq.	1803	H	1	267
Carpenter, Jacob	1811	I	1	72
Carpenter, Jacob	1823	O	1	113
Carpenter, Joel	1835	R	1	105
Carpenter, John	1786	E	1	324
Carpenter, John	1798	G	1	292
Carpenter, John	1841	S	1	555
Carpenter, John	1848	U	1	547
Carpenter, Magdalena	1804	H	1	435
Carpenter, Martin	1832	Q	1	193
Carpenter, Mary	1837	R	1	423
Carpenter, Mary	1840	S	1	378
Carpenter, Mary	1842	T	1	14
Carpenter, Samuel, Esq.	1824	O	1	257
Carpenter, Susanna	1822	N	1	247
Carr, Michael	1746	A	1	119
Carr, Patrick	1736	A	1	24
Carroll, Charles	1839	S	1	187
Carson, James	1773	C	1	142
Carson, James	1808	H	1	609
Carson, John	1765	B	1	413
Carson, John	1778	C	1	525
Carson, Patrick	1767	A	1	220
Carson, Thomas D.	1838	S	1	45
Carson, William	1761	I	1	85
Carter, Daniel	1839	S	1	198

Name	Year	Bk.	Vol	Page	Name	Year	Bk.	Vol	Page
Carter, Ebenezer	1829	P	1	357	Clingen, Thomas	1788	F	1	77
Carter, Henry B.	1844	T	1	417	Clopper, Feronica	1823	O	1	6
Casper, Cathrine	1849	U	1	797	Clopper, Leonard	1805	H	1	651
Casper, Frederick	1850	U	1	904	Cloud, Joseph	1829	P	1	345
Cassel, Joseph	1848	U	1	638	Clouder, Peter	1750	Y	2	129
Cassler, William	1829	P	1	335	Clouse, Michael	1805	H	1	611
Caster, Benjamin	1814	K	1	461	Coates, Margaret	1852	V	1	115
Casting, Frederick	1821	N	1	54	Coble, John	1818	M	1	132
Catherwood, John	1742	A	1	71	Coble, John	1844	T	1	369
Cathey, John	1742	I	1	72	Cochenour, Mary	1773	C	1	139
Cauffman, Andrew	1744	A	1	92	Cochran, Andrew	1775	C	1	330
Caughey, John, Sr	1833	Q	1	411	Cochran, Joseph	1794	I	1	85
Caveat, John	1784	E	1	67	Cochran, Thomas	1764	B	1	473
Cerfass, Nicholas	1784	Y	2	89	Cochran, William	1749	I	1	75
Chamberlain, John	1823	N	1	297	Cockley, John	1796	F	1	658
Chamberlain, Joshua, Sr.	1801	H	1	90	Coelln, Claus	1806	I	1	271
Chamberlain, Mary	1835	R	1	75	Coffman, Andreas	1744	Y	2	334
Chamberlin, Jonas	1771	B	1	653	Coffroth, Gerhart	1796	F	1	643
Chambers, Arthur	1762	A	1	219	Coldren, Mathias	1839	S	1	210
Chambers, James	1758	B	1	224	Coleman, Ann	1844	T	1	478
Chambers, John	1769	A	1	230	Coleman, Robert, Esq.	1825	O	1	347
Chambers, Lydia	1802	I	1	87	Coleman, William	1787	E	1	445
Chambers, Samuel	1766	B	1	466	Coleman, William	1837	R	1	384
Chambers, Stephen, Esq.	1789	F	1	128	Collins, Cornelius	1778	C	1	495
Chambers, Thomas	1763	A	1	218	Collins, Cornelius	1810	L	1	69
Chambers, William	1765	B	1	468	Collins, James	1823	O	1	58
Chapman, Stephman	1848	U	1	559	Coln, John(see Kohn)	1808	J	1	35
Charles, Jacob	1840	S	1	313	Compton, John	1741	A	1	60
Charles, Joseph	1839	S	1	138	Conn, Henry	1837	R	1	353
Charles, Timothy	1838	S	1	13	Connard, Isaac	1849	U	1	675
Chestnut, Henry	1811	L	1	70	Connelly, John	1747	A	1	141
Chitty, Benjamin	1822	N	1	191	Connelly, Joseph	1822	N	1	174
Christ, John	1850	U	1	909	Connelly, Susanna	1753	B	1	13
Christi, Anna Maria	1793	Y	2	90	Connelly, William	1848	U	1	501
Christopher, Charles	1767	B	1	464	Conner, Cathrine	1799	G	1	497
Christy, Edward	1803	H	1	292	Conner, John	1821	M	1	469
Christy, Henry	1799	G	1	498	Conner, Roger	1775	C	1	149
Christy, John	1790	F	1	222	Conrad, Catherine	1826	Y	2	135
Chrysty, Mary Barbara	1795	G	1	362	Conrad, Daniel	1812	L	1	73
Churchman, Margaret	1840	S	1	241	Conrad, George	1765	B	1	475
Clark, Ann	1845	T	1	554	Conrad, Jacob	1770	C	1	153
Clark, Brice	1820	M	1	444	Conrad, Peter	1798	G	1	418
Clark, Brice	1833	Q	1	378	Conway, William	1844	T	1	343
Clark, Daniel	1769	B	1	562	Cook, Allen	1847	U	1	411
Clark, Daniel	1793	F	1	515	Cook, David	1788	F	1	15
Clark, Elizabeth	1847	U	1	307	Cook, Edward	1805	H	1	621
Clark, Henry	1824	O	1	242	Cook, James	1741	A	1	57
Clark, James	1767	B	1	471	Cook, James	1774	C	1	148
Clark, John	1753	I	1	77	Cook, Samuel, Esq.	1804	H	1	543
Clark, Nathaniel	1778	C	1	515	Cookson, Thomas	1753	B	1	1
Clark, Robert	1771	C	1	131	Cooper, Calvin	1782	D	1	35
Clark, Robert	1849	U	1	653	Cooper, Christian	1771	C	1	134
Clark, Sarah	1752	I	1	76	Cooper, Henry	1748	A	1	161
Clark, Thomas	1759	I	1	81	Cooper, James	1804	H	1	520
Clark, Thomas(Drumore)	1803	H	1	293	Cooper, James	1848	U	1	609
Clark, Thomas(Martic)	1803	H	1	350	Cooper, John	1756	I	1	83
Clark, William	1732	A	1	5	Cooper, John	1757	B	1	192
Clark, William	1763	A	1	219	Cooper, John	1769	B	1	564
Clark, William	1818	M	1	125	Cooper, John	1827	P	1	100
Clarke, William	1780	D	1	9	Cooper, John George	1780	D	1	-
Clasgon, James	1774	C	1	185	Cooper, Rebecca	1813	K	1	427
Cleland, John	1753	B	1	8	Cooper, Samuel J.	1833	Q	1	485
Clemens, George	1817	M	1	116	Cooper, Truman	1850	U	1	894
Clemmens, Elizabeth	1829	P	1	392	Coppenheffer, John	1847	U	1	446
Clemson, James, Esq.	1792	F	1	369	Coppock, John	1789	F	1	217
Clemson, James, Esq.	1820	M	1	385	Corey, James	1849	U	1	670
Clemson, John	1794	F	1	523	Cornell, Sarah	1848	U	1	526
Clemson, John	1808	J	1	35	Corner, John	1753	D	1	78
Clemson, Thomas	1785	E	1	308	Cornhass, John	1783	D	1	321
Clendenin, James	1842	T	1	16	Corpman, Elizabeth	1854	Q	1	488
Clepper, Joseph	1817	M	1	115	Corran, James	1805	H	1	613
Clingan, James	1806	J	1	32	Corran, William	1787	E	1	415

Name	Year	Bk.	Vol	Page	Name	Year	Bk.	Vol	Page
Coss, Peter..............	1830	P	1	438	Cummings, James.........	1821	M	1	505
Cottrell, Eleanor.......	1844	T	1	423	Cummings, Jonathan......	1770	A	1	231
Cottrell, Joseph........	1850	U	1	901	Cummings, Jonathan......	1824	O	1	121
Coulter, Hugh...........	1806	J	1	31	Cummins, Elizabeth......	1805	H	1	610
Coulter, James..........	1736	A	1	23	Cummins, John...........	1790	F	1	239
Coulter, James..........	1845	U	1	38	Cunkle, Barbara.........	1821	N	1	51
Coulter, John...........	1845	T	1	527	Cunkle, Christian.......	1812	L	1	166
Coulter, Samuel.........	1778	C	1	526	Cunkle, Henry(Kunkle)...	1834	R	1	53
Cowan, David............	1757	I	1	82	Cunkle, John............	1845	T	1	565
Cowan, David............	1786	E	1	381	Cunkle, Magalena........	1834	R	1	55
Cowan, Henry............	1760	-	-	-	Cunningham, Andrew......	1760	I	1	81
Cowan, John.............	1760	A	1	217	Cunningham, Andrew......	1779	C	1	523
Cowan, Mary.............	1849	U	1	791	Cunningham, James.......	1793	F	1	469
Cowan, William..........	1793	J	1	31	Cunningham, Mathew......	1795	G	1	348
Cowden, Mathew..........	1773	C	1	144	Cunningham, Roger.......	1744	A	1	90
Cowden, William.........	1782	D	1	36	Cunningham, Samuel......	1777	D	1	374
Cowie, Samuel...........	1772	J	1	28	Cunningham, William.....	1752	A	1	199
Cox, Joshua.............	1747	A	1	131	Curley, Hugh............	1847	U	1	443
Cox, William............	1825	O	1	371	Curry, Robert...........	1768	A	1	208
Craig, Agnes............	1810	K	1	175	Curry, William..........	1746	A	1	125
Craig, Alexander........	1754	B	1	35	Cutler, Agnes...........	1825	O	1	336
Craig, Andrew...........	1775	C	1	150	Cutler, Susanna.........	1823	O	1	79
Craig, David............	1758	B	1	226	Czander,Jacob F.(Xander)	1827	P	1	46
Craig, John.............	1774	C	1	145	D				
Craig, John.............	1783	D	1	396	Dale, Samuel............	1842	T	1	140
Craig, John.............	1794	F	1	555	Dalker, Abraham.........	1772	C	1	154
Crall, Cathrine.........	1819	M	1	345	Dambach, Adam...........	1803	Y	2	95
Crall, Mathias..........	1785	E	1	240	Dampman, John...........	1811	L	1	78
Crall, Ulrich...........	1773	Y	2	91	Daniel, Andrew..........	1802	I	1	186
Cramer, Andrew..........	1783	D	1	325	Daniel, Hannah..........	1848	U	1	493
Cramer, Frederick.......	1758	D	1	212	Dannar, Barbara(Tanner).	1820	M	1	455
Cramer, Peter...........	1836	R	1	274	Danneberg,David.........	1804	H	1	540
Cranford, Mary..........	1848	U	1	555	Danner, Adam............	1820	M	1	373
Crawford, Christopher...	1816	M	1	1	Danner, Adam............	1847	U	1	248
Crawford, David.........	1779	C	1	528	Danner, Adam............	1850	U	1	830
Crawford, George........	1743	A	1	84	Danner, Godleib.........	1817	M	1	25
Crawford, James.........	1825	O	1	395	Danner, Jacob...........	1783	D	1	294
Crawford, John..........	1795	F	1	615	Danner, Michael.........	1845	P	1	615
Crawford, John..........	1844	T	1	365	Dans, Mary Barbara......	1797	Y	2	99
Crawford, Margaret......	1847	U	1	453	Dans, William..........	1786	E	1	328
Crawford, William......	1761	B	1	462	Dantz, Simon............	1789	Y	2	97
Crawford, William......	1805	I	1	90	Daubaugh, Jacob.........	1758	B	1	235
Creamer, Christian.....	1849	U	1	649	Daugherty, Mary.........	1766	B	1	483
Creamer, Solomon.......	1817	M	1	-	Dauner, Abraham.........	1786	E	1	389
Creamer, Valentine.....	1849	U	1	656	David, Evan.............	1740	A	1	48
Creamer, Yost..........	1781	D	1	11	David, Rees.............	1753	J	1	38
Crean, William.........	1752	I	1	76	Davidson Alexander......	1739	A	1	39
Creavy, Jacob..........	1828	P	1	185	Davidson, Samuel........	1753	J	1	36
Creighton, William.....	1790	F	1	260	Davis, Ann..............	1809	K	1	103
Creson, Sarah P........	1845	T	1	566	Davis, Cathrine........	1740	A	1	52
Cresson, Hannah H......	1841	S	1	446	Davis, David............	1773	C	1	156
Cresson, James.........	1843	T	1	244	Davis, Edward...........	1764	A	1	221
Crider, Henry..........	1813	K	1	404	Davis, Elizabeth........	1797	G	1	151
Crisswell, John........	1757	B	1	152	Davis, Gabriel..........	1813	K	1	397
Cro, Mathias...........	1771	C	1	132	Davis, Hannah...........	1779	C	1	531
Crocket, John..........	1768	A	1	209	Davis, James............	1784	D	1	412
Cross, George..........	1816	M	1	21	Davis, Jane.............	1846	U	1	171
Cross, Jane............	1779	C	1	527	Davis, Jenkin...........	1748	I	1	92
Cross, John............	1776	C	1	330	Davis, John, Jr........	1771	C	1	153
Crow, Alexander........	1814	K	1	641	Davis, John............	1772	C	1	151
Crow,Christian(see Groh)	1777	C	1	437	Davis, John............	1784	E	1	36
Crow, Christian........	1811	L	1	116	Davis, Mary.............	1793	F	1	420
Crow, Peter............	1769	A	1	241	Davis, Mary Barbara.....	1797	I	1	107
Cuckerly, Jacob........	1790	F	1	262	Davis, Walter...........	1815	M	1	24
Cuffroth, Jacob........	1824	O	1	228	Davis, William..........	1791	F	1	291
Culbert, Moses.........	1806	I	1	89	Davis, Zaccheus.........	1788	F	1	2
Culbertson, Abigail.....	1830	P	1	457	Davis, Zaccheus.........	1793	F	1	460
Culbertson, Ann Maria...	1840	S	1	276	Dawson, Elizabeth.......	1733	A	1	10
Culbertson, Fianna.....	1845	T	1	580	Dawson, Robert..........	1802	H	1	176
Cully, Isabella........	1843	T	1	185	Dealing, Jacob..........	1810	L	1	15
Cully, Thomas..........	1798	G	1	328	Deardurff, Henry........	1749	I	1	96
Culp, Henry (Kolp)......	1794	F	1	569	Dearmond, Mary..........	1780	D	1	15

Name	Year	Bk.	Vol	Page	Name	Year	Bk.	Vol	Page
Decker, Hannetta........	1795	G	1	392	Diller, Adam...........	1823	O	1	66
Decker, Jacob...........	1775	C	1	332	Diller, Elizabeth......	1830	P	1	529
Deemer, Jacob...........	1760	L	1	99	Diller, Feronica.......	1843	T	1	181
Dehaven, Edward........	1846	U	1	75	Diller, Francis........	1783	Y	2	98
Dehuff, Abraham........	1821	M	1	521	Diller, George........	1842	T	1	109
Dehuff, Cathrine........	1790	F	1	240	Diller, Isaac, Jr.......	1833	Q	1	450
Dehuff, Henry...........	1800	H	1	82	Diller, Isaac..........	1835	R	1	70
Dehuff, Henry...........	1808	I	1	112	Diller, Magdalena......	1783	D	1	394
Dehuff, John.............	1752	A	1	201	Diller, Peter..........	1817	M	1	26
Dehuff, John.............	1774	C	1	157	Diller, Rebecca........	1833	Q	1	445
Deimler, John...........	1822	N	1	242	Diller, Salome.........	1833	Q	1	478
Deininger, Leonard......	1770	A	1	232	Diller, William........	1846	U	1	96
Deis, Andrew............	1821	N	1	9	Dingee, Obidiah........	1846	U	1	90
Delcher, Adam...........	1765	B	1	477	Dinges, Jacob (Tinis)...	1760	B	1	312
Delinger, Michael.......	1736	A	1	26	Dinkley, Christopher				
Demuth, Christopher.....	1818	M	1	166	(Trunkley)...........	1752	-	-	-
Demuth, Elizabeth.......	1841	S	1	471	Dissler, Jacob.........	1830	P	1	429
Demuth, Jacob...........	1842	T	1	32	Ditler, John (Titler)...	1773	C	1	282
Demcker, John Julius....	1784	E	1	156	Ditz, Christian........	1804	Y	2	94
Denham, James..........	1835	R	1	76	Dixon, John............	1748	I	1	95
Denham, Tarlton........	1822	N	1	145	Dixon, John............	1781	D	1	16
Denlinger, Abraham......	1819	M	1	265	Dixon, Robert..........	1767	B	1	488
Denlinger, Abraham......	1836	R	1	218	Dobler, Jodocus........	1767	B	1	500
Denlinger, Jacob.......	1787	E	1	428	Dobsin, James..........	1748	A	1	147
Denlinger, Jacob, Sr....	1818	M	1	126	Doelker, Sarah.........	1774	C	1	161
Denlinger, Jacob.......	1835	R	1	121	Doersh, John...........	1826	O	1	414
Denny, Margery..........	1761	B	1	375	Doner, Abraham.........	1833	Q	1	347
Denny, Walter...........	1752	I	1	97	Doner, John............	1839	S	1	226
Derr, Henry.............	1781	D	1	20	Doner, Michael.........	1762	Y	2	104
Derr, John George......	1761	I	1	101	Doner, Nancy...........	1849	U	1	787
Derstler, Adam..........	1794	F	1	544	Donnelly, David A......	1845	T	1	533
Derstler, Cathrine......	1847	U	1	333	Donnelly, Henry........	1833	Q	1	448
Desh, Philip............	1777	Y	2	102	Donner, Christian......	1810	L	1	75
Deshong, Dietrich.......	1845	U	1	1	Donwody, Robert........	1748	I	1	94
Deyer, Emanuel..........	1836	R	1	247	Doom, Jacob............	1812	L	1	80
Deyermond, James........	1748	A	1	151	Dorne, Jacob...........	1771	C	1	155
Dice, John..............	1788	F	1	9	Dorneck, Elizabeth.....	1827	P	1	25
Dick, Ann Margaret......	1815	L	1	318	Dorward, Martin........	1797	G	1	153
Dickel, Philip..........	1829	P	1	417	Dorwart, Henry.........	1845	T	1	589
Dickert, Jacob..........	1822	N	1	144	Dorwart, Jonas.........	1829	P	1	265
Dickey, George..........	1748	A	1	158	Dorwart, Martin........	1771	C	1	99
Dickey, Moses...........	1766	B	1	485	Dosh, George...........	1800	H	1	63
Dickinson, Joseph.......	1811	L	1	76	Dosh, James(Tosh)......	1750	-	-	-
Dickinson, Elizabeth....	1849	U	1	692	Dosh, Jonathan (Tosh)...	1750	-	-	-
Dickinson, Gains........	1800	G	1	614	Dougherty, James.......	1841	S	1	495
Dickinson, Joseph.......	1847	U	1	399	Dougherty, Mary........	1841	S	1	518
Dickinson, Mary.........	1818	M	1	146	Dougherty, Michael.....	1781	D	1	68
Dickinson, Sarah........	1846	U	1	168	Doughterman, Jacob.....	1827	P	1	42
Dickinson, William......	1823	N	1	268	Douglas, Andrew........	1741	A	1	65
Diefenderfer, Michael...	1789	F	1	158	Douglas, James.........	1741	A	1	54
Diehm, Mary.............	1838	R	1	437	Douglass, Edward.......	1766	B	1	482
Diel, Jacob.............	1775	Y	2	103	Douglass, Thomas.......	1794	F	1	597
Dierdorf, Abraham.......	1801	H	1	150	Dowbenberger,Valentine..	1759	I	1	98
Dietrich, Henry........	1828	P	1	227	Dowdall, Michael.......	1751	A	1	195
Dietrich, Joseph........	1825	O	1	304	Downey, Thomas.........	1844	T	1	429
Dietrich, Lorentz.......	1815	M	1	23	Downey, William........	1834	R	1	4
Dietrich, Michael.......	1835	R	1	157	Downing, Margaret......	1807	I	1	110
Dietrich, Sarah........	1848	U	1	533	Downing, William.......	1787	F	1	12
Diffenbach, Adam........	1782	D	1	70	Doyle, Thomas..........	1791	F	1	273
Diffenbach, Mary.......	1838	R	1	445	Draeger,Godfreid(Traeger	1824	O	1	196
Diffenbaugh, George.....	1837	R	1	317	Draeger, Jacob(Traeger).	1816	L	1	607
Diffenderfer,Christiana.	1795	G	1	403	Dreish, Adam (Irish)....	1819	M	1	348
Diffenderfer, David.....	1846	U	1	110	Dritch, Charles........	1811	K	1	348
Diffenderffer, Eve......	1800	Y	2	93	Drob, Abraham..........	1777	C	1	476
Diffenderfer, Eve.......	1806	L	1	79	Druckenmiller, Jacob....	1806	I	1	108
Diffenderfer, John......	1818	M	1	181	Druckenmiller, Michael.	1778	C	1	587
Diffenderfer, John......	1837	R	1	415	Druxel, Abraham........	1784	Y	2	100
Diffenderfer, Margaret..	1821	N	1	99	Dubbs, Henry...........	1764	I	1	102
Diffenderfer, Philip....	1806	I	1	103	Duck, Nicholas.........	1793	F	1	448
Dillen, Joseph..........	1840	S	1	246	Duffy, Philip..........	1846	U	1	239
Diller, Adam............	1781	D	1	18	Duffield, George.......	1774	C	1	159
Diller, Adam............	1792	F	1	329	Dufresne, Dr. Albert....	1823	N	1	331

Name	Year	Bk.	Vol	Page
Dufresne, Dr. Samuel....	1835	R	1	142
Duke, George...........	1755	J	1	39
Dunbar, Margary........	1848	U	1	548
Duncan, James..........	1758	B	1	227
Duncan, James..........	1765	B	1	480
Duncan, Jane...........	1765	B	1	479
Duncan, John...........	1746	I	1	92
Dunckel, George........	1773	I	1	102
Dunkel, George.........	1847	U	1	268
Dunlap, James..........	1766	A	1	221
Dunlap, John...........	1778	C	1	530
Dunlap, Samuel.........	1776	C	1	333
Dunning, Mary..........	1735	A	1	20
Dunwoody, James........	1749	I	1	96
Dunwoody, James........	1829	P	1	296
Dups, Jacob............	1775	C	1	162
Durnbach, John.........	1809	J	1	40
Dussing, Paul..........	1784	D	1	454
Dussing, Peter.........	1770	C	1	151
Dutt, George..........	1830	P	1	426
Dysart, Alexander......	1834	Q	1	495
E				
Eaby, George...........	1814	K	1	465
Eagen, James...........	1822	N	1	195
Eagle, Dominick........	1829	P	1	338
Eakenroth, Eve Maria...	1841	S	1	504
Eakin, David...........	1810	L	1	83
Eakin, Mary............	1748	J	1	43
Earl, John.............	1748	J	1	44
Earley, Jacob..........	1777	C	1	424
Eaton, John............	1828	P	1	248
Eatter, John...........	1772	B	1	659
Eberle, Michael........	1844	T	1	468
Eberlein, John.........	1822	N	1	149
Eberline, Samuel.......	1839	S	1	130
Eberly, Anna...........	1826	O	1	544
Eberly, George........	1778	C	1	533
Eberly, Henry..........	1760	B	1	338
Eberly, Jacob..........	1807	J	1	48
Eberly, Jacob..........	1821	N	1	64
Eberly, Mary M.........	1839	S	1	174
Eberly, Michael........	1826	O	1	437
Eberly, Peter..........	1828	P	1	154
Eberly, Samuel.........	1846	U	1	157
Eberly, Ulrich.........	1809	K	1	121
Eberman, Godleib.......	1801	H	1	93
Eberman, John..........	1806	I	1	125
Eberman, John..........	1846	U	1	222
Ebersole, Jacob........	1785	E	1	244
Ebersole, Jacob........	1793	Y	2	109
Ebersole, Jacob, Sr....	1828	P	1	156
Ebersole, John.........	1770	Y	2	123
Ebersole, John.........	1846	U	1	106
Ebersole, Salome.......	1794	G	1	209
Eby, Abraham...........	1825	O	1	321
Eby, Andrew............	1769	Y	2	125
Eby, Anna..............	1826	O	1	534
Eby, Christian.........	1805	H	1	615
Eby, Christian.........	1807	J	1	47
Eby, Christian.........	1827	P	1	9
Eby, Daniel............	1819	M	1	268
Eby, Elizabeth.........	1842	T	1	133
Eby, Jacob.............	1794	F	1	590
Eby, Jacob.............	1818	Y	2	141
Eby, John..............	1820	M	1	402
Eby, John..............	1822	N	1	227
Eby, John..............	1838	N	1	11
Eby, John..............	1845	T	1	600
Eby, Martin............	1815	L	1	330
Eby, Mary..............	1841	S	1	516
Eby, Michael...........	1843	T	1	304
Eby, Peter.............	1748	J	1	42

Name	Year	Bk.	Vol	Page
Eby, Peter.............	1794	I	1	114
Eby, Peter (Leacock)....	1835	R	1	72
Eby, Peter (Elizabeth)..	1836	R	1	292
Eby, Rosina............	1819	M	1	254
Eby, Samuel............	1824	O	1	155
Eby, Samuel, Sr........	1832	Q	1	206
Eby, Samuel............	1844	T	1	360
Echtermach, Andrew......	1833	Q	1	435
Eckenrode, Henry.......	1806	I	1	123
Eckenroth, George......	1828	P	1	275
Eckerle, Samuel........	1789	Y	2	111
Eckerling, Samuel......	1782	D	1	73
Eckert, Gabriel C......	1849	U	1	679
Eckert, George........	1824	O	1	236
Eckert, George.........	1849	U	1	690
Eckert, Jacob..........	1821	N	1	71
Eckert, Jacob..........	1849	U	1	736
Eckert, Peter..........	1823	O	1	70
Eckert, Peter..........	1828	P	1	195
Eckert, Susanna........	1840	S	1	311
Eckman, Barbara........	1796	G	1	206
Eckman, Catharine......	1830	P	1	486
Eckman, Daniel.........	1829	P	1	383
Eckman, Elizabeth......	1796	G	1	71
Eckman, Elizabeth......	1844	T	1	458
Eckman, Heironermus....	1784	E	1	25
Eckman, Henry..........	1790	F	1	245
Eckman, Henry..........	1795	G	1	405
Eckman, Jacob..........	1784	E	1	73
Eckman, Jacob..........	1806	I	1	121
Eckman, John...........	1755	B	1	96
Eckman, Martin.........	1809	K	1	110
Eckman, Peter..........	1799	G	1	501
Eckstein, Barbara......	1797	G	1	88
Eckstein, Christian....	1787	E	1	424
Eckstein, Elizabeth.....	1796	Y	2	108
Edden, John............	1748	A	1	144
Edelman, Adam..........	1783	D	1	72
Edmiston, Martha.......	1835	R	1	156
Edwards, Elizabeth......	1772	B	1	660
Edwards, Evan..........	1771	C	1	165
Edwards, John..........	1790	F	1	275
Edwards, Sarah.........	1802	H	1	227
Edwards, Susanna.......	1804	H	1	567
Edwards, Thomas........	1794	F	1	543
Eger, Mary.............	1838	S	1	58
Ehler, Daniel..........	1832	Q	1	292
Ehley, George.........	1845	T	1	605
Ehrhard, Christian.....	1809	K	1	2
Ehrman, Peter..........	1814	K	1	462
Eichelberger, George Michael............	1789	Y	2	115
Eichenberg, John.......	1827	Y	2	143
Eichler, Godleib.......	1821	Y	2	139
Eicholtz, Jacob(Icholtz)	1760	B	1	407
Eicholtz, Jacob........	1842	T	1	77
Eicholtz, John.........	1821	N	1	58
Eideneier, Jacob.......	1844	T	1	432
Elder, John............	1757	B	1	151
Elder, Thomas..........	1752	J	1	45
Eliott, Thomas.........	1785	E	1	203
Elives, William........	1813	L	1	292
Ellenberger, Barbara...	1803	I	1	118
Ellenberger, Feronica..	1799	U	1	842
Ellick, Andrew(Illig)...	1761	A	1	244
Ellig, Andreas.........	1761	A	1	244
Elliot, Joseph.........	1795	G	1	335
Elliott, Anna..........	1806	I	1	131
Elliott, Mary..........	1807	J	1	52
Ellis, Cadwalder......	1730	A	1	2
Ellmaker, Anthony......	1817	L	1	560
Ellmaker, Leonard......	1783	D	1	64

Name	Year	Bk.	Vol	Page	Name	Year	Bk.	Vol	Page
Ellmaker, Leonard	1829	-	-	-	Eshleman, Benedict	1795	G	1	384
Ellmaker, Leonard	1834	Q	1	474	Eshleman, Benedict	1843	T	1	292
Ellmaker, Nathaniel	1837	R	1	369	Eshleman, Benjamin	1781	Y	2	120
Ellmaker, Susanna	1832	Q	1	212	Eshleman, Catharine	1810	L	1	82
Ellmer, Mary	1824	O	1	203	Eshleman, Christian	1803	H	1	285
Elser, Peter	1786	Y	2	113	Eshleman, Daniel	1749	A	1	171
Elser, Peter	1845	U	1	22	Eshleman, Daniel	1770	B	1	658
Ely, Abraham	1815	L	1	320	Eshleman, David	1834	R	1	37
Ely, Peter	1819	M	1	349	Eshleman, David	1848	U	1	636
Emrick, Anthony	1769	B	1	567	Eshleman, Elizabeth	1806	I	1	129
Ena, Henry	1755	J	1	46	Eshleman, Henry	1787	F	1	53
Enck, Cathrine	1806	I	1	130	Eshleman, Henry	1788	Y	2	116
Enck, Jacob	1787	E	1	406	Eshleman, Isaac	1807	Y	2	104
Endsworth, Andrew	1777	C	1	426	Eshleman, Jacob	1758	B	1	219
Endsworth, Samuel	1777	C	1	425	Eshleman, Jacob	1776	C	1	333
Engle, Andrew	1782	D	1	65	Eshleman, Jacob	1794	F	1	537
Engle, Jacob	1813	K	1	438	Eshleman, John	1808	I	1	134
Engle, Jacob, Sr	1833	Y	2	145	Eshleman, John	1830	P	1	516
Engle, Jacob	1841	S	1	405	Eshleman, Martin	1808	I	1	132
Engle, Jacob	1842	T	1	86	Eshleman, Martin	1832	Q	1	218
Engle, John	1802	H	1	219	Eshleman, Martin	1843	T	1	178
Engle, John, Sr	1826	Y	2	140	Eshleman, Martin	1849	U	1	788
Engle, Magdalena	1821	Y	2	142	Eshleman, Ulrich	1802	H	1	180
Engle, Peter	1813	K	1	440	Eshnower, Leonard	1769	Y	2	124
Engle, Ulrich	1799	G	1	504	Espie, William	1761	B	1	372
English, Barkley	1823	O	1	124	Esworthy, Elizabeth	1844	T	1	463
Enkwish, Barbara	1841	S	1	571	Ettelin, David	1781	Y	2	119
Ensminger, Nicholas	1781	D	1	23	Etter, Abraham	1814	K	1	466
Ensminger, Nicholas	1786	E	1	384	Etter, George	1811	L	1	93
Entrican, Samuel(Antrican)	1798	G	1	409	Etter, Gerhard	1783	D	1	296
Eppinger, John Adam	1846	U	1	181	Etter, Isaac	1836	R	1	187
Eppler, Maria	1804	Y	2	107	Etter, Jacob	1772	C	1	338
Erb, Christian	1736	A	1	25	Etter, John	1767	B	1	490
Erb, Christian	1750	Y	2	537	Etter, John	1847	U	1	370
Erb, Christian	1812	L	1	94	Etter, Margaret	1804	H	1	525
Erb, Daniel, Sr	1829	P	1	370	Ettigen, David	1785	E	1	231
Erb, Daniel	1837	R	1	406	Euteneyer, Jacob	1789	F	1	141
Erb, Isaac	1838	R	1	516	Evans, Aaron S	1845	U	1	40
Erb, Jacob	1811	L	1	90	Evans, Alexander	1747	A	1	129
Erb, Jacob	1815	L	1	124	Evans, Allice	1768	A	1	210
Erb, Jacob	1819	M	1	241	Evans, Amos	1796	F	1	641
Erb, John	1783	Y	2	121	Evans, Catharine	1820	M	1	435
Erb, John	1810	L	1	86	Evans, Charles	1816	L	1	558
Erb, Joseph	1804	Y	2	107	Evans, Isaac	1782	D	1	58
Erb, Messach	1833	Q	1	409	Evans, James	1801	H	1	136
Erb, Nicholas	1769	B	1	565	Evans, John	1748	A	1	152
Erb, Peter	1832	Q	1	195	Evans, John	1783	D	1	62
Erb, Samuel	1819	M	1	293	Evans, John	1798	G	1	171
Erb, Susanna	1837	R	1	599	Evans, John	1801	H	1	148
Ereman, John	1773	C	1	116	Evans, John	1813	K	1	445
Erfort, Anthony	1788	Y	2	118	Evans, Joseph	1833	Q	1	372
Erhard, Christian	1793	F	1	504	Evans, Joshua	1813	K	1	442
Erhard, Daniel	1810	L	1	84	Evans, Margaret	1759	B	1	267
Erhard, Susanna	1817	L	1	559	Evans, Mary	1798	I	1	117
Erhart, Abraham	1858	S	1	86	Evans, Morgan	1748	A	1	144
Erhart, Jacob	1804	Y	2	106	Evans, Nathan	1764	D	1	438
Erisman, Abraham	1829	P	1	348	Evans, Nathan	1798	G	1	420
Erisman, Jacob	1792	F	1	400	Evans, Thomas	1827	P	1	71
Ernst, Herman	1789	Y	2	110	Evans, William	1758	B	1	232
Ernst, John F	1805	I	1	119	Evans, William	1808	I	1	136
Ernst, William	1750	Y	2	537	Ewing, Elizabeth	1810	K	1	144
Ernstberger, Henry	1754	Y	2	127	Ewing, George	1785	E	1	219
Erwin, Jacob	1823	N	1	320	Ewing, James	1776	C	1	335
Erwin, John	1771	C	1	163	Ewing, Mary	1741	A	1	67
Erwin, John	1816	L	1	557	Ewing, Patrick	1786	E	1	327
Esbin, David	1810	L	1	12	Eyier, John	1782	D	1	61
Esby, George	1761	A	1	222	Eysell, Jacob	1764	Y	2	126
Eshbach, Andrew(Ashbuck)	1772	C	1	108	**F**				
Eshleman, Abraham	1784	Y	2	112	Faas, Adam	1787	Y	2	154
Eshleman, Abraham	1838	R	1	490	Faber, Elizabeth	1774	Y	2	148
Eshleman, Anna	1787	E	1	403	Faber, Frederick C	1835	R	1	174
Eshleman, Benedict	1780	D	1	21	Faber, Jacob	1763	Y	2	146

Name	Year	Bk.	Vol	Page	Name	Year	Bk.	Vol	Page
Fagan, Daniel...........	1849	U	1	686	Finchbagh, Ann.........	1753	J	1	53
Fahnestock, Dr. Daniel..	1829	P	1	365	Findley, Alexander......	1775	C	1	174
Fahnestock, Deitrich....	1776	C	1	337	Findley, James..........	1816	L	1	569
Fahnestock, Deitrich....	1817	L	1	572	Pinefrock, George.......	1838	S	1	84
Fahnestock, John........	1812	K	1	202	Pinefrock, Nathaniel....	1844	T	1	456
Fahnestock, Peter.......	1805	H	1	622	Finn, Philip............	1748	I	1	139
Fahnestock, Samuel......	1836	R	1	282	Finney, James...........	1774	B	1	662
Fainot, George Frederick	1818	M	1	116	Firestone, John.........	1801	H	1	103
Falls, Robert...........	1782	D	1	67	Fisher, Christian.......	1838	S	1	88
Fanney, Ann.............	1753	I	1	142	Fisher, David...........	1761	B	1	394
Fannon, James...........	1794	I	1	150	Fisher, Eve.............	1843	T	1	197
Fantz, John(see Pontz)..	1821	M	1	507	Fisher, George..........	1781	D	1	74
Farrell, George........	1747	A	1	132	Fisher, John............	1739	A	1	45
Farrer, John............	1737	A	1	28	Fisher, John............	1838	S	1	464
Fasig, Catherine........	1835	R	1	170	Fisher, John............	1842	P	1	81
Fasnacht, John..........	1821	M	1	470	Fisher, John............	1842	P	1	101
Fasnacht, John..........	1849	U	1	725	Fisher, John George....	1847	U	1	370
Fasnacht, Philip........	1794	F	1	567	Fisher, Thomas..........	1748	A	1	157
Fass, David.............	1795	Y	2	165	Fissel, George Jacob....	1766	B	1	504
Fausset, Charles........	1797	G	1	267	Fissel, John............	1796	Y	2	165
Faust, George...........	1813	K	1	451	Fistle, John............	1770	A	1	235
Faustnauer, Margaret....	1838	S	1	1	Fitzpatrick, Hugh.......	1850	U	1	926
Fautz, Michael(Pfautz)..	1769	C	1	21	Fitzpatrick, Hugh.......	1850	U	1	927
Fawber, Adam............	1767	Y	2	146	Fleisher, Andrew........	1842	T	1	70
Fawber, Bernard.........	1785	Y	2	151	Fleman, John............	1740	A	1	46
Feather, Bernard........	1816	L	1	570	Fleming, George........	1768	A	1	211
Feather, Gertrant.......	1794	Y	2	163	Fleming, John...........	1777	C	1	427
Feather, Henry..........	1811	K	1	197	Fleming, Thomas.........	1840	S	1	331
Feather, Julianna.......	1820	Y	2	167	Fleming, William........	1815	L	1	331
Feder, Henry............	1822	Y	2	169	Flick, H. N.............	1841	S	1	457
Fee, John...............	1823	O	1	86	Flick, Sarah............	1828	P	1	251
Feezer, Dorothea........	1823	Y	2	170	Flick, William..........	1825	O	1	381
Fegley, John............	1793	F	1	493	Flickinger, John........	1787	Y	2	155
Fehl, Frederick........	1827	P	1	97	Flickinger, Joseph......	1829	Y	2	180
Fehl, George............	1815	L	1	561	Flickinger, Joseph......	1847	U	1	254
Feiffer, Emanuel........	1781	D	1	167	Flieger,Tobias(Pflieger)	1779	C	1	572
Feil, Peter(see Pfeil)..	1761	B	-	-	Plinn, Mary.............	1830	P	1	521
Feit, George............	1785	Y	2	152	Flora, John.............	1781	I	1	147
Fell, Benjamin..........	1847	U	1	344	Flora, John.............	1825	Y	2	171
Fell, Francis G.........	1847	U	1	381	Flory, Anna.............	1843	T	1	273
Felter, Jacob...........	1834	R	1	26	Flory, Christopher......	1843	T	1	228
Feltman, John...........	1777	C	1	428	Flory, David............	1795	G	1	357
Fenegar, Henry..........	1847	A	1	417	Flory, Henry............	1837	R	1	374
Fenstermacher,Christian.	1768	A	1	233	Flory, John, Sr........	1831	Q	1	47
Ferguson, James.........	1750	A	1	189	Flory, John, Sr........	1836	R	1	214
Ferguson, Robert........	1845	T	1	564	Flower, John............	1809	K	1	31
Feris, Edward...........	1750	I	1	141	Flubacker, Ann..........	1823	O	1	45
Fernsler, Michael.......	1777	I	1	145	Flubacker, Jacob........	1744	A	1	82
Ferree, Abraham.........	1775	C	1	171	Foehl, Andrew..........	1795	G	1	366
Ferree, Daniel..........	1750	H	1	626	Foght, Christian (Voght)	1813	K	1	620
Ferree, Ephriam.........	1808	J	1	64	Follerin, Elizabeth.....	1840	S	1	320
Ferree, Israel..........	1808	K	1	145	Foltz, Abraham..........	1832	Q	1	280
Ferree, Jacob...........	1749	I	1	140	Foltz, Andrew...........	1831	Q	1	26
Ferree, John............	1773	C	1	169	Foltz, Christian........	1849	U	1	669
Ferree, John............	1834	R	1	23	Foltz, Henry............	1762	J	1	53
Ferree, Michael.........	1829	P	1	423	Foltz, John.............	1850	U	1	860
Ferree, Peter...........	1795	I	1	153	Foltz, Margaret.........	1779	C	1	537
Ferree, Philip..........	1753	B	1	15	Foltz, Michael..........	1769	A	1	214
Ferree, Philip..........	1796	J	1	65	Fondersmith, Benjamin...	1834	R	1	24
Ferree, Rebecca.........	1837	R	1	420	Foose, Jacob............	1841	S	1	99
Ferree, Richard.........	1791	F	1	268	Ford, George............	1843	P	1	252
Ferree, Richard.........	1844	T	1	443	Fordine, Michael........	1778	C	1	504
Ferrie, Joel............	1801	H	1	85	Fordney, Casper.........	1812	K	1	199
Fetchly, Henry..........	1819	M	1	335	Fordney, David..........	1781	D	1	26
Fetter, Jacob...........	1777	I	1	144	Fordney, Elizabeth......	1830	P	1	449
Ficks, Christian........	1793	I	1	515	Fordney, Jacob..........	1819	M	1	284
Field, Pierce...........	1746	I	1	138	Fordney, Jacob..........	1850	U	1	966
Field, William..........	1748	A	1	145	Fordney, John...........	1816	L	1	571
Fieser, Peter...........	1791	F	1	325	Fordney, Melchoir.......	1754	B	1	90
Fife, Jacob.............	1847	U	1	424	Fordney, Philip.........	1846	U	1	229
Fight, Arnold...........	1806	J	1	59	Fordney, Samuel.........	1819	M	1	298
Filson, John............	1838	R	1	531	Fordney Sophia.........	1826	O	1	591

Name	Year	Bk.	Vol	Page	Name	Year	Bk.	Vol	Page
Forney, Abraham.........	1785	E	1	162	Fream, David............	1768	A	1	234
Forney, Anna Maria......	1835	R	1	146	Frederick, Abraham......	1788	F	1	64
Forney, Christian.......	1757	B	1	173	Frederick, Anna Maria...	1790	F	1	202
Forney, Elizabeth.......	1847	U	1	340	Frederick, Christian....	1835	R	1	67
Forney, John............	1769	Y	2	147	Frederick, Christopher..	1784	E	1	30
Forney, John............	1823	O	1	26	Frederick, George.......	1771	J	1	57
Forrer, Barbara.........	1845	T	1	610	Frederick, John.........	1757	B	1	158
Forrer, Christian.......	1786	Y	2	152	Frederick, John.........	1819	M	1	347
Forrer, Christian.......	1809	K	1	96	Freed, Nancy............	1816	L	1	567
Forrer, John............	1811	L	1	102	Freeston, Hezekiah				
Forrer, Mary............	1803	H	1	335	(Hiestand)..........	1850	U	1	840
Forrestall, Richard.....	1823	O	1	41	French, James...........	1763	J	1	54
Forrester, Mary.........	1757	B	1	194	Frey, Adam..............	1832	Q	1	261
Forrey, Daniel..........	1793	Y	2	161	Frey, Catherine.........	1848	U	1	516
Forrey, John............	1753	B	1	9	Frey, Christian.........	1846	U	1	72
Forrey, John, Sr........	1834	R	1	38	Frey, Christopher.......	1785	E	1	269
Forrey, Martha..........	1847	U	1	409	Frey, Conrad............	1770	Y	2	148
Forster, Thomas.........	1772	C	1	167	Frey, David.............	1841	S	1	424
Forsyth, Robert.........	1752	A	1	203	Frey, Elizabeth.........	1818	M	1	126
Fortney, Francis........	1755	B	1	114	Frey, George............	1816	L	1	566
Fortney, Jacob..........	1761	B	1	355	Frey, Henry.............	1835	R	1	85
Foster, Alexander.......	1767	B	1	568	Frey, Jacob.............	1792	F	1	340
Foster, David...........	1745	A	1	109	Frey, Jacob.............	1841	S	1	412
Foster, David...........	1778	C	1	494	Frey, Jacob.............	1847	U	1	425
Foster, John............	1818	M	1	123	Frey, John..............	1770	J	1	56
Foster, William........	1764	J	1	55	Frey, John..............	1807	J	1	62
Foulk, John.............	1747	I	1	138	Frey, John..............	1813	K	1	413
Poultz, George.........	1741	A	1	81	Frey, John..............	1845	P	1	578
Foust, John.............	1762	B	1	404	Frey, Jonas.............	1849	U	1	784
Foutz, Jacob, Sr........	1800	H	1	74	Frey, Martin............	1806	J	1	59
Foutz, Jacob............	1835	R	1	117	Frey, Martin, Sr........	1830	P	1	538
Foutz, Michael..........	1812	K	1	204	Frey, Peter.............	1846	U	1	214
Fox, Martin.............	1842	T	1	74	Frey, Rudy..............	1796	G	1	220
Franch, Elizabeth.......	1817	L	1	572	Frey, Samuel............	1838	S	1	61
Franciscus, Christopher.	1757	B	1	178	Freymeyer, Jacob........	1834	Q	1	524
Franciscus, Christopher.	1794	G	1	148	Freymeyer, John.........	1804	H	1	568
Franciscus, Christopher.	1836	R	1	268	Frick, Abraham..........	1842	T	1	25
Franciscus, John........	1814	K	1	468	Frick, Adolph Christian.	1825	O	1	285
Franciscus, Rosina......	1805	H	1	625	Frick, Jacob............	1782	D	1	73
Franciscus, Stophel.....	1802	H	1	166	Frick, John.............	1813	K	1	446
Franciscus, Susanna.....	1842	T	1	24	Frick, John.............	1849	U	1	801
Franck, Ann Charlotte...	1843	T	1	308	Friday, Jacob...........	1842	P	1	97
Franck, Henry...........	1795	I	1	151	Friday, Mathias.........	1825	Y	2	171
Franck, Henry...........	1848	U	1	576	Frieck, Jacob...........	1743	A	1	82
Franck, Jacob...........	1753	B	1	23	Fritz, Henry............	1843	T	1	212
Franck, Michael.........	1836	R	1	216	Fritz, Jacob............	1765	Y	2	146
Frank, George..........	1809	K	1	18	Fritz, Jacob............	1842	S	1	506
Frank, George..........	1836	R	1	233	Fritz, John.............	1837	R	1	223
Frank, Jacob............	1787	E	1	411	Fritz, Valentine........	1859	S	1	103
Frank, Mary.............	1804	H	1	548	Fuchs, Jacob............	1787	Y	2	159
Frank, Michael..........	1781	D	1	28	Fulk, Mary Magdalena....	1802	H	1	204
Frank, Valentine........	1800	G	1	619	Fullerton, Humphrey.....	1778	C	1	534
Frankhouser, Christian..	1791	Y	2	160	Fullerton,Humphrey				
Frankhouser, Margaret...	1809	K	1	1	(Leacock)..........	1778	C	1	535
Frankhouser, Peter......	1784	E	1	63	Fullerton, William......	1784	D	1	462
Frankhouser, Peter......	1824	O	1	218	Fulton, David...........	1757	B	1	161
Frankhouser, Peter......	1830	P	1	498	Fulton, Hugh............	1820	M	1	366
Franklin, Walter.......	1836	R	1	194	Fulton, John............	1765	B	1	502
Frantz, Abraham.........	1770	A	1	245	Fulton, Richard.........	1775	B	1	663
Frantz, Abraham.........	1771	Y	2	116	Fulton, Samuel..........	1760	B	1	322
Frantz, Elizabeth.......	1848	U	1	485	Fulton, Martin..........	1844	T	1	388
Frantz, George Adam.....	1819	M	1	314	Funck, Henry............	1736	A	1	25
Frantz, Jacob...........	1797	G	1	508	Funck, Henry............	1788	F	1	72
Frantz, Jacob, Sr.......	1842	P	1	36	Funck, Henry............	1800	G	1	616
Frantz, John...........	1787	Y	2	153	Funck, Henry............	1816	L	1	568
Frantz, John...........	1821	M	1	157	Funck, Henry............	1825	O	1	394
Frantz, John...........	1839	S	1	70	Funck, Jacob............	1810	L	1	99
Frantz, Joseph..........	1827	F	1	45	Funck, John.............	1831	Q	1	61
Frasher, Elizabeth......	1845	T	1	525	Fundersmith, Ludwig.....	1787	E	1	426
Frazer, Joseph, Jr......	1773	C	1	170	Funk, Ann...............	1836	R	1	251
Frazer, Joseph..........	1783	D	1	587	Funk, Anna..............	1841	S	1	396
Frazier, Phebe..........	1820	M	1	438	Funk, Barbara...........	1821	M	1	471

Name	Year	Bk.	Vol	Page	Name	Year	Bk.	Vol	Page
Funk, Catherine.........	1840	S	1	346	Gebhard, Jacob.........	1814	K	1	644
Funk, Jacob.............	1798	G	1	331	Geesey, Philip.........	1811	K	1	222
Funk, John.............	1749	-	-	-	Gehman, Benjamin.......	1836	R	1	239
Funk, John.............	1758	Y	2	145	Gehman, Daniel.........	1810	K	1	163
Funk, Martin...........	1790	Y	2	158	Gehman, John...........	1838	S	1	85
Funk, Martin...........	1837	R	1	371	Gehr, Andrew...........	1771	C	1	180
Funk, Rudolph..........	1805	H	1	617	Gehr, George...........	1811	K	1	221
Funk, Samuel...........	1794	Y	2	163	Gehr, Paul.............	1773	Y	2	204
Furguson, David........	1775	C	1	337	Gehr, Peter............	1765	B	1	508
Furnis, Gardner........	1811	K	1	198	Gehrig, Joachim........	1773	Y	2	202
Furniss, Thomas........	1831	Q	1	12	Geib, Daniel...........	1849	U	1	720
Fyde, George...........	1752	I	1	143	Geib, Jacob............	1843	T	1	240
G					Geib, Jacob............	1847	U	1	452
Gabel, John............	1784	D	1	452	Geig, Adam.............	1783	D	1	299
Gabel, William.........	1786	E	1	352	Geiger, Ann Maria......	1769	Y	2	185
Gabil, William.........	1810	K	1	207	Geiger, Christian......	1779	C	1	542
Gable, Henry...........	1849	U	1	781	Geiger, Daniel........	1769	Y	2	187
Gable, John............	1850	U	1	976	Geiger, George........	1827	O	1	606
Gablin, Mary Barbara....	1760	I	1	163	Geigley, William.......	1833	Q	1	463
Gacklin, Margaret......	1798	Y	2	194	Geisel, Jacob..........	1837	R	1	317
Gailbard, Susanna......	1845	U	1	35	Geissinger, John......	1822	N	1	169
Galbraith, Dr. Bartram..	1835	R	1	138	Geist, George, Sr......	1821	N	1	62
Galbraith, John........	1753	B	1	98	Geist, George..........	1850	U	1	846
Galbraith, John........	1769	C	1	174	Geitner, John George...	1818	M	1	123
Galbraith, Robert......	1746	A	1	129	Gelb, Francis..........	1819	M	1	294
Galbraith, Sally.......	1839	S	1	168	Gelbaugh, Frederick....	1797	J	1	73
Galentine,Jacob (see					Gelbaugh, John.........	1797	G	1	85
Valentine).........	1829	P	1	406	Geldmacher, Henry......	1839	S	1	141
Galey, Benjamin........	1777	C	1	434	Gensemer, George......	1812	L	1	131
Gall, Jacob............	1847	U	1	303	Gensemer, George.......	1824	O	1	115
Gall, Jacob D. (Gill)...	1850	U	1	925	Geopfort, George......	1774	Y	2	200
Gallacher, John........	1781	D	1	85	Geopfort, Mathias......	1776	Y	2	200
Gallagher, George......	1793	F	1	495	Gepffertin, Maria Sarah.	1771	B	1	593
Gallen, James..........	1846	U	1	174	Gephart, Henry.........	1820	M	1	525
Galligher, John........	1820	M	1	361	Geppertin, Maria Sarah..	1771	B	1	237
Galt, Isabella.........	1764	J	1	72	Gerber, Adam...........	1796	G	1	211
Galt, James............	1762	J	1	68	Gerber, Andrew.........	1848	U	1	466¼
Galt, James............	1773	B	1	669	Gerber, Christian.....	1769	Y	2	185
Galt, James............	1821	N	1	107	Gerber, Christian.....	1806	I	1	173
Galt, John.............	1807	J	1	76	Gerber, Christian.....	1815	L	1	343
Galt, Margaret.........	1801	H	1	157	Gerber, Christiana.....	1837	R	1	313
Galt, Mary.............	1847	U	1	414	Gerber, Felix..........	1790	Y	2	233
Galt, Thomas...........	1781	D	1	81	Gerber, Henry..........	1810	L	1	105
Galt, William.........	1794	F	1	603	Gerber, Jacob..........	1801	Y	2	244
Galt, William.........	1847	U	1	361	Gerber, Jacob..........	1828	P	1	216
Gamber, Joseph.........	1834	Q	1	522	Gerber, John...........	1748	Y	2	192
Gamble, James..........	1846	U	1	62	Gerber, John...........	1748	A	1	165
Gander, Barbara........	1843	T	1	257	Gerber, John...........	1798	Y	2	194
Ganss, Valentine......	1845	T	1	620	Gerber, John(German)....	1828	Y	2	212
Gantz, Baltzar.........	1839	S	1	159	Gerber, Magdalena......	1818	M	1	154
Gantz, George.........	1818	M	1	130	Gerber, Mary...........	1835	R	1	68
Gantz, George.........	1833	Q	1	457	Gerber, Michael........	1790	F	1	248
Gantz, Magdalena......	1778	C	1	491	Gerber, Michael........	1794	F	1	551
Garber, Jacob..........	1846	U	1	235	Gerber, Michael........	1823	O	1	60
Garber, Jacob R........	1850	U	1	922	Gerber, Nicholas......	1748	Y	2	183
Garber, John..........	1842	T	1	56	Gerber, Susanna........	1836	R	1	235
Garber, Peter.........	1838	R	1	501	Gerhard, John..........	1810	K	1	209
Gardner, Christian.....	1825	Y	2	216	Gerhard, John..........	1846	U	1	105
Gardner, Thomas........	1747	A	1	130	Gerhard, John, Jr.....	1846	U	1	188
Gardner, Valentine.....	1849	U	1	766	Geringer, Jacob........	1796	G	1	54
Garman, Adam...........	1806	H	1	178	Gerlach, George.......	1770	B	1	665
Garretson, Isaac W.....	1839	S	1	164	German, Adam...........	1782	Y	2	238
Garrison, Peter........	1747	I	1	155	German, George........	1796	F	1	163
Gasho, Henry..........	1839	S	1	172	German, Jacob..........	1800	H	1	67
Gaul, Adam.............	1800	G	1	625	German, Leonard, Sr....	1813	K	1	453
Gaul, Mathias..........	1812	K	1	225	Gerner, Frederick......	1819	M	1	227
Gault, Alexander......	1834	Q	1	492	Gerner, John Mathias...	1787	Y	2	225
Gault, James..........	1811	L	1	122	Gerst, Theobald.......	1770	A	1	245
Gault, Letitia........	1818	M	1	135	Gerst, Theobald.......	1771	Y	2	184
Gay, Robert............	1760	B	1	328	Gertal, Margaret......	1811	L	1	114
Gay, William..........	1789	F	1	98	Gervenus, Frederick....	1759	I	1	159
Gebel, John Nicholas....	1759	Y	2	190	Gessler, John...:......	1818	Y	2	219

Name	Year	Bk.	Vol	Page	Name	Year	Bk.	Vol	Page
Gest, Deborah	1826	O	1	436	Glais, Leonard	1818	M	1	190
Gest, Joseph	1815	L	1	339	Glasgow, James	1774	C	1	185
Gettinger, Barbara	1808	I	1	184	Glasser, Frederick	1775	C	1	340
Getz, Christian (Christina	1762	J	1	70	Glasser, Jacob	1803	H	1	317
Getz, George	1838	R	1	532	Glatz, Jacob	1798	G	1	422
Getz, Jacob	1804	Y	2	245	Glatz, Jacob	1845	U	1	27
Getz, Jacob	1824	O	1	178	Glee, Jacob	1805	H	1	653
Getz, John	1796	G	1	66	Glen, John	1795	Y	2	193
Getz, John	1842	T	1	152	Glenn, John	1741	A	1	57
Getz, Mary	1817	L	1	582	Glenn, Robert	1761	B	1	348
Getz, Peter	1752	Y	2	183	Gless, Christian	1787	Y	2	227
Getz, Philip Jacob	1757	B	1	160	Glick, Elizabeth	1792	Y	2	222
Geyer, Barbara	1814	K	1	475	Glick, Philip	1789	Y	2	229
Geyer, George (German)	1828	Y	2	210	Gloninger, Catherine	1845	T	1	536
Gibbel, Jacob	1833	Q	1	432	Gloninger, Philip	1825	O	1	365
Gibbel, John	1818	M	1	197	Glotz, Albrecht	1789	Y	2	228
Gibbins, Abraham	1798	G	1	425	Glouse, Michael	1805	H	1	611
Gibble, Henry	1825	O	1	279	Gnayge, John	1772	Y	2	205
Gibble, Henry	1848	U	1	583	Gochenour, Esther	1839	S	1	201
Gibble, Joseph	1850	U	1	949	Gochenour, Joseph	1764	A	1	246
Gibbons, Deborah	1823	N	1	280	Gochenour, Joseph	1847	U	1	291
Gibbons, James	1781	D	1	82	Gochenour, Mary	1773	C	1	139
Gibbons, James	1810	K	1	212	Gockele, Jacob	1790	F	1	262
Gibbons, Lydia	1821	N	1	110	Gockley, Abraham	1839	S	1	204
Gibbons, William	1832	Q	1	163	Gockley, Dietrich	1828	P	1	211
Gibbs, Henry	1843	T	1	216	Gockley, John (Cockley)	1796	F	1	658
Giboney, John	1767	A	1	240	Gockley, Sebastian	1836	R	1	249
Gibson, George	1761	B	1	515	Gocklin, Margaret	1798	G	1	328
Gibson, Dr. Isaac	1829	P	1	260	Godshall, Ludwig	1799	Y	2	196
Gibson, James, Col	1815	L	1	345	Godshall, Peter	1788	F	1	43
Gibson, James	1845	T	1	598	Goepfert, George	1774	C	1	186
Gibson, Mary	1757	B	1	157	Goepfert, John	1805	H	1	641
Gibson, William	1795	I	1	166	Goepfert, Mathias	1780	D	1	75
Gibson, William	1846	U	1	137	Goepfertin, Sarah	1771	Y	2	393
Gieg, Adam	1783	Y	2	237	Gohern, John	1783	D	1	382
Giese, John	1827	Y	2	206	Gonder, George	1838	S	1	30
Giesey, John	1827	P	1	520	Gonter, Peter	1818	M	1	184
Giesy, Henry (Keesey)	1807	Y	2	248	Good, Abraham	1814	K	1	472
Gilbert, Jesse	1829	P	1	303	Good, Barbara	1834	Q	1	523
Gilchrist, James	1777	C	1	436	Good, Catherine	1815	L	1	334
Gilchrist, James	1782	D	1	83	Good, Christian	1757	Y	2	191
Gilchrist, John	1746	A	1	125	Good, Christian	1808	I	1	179
Gilchrist, Robert	1783	D	1	299	Good, Christian	1812	K	1	235
Gilchrist, Robert	1790	F	1	191	Good, Christian	1815	L	1	575
Gilchrist, William	1795	G	1	371	Good, Christian	1838	S	1	47
Gilcrest, John	1746	A	1	125	Good, Christian	1850	U	1	861
Gilford, John	1770	C	1	175	Good, Christiana	1820	M	1	461
Gilleland, Hugh	1751	I	1	157	Good, Elizabeth	1804	H	1	555
Gillespy, Patrick	1771	C	1	341	Good, Elizabeth	1834	R	1	36
Gillis, Daniel	1803	H	1	359	Good, Esther	1839	S	1	115
Gillmore, Isaac	1806	Y	2	248	Good, Henry	1757	B	1	162
Gilmore, James	1754	I	1	158	Good, Henry	1803	H	1	309
Gilmore, William	1795	G	1	361	Good, Henry	1816	L	1	586
Gilston, David	1760	I	1	162	Good, Jacob	1741	A	1	64
Gingery, Christian	1778	C	1	538	Good, Jacob	1761	B	1	390
Gingery, Michael	1785	E	1	233	Good, Jacob	1828	P	1	226
Gingle, Conrad	1777	Y	2	197	Good, John	1750	I	1	157
Gingrich, George	1846	U	1	210	Good, John	1762	J	1	67
Gingrich, Jacob	1802	H	1	201	Good, John	1792	F	1	374
Gingrich, John	1769	A	1	249	Good, John	1843	T	1	316
Gingrich, Peter	1786	E	1	373	Good, John Nicholas	1759	B	1	282
Gingry, Ann	1819	M	1	273	Good, Martin	1824	O	1	198
Ginter, Christian	1784	E	1	211	Good, Michael	1843	T	1	187
Ginter, Henry	1800	Y	2	242	Good, Peter	1745	Y	2	184
Girling, William	1837	R	1	344	Good, Peter	1754	Y	2	182
Gisch, Jacob	1846	U	1	118	Good, Peter	1766	B	1	506
Gisell, Christopher	1828	P	1	135	Good, Peter	1837	R	1	346
Gish, Abraham	1789	Y	2	229	Good, Robert	1785	E	1	186
Gish, Abraham	1816	L	1	576	Good, Samuel	1823	O	1	42
Gish, Jacob	1771	C	1	178	Good, Samuel, Sr	1833	Q	1	433
Gitton, Peter	1747	A	1	137	Good, Veronica	1831	Q	1	101
Giveny, Ann	1821	M	1	462	Good, William	1779	D	1	78

Name	Year	Bk.	Vol	Page	Name	Year	Bk.	Vol	Page
Gooddittle, Michael.....	1802	I	1	170	Gray, Mathew............	1768	A	1	248
Goodhart, Catherine.....	1845	U	1	34	Gray, Mathew............	1784	E	1	134
Gorgas, Benjamin........	1836	R	1	280	Gray, William...........	1819	M	1	275
Gorgas, Jacob...........	1829	P	1	394	Graybill,Jacob(Kraybill)	1832	Q	1	295
Gorner, John............	1796	G	1	20	Graybill, Mary..........	1793	F	1	467
Goshen, Huston..........	1845	U	1	20	Grebil, John............	1766	Y	2	187
Goshett, Isaac..........	1810	L	1	110	Grebill, Abraham........	1814	K	1	480
Goss, John..............	1734	A	1	19	Grebill, Christian......	1826	O	1	451
Goss, Peter.............	1830	P	1	438	Grebill, Jacob..........	1810	L	1	107
Gosser, Jacob...........	1779	C	1	541	Grebill, Jacob..........	1811	L	1	159
Gossler, Mary...........	1844	T	1	347	Grebill, John...........	1797	G	1	126
Gossler, Philip.........	1821	N	1	83	Grebill, John...........	1812	L	1	134
Gottinger, Andrew.......	1787	E	1	420	Grebill, John...........	1826	O	1	498
Gour, Edward............	1777	C	1	436	Grebill, John...........	1840	S	1	322
Gourly, Martha..........	1812	L	1	128	Grebill, Michael........	1783	D	1	385
Grabill, Susanna........	1788	F	1	5	Grebill, Shem...........	1786	E	1	361
Graeff, Eve.............	1837	R	1	315	Grebill, Susanna........	1819	Y	2	218
Graeff, Mathias.........	1780	D	1	75	Green, Martha...........	1825	O	1	369
Graff, Abraham..........	1819	M	1	326	Green, Thomas...........	1741	A	1	65
Graff, Benjamin.........	1812	K	1	228	Green, Thomas...........	1791	F	1	276
Graff, Catherine........	1798	G	1	273	Green, William..........	1764	A	1	241
Graff, Daniel...........	1785	E	1	215	Green, William..........	1833	Q	1	479
Graff, David............	1784	E	1	128	Greenawalt, Abraham.....	1815	L	1	337
Graff, David............	1839	S	1	131	Greenland, Flower.......	1815	L	1	335
Graff, Elizabeth........	1805	H	1	629	Gregg, William..........	1744	A	1	87
Graff, Eve..............	1768	A	1	239	Grehman, John...........	1764	A	1	246
Graff, Frantz...........	1819	Y	2	219	Greider, Anna...........	1847	U	1	379
Graff, George...........	1777	C	1	429	Greider, Catharine......	1826	O	1	601
Graff, George...........	1842	T	1	115	Greider, Christian......	1846	U	1	227
Graff, George Michael...	1768	A	1	237	Greider, Henry..........	1813	K	1	404
Graff, Henry............	1805	H	1	631	Greider, Jacob..........	1822	N	1	198
Graff, Jacob............	1766	B	1	509	Greider, John...........	1825	O	1	372
Graff, Jacob............	1782	Y	2	239	Greider,John (Kreider)..	1827	P	1	96
Graff, John.............	1746	A	1	113	Greider, John...........	1830	P	1	461
Graff, John.............	1748	I	1	156	Greider, Martin.........	1758	Y	2	191
Graff,John(Hans)........	1748	I	1	156	Greider, Martin.........	1803	H	1	278
Graff, John.............	1765	Y	2	188	Greider, Martin.........	1822	N	1	216
Graff, John.............	1777	C	1	433	Greider, Michael........	1739	A	1	43
Graff, John.............	1784	E	1	40	Greider, Michael........	1793	F	1	477
Graff, John.............	1821	M	1	480	Greider, Michael........	1794	I	1	163
Graff, Mark.............	1791	F	1	315	Greider, Michael........	1802	H	1	217
Graff, Martin...........	1760	I	1	162	Greider, Michael........	1825	O	1	340
Graff, Martin...........	1825	O	1	377	Greider, Michael........	1835	R	1	158
Graff, Michael..........	1760	I	1	161	Greider, Samuel.........	1834	R	1	62
Graff, Michael..........	1771	C	1	176	Greider,Susanna(Kreider)	1832	Q	1	151
Graff, Sebastian........	1763	A	1	236	Greider, Tobias.........	1838	R	1	517
Graff, Sebastian........	1791	F	1	309	Greiner, Adam...........	1804	H	1	466
Graff, William..........	1809	K	1	30	Greiner, Coleman........	1795	G	1	377
Graffe, Hans............	1746	A	1	113	Greiner, Martin.........	1820	M	1	404
Graffe, Hans............	1748	Y	2	181	Greiner, Martin.........	1841	S	1	427
Grafft, Elizabeth.......	1790	F	1	204	Greiner, Valentine......	1794	Y	2	223
Graft, Isaac............	1849	U	1	681	Greiner, Valentine......	1832	Q	1	185
Graft, Jacob............	1778	C	1	539	Greiter, George.........	1744	A	1	87
Graft, John.............	1758	B	1	251	Greiter, Henry..........	1781	Y	2	240
Graft, Margaretta.......	1807	J	1	75	Greiter, Jacob..........	1780	D	1	79
Graham, James...........	1745	A	1	105	Greiter, John Jacob.....	1744	A	1	95
Graham, Jarrett.........	1772	B	1	668	Greiter, Martin.........	1785	E	1	303
Graham, John............	1743	A	1	85	Greybel, John...........	1831	Q	1	118
Graham, Mary............	1846	U	1	111	Greybill. Christian.....	1802	I	1	171
Graham, Robert..........	1811	L	1	121	Greybill, Isaac.........	1837	R	1	297
Craig, Agnes............	1810	K	1	175	Greybill, Peter.........	1804	Y	2	246
Craig, Andrew(see Craig)	1775	C	1	150	Greyder, Henry(Kreyder).	1752	J	1	121
Graig, John(Craig)......	1774	C	1	145	Greyton, William........	1790	F	1	260
Graig, John(Craig)......	1794	F	1	555	Griffith, Rebecca.......	1832	Q	1	198
Grall, Mathias(Krall)...	1785	E	1	240	Grill, Adam, Sr.........	1801	H	1	105
Graner, Jacob...........	1832	Q	1	325	Grim, Leonard...........	1850	U	1	967
Gray, Ann...............	1824	O	1	204	Grimler, Benjamin.......	1831	Q	1	56
Gray, Duncan............	1743	A	1	82	Grimler, Henry..........	1785	E	1	281
Gray, George............	1811	K	1	219	Grimm, Henry............	1832	Q	1	228
Gray, Hugh..............	1760	I	1	160	Grimm, Martin...........	1755	Y	2	192
Gray, John..............	1785	E	1	192	Grisell, Elisha.........	1814	K	1	478
Gray, Joseph............	1806	I	1	176	Griste, Edward..........	1803	H	1	292

Name	Year	Bk.	Vol	Page	Name	Year	Bk.	Vol	Page
Gritter, Michael	1739	Y	2	117	Grubb, John	1790	F	1	228
Groff, Abraham	1827	P	1	58	Grubb, Julianna	1803	I	1	172
Groff, Abraham	1844	T	1	401	Grubb, Martha	1802	H	1	174
Groff, Abraham	1846	U	1	149	Grubb, Peter	1786	E	1	315
Groff, Andrew	1771	C	1	179	Grubb, Samuel	1805	H	1	639
Groff, Andrew	1775	B	1	670	Grubb, Thomas	1779	C	1	544
Groff, Andrew,Esq	1816	L	1	577	Grube, Christian	1845	T	1	592
Groff, Anna	1822	N	1	223	Grube,Elizabeth(German)	1835	Y	2	215
Groff, Anna	1846	U	1	169	Grube, Jacob	1829	P	1	385
Groff, Barbara	1837	R	1	364	Gruel, Marcus	1782	Y	2	238
Groff, Catherine	1814	K	1	469	Gryder, Elizabeth	1800	G	1	623
Groff, Christian	1834	Q	1	529	Gryder, Jacob	1814	K	1	477
Groff, Christian	1842	T	1	78	Gryder, Martin	1839	S	1	191
Groff, Daniel	1772	C	1	182	Gryder, Michael	1788	E	1	463
Groff, David	1831	Q	1	79	Gryder, Tobias	1791	Y	2	234
Groff, David S	1846	U	1	60	Guayge, John	1772	C	1	183
Groff, Jacob	1776	C	1	339	Guckerle, Jacob	1790	Y	2	233
Groff, Jacob	1825	O	1	382	Gudelius, Peter	1773	Y	2	203
Groff, John	1780	D	1	87	Guetz, Martin	1813	K	1	452
Groff, John	1800	G	1	622	Gumpf, Deitrich	1801	H	1	135
Groff, John M	1840	S	1	296	Gumpf, Margaret	1812	L	1	135
Groff, Joseph	1836	R	1	237	Gumpf, Michael	1843	T	1	297
Groff, Maria (Earl)	1834	R	1	34	Gundaker, Barbara	1829	P	1	349
Groff, Mary	1834	R	1	42	Gundaker, John	1814	K	1	654
Groff, Peter	1772	B	1	667	Gundaker, Margaret	1797	G	1	90
Groff, Samuel	1841	S	1	558	Gundaker, Michael	1775	C	1	341
Groh, Christian	1777	Y	2	197	Gundy, John	1819	M	1	296
Groh, Christian	1811	L	1	116	Gunkle, Barbara(Kunkle)	1821	N	1	51
Groh, Mathias(see Crew)	1781	C	1	132	Gunkle, Christiana	1812	L	1	166
Gromer, Martin	1780	Y	2	241	Gut, Christian(Good)	1790	Y	2	231
Groom, Thomas	1846	U	1	158	Gutelius, Peter	1773	C	1	184
Grosh, Christopher	1829	P	1	330	Guth, Jacob (Good)	1758	-	-	-
Grosh, Elizabeth	1848	U	1	605	Guth, Jacob (Good)	1812	L	1	129
Grosh, John	1808	I	1	185	Guth, Samuel (Good)	1777	Y	2	199
Grosh, John	1849	U	1	672	Gutt, Jacob	1760	Y	2	191
Grosh, Mathias	1832	Q	1	143	Gutzahr, Christian	1816	L	1	581
Grosh, Philip	1812	L	1	1?4	Guy, Isabella	1742	A	1	70
Grosh, Samuel	1850	U	1	929	Guy, Sarah	1829	P	1	260
Grosh, Valentine	1771	B	1	666	Gyer, George	1799	G	1	513
Gross, Andrew	1829	P	1	396	Gyger, John	1786	Y	2	225
Gross, Christian	1837	R	1	413	Gyle, Adam	1849	U	1	742
Gross, Conrad	1812	K	1	233	H				
Gross, George	1816	M	1	21	Haag, John	1755	Y	2	310
Gross, George	1847	U	1	438	Haats, John George	1755	B	1	109
Gross, Henry	1798	G	1	428	Habecker, Christian	1822	N	1	243
Gross, Henry	1828	P	1	262	Habecker, Esther	1830	P	1	533
Gross, Jane(see Cross)	1779	C	1	527	Habecker, Jacob	1789	F	1	105
Gross, John	1776	C	1	530	Habecker, Joseph	1798	G	1	329
Gross,Magdalena(German)	1831	Y	2	214	Habecker, Joseph	1800	Y	2	330
Gross, Martin	1827	P	1	29	Haberkam,Frederick (see				
Gross, Martin	1847	U	1	415	Havercamp)	1796	J	1	93
Gross, Michael	1771	C	1	1	Haberstick, Michael	1793	F	1	433
Gross, Michael, Esq	1820	M	1	424	Hackenberger, George	1831	Q	1	3
Gross, Michael	1841	S	1	520	Hackman, Abraham	1765	Y	2	296
Gross, Polly	1850	U	1	905	Hackman, Abraham	1847	U	1	345
Grossman, George	1824	Y	2	217	Hackman, David	1832	Q	1	179
Grossman, Michael	1810	L	1	111	Hackman, Jacob, Sr	1840	S	1	358
Grove, Christopher	1771	C	1	522	Hackman, Ulrich	1797	Y	2	307
Grove, Jacob	1784	E	1	119	Haerfiel, Casper	1821	N	1	102
Grove, Jacob	1805	H	1	637	Hagaman, Catherine	1797	G	1	129
Grove, John, Sr (Earl)	1796	G	1	237	Hage, Magdalena	1775	B	1	366
Grove, Marks	1827	P	1	76	Hageman, John Henry	1754	Y	2	292
Grove, Peter	1769	A	1	241	Hagen, George	1841	S	1	497
Grubb, Ann	1795	G	1	355	Hager, Christopher	1819	M	1	264
Grubb, Ann Margaret	1789	F	1	101	Hagy, Jacob	1805	I	1	204
Grubb, Casper	1808	I	1	182	Hagy, Jacob	1844	T	1	437
Grubb, Curtis, Jr	1790	F	1	211	Hagy, John	1811	K	1	253
Grubb, Hannah	1796	F	1	169	Hahler, Christian	1784	D	1	445
Grubb, Henry	1788	F	1	35	Hahn, Daniel	1840	S	1	257
Grubb, Henry	1816	L	1	580	Hahn, Frantz	1782	D	1	102
Grubb, Israel	1812	L	1	133	Hahn, Michael	1785	E	1	172
Grubb, Jacob	1786	Y	2	235	Hahn, Peter	1760	-	-	-

Name	Year	Bk.	Vol	Page	Name	Year	Bk.	Vol	Page
Hahnlen, Lewis	1847	U	1	338	Hare, Henry, Sr.	1785	E	1	227
Haines, Ann	1836	R	1	180	Hare, Isaac	1747	A	1	134
Haines, Anthony	1814	L	1	296	Hare, John	1756	B	1	144
Haines, Christiana	1752	I	1	199	Hare, John	1773	C	1	200
Haines, Daniel	1824	O	1	153	Hare, John	1783	D	1	376
Haines, Frederick	1847	U	1	354	Hare, John	1788	F	1	82
Haines, Hannah	1823	O	1	20	Hare, John	1810	L	1	3
Haines, Hannah	1847	U	1	383	Hare, Rudy	1777	C	1	439
Haines, Isaac	1831	Q	1	16	Hare, Samuel	1787	E	1	419
Haines, Isaac	1840	S	1	249	Harken, Charles	1806	I	1	221
Haines, Jacob	1763	A	1	253	Harkins, James	1842	T	1	111
Haines, Jacob	1771	C	1	189	harkins, John	1742	I	1	189
Haines, John	1826	O	1	407	Harlacher, Ann	1815	L	1	351
Haines, Joshua	1794	F	1	575	Harlacher, Benjamin	1779	Y	2	254
Haines, Reuben	1840	S	1	367	Harlacher, Catherine	1794	F	1	564
Haines, Samuel	1817	L	1	604	Harlacher, Charles	1762	A	1	250
Haines, Thomas I.	1848	U	1	622	Harlacher, Charles	1794	F	1	593
Haines, Timothy	1846	U	1	87	Harlacher, Samuel	1806	I	1	207
Haines, William	1781	D	1	96	Harlan, James	1819	M	1	307
Hains, Magdalena	1791	F	1	293	Harlan, Moses	1749	A	1	167
Halbach, John Peter	1826	O	1	415	Harman, Barbara	1849	U	1	795
Haldeman, Henry	1849	U	1	688	Harman, Daniel	1752	A	1	200
Haldeman, Jacob	1783	D	1	307	Harman, Daniel	1758	B	1	223
Haldeman, John	1832	Q	1	259	Harman, Esther	1848	U	1	477
Haldeman, John B.	1836	R	1	284	Harman, Philip	1828	P	1	169
Haldeman, Peter	1790	F	1	233	Harmon, Henry	1847	U	1	271
Hall, Barbara	1806	I	1	222	Harnish, Barbara	1825	O	1	287
Hall, Charles	1783	D	1	304	Harnish, David	1845	T	1	621
Hall, Charles	1793	F	1	511	Harnish, Jacob	1749	I	1	194
Hall, Christian	1848	U	1	600	Harnish, Jacob	1814	K	1	487
Hall, David	1814	K	1	494	Harnish, Jacob	1842	T	1	145
Hall, Ephriam	1808	I	1	253	Harnish, John	1829	P	1	408
Hall, Hugh	1758	B	1	223	Harnish, Michael	1806	I	1	229
Hall, James	1745	A	1	101	Harnish, Samuel	1788	Y	2	262
Hall, Sarah	1783	D	1	303	Harnley, Abraham	1839	S	1	152
Hall, Thomas	1759	B	1	266	Harnley, Christian	1846	U	1	161
Hallacher, Elizabeth	1849	U	1	713	Harper, Moses	1749	A	1	182
Haller, Jacob	1794	F	1	583	Harrah, Agnes	1790	F	1	255
Hamacker, John, Esq.	1804	J	1	102	Harrah, Patrick	1770	B	1	575
Hamaker, Adam	1784	Y	2	288	Harris, John	1754	B	1	542
Hamaker, Christian	1841	S	1	529	Harris, Richard	1808	I	1	252
Hambleton, James	1833	Q	1	352	Harris, Simpson	1783	D	1	349
Hambright, Henry	1835	R	1	96	Hart, Benjamin	1844	T	1	428
Hambright, John	1806	I	1	210	Hart, Henry	1771	B	1	672
Hambright, Mary Ann	1835	R	1	119	Hart, John, Jr.	1846	U	1	197
Hamilton, James	1748	I	1	190	Hart, Valentine	1826	O	1	471
Hamilton, James	1777	C	1	443	Hartafel, Sophia	1803	H	1	248
Hamilton, James	1807	I	1	241	Hartafle, Catherine	1786	E	1	556
Hamilton, James	1815	L	1	477	Harter, Andrew	1814	L	1	350
Hamilton, John	1769	B	1	572	Harting, Christian	1780	Y	2	251
Hamilton, Margaret	1816	K	1	588	Harting, Jacob	1850	U	1	962
Hamilton, Margaret	1828	P	1	264	Hartley, Nicholas	1834	Q	1	494
Hamilton, William	1782	D	1	98	Hartley, William	1749	I	1	195
Hamilton, William	1794	J	1	87	Hartman, Ann	1839	S	1	156
Hanay, Patrick	1786	E	1	385	Hartman, Christian	1779	Y	2	252
Hand, Sarah	1797	G	1	200	Hartman, Christian	1827	P	1	94
Hankel, Casper	1846	U	1	91	Hartman, Elizabeth	1848	U	1	505
Hanley, Frederick	1761	Y	2	295	Hartman, Frederick	1818	M	1	196
Hanneberger, David	1837	R	1	365	Hartman, Henry	1810	L	1	7
Hanney, Margaret	1768	A	1	569	Hartman, Henry	1846	U	1	153
Hanrick, Samuel	1738	A	1	32	Hartman, Jacob	1796	F	1	654
Hans, John (Haines)	1807	Y	2	301	Hartman, Jacob	1846	U	1	92
Hansen, Martin	1837	Y	2	321	Hartman, John	1844	T	1	485
Harbill, Lewis	1849	U	1	707	Hartmetz, Catherine	1821	Y	2	330
Harding, Conrad	1759	B	1	285	Hartmetz, John	1817	L	1	601
Hardman, Philip	1812	Y	2	311	Hartz, Mary	1824	O	1	247
Hardt, Samuel (Hart)	1769	I	1	78	Harvye, Moses	1831	Q	1	64
Hardting, Michael	1829	P	1	399	Haslet, John	1797	G	1	201
Hare, Abraham (Herr)	1756	B	1	125	Hasselbach, Henry(German)	1834	Y	2	321
Hare, Abraham, Sr.(Herr)	1785	E	1	272	Hassler, Christian	1784	Y	2	279
Hare, Christian	1749	I	1	192	Hastings, John	1744	A	1	88
Hare, Christian	1772	C	1	190	Hastings, Sarah	1823	P	1	527

Name	Year	Bk.	Vol	Page	Name	Year	Bk.	Vol	Page
Haston, Peter	1769	B	1	574	Heistand, Jacob, Sr.	1808	I	1	249
Hathorn, Agnes	1772	C	1	188	Heistand, Jacob	1816	L	1	593
Hathorn, Samuel	1767	I	1	78	Heistand, Jacob	1834	R	1	30
Hathorn, Samuel	1803	H	1	399	Heistand, John	1784	E	1	23
Hattler, Jacob	1785	E	1	222	Heistand, Peter	1813	K	1	485
Hatz, John	1840	S	1	331	Heistand, Peter	1833	P	1	415
Hatz, John	1845	U	1	16	Heiston, Elizabeth	1832	Q	1	323
Hauck, Susanna	1824	Y	2	323	Heitler, Andrew	1817	L	1	603
Haunenstein, Henry	1792	J	1	83	Heitshu, Philip	1846	U	1	218
Hauser, Martin	1779	C	1	549	Heitzel, Henry	1786	E	1	382
Hauser, Ulrich	1754	B	1	51	Held, Henry	1809	K	1	8
Hausser, Mathias	1784	E	1	14	Held, Henry	1845	T	1	520
Hautz, Philip	1766	Y	2	289	Held, Juliana	1815	L	1	462
Haverstick, Jacob	1833	Q	1	390	Heller, Barbara	1790	F	1	263
Hay, Hugh	1779	C	1	547	Heller, Catherine	1815	L	1	355
Hay, John	1774	B	1	678	Heller, Jacob	1787	E	1	433
Hay, John, Esq.	1766	B	1	521	Heller, John	1822	N	1	234
Hayde, George	1772	C	1	193	Heller, John, Sr.	1828	P	1	142
Hayes, Catherine	1798	G	1	436	Heller, Joseph	1846	U	1	143
Hayes, James	1742	A	1	72	Hellman, Ann	1845	T	1	608
Haynin, Ann Regina	1784	D	1	414	Hellman, Lorenz	1797	G	1	47
Hays, Andrew	1841	S	1	563	Helm, John	1830	P	1	451
Hays, Catherine	1839	S	1	100	Helser, Henry	1846	U	1	225
Hays, Charles	1834	Q	1	514	Helwig, Charles	1765	B	1	511
Hays, David	1780	D	1	95	Hemperly, Catherine	1841	S	1	395
Hays, Robert	1806	I	1	224	Henderson, Archibald	1827	P	1	121
Heagy, George	1844	T	1	447	Henderson, Catherine E.	1850	U	1	857
Heard, Stephen	1757	B	1	167	Henderson, David	1838	R	1	493
Heard, Stephen	1797	G	1	157	Henderson, David	1839	S	1	183
Heckendorn, Daniel	1782	D	1	99	Henderson, Elizabeth	1838	R	1	536
Heckendorn, John	1778	C	1	493	Henderson, Mathew	1806	I	1	213
Hecker, John Charles	1776	C	1	345	Henderson, Thomas	1841	S	1	462
Hecker, Ludwig	1796	Y	2	308	Hendricks, Tobias	1739	A	1	39
Heckert, Jacob	1775	C	1	205	Hening, Jacob	1769	A	1	257
Heckman, John	1735	I	1	188	Henly, Christian	1849	U	1	721
Heferfinger, Martin	1742	Y	2	300	Henly, Michael	1809	K	1	105
Heffley, Jacob	1775	C	1	204	Henneberger, Christian	1847	U	1	270
Heffley, John	1793	F	1	486	Henneberger, Elizabeth	1830	P	1	449
Heffley, John	1809	K	1	127	Henning, Thomas	1747	A	–	–
Heffley, Joseph	1807	I	1	233	Henry, Andrew	1770	B	1	579
Heffley, Mary	1849	U	1	751	Henry, Dominick	1823	N	1	328
Heft, George	1840	S	1	309	Henry, Elizabeth	1846	U	1	159
Heger, Feronica	1798	Y	2	306	Henry, James	1766	B	1	519
Heggensiller, John	1793	F	1	423	Henry, James	1803	H	1	275
Hehl, Matthias Leonard	1794	J	1	585	Henry, John	1770	B	1	577
Heidelbaugh, Henry	1810	L	1	137	Henry, John	1779	C	1	546
Heighold, Martin	1780	Y	2	255	Henry, John Joseph, Esq.	1811	K	1	246
Heil, Ann Mary	1749	I	1	197	Henry, William, Esq.	1786	E	1	392
Heil, Benina	1787	E	1	431	Hensel, William	1842	T	1	117
Heil, Jacob	1783	D	1	363	Hensen, Martin	1837	R	1	343
Heilbrunner, Casper	1825	O	1	337	Hensler, John	1837	R	1	435
Heilbrunner, John	1785	Y	2	280	Hensler, Mathias	1840	S	1	286
Heilman, John Adam	1770	B	1	580	Heppenheimer, David	1818	M	1	120
Heinaman, Jacob	1832	Q	1	283	Heppenheimer, William	1825	O	1	291
Heinitsh, Charles	1803	H	1	360	Herber, Adam (Gerber)	1782	Y	2	299
Heinitz, Augustus	1824	O	1	241	Herbert, Stewart	1778	C	1	545
Heins, John	1840	S	1	280	Herbst, Elizabeth	1834	R	1	41
Heintzelman, Jerome	1797	G	1	155	Herbst, Henry	1826	O	1	515
Heise, Solomon	1833	Q	1	374	Hergelroth, Christian	1826	O	1	412
Heiser, Michael	1846	U	1	112	Hergelroth, Christianna	1847	U	1	282
Heisey, Daniel	1840	S	1	351	Herman, Christian	1806	I	1	218
Heisey, Joseph	1834	Q	1	534	Hernley, Jacob	1785	Y	2	285
Heisey, Martin	1792	Y	2	276	Hernley, Peter	1842	T	1	98
Heisey, Peter	1789	Y	2	293	Hernley, Ulrich	1784	Y	2	260
Heiss, Daniel	1828	P	1	250	Herouf, Andrew	1777	C	1	415
Heiss, Dietrich	1819	Y	2	328	Herr, Abraham	1803	H	1	251
Heiss, Jacob	1841	S	1	483	Herr, Abraham	1807	I	1	240
Heissey, Michael	1831	Y	2	332	Herr, Abraham	1820	M	1	–
Heistand, Elizabeth	1788	Y	2	262	Herr, Abraham(Manor)	1824	O	1	109
Heistand, Henry	1795	G	1	399	Herr, Abraham	1845	U	1	49
Heistand, Henry	1805	Y	2	300	Herr, Abraham	1849	U	1	673
Heistand, Jacob	1772	Y	2	127	Herr, Abraham S.	1839	S	1	157

Name	Year	Bk.	Vol	Page	Name	Year	Bk.	Vol	Page
Herr, Barbara	1805	Y	2	305	Hershey, Christian(Manor	1837	R	1	357
Herr, Catherine	1829	P	1	430	Hershey, Christian	1840	S	1	366
Herr, Catherine	1838	R	1	441	Hershey, Christian	1843	T	1	288
Herr, Christian, Sr.	1763	Y	2	129	Hershey, Elizabeth	1821	N	1	23
Herr, Christian	1764	A	1	254	Hershey, Elizabeth	1847	U	1	240
Herr, Christian	1811	K	1	255	Hershey, Esther	1793	Y	2	313
Herr, Christian, Sr.	1815	L	1	583	Hershey, Jacob	1797	G	1	135
Herr, Christian	1819	M	1	317	Hershey, Jacob	1819	Y	2	324
Herr, Christian	1821	M	1	512	Hershey, Jacob (Manor)	1821	N	1	15
Herr, Christian	1823	O	1	90	Hershey, Jacob(Warwick)	1821	N	1	154
Herr, Christian	1841	S	1	525	Hershey, Jacob	1825	O	1	307
Herr, Christian	1842	T	1	50	Hershey, Jacob	1835	R	1	77
Herr, Christian	1846	U	1	122	Hershey, Jacob	1842	T	1	112
Herr, Christian	1850	U	1	873	Hershey, John	1784	Y	2	284
Herr, Christian S.	1850	V	1	358	Hershey, John	1843	T	1	274
Herr, David	1772	Y	2	290	Hershey, John	1848	U	1	614
Herr, David	1789	F	1	181	Hershey, John	1850	U	1	969
Herr, David	1835	R	1	135	Hershey, Joseph	1763	A	1	252
Herr, Elizabeth	1849	U	1	553	Hershey, Joseph	1822	N	1	212
Herr, Emanuel	1828	P	1	254	Hershey, Judith	1794	F	1	565
Herr, Feronica	1806	I	1	206	Hershey, Mary	1831	Q	1	104
Herr, Feronica	1826	O	1	530	Hertzler, Abraham	1846	U	1	64
Herr, Francis	1810	K	1	155	Hertzler, Christian	1841	S	1	440
Herr, Henry	1777	C	1	441	Hertzler, Christian	1842	T	1	115
Herr, Henry	1785	Y	2	286	Hertzler, George	1783	D	1	344
Herr, Henry	1848	U	1	632	Hertzler, Jacob	1794	F	1	532
Herr, Isaac	1819	M	1	203	Hertzler, Jacob	1849	U	1	768
Herr, John	1775	B	1	683	Hertzler, John	1794	Y	2	310
Herr, John	1796	J	1	94	Hertzler, John	1795	Y	2	309
Herr, John	1797	G	1	57	Hertzog, Nicholas	1811	K	1	250
Herr, John	1813	K	1	483	Hess, Abraham	1828	P	1	152
Herr, John (miller)	1828	P	1	170	Hess, Abraham	1803	H	1	367
Herr, John	1838	R	1	477	Hess, Anna	1848	U	1	628
Herr, John	1848	U	1	514	Hess, Catherine	1831	Q	1	15
Herr, John	1850	U	1	890	Hess, Christian	1794	F	1	557
Herr, Martin	1810	L	1	28	Hess, Christian	1816	L	1	593
Herr, Mary	1807	I	1	237	Hess, Christian	1818	M	1	155
Herr, Rudy	1797	G	1	76	Hess, Christian	1826	O	1	580
Herr, Samuel	1787	Y	2	266	Hess, Christian	1848	U	1	532
Herr, Tobias	1833	Q	1	459	Hess, Christian	1850	U	1	885
Herring, Maria Margaret	1759	I	1	200	Hess, David	1815	L	1	463
Hersh, Conrad	1797	J	1	99	Hess, Feronica	1814	K	1	652
Hersh, Jacob	1846	U	1	107	Hess, Frederick	1784	Y	2	259
Hersh, John	1802	Y	2	268	Hess, George	1770	C	1	187
Hersh, Joseph	1832	Q	1	330	Hess, George	1770	B	1	583
Hershberger, Barbara	1811	L	1	147	Hess, George	1820	M	1	357
Hershberger, Henry	1828	P	1	166	Hess, Henry	1827	P	1	5
Hershberger, Isaac	1793	Y	2	314	Hess, Jacob	1849	U	1	702
Hershberger, Jacob	1762	A	1	251	Hess, John	1733	A	1	11
Hershberger, John	1765	B	1	516	Hess, John	1798	G	1	432
Hershberger, John	1813	K	1	402	Hess, John	1825	N	1	292
Hershberger, Magdalena	1840	S	1	333	Hess, John (German)	1828	Y	2	317
Hershey, Abraham	1811	Y	2	311	Hess, John,Sr.(German)	1830	Y	2	320
Hershey, Abraham	1821	Y	2	331	Hess, Magdalena	1767	B	1	522
Hershey, Andrew	1755	B	1	74	Hess, Martin	1773	C	1	194
Hershey, Andrew	1792	Y	2	275	Hess, Mary	1819	M	1	251
Hershey, Andrew	1806	Y	2	303	Hess, Michael	1760	I	1	200
Hershey, Andrew	1837	R	1	335	Hess, Michael	1825	Y	2	315
Hershey, Andrew	1837	R	1	338	Hess, Philip, Sr.	1845	T	1	563
Hershey, Andrew	1845	U	1	7	Hess, Samuel	1788	F	1	46
Hershey, Barbara	1828	P	1	278	Hess, Samuel	1819	Y	2	325
Hershey, Barbara	1850	U	1	880	Hessner, Adam	1789	F	1	174
Hershey, Benjamin, Sr.	1812	L	1	287	Heston, Mordecai	1813	K	1	482
Hershey, Benjamin	1815	L	1	470	Hetler, John George	1758	B	1	218
Hershey, Christian	1745	A	1	98	Hetzel, Henry	1782	Y	2	298
Hershey, Christian	1771	Y	2	118	Hetzelberger, Nicholas	1794	J	1	89
Hershey, Christian, Sr.	1783	Y	2	255	Hetzler, George	1783	Y	2	257
Hershey, Christian, Sr.	1795	G	1	373	Heyle, John	1788	F	1	42
Hershey, Christian	1806	I	1	227	Hibshman, Wendele	1819	M	1	311
Hershey,Christian(German	1828	P	1	132	Hiestand, Ann	1846	U	1	58
Hershey, Christian	1830	Y	2	319	Hiestand, John	1797	G	1	130
Hershey, Christian	1834	Y	2	132	Hildebrandt, Michael	1790	F	1	225

Name	Year	Bk.	Vol	Page	Name	Year	Bk.	Vol	Page
Hill, Gotleib	1749	A	1	186	Hoh, Catherine	1849	U	1	623
Hill, John	1770	B	1	578	Holl, Wendel	1769	A	1	259
Hill, John	1837	R	1	326	Hoke, Conrad	1814	K	1	492
Hill, Martha	1746	A	1	124	Holl, Christian	1808	I	1	250
Hill, Robert	1783	D	1	313	Holl, Mary	1840	S	1	313
Hill, Thomas	1794	J	1	90	Holl, Peter	1784	D	1	418
Hiller, Jacob	1799	Y	2	269	Holl, Peter	1819	M	1	271
Hiller, John	1812	K	1	382	Holl, Peter, Sr	1825	O	1	401
Hiller, Magdalena	1843	T	1	175	Holl, Wendel	1773	C	1	196
Hillman, Richard	1835	R	1	172	Holl, Wendel	1848	U	1	637
Hilton, Edward	1773	B	1	675	Holland, Rev. John J.	1823	O	1	39
Hilton, John	1784	E	1	136	Holliday, Hugh	1820	M	1	372
Himmelsberger, Jacob, Sr	1809	K	1	9	Holliday, Samuel	1818	M	1	195
Hinckle, Henry	1782	D	1	106	Holliday, Thomas	1774	C	1	203
Hinckle, John	1780	Y	2	250	Hollinger, Adam	1826	Y	2	316
Hines, Elizabeth	1845	T	1	572	Hollinger, Daniel	1775	Y	2	282
Hinkle, George	1778	C	1	508	Hollinger, David	1775	C	1	344
Hinkle, John	1828	P	1	221	Hollinger, George	1843	T	1	284
Hipple, Elizabeth	1815	L	1	354	Hollinger, Jacob	1782	D	1	107
Hipple, Frederick	1814	K	1	489	Hollinger, Jacob	1824	O	1	125
Hitcher, John Michael	1750	I	1	198	Hollinger, John	1793	Y	2	312
Hitzelberger, Baltzer	1773	B	1	680	Hollinger, Nicholas	1785	E	1	279
Hoak, Henry	1834	R	1	90	Holmes, James	1749	E	1	197
Hoak, John	1836	R	1	289	Holsinger, Magdalena	1806	I	1	226
Hoake, Elizabeth	1820	M	1	359	Holtzhauer, Andrew	1763	I	1	201
Hoar, Jonathan	1811	K	1	243	Holtzinger, Jacob	1760	Y	2	294
Hoar, Joseph	1815	L	1	460	Holtzinger, John George	1789	F	1	85
Hoar, Margaret	1841	S	1	398	Homsher, Anthony	1848	U	1	466
Hoar, Mary	1850	U	1	815	Homsher, Mary	1846	U	1	116
Hoar, Robert	1849	U	1	722	Hone, Valentine	1807	I	1	243
Hobsh, Joseph	1788	Y	2	264	Hoober, Jacob	1788	F	1	23
Hochlander, Michael	1794	J	1	85	Hoober, Jacob	1810	K	1	239
Hock, George	1811	L	1	143	Hoober, John	1750	A	1	193
Hodgson, Deborah	1843	T	1	242	Hoober, Jonas	1792	F	1	350
Hoeffner, Garlach	1828	P	1	190	Hoober, Michael	1811	L	1	142
Hoefgen, Sebastian	1824	O	1	198	Hood, Samuel	1748	A	1	149
Hoff, Andrew	1808	I	1	255	Hooft, Philip	1762	Y	2	295
Hoff, George	1816	L	1	591	Hook, Anthony	1840	S	1	279
Hoff, George	1822	N	1	126	Hook, Michael	1798	G	1	139
Hoff, John	1818	M	1	179	Hoole, Mary	1802	H	1	159
Hoffard, Anna	1825	O	1	297	Hoopes, Thomas	1849	U	1	755
Hoffer, John	1832	Q	1	153	Hoover, George	1846	U	1	172
Hoffer, Mathias	1803	Y	2	270	Hoover, George	1849	U	1	811
Hoffert, John	1748	A	1	157	Hoover, Jacob	1803	H	1	389
Hoffert, Joseph	1812	L	1	149	Hoover, John	1785	E	1	171
Hoffman, Anna Maria	1767	A	1	258	Hoover, John	1846	U	1	232
Hoffman, Baltzer	1849	U	1	730	Hoover, Joseph	1844	T	1	500
Hoffman, Frederick	1785	E	1	193	Hoover, Martin	1785	E	1	223
Hoffman, Frederick	1816	L	1	589	Hoover, Martin	1810	L	1	139
Hoffman, George	1805	H	1	646	Hoover, Martin(tailor)	1847	U	1	342
Hoffman, George	1841	S	1	422	Hopkins, Catherine	1817	M	1	117
Hoffman, George	1845	T	1	604	Hopkins, John	1820	M	1	460
Hoffman, Henry	1832	Q	1	223	Hopson, Elizabeth	1808	I	1	246
Hoffman, Jacob	1784	Y	2	260	Hopson, John	1804	J	1	100
Hoffman, Jacob	1827	P	1	73	Hora, Mathias	1817	L	1	600
Hoffman, Jacob	1846	U	1	73	Horener, George	1771	J	1	80
Hoffman, John	1793	F	1	437	Horst, Anna	1834	R	1	56
Hoffman, John	1841	S	1	498	Horst, Christian	1834	R	1	35
Hoffman, Michael	1803	Y	2	271	Horst, Christian	1836	R	1	193
Hoffman, Michael	1804	H	1	506	Horst, David	1845	T	1	587
Hoffman, Michael	1845	T	1	584	Horst, Jacob	1759	Y	2	293
Hoffman, Rosina	1833	Q	1	364	Horst, Jacob	1789	F	1	89
Hoffman, Samuel	1821	N	1	69	Horst, Jacob	1828	P	1	244
Hoffman, Valentine	1833	Q	1	380	Horst, Jacob	1813	K	1	405
Hoge, John, Esq.	1749	A	1	175	Horst, John	1821	M	1	477
Hogendobler, Isaac	1822	N	1	261	Horst, Joseph	1824	O	1	250
Hogendobler, John	1820	M	1	399	Horst, Mary	1794	J	1	84
Hogendobler, John	1823	N	1	335	Horst, Michael	1830	P	1	541
Hogendobler, Joseph	1845	T	1	617	Horting, Adam	1848	U	1	635
Hogentogler, Samuel	1822	N	1	197	Horting, Barbara	1835	R	1	95
Hogg, William	1843	T	1	217	Hoss, Daniel	1827	O	1	604
Hoh, Adam	1838	R	1	485	Hostetter, Abraham	1796	J	1	91

Name	Year	Bk.	Vol	Page	Name	Year	Bk.	Vol	Page
Hostetter, Abraham	1831	Q	1	30	Huber, Jacob	1804	J	1	100
Hostetter, Abraham	1834	Q	1	530	Huber, Jacob	1812	L	1	154
Hostetter, Anna	1841	S	1	527	Huber, John	1770	B	1	581
Hostetter, Barbara	1828	P	1	138	Huber, John	1784	Y	2	279
Hostetter, Benjamin	1844	T	1	379	Huber, John	1791	F	1	288
Hostetter, Christian	1777	C	1	456	Huber, John	1792	F	1	407
Hostetter, Christian	1838	S	1	38	Huber, John, Sr	1799	G	1	592
Hostetter, Christian	1847	U	1	444	Huber, John, Esq	1803	H	1	370
Hostetter, Daniel	1824	O	1	135	Huber, John	1821	N	1	33
Hostetter, Elizabeth	1782	Y	2	277	Huber, John Nicholas	1784	E	1	99
Hostetter, Henry	1833	Q	1	427	Huber, John Ulrich, Sr.	1775	C	1	344
Hostetter, Jacob	1761	Y	2	283	Huber, John Ulrich	1775	B	1	681
Hostetter, Jacob	1796	G	1	37	Huber, John Ulrich	1767	B	1	308
Hostetter, Jacob	1823	O	1	75	Huber, Joseph	1800	G	1	628
Hostetter, John	1765	B	1	518	Huber, Joseph	1826	O	1	575
Hostetter, John	1777	C	1	416	Huber, Magdalena	1784	E	1	7
Hostetter, John	1818	Y	2	329	Huber, Mary	1837	R	1	398
Hostetter, John	1838	S	1	51	Huber, Michael	1773	C	1	202
Hostetter, Oswald	1749	A	1	181	Huber, Michael	1824	O	1	107
Hostetter, Rudolph	1844	T	1	459	Huber, Michael	1847	U	1	342
Hottenstein, Jacob	1782	Y	2	297	Huber, Peter, Sr	1798	G	1	590
Hottenstein, Philip	1829	Y	2	318	Huber, Peter	1824	O	1	252
Houck, George	1819	M	1	299	Huber, Samuel	1788	F	1	54
Houder, Daniel	1826	O	1	562	Hubert, Jacob	1828	P	1	176
Hough, Abraham	1840	S	1	377	Hubley, Ann Maria	1832	Q	1	321
Hough, Benjamin	1803	F	1	284	Hubley, Bernard	1803	H	1	321
Hough, Jacob	1768	A	1	258	Hubley, Frederick	1769	B	1	570
Hough, Joseph	1816	L	1	588	Hubley, Henry	1832	Q	1	160
Houseal, William	1846	U	1	57	Hubley, John, Esq	1821	N	1	25
Househalter, Lawrence	1805	I	1	202	Hubley, Mary	1825	O	1	376
Housekeeper, Mary	1845	T	1	577	Hubley, Michael, Esq.	1804	H	1	492
Housekeeper, Philip	1842	T	1	168	Hudson, Charles	1749	A	1	165
Houser, Christian	1849	U	1	777	Hudson, George	1747	D	1	434
Houston, Anna Rhoda	1839	S	1	160	Hudson, Nicholas	1780	D	1	91
Houston, James	1784	D	1	431	Huey, Esther	1774	C	1	198
Houston, John	1769	B	1	572	Huey, Joseph	1773	B	1	676
Houston, Susanna	1829	P	1	418	Huey, Robert	1770	B	1	585
Houtz, George	1782	Y	2	297	Huffman, Christian	1815	L	1	358
Hover, Jacob (Huber)	1759	F	1	383	Huffnagle, George	1809	K	1	28
Howard, Frederick	1833	Q	1	462	Huffnagle, Mary M.	1833	Q	1	339
Howard, Gordon	1754	B	1	41	Hughes, Samuel	1785	E	1	82
Howard, John	1778	C	1	512	Hull, Thomas	1823	N	1	294
Hower, Bernhard	1786	E	1	391	Humble, Christian(Umble)	1821	M	1	497
Hower, Elizabeth	1850	U	1	938	Humel, Frederick	1779	Y	2	253
Howry, Daniel	1628	P	1	139	Humes, James	1845	T	1	567
Howry, Elizabeth	1846	U	1	139	Humes, John	1840	S	1	318
Howser, Feronica	1786	E	1	395	Humes, Michael	1811	L	1	286
Hoye, Philipina	1817	L	1	602	Hummer, Ann Maria	1846	U	1	71
Hoyl, George	1807	K	1	238	Hummer, John	1810	K	1	237
Hoyl, Jacob	1787	J	1	82	Hummer, Peter	1784	E	1	81
Hoyle, Hawthorn	1774	B	1	679	Hunter, Alexander	1841	S	1	507
Huber, Abraham	1777	C	1	414	Hunter, John	1756	B	1	140
Huber, Abraham	1790	F	1	219	Hunter, John	1760	B	1	329
Huber, Abraham	1827	P	1	43	Huntzbacher, Rudolph	1769	A	1	255
Huber, Abraham	1843	T	1	294	Hurch, Christopher	1789	F	1	123
Huber, Abraham	1848	U	1	480	Hurst, Ann	1832	Q	1	187
Huber, Anna	1828	P	1	127	Hurst, Joseph	1804	Y	2	273
Huber, Barbara	1785	E	1	282	Hurst, Michael	1772	B	1	673
Huber, Barbara	1841	S	1	482	Hushour, Theobold	1785	E	1	209
Huber, Christian	1789	F	1	124	Husman, John D.	1850	U	1	868
Huber, Christian	1820	M	1	445	Huston, Andrew	1782	D	1	103
Huber, Daniel	1787	Y	2	267	Hutchinson, Alexander	1748	I	1	191
Huber, Elizabeth	1806	I	1	213	Hutchinson, James, Sr.	1784	E	1	57
Huber, Elizabeth(German)	1829	Y	2	322	Hutchinson, John	1784	D	1	451
Huber, Esther	1832	Q	1	189	Hutchinson, Joseph	1747	I	1	189
Huber, Feronica	1845	T	1	602	Hutchinson, Joseph	1784	D	1	448
Huber, George	1747	I	-	-	Hutchinson, Robert	1774	C	1	199
Huber, Henry	1757	B	1	202	Hutchinson, Samuel	1747	A	1	133
Huber, Henry	1837	R	1	311	Hutchinson, William	1823	N	1	325
Huber, Henry	1850	U	1	817	Huttenstein, Henry	1809	K	1	90
Huber, Jacob	1767	B	1	529	Hutton, Benjamin	1840	S	1	360
Huber, Jacob	1791	F	1	265	Hutton, Isaac I.	1841	S	1	342

Name	Year	Bk.	Vol	Page	Name	Year	Bk.	Vol	Page
Hutton, Joseph	1821	N	1	95	Johnson, Jacob	1825	O	1	299
Hutton, Rachel	1840	S	1	281	Johnson, Jacob	1844	T	1	439
Hutton, William	1825	O	1	397	Johnson, James	1763	B	1	588
Hyde, Elizabeth	1843	T	1	239	Johnson, James	1840	S	1	245
I					Johnson, James	1842	T	1	76
Iackle, Andrew (Yackle)	1836	R	1	288	Johnson, Jane	1741	A	1	81
Icholds, Jacob	1760	B	1	407	Johnson, John	1763	B	1	587
Ihling, Christopher	1818	M	1	133	Johnson, John	1822	N	1	129
Illges, Philip	1829	P	1	288	Johnson, John, Sr.	1834	Q	1	497
Illig, George	1804	H	1	557	Johnson, Joseph H.	1815	L	1	483
Illig, George	1833	Q	1	367	Johnson, Mary	1816	M	1	31
Immel, John Michael	1758	B	1	221	Johnson, Richard	1767	B	1	524
Immel, Martin	1823	N	1	317	Johnson, Samuel	1781	D	1	115
Imoberstig, Abraham	1768	B	1	590	Johnson, Samuel	1784	E	1	97
Ingram, James	1846	U	1	117	Johnson, Thomas	1757	B	1	171
Innes, Brice	1778	C	1	506	Johnson, Thomas	1758	B	1	213
Ire, John	1782	D	1	61	Johnson, William	1749	I	1	257
Ireland, James	1765	B	1	527	Johnson, William	1819	M	1	232
Irwin, Benjamin	1809	K	1	119	Johnston, James	1783	D	1	379
Irwin, Hannah	1812	L	1	289	Johnston, John	1804	H	1	479
Irwin, Jacob	1823	N	1	320	Johnston, John	1816	M	1	32
Irwin, James	1746	A	1	111	Jones, David	1746	A	1	117
Irwin, John	1771	C	1	163	Jones, Derrick	1777	I	1	262
Irwin, John	1816	L	1	557	Jones, John	1800	G	1	631
Irwin, Joseph	1750	I	1	258	Jones, John(see Hans)	1807	I	1	35
Irwin, Rachel	1813	K	1	388	Jones, John G.	1841	S	1	433
Irwin, Samuel	1783	D	1	316	Jones, Jonathan	1806	I	1	263
Irwin, Thomas	1802	H	1	161	Jones, Jonathan D.	1836	R	1	257
Irwin, William	1741	A	1	62	Jones, Paul	1847	U	1	361
Irwin, William	1748	A	1	148	Jones, William	1771	B	1	687
Irwin, William	1802	H	1	183	Jones, William	1850	U	1	913
J					Jordan, Elizabeth	1808	J	1	107
Jack, James, Esq.	1802	H	1	214	Jordan, John	1777	C	1	482
Jackson, James	1843	T	1	233	Jordan, Martin	1812	L	1	156
Jackson, Levin H.	1849	U	1	656	Jordan, Owen	1808	J	1	106
Jackson, Robert	1761	I	1	260	Jordan, Robert	1749	I	1	256
Jacobs, Cyrus, Esq.	1830	P	1	481	Jorde, Peter	1765	Y	2	337
Jacobs, Jane	1845	U	1	6	Jordy, John	1766	C	1	404
James, Philip	1808	J	1	104	Jost, Philip	1816	M	1	108
James, Samuel	1838	S	1	6	Jutz, Anthony	1781	Y	2	338
Jamison, David	1783	D	1	125	**K**				
Jamison, George	1779	C	1	551	Kaekglosco, John Henry	1748	Y	2	125
Jamison, John	1751	I	1	258	Kafroth, Jacob	1824	O	1	228
Jamison, John	1777	C	1	444	Kagereis, Michael	1845	T	1	551
Jamison, John	1783	D	1	345	Kagey, Abraham	1784	E	1	123
Jamison, Margaret	1783	D	1	313	Kagey, Isaac	1789	F	1	139
Jamison, Samuel	1772	B	1	689	Kagey, Jacob	1783	D	1	399
Jamison, Susanna	1769	B	1	590	Kagey, John	1748	A	1	156
Jefferies, David W.	1836	R	1	223	Kain, Cornelius	1750	J	1	119
Jefferies, Thomas	1850	U	1	896	Kain, John	1841	S	1	566
Jenkins, David	1797	G	1	98	Kalb, Henry	1794	F	1	569
Jenkins, Isaac	1782	D	1	123	Kamber, Joseph	1834	Q	1	522
Jenkins, John, Sr.	1777	C	1	448	Kamerer, Andrew	1783	D	1	325
Jenkins, John	1810	K	1	177	Kamerer, Mathias	1823	O	1	16
Jenkins, Joshua	1763	I	1	261	Kann, Adam	1818	M	1	119
Jenkins, Martha	1802	H	1	169	Kann, Henry	1824	O	1	184
Jenkins, Nathaniel	1833	Q	1	362	Kann, John	1812	L	1	167
Jenkins, Ralph	1848	U	1	588	Kapp, Anna Maria	1832	Y	2	341
Jenkins, William	1777	C	1	445	Kapp, Daniel	1829	P	1	295
Jetter, Martha	1804	H	1	537	Kapp, John	1758	B	1	198
Jevon, William, Esq.	1767	B	1	531	Kapp, John Michael	1764	Y	2	360
Job, Jacob	1834	R	1	18	Kapp, Margaret	1785	Y	2	380
John, Morgan	1754	B	1	37	Kapp, Martin	1832	Q	1	303
Johns, Abraham	1838	R	-	513	Karch, John	1814	K	1	499
Johns, Catherine Barbara	1827	P	1	75	Karmony, John	1781	D	1	12
Johns, Christian	1798	Y	2	334	Karr, John	1778	J	1	128
Johns, Jacob	1809	J	1	108	Karr, John	1785	E	1	242
Johns, John	1766	C	1	392	Kauffman, Adaline	1849	U	1	731
Johns, John	1799	G	1	517	Kauffman, Andrew	1744	A	1	92
Johns, John	1830	P	1	493	Kauffman, Andrew	1763	Y	2	360
Johns, John	1850	U	1	856	Kauffman, Andrew	1785	Y	2	379
Johnson, Bernard	1754	Y	2	339	Kauffman, Andrew	1845	T	1	593

Name	Year	Bk.	Vol	Page	Name	Year	Bk.	Vol	Page
Kauffman, Anna	1847	U	1	273	Kehler, Peter	1803	H	1	396
Kauffman, Barbara	1829	P	1	346	Kehner, Adam	1810	L	1	16
Kauffman, Benjamin	1792	Y	2	384	Keil, George	1849	U	1	699
Kauffman, Catharine	1822	N	1	208	Keil, Margaret	1829	P	1	380
Kauffman, Catharine	1836	R	1	232	Keiler, Sybilla	1821	U	1	36
Kauffman, Catharine	1848	U	1	513	Keimer, James	1784	E	1	42
Kauffman, Christian	1745	Y	2	391	Keiper, Casper	1819	M	1	249
Kauffman, Christian	1748	A	1	146	Keiper, Jacob	1847	U	1	305
Kauffman, Christian	1783	Y	2	346	Keiser, Elizabeth	1837	R	1	407
Kauffman, Christian	1792	F	1	404	Kelb, Catharine	1818	M	1	128
Kauffman, Christian	1798	G	1	439	Kelb, John Adam	1818	M	1	128
Kauffman, Christian	1799	G	1	523	Kelb, Jonathan	1815	M	1	127
Kauffman, Christian	1806	H	1	654	Kelicker, Henry	1762	B	1	591
Kauffman, Christian	1816	M	1	35	Kellen, Adam	1748	A	1	164
Kauffman, Christian	1818	M	1	187	Kellen, Claus	1806	I	1	271
Kauffman, Christian	1819	M	1	279	Keller, Augustus F.	1847	U	1	236
Kauffman, Christian	1826	P	1	14	Keller, Esther	1826	O	1	422
Kauffman, Christiana	1783	D	1	319	Keller, George	1849	U	1	658
Kauffman, David	1821	N	1	80	Keller, Jacob	1804	H	1	500
Kauffman, David	1844	P	1	387	Keller, Jacob	1830	P	1	472
Kauffman, Eleanor	1839	S	1	218	Keller, Jacob	1841	S	1	510
Kauffman, Elizabeth	1824	O	1	245	Keller, Jacob	1849	U	1	750
Kauffman, Frederick	1846	U	1	147	Keller, John	1829	P	1	282
Kauffman, Henry	1774	Y	2	391	Keller, Margaret	1737	A	1	27
Kauffman, Henry	1798	Y	2	388	Keller, Martin	1772	Y	2	349
Kauffman, Henry	1822	N	1	159	Keller, Peter	1803	J	1	129
Kauffman, Henry	1843	T	1	248	Keller, Peter	1821	M	1	494
Kauffman, Isaac	1777	Y	2	347	Keller, Renatus	1782	D	1	121
Kauffman, Isaac	1822	N	1	236	Keller, Dr. Sebastian	1808	I	1	285
Kauffman, Jacob	1766	Y	2	356	Keller, Sebastian	1839	S	1	192
Kauffman, Jacob	1767	B	1	594	Keller, Wendle	1771	B	1	604
Kauffman, Jacob	1794	I	1	265	Kelly, Edward (original				
Kauffman, Jacob	1812	L	1	173	on file Mifflin Co)	1830	J	1	387
Kauffman, Jacob	1836	R	1	224	Kelly, George	1768	B	1	600
Kauffman, Jane	1847	U	1	372	Kelly, Hugh	1793	J	1	129
Kauffman, John	1759	Y	2	124	Kelly, Patrick	1769	B	1	602
Kauffman, John	1826	O	1	503	Kember, Catharine	1817	M	1	37
Kauffman, John	1829	P	1	358	Kemper, Barbara	1843	T	1	201
Kauffman, John	1838	S	1	5	Kemper, John	1822	O	1	3
Kauffman, John	1844	T	1	410	Kemper, Levi G.	1822	E	2	270
Kauffman, Magdalena	1843	T	1	250	Kempf, Verner	1833	Q	1	466
Kauffman, Martha	1847	U	1	418	Keneagy, Rudolph	1815	L	1	485
Kauffman, Michael	1791	Y	2	383	Kendig, Abraham	1789	F	1	146
Kauffman, Michael	1816	M	1	33	Kendig, Adam	1807	I	1	273
Kauffman, Samuel	1794	F	1	524	Kendig, Ann	1822	N	1	210
Kautz, John	1835	R	1	124	Kendig, Barbara	1849	U	1	775
Kautz, Joseph	1795	G	1	247	Kendig, Catharine	1803	H	1	296
Kautz, Joseph	1846	U	1	86	Kendig, George	1755	B	1	94
Kautzman, Adam	1775	C	1	345	Kendig, George	1770	Y	2	353
Kayhey, John	1763	B	1	595	Kendig, Henry	1756	B	1	118
Kean, Dennis	1794	G	1	242	Kendig, Henry	1787	E	1	417
Kearagan, Michael	1802	H	1	233	Kendig, Henry	1825	O	1	399
Kedar, Bernhard	1765	B	1	534	Kendig, Jacob	1814	K	1	496
Keef, Owen	1761	B	1	592	Kendig, Jacob	1847	U	1	413
Keefaver, Peter	1786	Y	2	380	Kendig, John	1775	B	1	697
Keefe, Cornelius	1750	J	1	120	Kendig, John	1833	Q	1	379
Keefer, Henry	1841	S	1	549	Kendig, Martin	1748	J	1	115
Keehn, Henry	1839	S	1	194	Kendig, Mary	1819	M	1	339
Keener, Adam	1762	B	1	595	Kendig, Nancy	1845	F	1	522
Keener, Frederick	1780	D	1	110	Kendrick, Isaac, Jr.	1816	M	1	36
Keener, Lawrence	1818	J	1	133	Kendrick, Samuel	1839	S	1	111
Keentzly, Jacob	1803	H	1	255	Kenedy, David	1775	C	1	348
Keeports, Daniel	1843	P	1	298	Kenedy, James	1777	J	1	126
Kees, James	1832	Q	1	265	Kenedy, Mary	1777	J	1	127
Kegeny,John(see Gnayge)	1772	C	1	183	Kenegy, Ulrich	1820	M	1	381
Kegerise, Michael, Sr.	1804	H	1	476	Kennedy, Francis	1790	F	1	266
Kegerize, Agnes	1801	H	1	73	Kennedy, James	1799	G	1	525
Kehler, Andrew	1803	H	1	289	Kennedy, John	1757	B	1	168
Kehler, Frederick	1812	K	1	269	Kennedy, Maxwell	1845	T	1	625
Kehler, Henry	1824	O	1	180	Kentzer, Michael	1808	I	1	289
Kehler, John Albright	1778	C	1	552	Kepfferton,Maria Sarah	1771	Y	2	390
Kehler, Michael	1815	L	1	361	Kerchner, John	1828	P	1	148

Name	Year	Bk.	Vol	Page	Name	Year	Bk.	Vol	Page
Kerlin, James............	1810	K	1	261	Kinsch, Jacob..........	1849	U	1	758
Kern, Henry.............	1812	L	1	170	Kinsel, Christopher.....	1783	D	1	324
Kern, Peter.............	1796	G	1	15	Kinsey, David..........	1827	P	1	109
Kerns, Barbara..........	1832	Q	1	175	Kinsey, Jacob..........	1790	Y	2	385
Kerns, William.........	1773	J	1	30	Kinsey, John...........	1835	R	1	98
Kerr, George...........	1734	A	1	15	Kinsey, Margaret.......	1801	Y	2	378
Kerr, James............	1748	J	1	116	Kinsley, Joseph........	1820	M	1	383
Kerr, John.............	1784	B	1	79	Kintzer, Jacob.........	1783	D	1	327
Kessler, John..........	1844	T	1	434	Kinzer, Henry..........	1823	N	1	284
Kessler, Leonard.......	1855	V	1	894	Kinzy, John............	1848	U	1	549
Kettera, John..........	1772	B	1	693	Kipp, Henry............	1807	Y	2	368
Kettering, Adam........	1775	C	1	347	Kipping, John..........	1759	Y	2	390
Keyser, Jacob..........	1786	Y	2	381	Kircher, Frederick.....	1798	G	1	302
Kibler, Esther.........	1837	R	1	330	Kirk, Jacob............	1841	S	1	522
Kiefer, Jacob..........	1796	Y	2	387	Kirk, Jeremiah.........	1831	Q	1	65
Kieffer, Daniel........	1830	P	1	454	Kirk, John.............	1799	G	1	520
Kienborts, Elizabeth....	1828	P	1	146	Kirk, John.............	1847	U	1	290
Kiepper, John George...	1780	D	1	-	Kirkpatrick, Alexander..	1747	J	1	114
Kiessel, Frederick.....	1848	U	1	577	Kirkpatrick, Samuel....	1788	F	1	39
Kiestetter, Martin.....	1759	B	1	274	Kirkpatrick, William...	1760	B	1	334
Kilheffer, Christian...	1832	J	1	180	Kirkpatrick, William....	1838	S	1	24
Kilheffer, John........	1797	G	1	92	Kirkwood, Robert.......	1771	B	1	690
Kilhefner, John........	1821	M	1	525	Kirkwood, William......	1847	U	1	359
Killcrest, James.......	1777	C	1	436	Kissel, Nicholas.......	1791	Y	2	382
Killcrest, John........	1746	A	1	125	Kittera, Hannah........	1804	H	1	496
Killcrest,Robert.......	1783	D	1	299	Kleeh, Jacob...........	1805	Y	2	369
Killcrest,Robert					Klefer, Jacob..........	1796	I	1	267
(see Gilchrist).....	1790	F	1	191	Klein, Daniel..........	1848	U	1	542
Killcrest,William					Klein, Dorothy.........	1799	Y	2	340
(see Gilchrist).....	1795	G	1	371	Klein, George..........	1789	F	1	175
Killday, Dinah.........	1845	P	1	614	Klein, Godfried........	1773	Y	2	348
Killheffer, Jacob......	1823	Y	2	376	Klein, Leonard.........	1793	F	1	458
Killian, E. Elizabeth..	1833	Q	1	337	Klein, Peter M.........	1806	I	1	269
Killian, Jacob.........	1828	P	1	269	Klein, Rosina..........	1795	G	1	245
Killian, Magdalena.....	1803	Y	2	371	Kleiss, John...........	1829	P	1	381
Killian, Philip........	1838	S	1	19	Kleiss, Philip.........	1800	G	1	635
Killinger, Jacob.......	1779	C	1	555	Kleman, John Adam......	1771	Y	2	352
Killough, David........	1761	B	1	358	Klepper, Joseph........	1817	M	1	115
Killough, David........	1785	E	1	217	Klick, Philip..........	1789	F	1	133
Killough, Margaret.....	1842	T	1	108	Klick, Elizabeth.......	1792	F	1	394
Killough, Mary.........	1845	T	1	557	Kline, Abraham.........	1824	O	1	224
Killough, Samuel.......	1749	J	2	118	Kline, Adam............	1805	J	1	131
Kilpatrick, Edward.....	1784	E	1	104	Kline, Daniel..........	1818	M	1	147
Kimerlin, Jacob........	1771	Y	2	351	Kline, Daniel, Jr......	1828	P	1	233
Kimmel, Jacob, Sr......	1784	E	1	153	Kline, Jacob...........	1826	O	1	446
Kimmel, Jacob..........	1824	O	1	133	Kline, Martin..........	1784	E	1	91
Kimmel, Michael........	1843	T	1	222	Kline, Michael.........	1828	P	1	235
Kimmerly, George.......	1782	D	1	122	Kline, Michael, Sr.....	1842	T	1	118
Kindig, Mary...........	1843	T	1	161	Kline, Peter..........	1826	O	1	441
Kindrick, Wolery.......	1772	B	1	692	Kline, Philip..........	1835	R	1	110
Kinig, John............	1838	Y	2	366	Kline, William Henry...	1839	S	1	149
King, Jacob............	1749	J	1	117	Kling, Moses...........	1842	T	1	106
King, Jacob............	1775	Y	2	123	Klopp, Peter...........	1755	Y	2	377
King,James (Salisbury)..	1824	O	1	262	Klopper, Feronica......	1823	Y	2	344
King,James(Little Brit.)	1825	O	1	309	Klopper, Leonard.......	1805	H	1	651
King, Jane.............	1797	G	1	118	Klouse, Michael........	1805	H	1	611
King, John.............	1748	A	1	153	Klug, Charles..........	1826	O	1	519
King, John.............	1829	P	1	307	Klugh, Charles.........	1811	K	1	265
King, John (Koenig).....	1831	Y	2	341	Knall, Jacob...........	1849	U	1	642
King, John.............	1847	U	1	283	Knebel, Jacob..........	1818	M	1	136
King, Joshua...........	1838	S	1	31	Kneeriemery, Jacob.....	1824	Y	2	364
King, Michael..........	1780	D	1	113	Kneisle, John..........	1811	K	1	267
King, Robert...........	1763	B	1	598	Kneisley, George.......	1786	E	1	316
King, Robert...........	1827	P	1	62	Kneisley, John.........	1757	B	1	169
King, Simeon...........	1759	J	1	123	Kneisley, John.........	1787	E	1	448
King, Solomon..........	1804	H	1	562	Kneisly, Michael.......	1793	F	1	476
King, Vincent..........	1801	H	1	145	Knimshilt, Christopher..	1793	G	1	243
Kingnson, Robert.......	1749	J	1	118	Knoll, Catharine.......	1822	N	1	253
Kingry, Ann............	1819	M	1	273	Knoll, Elizabeth.......	1847	U	1	308
Kinig or King, John....	1838	R	1	458	Knoll, Jacob...........	1814	K	1	494
Kinkhend, John.........	1811	K	1	266	Knopf, Jacob...........	1792	F	1	360
Kinnard, Emanuel.......	1814	K	1	500	Knox, George..........	1795	G	1	400

Name	Year	Bk.	Vol	Page	Name	Year	Bk.	Vol	Page
Knox, James	1812	K	1	272	Kriger, George	1774	Y	2	356
Knox, Mathew	1838	R	1	534	Krop, Christian	1808	I	1	281
Knox, Robert	1848	U	1	474	Krous, John	1841	S	1	500
Knup, John	1782	D	1	319	Krow, George	1838	S	1	65
Kober, Christian	1794	Y	2	375	Krug, Valentine	1759	B	1	293
Koch, Adam	1748	A	1	-	Kryder, Henry	1752	J	1	121
Koch, Barbara	1803	Y	2	371	Kucher, Godleib	1776	C	1	349
Koch, John	1812	L	1	169	Kucher, Peter	1775	C	1	210
Koch, Melchior	1781	D	1	113	Kuckerle, Jacob	1790	F	1	262
Kochenderfer, Andrew	1778	C	1	501	Kuhn, Abraham	1833	Q	1	377
Koehler, Jacob	1811	L	1	163	Kuhn, Maria	1798	I	1	268
Koelb, John Adam	1818	Y	2	362	Kuhns, George	1842	T	1	143
Koenig, Conrad	1800	H	1	71	Kumler, Michael	1823	N	1	307
Koenig, David	1804	H	1	438	Kunkle, Barbara	1821	N	1	51
Koenig, John Christopher	1805	J	1	132	Kunkle, Christian	1812	L	1	166
Koffroth, Gerhart	1796	F	1	643	Kunkle, Henry	1834	R	1	53
Kohn, John	1808	Y	2	367	Kunkle, Magdalena	1834	R	1	55
Kolb, Christian	1774	Y	2	357	Kuntz, Christian	1797	G	1	109
Kolb, Christopher	1760	J	1	124	Kuntz, Elizabeth	1831	Q	1	49
Kolm, John	1808	I	1	285	Kuntz, George	1819	M	1	250
Konig, John Christopher.	1805	Y	2	370	Kuntz, George	1835	R	1	71
Kooch, Adam	1748	Y	2	124	Kuntz, Henry	1823	O	1	56
Kooch, Adam	1748	Y	2	451	Kuntz, Jacob	1763	B	1	597
Koontz, Philip	1764	Y	2	389	Kuntz, Jacob	1778	C	1	553
Kopp, George	1812	K	1	271	Kuntz, John	1797	G	1	159
Korffman, John Michael..	1796	I	1	266	Kuntz, John	1811	K	1	262
Kornhass, John	1783	D	1	321	Kuntz, Ludwig	1776	C	1	346
Koss, Peter	1830	P	1	443	Kuntz, Maria	1802	H	1	235
Krall, Catharine	1819	M	1	345	Kuntzelman, Bartholemew.	1774	C	1	209
Krall, Christian	1802	Y	2	373	Kupper, John George.....	1780	Y	2	345
Krall, Mathias	1785	E	1	240	Kurtz, Abraham	1799	G	1	528
Krall,Ulrich(see Crall)..	1773	C	1	143	Kurtz, Abraham	1782	D	1	117
Kramer, John	1787	E	1	394	Kurtz, Barbara(German)..	1830	Y	2	342
Kramer, Michael	1759	J	1	123	Kurtz, Barbara	1843	T	1	326
Kratzer, Joseph	1773	Y	2	359	Kurtz, Catharine	1811	L	1	158
Kratzer, Peter	1803	H	1	383	Kurtz, Christian	1807	I	1	277
Kreager, George	1774	C	1	208	Kurtz, Christian	1837	R	1	434
Krebill, Christian	1826	O	1	451	Kurtz, Christopher	1832	Q	1	275
Krebill, Jacob	1811	L	1	159	Kurtz, Conrad	1836	R	1	248
Krebill, Magdalena	1840	S	1	247	Kurtz, Hannah	1842	T	1	52
Krebill,Michael(Grebill)	1783	D	1	385	Kurtz, Jacob	1792	F	1	356
Krebs, Catharine	1779	C	1	554	Kurtz, Jacob	1822	N	1	250
Krebs, Catharine	1814	K	1	498	Kurtz, Jacob	1829	P	1	329
Krebs, Christiana	1767	J	1	125	Kurtz, Jacob, Sr	1832	Q	1	163
Krebs, Peter	1798	G	1	307	Kurtz, Jacob	1845	T	1	627
Kredy, Jacob	1828	P	1	185	Kurtz, John	1826	O	1	458
Kreider, Fred Peter	1836	R	1	221	Kurtz, John	1844	T	1	370
Kreider, George	1795	G	1	381	Kurtz, Lawrence	1802	H	1	206
Kreider, Jacob	1839	S	1	186	Kurtz, Peter	1793	F	1	446
Kreider, John	1808	I	1	281	Kurtz, Samuel	1835	R	1	153
Kreider, John	1809	Y	2	363	Kurtz, Stephen	1773	Y	2	358
Kreider, John	1827	P	1	96	Kuster, Henry	1828	P	1	165
Kreider, John	1847	U	1	393	Kyles, Robert	1823	O	1	114
Kreider, Margaret	1812	L	1	259	Kyser, Elizabeth	1828	P	1	203
Kreider, Mathias	1843	T	1	258	Kyser, Michael	1793	F	1	449
Kreider, Michael	1793	F	1	477	**L**				
Kreider, Susanna	1832	Q	1	151	Laber, Martin	1823	O	1	46
Kreissly, George	1777	Y	2	347	Lackey, Eleanor	1831	Q	1	43
Kreiter, Andrew	1824	Y	2	343	Laird, Agness	1779	C	1	558
Kreiter, Ann Christina..	1839	Y	2	367	Laird, James	1741	A	1	62
Kreiter, David	1845	P	1	586	Laird, John	1777	J	1	141
Kreiter, F. E	1836	Y	2	365	Laird, John	1849	U	1	683
Kreiter, Margaret	1808	I	1	287	Laird, Lewis	1842	T	1	128
Kreiter, Mary	1826	O	1	472	Lake, Henry	1772	Y	2	401
Kreiter, Michael	1835	R	1	158	Lamb, John	1770	C	1	214
Kreiter, Peter	1802	Y	2	372	Lambert, Henry	1826	O	1	527
Kremer,Jost(see Creamer)	1781	D	1	11	Lambert, Nicholas	1828	P	1	164
Kremer, Leonard	1829	P	1	354	Lamberter,Eva Magdalena.	1840	S	1	285
Kreybill. Jacob	1810	L	1	107	Lamp, Henry	1841	S	1	519
Kreybill, Jacob	1832	Q	1	295	Lanciscus, Thomas	1751	Y	2	394
Kreyle, John	1831	Q	1	118	Landis, Abraham	1832	Q	1	298
					Landis, Abraham	1846	U	1	76

Name	Year	Bk.	Vol	Page	Name	Year	Bk.	Vol	Page
Landis, Ann.............	1779	C	1	557	Leaman, Elizabeth.......	1828	P	1	280
Landis, Barbara.........	1776	C	1	350	Leaman, John...........	1798	Y	2	413
Landis, Benjamin........	1787	E	1	439	Leaman, John...........	1824	O	1	206
Landis, Benjamin........	1810	K	1	140	Lear, John.............	1793	J	1	143
Landis, David...........	1825	O	1	329	Leber, John............	1834	Q	1	503
Landis, Elizabeth.......	1852	Q	1	203	Lebo, Peter............	1783	Y	2	404
Landis, Felix...........	1739	A	1	59	Lebreton, Aime.........	1834	Q	1	527
Landis, Felix...........	1770	Y	2	121	Lechler, Henry.........	1835	R	1	128
Landis, Henry...........	1761	J	1	139	Lechler, John..........	1806	I	1	301
Landis, Henry...........	1825	O	1	288	Lechler, William.......	1838	R	1	491
Landis, Henry...........	1839	S	1	120	Leckey, William........	1756	B	1	139
Landis, Henry...........	1846	U	1	54	Lecklam, John..........	1747	J	1	134
Landis, Jacob...........	1794	J	1	144	Leech, Robert..........	1769	J	1	140
Landis, Jacob...........	1804	H	1	511	Leed, Jacob............	1806	I	1	296
Landis, Jacob(German)...	1857	Y	2	429	Leek, John.............	1838	R	1	492
Landis, Jacob...........	1840	S	1	320	Lefever, Adam..........	1847	U	1	280
Landis, Jacob...........	1848	U	1	578	Lefever, Catharine.....	1802	H	1	209
Landis, John...........	1756	Y	2	395	Lefever, Elizabeth.....	1848	U	1	495
Landis, John...........	1801	Y	2	416	Lefever, George........	1847	U	1	458
Landis, John...........	1826	O	1	535	Lefever, Henry.........	1844	T	1	471
Landis, John...........	1827	Y	2	427	Lefever, Isaac.........	1751	J	1	135
Landis, John...........	1837	R	1	345	Lefever, John, Jr......	1791	F	1	318
Landis, Maria...........	1838	Y	2	432	Lefever, Samuel........	1789	F	1	120
Landis, Salome..........	1820	M	1	430	Lefevre, Daniel........	1801	H	1	108
Landis, Solomn..........	1849	U	1	696	Lefevre, George........	1815	L	1	493
Landis, Susanna........	1844	T	1	509	Lefevre, John..........	1810	L	1	175
Landis, William........	1814	K	1	506	Lefevre, Peter.........	1799	G	1	530
Lane, Abraham..........	1800	Y	2	415	Lefevre, Philip.......	1814	K	1	505
Lane, Cornelius........	1780	C	1	559	Leghner, Leonard.......	1767	B	1	535
Lane, Elizabeth........	1782	D	1	127	Lehman, Barbara.......	1831	Q	1	84
Lane, Henry............	1773	Y	2	399	Lehman, Christian......	1783	D	1	330
Lane, Henry............	1795	Y	2	410	Lehman, Daniel........	1764	Y	2	403
Lane, Mary.............	1804	Y	2	418	Lehman, John..........	1771	B	1	701
Lane, Peter............	1782	D	1	130	Lehman, John...........	1776	Y	2	421
Lane, Peter............	1803	Y	2	417	Lehman,Ludwig(German)...	1826	Y	2	428
Lantz, Baltzer.........	1812	K	1	282	Lehman, Michael.......	1783	Y	2	404
Lantz, Ferenica........	1819	M	1	236	Lehman, Peter.........	1840	S	1	342
Lantz, Jacob...........	1837	R	1	401	Lehn, Abraham.........	1800	H	1	79
Lantz, John...........	1789	Y	2	408	Lehn, Cornelius.......	1782	Y	2	46
Lantz, John...........	1806	I	1	300	Lehn, John............	1822	N	1	147
Lantz, Powl...........	1810	K	1	276	Lehnert, Peter, Esq.....	1826	O	1	505
Lantz, Samuel..........	1782	D	1	131	Lehr, Esther..........	1818	Y	2	440
Lapp, Catharine........	1842	P	1	17	Lehr, Philip..........	1770	Y	2	403
Lapp, George..........	1921	Y	2	437	Leib, Abraham.........	1814	L	1	363
Lapp, John............	1815	L	1	491	Leib, Jacob...........	1846	U	1	85
Lapp, Michael..........	1824	Y	2	435	Leib, John............	1805	I	1	291
Lapsley, Richard........	1751	J	1	136	Leib, Ulrich..........	1769	B	1	616
Larshey, Peter.........	1802	J	1	147	Leibley, George.......	1798	Y	2	414
Latta, John...........	1768	B	1	609	Leibrich, John........	1785	Y	2	406
Latterer, Herman.......	1774	Y	2	399	Leid, William........	1828	P	1	162
Lau, Abraham...........	1815	L	1	367	Leidig,Leonard Michael..	1790	F	1	234
Laubsher, Jacob........	1784	E	1	8	Lein, Christian.......	1823	N	1	295
Lauderbach, Michael.....	1822	N	1	150	Lein, Jacob...........	1762	Y	2	393
Laughlin, Adam.........	1758	B	1	254	Lein, John............	1822	N	1	184
Laughlin, William......	1760	J	1	138	Lein, Samuel..........	1849	U	1	693
Lauman, Lewis..........	1819	M	1	295	Leinbach, Christian....	1841	S	1	569
Lauman, Ludwig.........	1797	G	1	270	Leisey, Joseph........	1826	O	1	520
Lauman, Martin.........	1796	G	1	161	Leman, Abraham........	1806	I	1	303
Lausch, Gabriel........	1842	T	1	136	Leman, Abraham........	1807	I	1	312
Lausch, Henry..........	1834	Q	1	533	Leman, Daniel.........	1783	D	1	335
Laver, Baltzer.........	1774	B	1	705	Leman, Hannah.........	1813	K	1	502
Laver, Elizabeth.......	1784	D	1	424	Leman, Jacob..........	1835	R	1	169
Lawfer, Conrad.........	1753	B	1	5	Leman, John...........	1816	M	1	38
Lawler, Mary...........	1778	C	1	556	Leman, Joseph.........	1833	Q	1	430
Lawman, Elizabeth......	1810	K	1	277	Leman, Martin.........	1801	H	1	126
Lay, Ludwig............	1767	Y	2	396	Leman, Peter..........	1741	A	1	56
Layer, Frederick........	1838	S	1	91	Leman, Peter..........	1749	Y	2	394
Lazarus, Peter.........	1821	N	1	13	Leman, Peter..........	1807	I	1	306
Leader, Henry..........	1788	E	1	470	Leman, Peter..........	1807	I	1	309
Leadly, John...........	1769	B	1	617	Leman, William........	1772	C	1	217
Leaffel, Christian.....	1748	Y	2	394	Leman, William........	1847	U	1	390
Leaman, Catharine......	1826	O	1	588	Lemmerman, Christian....	1843	P	1	319

Name	Year	Bk.	Vol	Page	Name	Year	Bk.	Vol	Page
Lemont, James	1785	E	1	263	Linville, William	1814	K	1	510
Lenhen, Jacob	1769	B	1	613	Linville, William	1833	Q	1	400
Lennert, Joanna Susana	1846	U	1	209	Little, Agnes	1820	M	1	380
Lentz, John B	1849	U	1	771	Little, Archibald	1749	A	1	166
Leonard, George	1772	B	1	703	Little, Thomas	1826	O	1	427
Leonard, John	1847	U	1	297	Livergood, Henry	1841	S	1	379
Leonard, Philip	1810	L	1	177	Livermore, Daniel	1827	O	1	609
Leperd, John	1748	J	1	134	Livingston, John	1760	J	1	137
Lepo, Peter	1783	D	1	338	Livingston, John	1832	Q	1	173
Lerew, Peter	1759	B	1	290	Livingston, William	1836	R	1	207
Lepne, George	1770	B	1	614	Lochart, Elizabeth	1843	T	1	255
Leroy, Abraham	1765	B	1	545	Lockhart, Josiah	1809	K	1	114
Lesh, Adam	1768	Y	2	397	Lockhart, Robert	1804	H	1	516
Lesh, Sophia	1771	Y	2	398	Lockhart, Sarah	1834	R	1	7
Lesher, Abraham	1848	U	1	580	Loeffler,Caroline Sophia	1849	U	1	734
Lesher, Ann	1821	Y	2	436	Loffler,Frederick Jacob.	1841	S	1	430
Lesher, Christian	1828	P	1	208	Logan, David	1778	C	1	518
Lesher, Henry	1784	Y	2	405	Logan, John	1832	Q	1	307
Lesher, Jacob	1809	K	1	16	Long, Abraham	1806	Y	2	421
Lesher, John, Sr	1831	Q	1	8	Long, Adam	1841	S	1	453
Lesher, John	1840	Y	2	430	Long, Ann	1817	M	1	118
Lesher, Nicholas	1795	F	1	623	Long, Ann	1834	Q	1	521
Lesley, Samuel	1812	L	1	186	Long, Ann Margaret	1794	Y	2	410
Leslie, Benjamin	1811	K	1	278	Long, Anna	1831	Q	1	122
Leson, Paul	1766	B	1	544	Long, Benjamin	1823	Y	2	435
Levergood, Peter	1825	O	1	333	Long, Christian	1794	F	1	520
Levy, Lazarus	1809	K	1	135	Long, Christian	1820	M	1	422
Lewig, Peter	1799	G	1	533	Long, Christian	1824	O	1	141
Ley, John George	1776	C	1	350	Long, Christiana	1828	P	1	187
Lichtentheler, Adolph	1836	Y	2	434	Long, Eleanor	1811	L	1	378
Lichty, Peter	1831	Q	1	2	Long, George	1824	O	1	116
Lick, Henry	1775	Y	2	400	Long, Dr. George	1847	U	1	325
Light, Catharine	1846	U	1	69	Long, Herman	1804	-	-	-
Light, Henry	1813	K	1	422	Long, Hugh	1832	Q	1	224
Light, Jacob	1809	K	1	23	Long, Isaac	1803	H	1	242
Light, John	1808	I	1	315	Long, James	1803	H	1	411
Light, John	1834	R	1	12	Long, James	1827	P	1	35
Light, Joseph	1733	A	1	11	Long, James	1845	T	1	537
Lightheiser, Catharine	1842	P	1	166	Long, John	1750	Y	2	402
Lightner, Barbara	1821	N	1	81	Long, John	1767	B	1	540
Lightner, Elizabeth	1847	U	1	421	Long, John	1782	Y	2	45
Lightner, Joel	1837	R	1	367	Long, John	1783	D	1	352
Lightner, John	1812	L	1	181	Long, John	1794	F	1	553
Lightner, John	1841	S	1	492	Long, John	1801	I	1	314
Lightner, Leah	1842	T	1	156	Long, John	1817	M	1	40
Lightner, Michael	1810	L	1	13	Long, Joseph	1785	E	1	200
Lightner, Nathaniel	1782	D	1	128	Long, Robert	1799	G	1	536
Ligit, John	1766	B	1	607	Long, Robert	1806	I	1	298
Likens, Samuel	1843	T	1	202	Long, Urban	1769	B	1	611
Lile, Elizabeth	1787	E	1	460	Long, William	1779	C	1	557
Limrich, John	1777	C	1	351	Longenecker, Abraham	1800	G	1	639
Lind, Conrad	1836	R	1	260	Longenecker, Abraham	1806	Y	2	423
Lind, Elizabeth	1847	U	1	422	Longenecker, Ann	1820	M	1	458
Lind, John	1823	O	1	47	Longenecker, Christian.	1808	I	1	321
Lindeman, Henry	1805	I	1	293	Longenecker, Christian.	1814	K	1	508
Linderberger, David	1796	F	1	652	Longenecker, Daniel	1805	H	1	657
Linderman, John	1810	L	1	178	Longenecker, David	1766	Y	2	407
Linderman, John	1847	U	1	462	Longenecker, David	1848	U	1	564
Lindermuth, Ludwig	1777	Y	2	424	Longenecker, Jacob	1825	O	1	354
Lindner, Daniel	1804	H	1	531	Longenecker, John	1767	B	1	537
Lindolf, Anna Eva	1765	Y	2	395	Longenecker, John	1819	Y	2	438
Line, Anna	1823	N	1	289	Longenecker, Rev. John.	1831	Q	1	58
Line, Christian	1795	Y	2	409	Longenecker, John	1836	R	1	200
Line, Elizabeth	1824	O	1	154	Longenecker, John	1842	T	1	127
Line, Henry	1816	M	1	39	Longenecker, Susanna	1826	O	1	555
Line, John	1758	B	1	197	Longenecker, Ulrich	1793	Y	2	120
Line, John	1805	H	1	665	Longnecker, Benjamin	1845	P	1	619
Line, Justina	1815	L	1	368	Loop, Catharine	1827	P	1	2
Line, Samuel	1814	K	1	504	Lorah, George	1822	N	1	248
Linton, Catharine	1847	U	1	408	Lorentz, Francis Peter..	1795	G	1	383
Linton, Samuel	1804	H	1	513	Loss, Jacob	1782	Y	2	426
Linville, Ann	1795	F	1	606	Lou, James	1782	D	1	133

Name	Year	Bk.	Vol	Page	Name	Year	Bk.	Vol	Page
Loudon, Ann	1808	I	1	322	McCeery, James	1814	K	1	547
Loughrey, Samuel	1846	U	1	203	McChesney, Margaret	1820	M	1	448
Louhead, Robert	1770	-	-	-	McClanachan, Thomas	1759	B	1	265
Loury, Alexander	1806	I	1	295	McClanahan, John	1748	I	1	333
Love, Robert	1741	A	1	61	McCleary, Andrew	1748	I	1	331
Lovett, Aaron	1818	M	1	124	McCleary, Andrew	1769	C	1	3
Lovett, Charity	1826	O	1	589	McCleery, Joseph	1799	G	1	446
Lovett, James	1848	U	1	475	McClellan, Mary	1822	N	1	170
Lovett, John	1849	U	1	783	McClellan, Samuel	1806	J	1	190
Lowdon, Catharine	1811	L	1	179	McClellan, Samuel	1845	T	1	541
Loyman, Jacob (Leiman)	1785	Y	2	406	McClelland, James	1769	B	1	636
Luckey, Robert	1759	B	1	188	McClenachen, William	1783	D	1	372
Ludintown, Thomas	1742	A	1	75	McClery, John	1832	Q	1	277
Ludwig, Jacob	1805	H	1	661	McCleskey, Peter	1839	S	1	185
Lusk, James	1768	B	1	610	McClintock, Abraham	1773	B	1	725
Lusk, James	1778	C	1	511	McCloud, Alexander	1813	K	1	538
Luther, Christian	1808	I	1	319	McCloud, John	1837	R	1	360
Luther, Christian	1812	L	1	183	McClune, William	1746	I	1	225
Luther, Dr. John	1828	P	1	177	McClung, Charles	1763	B	1	624
Luttman, Jacob	1787	E	1	483	McClung, Elizabeth	1815	L	1	508
Luttman, John	1789	F	1	119	McClung, Elizabeth	1829	P	1	312
Luttman, John	1794	G	1	235	McClung, Hugh	1830	P	1	532
Lutz, Adam, Sr.	1847	U	1	261	McClung, Mathew	1799	G	1	539
Lutz, Casper	1791	F	1	301	McClung, Mathew	1802	H	1	199
Lutz, Casper	1798	Y	2	412	McClure, David	1749	A	1	182
Lutz, Casper	1800	G	1	641	McClure, Elizabeth	1828	P	1	140
Lutz, Christian	1798	G	1	443	McClure, James	1841	S	1	454
Lutz, George	1834	R	1	31	McClure, Jane	1800	G	1	649
Lutz, Henry	1818	Y	2	439	McClure, John	1839	S	1	140
Lutz, John	1821	M	1	466	McClure, Mary	1773	C	1	223
Lutz, Margaret	1807	I	1	308	McClure, Randel	1793	F	1	483
Lutz, Nicholas	1839	S	1	177	McClure, Richard	1774	B	1	726
Lutz, Stephen	1797	J	1	146	McClure, Robert	1795	G	1	364
Lutzberger, Adam	1811	K	1	280	McClure, Thomas	1764	B	1	626
Lynch, Catharine	1844	P	1	422	McClure, Thomas	1778	C	1	499
Lyne, John	1746	A	1	115	McClure, William	1768	B	1	547
Lyon, Elizabeth	1833	Q	1	446	McClure, William	1806	J	1	188
Lyon, John	1748	A	1	156	McComick, Hugh	1847	V	1	404
Lyon, John	1760	J	1	137	McComuck, John	1784	D	1	426
Lyon, Sarah	1783	D	1	333	McConnel, Alexander	1754	B	1	42
Lyon, Thomas	1825	O	1	390	McConnel, Alexander	1767	B	1	555
Lytle, Ephraim	1776	C	1	352	McConnel, Daniel	1797	G	1	175
Lytle, James	1821	M	1	474	McConnel, Hugh	1827	P	1	20
Lytle, Nathaniel	1748	A	1	160	McConnel, John	1754	B	1	81
Lytle, William	1778	J	1	146	McConnel, John	1774	C	1	146
Mc					McConomy, Peal	1836	R	1	197
McAllen, James	1744	A	1	89	McCord, Mary	1840	S	1	244
McArthur, Thomas	1785	E	1	182	McCord, Richard	1832	Q	1	331
McBrown, John	1746	A	1	118	McCord, William	1761	B	1	380
McCabe, Francis	1778	C	1	500	McCorkle, Elizabeth	1832	Q	1	264
McCaffery, Bernard	1842	T	1	123	McCowan, Alexander	1847	U	1	250
McCall, John	1805	J	1	179	McCowan, John	1748	I	1	332
McCalley, John	1761	B	1	345	McCowan, Robert	1846	W	1	224
McCallister, Peal	1757	B	1	757	McCral, Henry	1839	S	1	211
McCallister, Rose	1769	J	1	150	McCready, Archibald	1815	L	1	605
McCallon, James	1747	I	1	329	McCreary, John	1777	C	1	453
McCally, James	1802	H	1	193	McCreary, John	1816	M	1	41
McCally, John	1829	P	1	285	McCrinnel, William	1748	I	1	335
McCally, Robert	1774	C	1	231	McCulley, James	1799	G	1	542
McCalmont, Robert	1827	P	1	120	McCullough, Alexander	1747	A	1	135
McCamant, Alexander	1748	A	1	159	McCullough, George	1807	K	1	395
McCamant, Alexander J.	1809	J	1	205	McCullough, Hugh	1848	U	1	537
McCamant, Isaac	1807	J	1	194	McCullough, Hugh	1850	U	1	380
McCamant, Rebecca	1819	M	1	297	McCullough, John	1803	H	1	380
McCann, Bernard	1814	K	1	546	McCullough, Margaret	1773	B	1	720
McCartney, Andrew	1792	F	1	390	McCullough, Mary	1819	M	1	226
McCash, Jennet	1757	B	1	185	McCullough, Samuel	1785	E	1	310
McCash, John	1754	B	1	67	McCully, Thomas	1803	H	1	401
McCaskey, John	1847	U	1	354	McCumant, Samuel	1797	G	1	144
McCaslin, John	1778	C	1	491	McCurdy, Archibald	1738	A	1	31
McCauley, Lucia	1779	C	1	233	McCurdy, Archibald	1795	G	1	343
McCausland, William	1824	O	1	126	McCurdy, Daniel	1826	O	1	454

Name	Year	Bk.	Vol	Page	Name	Year	Bk.	Vol	Page
McCurdy, James	1770	C	1	8	McKissick, Mary U.	1850	U	1	822
McDarrah, Mary	1836	R	1	195	McKneely, John	1758	B	1	215
McDermut, Daniel	1790	F	1	193	McKneely, William, Jr.	1771	B	1	709
McDill, George	1760	B	1	310	McKneely, William	1780	D	1	136
McDill, George	1809	K	1	72	McKnight, James	1753	B	1	30
McDill, Jacob	1771	B	1	716	McKnight, William P.	1834	R	1	16
McDill, James	1795	I	1	348	McKown, George	1779	C	1	569
McDonald, Duncan	1832	Q	1	183	McKown, Mahlon	1794	I	1	342
McDowall, Archibald	1772	C	1	221	McKraken, James	1758	B	1	255
McDowall, James	1747	I	1	329	McLenegan, Zepheniah	1842	T	1	15
McDowell, Alexander	1779	C	1	565	McLlaughlin, George	1813	K	1	541
McElhany, Alexander	1761	B	1	395	McMichael, James	1746	A	1	112
McElroy, Hugh	1744	I	1	324	McMillan, William	1782	D	1	157
McElroy, John	1804	H	1	481	McMullan, Jane	1807	J	1	191
McElvain, Patrick	1832	Q	1	300	McMullen, Margaret	1742	A	1	73
McElvain, Andrew	1749	A	1	178	McNabb, John	1757	B	1	163
McElvain, Robert	1760	B	1	320	McNabb, William	1748	A	1	153
McElwain, Robert	1772	B	1	713	McNally, Patrick	1840	S	1	270
McElwin, George	1747	A	1	139	McNaught, James	1778	C	1	488
McEnally, Bernard	1804	H	1	424	McNauton, James	1809	K	1	74
McEnelly, Elizabeth	1812	L	1	202	McNeal, Daniel	1761	B	1	353
McEntire, Andrew	1784	E	1	52	McNeal, Hugh	1747	I	1	327
McFadden, James	1775	C	1	367	McNeal, Margaret	1800	G	1	643
McFarlan, James	1793	F	1	417	McNeal, Thomas	1820	W	1	460
McFarland, Daniel	1752	I	1	338	McNeely, Adam	1771	J	1	152
McFarland, Duncan	1769	C	1	4	McNeely, Martin	1762	B	1	622
McFarland, James	1752	I	1	336	McNeely, Michael	1763	B	1	623
McFarland, Jane	1830	P	1	485	McNeil, Daniel	1811	-	-	-
McFarland, Robert	1752	I	1	340	McNeil, Mary	1849	U	1	753
McFarlon, James	1811	K	1	421	McNutt, Alexander	1740	A	1	46
McFaun, Caleb	1843	T	1	271	McNutt, Joseph	1767	B	1	632
McFerson, Daniel	1755	B	1	104	McPherson, Alexander	1812	K	1	377
McGachey, Alexander	1750	-	-	-	McPherson, William	1783	D	1	395
McGee, John	1748	I	1	330	McQueen, John	1770	B	1	710
McGee, Rosanna Margaret	1837	R	1	303	McQuown, Richard	1778	C	1	562
McGinley, Charles	1821	N	1	76	McSparran, Elinor	1841	S	1	560
McGinnis, James	1839	S	1	216	McSparran, James	1794	I	1	343
McGirr, Nathaniel	1801	H	1	134	McStullin, John	1823	O	1	7
McGirr, Nathaniel	1801	H	1	139	McStullian, William	1839	S	1	213
McGlaughlin, Alexander	1776	C	1	358	McVey, John	1841	S	1	374
McGlaughlin, Boyd	1797	G	1	177	McWeen, William	1746	A	1	121
McGlaughlin, James	1794	F	1	550	McWillan, John	1790	F	1	214
McGlaughlin, William	1809	K	1	107	McWinn, Robert	1758	B	1	230
McGovern, Peter	1823	O	1	221	**M**				
McGowan, Patrick	1828	P	1	158	Mackerel, George	1783	D	1	340
McGowen, Daniel	1822	N	1	256	Mackey, Thomas	1815	L	1	518
McGowen, John	1775	C	1	353	Mackinson, Thomas	1823	O	1	31
McGown, William	1817	M	1	46	Maginnis, Bernard	1828	P	1	232
McGrann, Peter	1838	R	1	453	Mainzer, George	1800	G	1	645
McGrann, Terrence	1831	Q	1	52	Manahan, Cornelius	1742	A	1	74
McGrouty, John	1806	J	1	182	Manahan, Mary	1825	O	1	364
McGroverty, Bridget	1844	T	1	402	Manderbaugh, Henry	1827	P	1	10
McGrow, James	1748	I	1	333	Mann, Bernard	1816	M	1	50
McGuigan, Hannah	1847	V	1	376	Mann, Sarah	1837	R	1	324
McIlvain, George	1807	J	1	198	Mantle, Christopher	1814	L	1	369
McIlvain, John	1774	C	1	225	Marburg, Margaret	1794	F	1	574
McIlvain, Robert	1825	O	1	283	Marck, Catharine	1812	L	1	205
McIlvain, Robert	1832	Q	1	239	Mark, Conrad	1787	E	1	413
McIntire, Dinah	1819	M	1	273	Markley, Martin	1819	M	1	303
McIntire, William	1803	H	1	326	Marple, Able	1830	P	1	479
McKean, Mary	1790	F	1	236	Marsden, Ann	1767	B	1	558
McKean, Samuel C.	1825	O	1	324	Martin, Abraham	1813	K	1	522
McKean, William, Sr.	1785	E	1	278	Martin, Abraham	1815	L	1	396
McKee, Alexander	1740	A	1	45	Martin, Abraham	1823	N	1	282
McKee, James	1762	B	1	621	Martin, Abraham	1831	Q	1	21
McKee, Samuel	1850	U	1	847	Martin, Abraham	1847	U	1	440
McKibbons, Joseph	1761	B	1	356	Martin, Alexander	1771	B	1	712
McKiney, James	1790	F	1	247	Martin, Alexander	1778	C	1	563
McKinney, David	1808	I	1	351	Martin, Alexander, Sr.	1821	M	1	488
McKinney, John	1754	B	1	47	Martin, Ann	1735	Y	2	443
McKinney, John	1805	J	1	176	Martin, Barbara	1782	Y	2	447
McKinnie, John	1749	A	1	184	Martin, Barbara	1847	U	1	432

Name	Year	Bk.	Vol	Page	Name	Year	Bk.	Vol	Page
Martin, Christian......	1759	Y	2	479	Meanart, Jacob.........	1808	K	1	64
Martin,Christian(Rapho).	1792	Y	2	455	Means, Samuel..........	1746	A	1	121
Martin, Christian......	1836	R	1	227	Meas, George...........	1757	Y	2	450
Martin, Christian......	1841	S	1	465	Meas, George...........	1767	B	1	634
Martin, Christian......	1844	T	1	399	Mease, John............	1784	Y	2	446
Martin, David..........	1784	Y	2	442	Meck, Philip...........	1844	T	1	505
Martin, David..........	1805	J	1	166	Meese, Philip..........	1761	B	1	397
Martin, David..........	1819	M	1	267	Mehaffey, Benjamin.....	1848	U	1	627
Martin, David..........	1824	O	1	119	Mehany, Ann............	1849	U	1	735
Martin, David..........	1835	R	1	100	Meier, John, Sr........	1721	I	1	324
Martin, David..........	1838	S	1	41	Meier, John Conrad.....	1721	I	1	324
Martin, David..........	1839	S	1	222	Meinzer, Conrad........	1781	D	1	140
Martin, David..........	1841	S	1	476	Meister, Conrad........	1832	Q	1	168
Martin, Elizabeth......	1845	T	1	613	Meister, Henry.........	1844	T	1	390
Martin, Eve............	1829	P	1	421	Meixel, Andrew.........	1739	Y	2	479
Martin,Frederick(German)	1806	Y	2	458	Meixel, Ephraim........	1824	O	1	239
Martin, George.........	1826	O	1	461	Meixel, Martin.........	1789	F	1	134
Martin, Henry, Sr......	1784	E	1	114	Meixel, Martin.........	1823	O	1	80
Martin, Henry..........	1819	M	1	264	Meixel, Susanna........	1835	R	1	141
Martin, Henry..........	1825	Y	2	478	Mellinger, Barbara.....	1849	U	1	812
Martin, Henry..........	1827	O	1	599	Mellinger, Benedict....	1795	G	1	397
Martin, Isaac..........	1814	K	1	550	Mellinger, Christian...	1841	S	1	381
Martin, Jacob..........	1790	Y	2	472	Mellinger, Christian....	1846	U	1	89
Martin, Magdalena......	1772	Y	2	441	Mellinger, Christian....	1849	U	1	765
Martin, Maria..........	1828	P	1	206	Mellinger, Jacob.......	1834	Y	2	484
Martin, Martin.........	1774	Y	2	464	Mellinger, Magdalena....	1784	Y	2	445
Martin, Martin.........	1811	L	1	192	Mellinger, Martin......	1842	T	1	153
Martin, Mathew.........	1776	C	1	363	Mellinger, Mary........	1822	Y	2	480
Martin, Peter..........	1745	I	1	325	Mellinger, William.....	1827	P	1	115
Martin, Peter..........	1844	T	1	473	Meloy, Elizabeth.......	1846	U	1	179
Martin, Rebecca........	1810	H	1	292	Menart, Frederick......	1775	B	1	728
Martin, Robert.........	1773	C	1	224	Mengal, George.........	1811	K	1	294
Martin, Samuel.........	1770	C	1	11	Mengle, William........	1780	D	1	138
Martin, Dr. Samuel.....	1825	O	1	295	Mentkser, Ludwig.......	1777	C	1	455
Martin, Samuel(Cocalico)	1826	O	1	410	Mentzer, Frederick.....	1848	U	1	575
Martin, Samuel.........	1842	T	1	103	Mentzer, George........	1806	J	1	187
Martin, Stephen........	1804	H	1	509	Mentzer, George Michael.	1807	J	1	197
Martin, William........	1797	G	1	142	Mentzer, Sarah.........	1835	R	1	173
Martzall, Catharine....	1817	M	1	45	Mercier, Claudine B.C.N.	1824	O	1	138
Martzall, Wendel.......	1804	H	1	467	Meredith, Charles......	1833	Q	1	429
Maslick, Godleib.......	1811	L	1	200	Merkel, George.........	1812	L	1	206
Mathews, Robert W......	1840	S	1	371	Merkley, Daniel(German).	1832	Q	1	389
Matin, Robert..........	1777	C	1	454	Merkley, Daniel........	1833	Y	2	483
Matter, George.........	1837	R	1	381	Merow, Elizabeth.......	1822	N	1	301
Mattern, Thomas........	1771	C	1	7	Mesner, Casper.........	1781	D	1	142
Maurer, Baltzer........	1822	N	1	230	Mesner, Christian......	1807	J	1	195
Maurer, John...........	1826	Y	2	477	Messenkop, Barbara.....	1825	O	1	301
Maurer, Peter..........	1781	Y	2	447	Messenkop, Elizabeth....	1831	Q	1	78
Maurer, Peter..........	1847	U	1	321	Messer, John...........	1740	A	1	47
Maurer, Philip.........	1786	Y	2	452	Messersmith, George....	1812	K	1	301
Maurer, Susan..........	1830	P	1	530	Messersmith, George....	1848	U	1	565
Maxwell, Robert........	1752	I	1	339	Messner, Barbara.......	1785	Y	2	444
Maxwell, Robert........	1820	M	1	358	Messner, Christian.....	1825	O	1	304
Maxwell, Robert........	1846	U	1	52	Metz, Abraham..........	1843	T	1	207
May, Dr. Arthur........	1812	L	1	203	Metz, Mary.............	1839	S	1	162
May, Christian.........	1830	P	1	448	Metzgar, George........	1784	E	1	121
May, Philip............	1777	C	1	452	Metzger,Catharine(German	1806	Y	2	458
Mayberry, Ann..........	1843	T	1	256	Metzger, Christian.....	1818	M	1	178
Mayer, Ann.............	1819	M	1	275	Metzger, David.........	1777	J	1	154
Mayer, Christopher.....	1815	L	1	498	Metzger, Philip........	1832	Q	1	194
Mayer, George..........	1793	F	1	497	Metzger, Elizabeth.....	1849	U	1	652
Mayer, Henry...........	1820	M	1	367	Metzler, Henry.........	1857	R	1	429
Mayer, Peter...........	1778	C	1	561	Metzler, Maria.........	1826	O	1	506
Mayer, Samuel..........	1809	K	1	20	Metzler, Susanna.......	1847	U	1	336
Mayes, Richard.........	1742	A	1	71	Meyer, Catharine.......	1826	O	1	551
Mays, Andrew...........	1754	B	1	52	Meyer, Christian.......	1804	H	1	668
Mays, Ann..............	1844	T	1	459	Meyer, Christian.......	1841	S	1	413
Mays, Catharine........	1828	P	1	263	Meyer, Conrad..........	1786	E	1	349
Mays, James............	1745	A	1	102	Meyer, Conrad..........	1831	Q	1	92
Mays, Thomas...........	1764	B	1	625	Meyer, David...........	1848	U	1	463
Mead, Catharine........	1803	H	1	352	Meyer, Elizabeth.......	1847	U	1	373
Mead, Philip...........	1795	F	1	610	Meyer, John............	1789	Y	2	474

Name	Year	Bk.	Vol	Page	Name	Year	Bk.	Vol	Page
Meyer, Martin (Manheim).	1809	K	1	85	Miller, Leonard.........	1813	K	1	521
Meyer, Martin (Donegal).	1809	K	1	87	Miller, Lydia...........	1848	U	1	497
Meyer, Martin (Cocalico)	1810	L	1	190	Miller, Margaret........	1782	D	1	152
Meyer, Philip..........	1828	P	1	273	Miller, Margaret........	1809	K	1	4
Meyer, Samuel..........	1811	K	1	295	Miller, Margaret(German)	1830	Y	2	482
Meyers, Maria..........	1807	J	1	203	Miller, Margaret........	1848	U	1	483
Meylin, Martin.........	1749	A	1	185	Miller, Margaret........	1848	U	1	573
Meylin, Martin, Sr.....	1770	B	1	708	Miller, Maria...........	1773	C	1	227
Michael, Frederick.....	1777	C	1	451	Miller, Martha..........	1833	Q	1	481
Michael, Philip........	1818	M	1	147	Miller, Martin..........	1770	Y	2	461
Michael, William.......	1846	U	1	212	Miller, Martin..........	1773	B	1	721
Michenfetter, Barbara...	1821	M	1	473	Miller, Martin..........	1815	L	1	393
Michler, John..........	1796	Y	2	470	Miller, Martin..........	1849	U	1	715
Middleton, Andrew......	1750	I	1	335	Miller, Mary............	1819	M	1	206
Middleton, William.....	1732	A	1	8	Miller, Mathias........	1770	Y	2	466
Middletown, George.....	1747	I	1	327	Miller, Michael........	1739	A	1	37
Middletown, Robert.....	1731	A	1	4	Miller, Michael........	1774	C	1	230
Mier, Hans.............	1752	Y	2	126	Miller, Michael........	1785	E	1	276
Mies, George..........	1848	U	1	611	Miller, Michael........	1814	L	1	371
Milchsack, Elizabeth....	1807	J	1	200	Miller, Michael........	1822	N	1	172
Miles, William..........	1844	P	1	180	Miller, Nathan.........	1808	I	1	354
Milichsack, Augustus....	1789	F	1	185	Miller, Nicholas.......	1778	Y	2	460
Milleisen, Christopher..	1778	C	1	498	Miller, Peter..........	1796	-	-	-
Miller, Aaron..........	1842	T	1	122	Miller, Peter(Leacock).	1813	K	1	526
Miller, Abraham........	1803	H	1	347	Miller, Peter..........	1813	K	1	542
Miller, Abraham........	1834	R	1	1	Miller, Peter..........	1832	Q	1	171
Miller, Adam...........	1814	K	1	516	Miller, Peter..........	1840	S	1	259
Miller, Agnes..........	1825	O	1	336	Miller, Peter..........	1847	U	1	266
Miller, Andrew.........	1832	Q	1	246	Miller, Philip.........	1826	O	1	442
Miller, Ann............	1843	T	1	269	Miller, Philipina......	1815	L	1	512
Miller, Catharine......	1828	P	1	183	Miller, Rachel.........	1840	S	1	317
Miller, Catharine......	1839	S	1	221	Miller, Rudolph........	1805	H	1	679
Miller, Charles........	1792	F	1	362	Miller, Rudolph........	1824	O	1	268
Miller, Christian......	1762	B	1	622	Miller, Rudy...........	1732	A	1	9
Miller, Christian......	1796	Y	2	470	Miller, Samuel.........	1739	A	1	40
Miller, Christian......	1803	H	1	338	Miller, Samuel.........	1833	Q	1	449
Miller, Christian......	1838	R	1	443	Miller, Samuel.........	1838	R	1	447
Miller, Christopher.....	1775	J	1	153	Miller, Simon..........	1795	P	1	347
Miller, Christopher.....	1815	L	1	510	Miller, Sophia.........	1815	L	1	387
Miller, Conrad.........	1760	-	-	-	Miller, Tobias.........	1771	C	1	219
Miller, Daniel.........	1793	F	1	455	Miller, Tobias.........	1805	H	1	672
Miller, David..........	1794	F	1	578	Miller, Toby...........	1746	A	1	111
Miller, David..........	1824	O	1	213	Miller, Ulrich.........	1776	C	1	357
Miller, David..........	1834	R	1	51	Miller, Valentine......	1760	J	1	148
Miller, Elizabeth......	1841	S	1	415	Miller, William........	1789	F	1	58
Miller, Elizabeth......	1844	T	1	448	Millican, Patrick......	1761	B	1	409
Miller, Feit...........	1794	F	1	540	Mills, William.........	1784	E	1	141
Miller, Felix..........	1748	A	1	152	Milton, Benjamin.......	1822	N	1	123
Miller, Felix..........	1748	I	1	334	Minnich, Adam..........	1813	K	1	536
Miller, Felix..........	1770	Y	2	463	Minich, George.........	1784	E	1	47
Miller, Frederick......	1849	U	1	746	Mink, Jacob............	1806	Y	2	459
Miller, George.........	1817	M	1	44	Minnich, George........	1782	Y	2	443
Miller, George.........	1830	P	1	525	Minnich, George........	1841	S	1	451
Miller, George.........	1833	Q	1	467	Minnich, Henry.........	1850	U	1	948
Miller, George.........	1841	S	1	461	Minnich, Susan.........	1849	U	1	733
Miller, George.........	1843	T	1	266	Minnich, Wendle........	1784	Y	2	449
Miller, Heironemus.....	1823	O	1	100	Minshall, Jane.........	1747	A	1	137
Miller, Henry..........	1778	C	1	560	Minshall, Joshua.......	1747	A	1	135
Miller, Henry..........	1791	F	1	305	Minshall, Thomas.......	1785	E	1	190
Miller, Henry..........	1804	H	1	414	Miranda, Isaac.........	1732	A	1	6
Miller, Henry..........	1828	P	1	270	Mishey, John...........	1831	Q	1	124
Miller, Henry..........	1832	Q	1	332	Mitchel, James.........	1746	A	1	203
Miller, Henry..........	1834	R	1	32	Mitchel, Samuel........	1745	A	1	99
Miller, Henry..........	1842	T	1	42	Mitchel, Thomas........	1734	A	1	17
Miller, Henry..........	1847	U	1	327	Mitchell, David........	1757	B	1	187
Miller, Henry..........	1847	U	1	391	Mitchell, George.......	1765	B	1	628
Miller, Henry..........	1848	U	1	590	Modderwell, Adam.......	1831	Q	1	87
Miller, James..........	1749	A	1	168	Modderwell, Thomas.....	1790	F	1	262
Miller, John...........	1745	A	1	98	Moffat, William........	1849	U	1	659
Miller, John...........	1787	Y	2	475	Mohler, Dr. Henry......	1769	B	1	637
Miller, Leonard........	1761	Y	2	451	Mohler, Henry..........	1774	C	1	228
Miller, Leonard........	1785	Y	2	481	Mohler, Henry, Sr......	1833	Q	1	413

Name	Year	Bk.	Vol	Page	Name	Year	Bk.	Vol	Page
Mohr, Michael..........	1800	G	1	548	Mosser, Michael........	1814	K	1	554
Mollo, Adam............	1813	K	1	525	Mosser, Peter..........	1827	O	1	600
Money, Barnabus........	1794	I	1	345	Mosses, Peter..........	1759	B	1	270
Money, James...........	1748	A	1	147	Mowrer, Adam...........	1839	S	1	154
Montelus, Marcus.......	1805	J	1	358	Mowrer, George.........	1846	U	1	200
Montgomery, Archibald...	1774	J	1	152	Mowrer, Martin.........	1771	Y	2	466
Montgomery, Mary........	1788	F	1	28	Mowry, Philip..........	1779	E	1	357
Montgomery, Moses.......	1820	M	1	426	Moyer, Catharine.......	1810	L	1	188
Montgomery, Robert......	1748	A	1	158	Moyer, Elizabeth.......	1843	T	1	196
Montgomery, Robert......	1776	C	1	361	Muecke, Mathias........	1832	Q	1	310
Montgomery, Sarah.......	1784	E	1	151	Muhleisen, John........	1801	Y	2	468
Montgomery, Thomas......	1771	C	1	9	Muhlenberg, Rev. Henry..	1815	L	1	506
Montgomery, William.....	1782	D	1	148	Muldoon, Patrick.......	1839	S	1	110
Mooney, George.........	1813	K	1	539	Mulgren, Neal..........	1843	T	1	234
Mooney, Mary...........	1751	J	1	148	Mullen, Daniel.........	1789	F	1	169
Moore, Agnes............	1784	E	1	116	Mumma, Anna............	1847	U	1	299
Moore, Alexander.......	1750	A	1	191	Mumma, Barbara.........	1788	F	1	78
Moore, Andrew..........	1767	B	1	553	Mumma, Catharine.......	1814	K	1	551
Moore, Andrew..........	1805	J	1	168	Mumma, Elizabeth.......	1855	R	1	116
Moore, Ann.............	1793	J	1	157	Mumma, Fanny...........	1837	R	1	405
Moore, Asahel..........	1847	U	1	269	Mumma, Frederick.......	1814	K	1	519
Moore, Elizabeth.......	1745	A	1	97	Mumma, George..........	1786	E	1	368
Moore, Elizabeth.......	1831	Q	1	1	Mumma, Jacob...........	1794	Y	2	454
Moore, Ephraim.........	1776	C	1	364	Mumma, Leonard.........	1817	M	1	51
Moore, George..........	1837	R	1	313	Mundorf, Elizabeth.....	1810	L	1	187
Moore, Hugh............	1786	E	1	366	Murphy, Bryan..........	1753	B	1	25
Moore, Isaac...........	1826	O	1	522	Murphy, Daniel.........	1747	I	1	326
Moore, James...........	1736	A	1	22	Murphy, Dennis.........	1747	A	1	131
Moore, Jane............	1748	A	1	144	Murphy, Elizabeth......	1743	A	1	78
Moore, John............	1730	A	1	3	Murphy, Letitia........	1835	R	1	120
Moore, Margaret........	1777	C	1	484	Murphy, Patrick........	1835	R	1	123
Moore, Mary............	1842	T	1	132	Murphy, William........	1841	S	1	480
Moore, Michael.........	1800	Y	2	469	Murray, Charles........	1842	T	1	5
Moore, Michael.........	1843	T	1	270	Murray, James..........	1747	I	1	328
Moore, Moses...........	1835	R	1	69	Murray, John...........	1745	A	1	100
Moore, Robert..........	1826	O	1	438	Murray, John...........	1745	A	1	105
Moore, Samuel..........	1777	Y	2	453	Murray, Lackey.........	1815	L	1	516
Moore, Samuel..........	1829	P	1	313	Murray, Rachel.........	1816	M	1	43
Moore, William.........	1776	C	1	362	Murray, Susanna........	1813	K	1	532
Moore, William.........	1779	C	1	564	Musgrave, John.........	1748	A	1	109
Moorehead, Thomas......	1770	C	1	6	Musgrave, John.........	1748	A	1	160
Moorehead, William.....	1829	P	1	404	Musgrave, Thomas.......	1759	B	1	405
Mordak, John...........	1744	A	1	92	Musselman, Andrew......	1747	I	1	328
Morgan, David..........	1785	J	1	156	Musselman, Christian...	1734	A	1	96
Morgan, Elizabeth......	1746	A	1	123	Musselman, Christian...	1798	G	1	288
Morgan, Francis........	1779	C	1	566	Musselman, Christian...	1808	I	1	352
Morgan, Given..........	1746	D	1	429	Musselman, Christian...	1823	O	1	52
Morgan, Margaret.......	1782	D	1	150	Musselman, Christian...	1829	Y	2	482
Morgan, Reese..........	1769	B	1	639	Musselman, Henry.......	1752	Y	2	479
Morgan, Thomas.........	1848	U	1	570	Musselman, Henry.......	1805	J	1	177
Morr, Adam.............	1758	B	-	-	Musselman, Henry.......	1841	S	1	542
Morrel, Dietrich.......	1785	E	1	205	Musselman, Jacob.......	1798	Y	2	471
Morris, Willer.........	1811	K	1	297	Musselman, Joseph......	1807	Y	2	456
Morris, William........	1772	C	1	222	Musselman, Mathias.....	1811	L	1	195
Morrison, Alexander....	1826	O	1	474	Musser, Abraham........	1828	P	1	261
Morrison, Gabriel......	1799	G	1	596	Musser, Adam...........	1823	N	1	276
Morrison, Samuel.......	1811	K	1	299	Musser, Benjamin.......	1821	M	1	463
Morrison, Samuel.......	1832	Q	1	250	Musser, Christiana.....	1787	Y	2	476
Morrison, Sarah........	1833	Q	1	476	Musser, Christiana.....	1828	P	1	182
Morrison, Thomas.......	1748	-	-	-	Musser, Elizabeth......	1820	M	1	371
Moser, Christian.......	1832	Q	1	268	Musser, Feronica.......	1798	G	1	448
Mosen, Peter...........	1845	T	1	561	Musser, George.........	1806	J	1	185
Moss, Bernard..........	1839	S	1	163	Musser, Hans Adam......	1770	C	1	5
Mosser, Christian......	1830	P	1	475	Musser, Henry..........	1805	H	1	682
Mosser, David..........	1849	U	1	674	Musser, Jacob..........	1789	Y	2	453
Mosser, Henry(in German)	1805	Y	2	467	Musser, John...........	1752	Y	2	126
Mosser, Henry..........	1826	O	1	489	Musser, Magdalena......	1849	U	1	790
Mosser, Henry..........	1829	P	1	411	Musser, Martin.........	1807	J	1	201
Mosser, Jacob..........	1756	Y	2	448	Musser, Mary...........	1846	U	1	170
Mosser, Jacob..........	1784	Y	2	441	Musser, Peter..........	1805	J	1	172
Mosser, John Adam......	1770	Y	2	461	Musser, Peter..........	1835	R	1	92
Mosser, Mathias........	1834	Q	1	508	Musser, Yost...........	1761	Y	2	476

Name	Year	Bk.	Vol	Page	Name	Year	Bk.	Vol	Page
Myer, Abraham..........	1767	B	1	551	Negly, Leonard.........	1836	R	1	210
Myer, Abraham..........	1823	N	1	305	Nehr, Martin, Jr.......	1797	G	1	141
Myer, Adam.............	1759	B	1	286	Nehre, Christian.......	1817	U	1	54
Myer, Ann M............	1858	S	1	36	Neininger, Barbara.....	1794	J	1	161
Myer, Christian, Sr....	1794	G	1	251	Nelson, Abraham........	1761	B	1	368
Myer, Christian........	1798	G	1	313	Nelson, Isaac..........	1802	H	1	210
Myer, Christian........	1805	J	1	171	Nelson, John...........	1749	J	1	157
Myer, Dewalt...........	1776	C	1	356	Neries, John...........	1802	H	1	237
Myer, Michael..........	1847	U	1	431	Ness, Adam.............	1837	R	1	414
Myer, Samuel...........	1795	F	1	629	Nessinger, Nicholas....	1817	M	1	56
Myers, Abraham.........	1791	F	1	270	Nestleroth, Israel.....	1833	Q	1	371
Myers, Christian.......	1849	U	1	647	Netzley, John..........	1777	C	1	417
Myers, George.........	1840	S	1	234	Netzly, Henry..........	1817	M	1	57
Myers, George.........	1842	T	1	6	Netzly, John...........	1817	M	1	59
Myers, Henry..........	1781	D	1	139	Neuhaff, Philip........	1838	R	1	468
Myers, John...........	1821	Y	2	484	Newcomer, Abraham......	1794	G	1	249
Myers, Susan..........	1850	U	1	957	Newcomer, Aur..........	1813	K	1	556
Mylin, Abraham........	1849	U	1	747	Newcomer, Catharine....	1805	I	1	364
Mylin, Christian......	1760	-	-	-	Newcomer, Christian....	1800	H	1	4
Mylin, Martin.........	1820	M	1	427	Newcomer, Christian....	1815	L	1	520
Mylin, Martin.........	1845	T	1	556	Newcomer, Christian....	1829	P	1	419
N					Newcomer, John........	1770	C	1	23
Naaker, John D........	1757	Y	2	497	Newcomer, John........	1805	I	1	366
Nachtreip, Frederick..	1841	S	1	565	Newcomer, John........	1848	U	1	597
Nagel, Joachin........	1804	H	1	416	Newcomer, Joseph......	1849	U	1	672
Nagel, John George....	1789	Y	2	486	Newcomer, Peter.......	1732	A	1	10
Nagle, Catharine......	1838	I	1	90	Newcomer, Wolfang.....	1771	C	1	20
Nagle, Christopher....	1812	L	1	290	Newkomet, Christian...	1805	Y	2	490
Nagle, Margaret(Peggy)..	1850	U	1	865	Newman, Catharine.....	1825	-	-	-
Nagle, Richard........	1842	T	1	44	Newman, Walter........	1775	C	1	237
Nauman, Ann Margaret...	1832	Q	1	215	Newswanger, Ann.......	1813	K	1	558
Nauman, Benjamin.......	1826	O	1	587	Newswanger, Christian..	1762	C	1	14
Nauman, George.........	1815	L	1	400	Newswanger, Emanuel...	1817	U	1	53
Nauman, John..........	1828	P	1	159	Ney, Adam.............	1783	D	1	161
Nauman, John..........	1836	R	1	246	Nicholas, John........	1831	Q	1	117
Nauman, Peter.........	1834	R	1	61	Nicholas, Michael.....	1805	I	1	361
Nauman, Salome........	1822	N	1	163	Nickie, George........	1774	Y	2	493
Nauman, William Hall...	1839	S	1	117	Nigh, Nicholas........	1814	Y	2	119
Neaff, Jacob..........	1790	Y	2	487	Nigh, Philip..........	1782	D	1	161
Neaff, Jacob..........	1798	G	1	451	Nininger, Jacob.......	1793	F	1	491
Neal, Charles.........	1770	C	1	240	Nissley, Christian.....	1822	N	1	257
Nean, Henry...........	1749	J	1	158	Nissley, Elizabeth.....	1794	J	1	160
Neaser, Nicholas.......	1819	M	1	302	Nissley, Henry........	1786	Y	2	485
Neass, Michael........	1761	Y	2	496	Nissley, Jacob........	1763	-	-	-
Neave, Henry..........	1755	B	1	100	Nissley, John.........	1789	Y	2	487
Neave, Henry, Sr......	1777	C	1	370	Nissley, John.........	1847	V	1	447
Neel, Adam............	1779	C	1	571	Nissley, Martin.......	1840	S	1	365
Neel, James...........	1848	U	1	521	Nissley, Mary.........	1801	Y	2	489
Neel, John............	1792	F	1	393	Nissley, Samuel.......	1838	R	1	505
Neel, Rachael.........	1827	P	1	104	Nissley, Samuel.......	1845	T	1	538
Neel, Thomas..........	1824	O	1	163	Nissly, John..........	1819	M	1	330
Neely, William........	1843	T	1	231	Nixon, James..........	1759	B	1	269
Neeper, James.........	1778	C	1	570	Noacre, Christopher...	1757	B	1	174
Neeper, Samuel........	1836	R	1	198	Noble, James..........	1806	I	1	367
Neeper, Samuel........	1840	S	1	318	Noble, John...........	1773	C	1	235
Nees, Adam............	1806	I	1	371	Noble, John...........	1775	J	1	159
Nees, John............	1807	I	1	374	Noble, William........	1850	N	1	844
Nefe, Jacob...........	1831	Q	1	5	Nofzeiger, Jacob......	1783	D	1	367
Neff, Barbara.........	1843	T	1	206	Noll, Catharine.......	1822	N	1	253
Neff, George..........	1773	Y	2	494	Noll, John Henry......	1805	I	1	365
Neff, Dr. Henry.......	1745	A	1	96	Noll, Philip..........	1749	Y	2	497
Neff, Henry..........	1829	P	1	256	Nolt, Christian.......	1820	U	1	433
Neff, Henry..........	1833	Q	1	396	Nolt, Jonas...........	1775	Y	2	491
Neff, Henry..........	1840	S	1	347	Nolt, Jonas...........	1838	I	1	33
Neff, Isaac, Jr.......	1793	F	1	487	Nolt, Jonas...........	1848	U	1	510
Neff, Isaac...........	1793	F	1	489	Nolt, Maria...........	1805	Y	2	489
Neff, Jacob...........	1814	K	1	560	Norris, Edward........	1755	B	1	73
Neff, Jacob...........	1843	P	1	218	Norris, William.......	1840	S	1	351
Neff, Jacob...........	1849	U	1	726	Notz, Leonard.........	1758	B	1	201
Neff, Martin..........	1827	P	1	22	Notz, Michael.........	1800	H	1	5
Neff, Oswald..........	1758	Y	2	497	Null, George..........	1771	C	1	234
Negel, Leonard........	1771	Y	2	495					

Name	Year	Bk.	Vol	Page	Name	Year	Bk.	Vol	Page
Nunnemacher, William....	1847	N	1	410	Patterson, James........	1733	A	1	13
Nure, Henry.............	1817	M	1	58	Patterson, James........	1735	A	1	21
O					Patterson, James........	1789	F	1	130
Obel, Christopher.......	1768	Y	2	48	Patterson, James........	1791	F	1	322
Ober, Barbara..........	1841	S	1	398	Patterson, John........	1843	T	1	215
Ober, Christian........	1840	S	1	362	Patterson, Mary........	1809	K	1	131
Ober, David............	1844	T	1	353	Patterson, Mary Ann.....	1847	U	1	262
Ober, Henry............	1822	N	1	202	Patterson, Peter.......	1786	D	1	174
Ober, Jacob............	1769	Y	2	500	Patterson, Rebecca.....	1805	I	1	380
Ober, Magdalena........	1843	T	1	227	Patterson, Robert......	1747	A	1	139
Ober, Michael..........	1815	L	1	402	Patterson, Robert......	1843	T	1	195
Ober, Michael..........	1818	M	1	144	Patterson, Samuel......	1772	C	1	241
Ober, Michael..........	1850	U	1	934	Patterson, Samuel......	1777	C	1	458
Oberholzer, Christian...	1850	U	1	843	Patterson, Samuel......	1821	M	1	501
Oberholtzer,Christian...	1789	F	1	155	Patterson, Samuel......	1831	Q	1	111
Oberholtzer,Christian...	1812	Y	2	501	Patterson, Thomas J.....	1853	V	1	520
Oberholtzer, Jacob.....	1806	I	1	377	Patterson, William.....	1745	A	1	104
Oberholtzer, Samuel.....	1822	Y	2	498	Patterson, William.....	1781	D	1	168
Oberlander, Peter.......	1780	-	-	-	Patton, James..........	1746	A	1	117
Oberlin, George........	1823	N	1	216	Patton, James..........	1755	B	1	84
Oberlin, Michael........	1788	F	1	60	Patton, John............	1760	B	1	402
Oberstag, Abraham.......	1768	B	1	590	Patton, John............	1810	K	1	170
Oblinger, Christian.....	1798	G	1	598	Patton, Mary...........	1746	A	1	120
Odell, Charles.........	1848	U	1	619	Patton, Nathan........	1784	D	1	172
Odenwalt, George.......	1792	F	1	344	Patton, Robert.........	1755	B	1	116
Offner, Martin.........	1762	C	1	13	Patton, Robert.........	1776	C	1	371
Ogilly, Joseph.........	1840	S	1	262	Patton, Robert.........	1784	E	1	93
Oharra, Martha.........	1825	O	1	369	Patton, Thomas.........	1774	C	1	243
Okely, John............	1792	F	1	352	Patton, Thomas.........	1791	F	1	286
Oldweiler, Jacob.......	1793	Y	2	502	Patton, Thomas.........	1812	L	1	211
Olevholtzer,Samuel......	1748	-	-	-	Pattrison, Alexander....	1842	T	1	20
Olifent, Charles......	1770	C	1	18	Pattrison, Ann........	1792	F	1	354
Olweiler, Philip.......	1815	L	1	524	Pattrison, Arthur......	1826	O	1	406
Oneal, Charles........	1770	C	1	240	Paul, Margaret........	1821	N	1	22
Opitz, Renatta.........	1824	Y	2	503	Paules, Catherine.......	1848	U	1	551
Opitz, Renatta.........	1836	R	1	189	Paules, Henry..........	1820	M	1	343
Oppelt, John..........	1848	U	1	467	Paulis, Elizabeth......	1805	I	1	383
Orr, Robert............	1816	M	1	60	Pautz, Mathias.........	1831	Q	1	94
Orth, Daniel...........	1795	F	1	607	Pautz, Michael........	1769	C	1	21
Oster, Henry...........	1810	K	1	153	Paxton, John..........	1769	C	1	33
Ostetter, Christian.....	1777	C	1	456	Paxton, John..........	1823	N	1	323
Oswald, Sarah..........	1849	U	1	680	Paxton, Samuel........	1755	B	1	110
Ott, George............	1842	T	1	157	Paye, Jasper..........	1779	C	1	573
Otto, Catharine.......	1797	G	1	133	Peak, Samuel..........	1759	B	1	263
Overholtzer, Martin.....	1833	Q	1	469	Pearson, John..........	1822	O	1	144
Overholzer, Samuel.....	1748	Y	2	118	Peart, Sarah C.........	1861	H	1	220
Overkish, Michael.......	1782	Y	2	501	Peck, Christian.......	1845	T	1	523
Owen, Benjamin........	1824	O	1	270	Peck, Elizabeth.......	1845	T	1	540
Owen, Elizabeth........	1805	I	1	376	Peck, Peter............	1811	L	1	54
Owens, Archibald.......	1814	K	1	562	Peck, Samuel..........	1771	C	1	116
Oyster, Christian......	1747	A	1	133	Pedan, Hugh............	1800	H	1	11
P					Peden, John............	1775	C	1	368
Pagan, Archibald.......	1749	J	1	163	Peden, Martha..........	1776	C	1	369
Palsbacher, Peter......	1748	A	1	155	Peebles, James........	1758	B	1	250
Park, Robert..........	1753	B	1	2	Pegan, Andrew..........	1789	F	1	86
Parkason, Joseph.......	1793	F	1	426	Pegan, James, Sr.......	1834	Q	1	506
Parker, John..........	1749	J	1	164	Peifer, John..........	1805	I	1	382
Parker, John..........	1821	M	1	479	Peiffer, Bernard......	1785	E	1	214
Parker, Robert........	1812	K	1	314	Peiffer, Maria........	1846	U	1	108
Parker, Robert........	1823	O	1	5	Peirce, Israel.........	1840	S	1	316
Parker, Susanna........	1834	Q	1	487	Peirce, Jonathan......	1835	R	1	165
Parkeson, Richard......	1744	A	1	89	Peirce, Joseph........	1849	U	1	644
Parkheffer, Conrad.....	1746	-	-	-	Peirce, William.......	1822	N	1	226
Parr, Grace............	1814	K	1	646	Pence, William........	1850	U	1	947
Parry, Roger..........	1741	A	1	55	Penegar, Mary Ann.....	1842	T	1	40
Passard, Henry........	1749	-	-	-	Pennel, Robert........	1810	K	1	307
Passmore, Sarah........	1846	U	1	51	Pennel, Robert........	1823	N	1	312
Paterson, James........	1785	D	1	173	Pennel, William.......	1823	N	1	275
Patrick, Hugh..........	1778	C	1	519	Pennel, William.......	1825	O	1	344
Patterson, Arthur......	1822	N	1	246	Pennell, William......	1803	H	1	354
Patterson, Arthur......	1836	R	1	183	Pennman, John..........	1832	Q	1	234
Patterson, George......	1749	J	1	162	Penny, Hugh............	1809	K	1	83

Name	Year	Bk.	Vol	Page	Name	Year	Bk.	Vol	Page
Penny, Joseph	1785	E	1	227	Poor, Alexander	1739	A	1	37
Penny, Mary	1804	H	1	504	Poorman, Jacob	1784	D	1	447
Penny, William	1767	C	1	17	Poorman, Stephen	1782	D	1	170
Percinger, Casper	1750	-	-	-	Porter, Eleanor	1820	M	1	370
Perry, Janet	1752	J	1	166	Porter, George B.,Esq	1834	R	1	27
Perry, William	1752	J	1	165	Porter, James(Maryland)	1785	E	1	299
Pershinger, Henry	1763	C	1	27	Porter, James(Drumore)	1786	E	1	364
Persinger, Andrew	1774	B	1	648	Porter, Col. James	1817	M	1	66
Peter, Francis	1795	G	1	383	Porter, Jane	1842	T	1	100
Peter, Jacob	1848	U	1	626	Porter, John	1765	C	1	16
Peterie, Christopher	1791	F	1	312	Porter, John	1800	H	1	8
Peterman, Joachim	1819	M	1	310	Porter, Rebecca	1835	R	1	115
Peters, Abraham	1818	M	1	121	Porter, Robert	1745	A	1	116
Peters, Arnold	1817	M	1	65	Porter, Samuel	1775	C	1	245
Peters, Catherine	1843	T	1	300	Porter, Rev. Samuel	1813	R	1	619
Peters, Jacob	1837	R	1	336	Porter, Samuel	1827	P	1	151
Peters, Lewis	1794	F	1	588	Porter, Thomas	1823	N	1	297
Peters, Michael	1800	H	1	-	Potts, Robert	1769	C	1	27
Peterson, John	1824	Y	2	503	Powell, John	1748	J	1	162
Peterson, John Christian	1760	B	1	326	Powell, John	1772	C	1	242
Petigrew, Mary	1838	R	1	469	Powell, Peter	1813	K	1	618
Petree, Andrew	1801	H	1	112	Pownall, Elizabeth	1845	T	1	568
Petrie, Christian	1811	K	1	311	Pownall, Levi	1840	S	1	334
Petry, Anthony	1777	C	1	457	Pratt, James	1803	H	1	340
Petry, Catharine	1793	F	1	427	Pratter, Mary	1748	A	1	143
Petticoffer, Elizabeth	1824	O	1	158	Pratzman, Peter	1833	Q	1	442
Petz, George	1781	D	1	165	Prees, Thomas	1759	-	-	-
Peush, John	1843	T	1	267	Prenneman, Adam	1760	B	1	298
Pfautz, Jacob, Sr	1800	H	1	74	Price, George	1821	N	1	61
Pfautz, John	1821	M	1	507	Price, James	1777	C	1	483
Pfautz, Michael	1812	K	1	204	Price, John	1850	U	1	833
Pfeiffer, Emanuel	1781	D	1	167	Price, Dr. William	1807	I	1	383
Pfeiffer, Frederick	1845	U	1	36	Price, Dr. William	1829	T	1	337
Pfeil, Peter	1761	Y	2	506	Pricker, Peter	1761	B	1	398
Pfleiger, Tobias	1779	C	1	572	Primisholtz, Elizabeth	1781	Y	2	525
Pfoltz, Christian	1849	U	1	669	Printzell, George	1799	G	1	544
Pfundt, Mary	1849	U	1	709	Pritch, Peter	1759	B	1	275
Phenegar, Henry	1847	U	1	417	Pritz, George, Sr	1821	N	1	18
Phillips, George	1816	M	1	64	Prosey, John	1806	I	1	48
Phillips, William	1851	U	1	995	Pugh, Edward	1747	A	1	141
Phite, George(see Feite)	1785	E	1	162	Pugh, George	1785	E	1	265
Phyfer, George	1813	K	1	616	Pugh, Mary	1747	A	1	163
Phyfer, John	1805	Y	2	519	Purcat, Charles	1760	B	1	313
Phyfer, Martin	1823	O	1	94	Pusey, Samuel	1843	T	1	329
Pickel, Barbara	1842	T	1	134	Pyle, Moses	1784	D	1	415
Pickel, Henry	1827	T	1	106	Q				
Pickel, Peter	1821	N	1	56	Quarril, Joseph	1821	N	1	105
Pickle, John	1837	R	1	336	Quigly, Ann	1826	O	1	444
Pickle, Leonard	1790	F	1	213	Quigly, Christian	1739	A	1	38
Pinkerton, Elizabeth	1844	T	1	487	Quimby, Aaron	1849	U	1	780
Pinkerton, Henry	1816	M	1	61	R				
Pinkerton, John	1802	H	1	191	Rab, John George	1838	S	1	65
Pinkerton, Thomas	1807	I	1	384	Rabb, William	1753	J	1	214
Planck, John, Sr	1835	R	1	139	Radinger, John	1799	G	1	599
Plank, John	1790	F	1	193	Radmacher, Michael	1796	G	1	213
Plank, John	1794	I	1	36	Raeder, John	1778	Y	2	527
Plank, John	1806	I	1	52	Rainley, Frederick	1797	G	1	73
Plantz, Matthias	1774	Y	2	504	Rakestraw, Thomas	1842	T	1	42
Platner, Michael	1757	B	1	164	Ralston, John R	1815	L	1	529
Platt, Thomas	1810	K	1	309	Ramber, Jacob	1784	E	1	130
Pleis, Jacob	1765	Y	2	506	Ramsay, Elizabeth	1797	G	1	187
Pletz, Frederick	1784	E	1	110	Ramsay, Elizabeth	1800	H	1	20
Pletz, John	1784	E	1	78	Ramsay, James	1786	E	1	390
Pletz, John Adam	1784	E	1	110	Ramsay, John	1785	E	1	258
Plontz, George	1807	I	1	385	Ramsay, John	1831	Q	1	130
Plough, John	1763	-	-	-	Ramsay, Jane	1833	Q	1	368
Plum, John	1759	B	1	277	Ramsey, John	1746	J	1	206
Poh, Wendle	1768	Y	2	505	Ramsey, Robert	1789	F	1	153
Poitcht, George	1826	O	1	590	Ramsey, Samuel	1772	B	1	731
Pollock, Samuel	1778	C	1	489	Ramsey, Samuel	1800	H	1	16
Pooder, Nancy	1870	A	2	74	Ramsey, William	1817	U	1	75
Poolman, Christian	1749	-	-	-	Ranch, Henry	1796	G	1	81

Name	Year	Bk.	Vol	Page	Name	Year	Bk.	Vol	Page
Ranch, Henry G.	1822	N	1	176	Reichenbach, John	1796	G	1	215
Ranck, Abraham	1850	U	1	838	Reichenbach, William	1821	N	1	3
Ranck, Daniel	1827	P	1	67	Reichenback, Susanna	1811	L	1	220
Ranck, David	1844	T	1	493	Reichwine, George	1788	Y	2	545
Ranck, Elizabeth	1843	T	1	224	Reid, Thomas	1734	A	1	14
Ranck, Jacob	1827	P	1	44	Reid, William	1802	H	1	198
Ranck, John	1845	U	1	14	Reidenbach, Isaac	1864	Y	1	166
Ranck, Ludwick	1842	T	1	54	Reidenbach, Martin	1837	R	1	300
Ranck, Philip	1815	Y	2	523	Reidenbaugh, George	1754	B	1	63
Ranck, Samuel	1815	L	1	409	Reidlinger, John	1841	S	1	443
Ranck, Samuel	1831	Q	1	121	Reier, Emick	1772	Y	2	513
Ranck, Valentine	1839	S	1	136	Reiff, Abraham	1774	Y	2	512
Randall, Sarah	1834	R	1	22	Reiff, Abraham, Jr	1788	F	1	33
Rank, Elizabeth	1817	M	1	71	Reiff, Abraham	1820	Y	2	511
Rank, Mary Margaret	1848	U	1	539	Reiff, Barbara	1838	Y	2	526
Rank, Michal	1835	R	1	131	Reiff, Henry	1755	B	1	85
Rank, Philip	1785	Y	2	546	Reiff, Isaac	1801	H	1	99
Rank, Philip	1841	S	1	401	Reiff, John	1750	A	1	190
Rank, Valentine	1813	K	1	564	Reiff, John Jacob	1756	Y	2	519
Rankin, Adam	1747	J	1	208	Reiff, Samuel	1831	Q	1	51
Rankin, Henry	1778	C	1	575	Reigart, Adam	1813	K	1	565
Ranson, Nancy	1873	B	2	56	Reigart, Adam	1844	T	1	449
Rapp, Jacob	1825	O	1	332	Reigart, Christopher	1784	D	1	404
Rapp, Peter	1783	Y	2	526	Reigart, Christopher	1800	H	1	19
Rathvon, Michael	1835	R	1	182	Reigart, Emanuel	1846	U	1	56
Rathvon, Michael	1836	R	1	182	Reigart, John, Esq.	1829	P	1	298
Rauh, John Moritz	1777	C	1	459	Reigart, Michael	1841	S	1	372
Raushenberger, Jacob	1829	P	1	368	Reigart, Samuel	1842	T	1	49
Rea, George	1746	A	1	126	Reigart, Susanna	1804	Y	2	129
Rea, James	1848	U	1	473	Reigart, Susanna	1827	P	1	1
Read, James	1768	C	1	37	Reigart, Susanna	1848	U	1	557
Read, John	1832	Q	1	249	Reigart, Ulrick	1766	C	1	31
Reader, John	1778	C	1	520	Reigel, Barbara	1849	U	1	679
Reah, John	1787	E	1	405	Reigel, Magdalena	1814	K	1	583
Reah, Samuel	1817	U	1	76	Reiger, Eve Catherine	1796	G	1	12
Ream, Andrew	1845	T	1	560	Reiger, Melcher	1776	Y	2	529
Ream, Catharine	1826	O	1	460	Reikert, Isaac	1834	R	1	44
Ream, Isaac	1820	M	1	407	Reily, John	1787	E	1	450
Ream, John	1784	Y	2	534	Reiley, James	1826	O	1	466
Ream, Magdalena	1815	L	1	413	Rein, Elizabeth	1807	L	1	–
Ream, Matthias	1789	F	1	92	Rein, Michael	1779	C	1	576
Ream, Samuel	1810	L	1	24	Reinert, Catharine	1830	P	1	439
Ream, Samuel(German)	1839	S	1	134	Reinhart, Christianna	1817	M	1	74
Ream, Tobias	1807	Y	2	547	Reinhart, Frederick	1819	M	1	263
Reckenbach, Henry	1741	A	1	52	Reinhart, George	1834	Q	1	525
Redcay, Henry	1848	U	1	536	Reinhart, Henry	1841	S	1	417
Reddle, James	1763	C	1	26	Reinhart, Margaret	1816	M	1	68
Redick, Agnes	1795	G	1	394	Reinhold, Christopher				
Redick, Agnes	1796	J	1	223	Henry	1793	Y	2	539
Redsecker, Ann Mary	1817	M	1	74	Reinhold, Frederick				
Redsecker, George	1838	R	1	508	(in German)	1833	Y	2	509
Reed, Adam	1769	C	1	36	Reinhold, Henry	1845	T	1	553
Reed, George	1789	F	1	164	Reinhold, Henry	1846	U	1	219
Reed, John	1752	J	1	215	Reisinger, Charles	1829	P	1	414
Reed, John	1777	C	1	461	Reist, Abraham, Sr	1813	K	1	416
Reed, Martin	1841	S	1	421	Reist, Abraham, Jr	1844	T	1	480
Reed, Mary	1830	P	1	444	Reist, Barbara	1820	M	1	413
Reed, Patrick	1767	C	1	32	Reist, Christian	1814	L	1	294
Reed, Peter, Sr	1840	S	1	282	Reist, John	1813	K	1	391
Reed, Robert	1786	E	1	376	Reist, Peter	1842	T	1	58
Reed, Robert	1801	H	1	101	Reitenback, Peter	1820	Y	2	507
Reed, William	1803	H	1	332	Reiter, Michael	1760	B	1	356
Reem, Tobias	1775	B	1	733	Reitlinger, Jacob	1762	Y	2	517
Reesar, Jacob	1849	U	1	645	Reitzel, Christopher	1831	Q	1	71
Reese, Henry	1812	L	1	223	Reitzel, George	1758	B	1	205
Reese, James	1815	L	1	407	Reitzel, George	1799	G	1	547
Reese, John	1746	A	1	115	Reitzel, John	1832	Q	1	159
Reeser, Jacob, Sr	1836	R	1	177	Reitzel, Peter	1781	D	1	178
Reeser, Nicholas	1867	Z	1	131	Remck, Thomas	1777	C	1	460
Reesor, John	1832	Q	1	336	Remley, Frederick, Sr	1830	P	1	522
Rehm, Jacob	1777	C	1	485	Remley, Jacob	1832	Q	1	335
Reichenbach, Jacob	1805	I	1	400	Renick, John	1784	E	1	39

Name	Year	Bk.	Vol	Page	Name	Year	Bk.	Vol	Page
Renkin, John...........	1749	J	1	211	Ringwalt, Elizabeth.....	1835	R	1	65
Renner, John Wendle.....	1792	Y	2	541	Ringwalt, George........	1840	S	1	284
Rennick, Jane...........	1782	D	1	181	Ringwalt, Jacob.........	1789	F	1	143
Resh, Elizabeth.........	1828	P	1	201	Ringwalt, Martin........	1821	N	1	29
Resh, Henry.............	1808	I	1	227	Rippey, Matthew.........	1800	H	1	15
Resh, Henry.............	1811	L	1	219	Rippley, Peter..........	1805	I	1	399
Resh, Henry.............	1849	U	1	704	Rippy, Hugh.............	1757	B	1	180
Resh, John..............	1768	Y	2	515	Risdel, John............	1834	R	1	56
Reshling, John..........	1784	E	1	31	Risdel, Mary............	1841	S	1	533
Ressler, George.........	1842	T	1	91	Rissel, John Christopher	1793	F	1	436
Ressler, John...........	1806	I	1	404	Risser, Christian.......	1826	O	1	545
Rester, Jacob...........	1844	T	1	349	Risser, Levi E..........	1857	W	1	374
Retterford, Mary........	1846	U	1	190	Risser, Peter...........	1840	S	1	361
Reyer, Daniel...........	1784	Y	2	532	Ritchey, William........	1818	U	1	77
Reynolds, Catharine.....	1822	N	1	255	Riter, Agness...........	1776	C	1	374
Reynolds, Eli...........	1821	N	1	90	Ritter, Conrad..........	1769	C	1	35
Reynolds, Henry.........	1809	K	1	11	Ritter, Joseph..........	1775	B	1	735
Reynolds, Jacob.........	1822	-	-	-	Ritter, Michael.........	1794	Y	2	539
Reynolds, John..........	1745	A	1	103	Ritter, Peter...........	1778	J	1	217
Reynolds, Joseph........	1747	J	1	207	Ritter, Peter...........	1789	Y	2	532
Reynolds, Joshua........	1841	S	1	377	Ritter, Simon...........	1783	Y	2	536
Reynolds, Lydia.........	1857	W	1	324	Rixecker, Margaret......	1850	U	1	964
Reynolds, Nathan........	1828	P	1	228	Rixecker, Mary..........	1847	U	1	250
Reynolds, Samuel........	1822	N	1	190	Rixecker, Peter.........	1836	R	1	228
Reynolds, William.......	1801	H	1	128	Road, Henry.............	1822	N	1	193
Rhea, John..............	1762	C	1	24	Road, Jacob.............	1841	S	1	436
Rhea, John..............	1809	K	1	113	Road, John..............	1850	U	1	835
Rhedy, James............	1734	A	1	17	Road, Peter.............	1793	J	1	220
Rheem, John.............	1838	R	1	495	Road, Ulrick............	1763	Y	2	516
Rhoade, John, Jr........	1830	P	1	468	Roan, Rev. John.........	1776	C	1	375
Rhoads, Isaac...........	1884	F	2	238	Robb, Sarah.............	1769	J	1	215
Rhoads, Peter...........	1857	U	1	314	Roberson, Samuel........	1748	J	1	210
Rhodes, Philip..........	1847	U	1	423	Roberts, John...........	1809	K	1	57
Rhule, George...........	1800	H	1	141	Roberts, John...........	1847	U	1	455
Rice, Edward............	1844	T	1	442	Robinson, Elizabeth.....	1825	O	1	346
Richards, James.........	1829	P	1	412	Robinson, Hugh..........	1800	H	1	18
Richards, Lydia.........	1839	S	1	176	Robinson, James.........	1782	D	1	183
Richards, William.......	1748	J	1	209	Robinson, Jane..........	1837	R	1	421
Richardson, Ezekiel.....	1787	E	1	451	Robinson, John..........	1778	C	1	574
Richardson, Isaac, Esq..	1765	C	1	29	Robinson, John..........	1826	O	1	497
Richardson, Jesse.......	1847	U	1	434	Robinson, Michael.......	1785	E	1	251
Richardson, John........	1798	J	1	226	Robinson, Nancy.........	1876	C	2	166
Richardson, Joseph......	1814	K	1	579	Robinson, Philip........	1770	C	1	40
Richardson, William.....	1749	J	1	212	Robinson, Richard.......	1768	A	1	208
Richey, Samuel..........	1739	A	1	41	Robinson, Samuel........	1750	A	1	192
Richison, Eleanor.......	1796	J	1	222	Robinson, Thomas........	1758	B	1	211
Richison, Margaret......	1796	J	1	222	Robinson, Thomas........	1780	D	1	176
Rickert, John...........	1850	U	1	833	Robison, Dunkin.........	1807	K	1	33
Rickert, Leonard........	1811	K	1	318	Rockafield, Jacob.......	1848	U	1	491
Rickle, George Michael..	1785	Y	2	547	Rockey, Henry...........	1790	F	1	197
Ricksecker, Elizabeth...	1782	D	1	180	Rockey, Jacob...........	1832	Q	1	266
Ricksecker, Jacob.......	1806	Y	2	543	Rockey, Jacob...........	1846	U	1	142
Ricksecker, John........	1813	K	1	572	Rockey, Peter...........	1824	O	1	219
Riddle, Ann Barbara.....	1847	U	1	267	Rode, George............	1772	C	1	248
Riddle, John............	1827	P	1	49	Roe, Matthias...........	1805	I	1	398
Riddle, William.........	1795	G	1	350	Roeser, Susanna.........	1791	F	1	267
Rieblet, Abraham........	1759	B	1	296	Rogers, Jane............	1829	P	1	422
Ried, Nathan............	1739	A	1	35	Rogers, Robert, Jr......	1745	A	1	107
Riegel, Michael.........	1809	Y	2	541	Rogers, Seth............	1758	B	1	243
Rieger, Jacob...........	1761	B	1	364	Rogers, Timothy.........	1848	U	1	602
Rieger,Rev. John Bartholemew.........	1769	C	1	38	Rohine, Stephen.........	1832	Q	1	227
Rieger, Melchoir........	1776	C	1	374	Rohrer, Abraham.........	1831	Q	1	129
Rife, Michael...........	1834	Q	1	489	Rohrer, Christian.......	1833	Q	1	359
Rifewine, Adam..........	1768	C	1	34	Rohrer, Elizabeth.......	1788	Y	2	545
Righter, Joseph.........	1843	T	1	265	Rohrer, Elizabeth.......	1818	M	1	153
Rigler, George..........	1831	Q	1	108	Rohrer, Henry...........	1823	O	1	35
Rihm, Nickolas..........	1774	Y	2	530	Rohrer, Isaac...........	1804	Y	2	538
Rine, Catharine.........	1847	U	1	352	Rohrer, Jacob...........	1803	H	1	300
Rine, Christian.........	1826	O	1	507	Rohrer, Jacob...........	1835	R	1	125
Rine, George............	1818	M	1	76	Rohrer, Jacob...........	1839	S	1	214
Rine, Leonard...........	1809	K	1	123	Rohrer, Jacob...........	1848	U	1	529
					Rohrer, John............	1771	C	1	246

Name	Year	Bk.	Vol	Page	Name	Year	Bk.	Vol	Page
Rohrer, John............	1772	Y	2	513	Rumel, Felix............	1828	P	1	213
Rohrer, John............	1814	K	1	574	Rumel, Valentine.......	1816	U	1	67
Rohrer, John............	1848	U	1	633	Rummel, William........	1834	Q	1	515
Rohrer, John............	1850	U	1	919	Rung, Henry............	1793	T	1	473
Rohrer, Mary............	1849	U	1	803	Runner, George.........	1839	S	1	179
Roland, Ann.............	1823	N	1	300	Runner, William........	1806	I	1	401
Roland, David..........	1807	Y	2	544	Runner, William........	1844	T	1	351
Roland, Henry..........	1847	U	1	241	Runshaw, William.......	1798	G	1	308
Roland, John...........	1790	F	1	208	Rupp, George..........	1818	M	1	129
Roland, Philip.........	1770	C	1	40	Rupp, Jacob............	1836	R	1	253
Roland, Philip.........	1771	Y	2	528	Rupp, John.............	1784	Y	2	531
Rookey, Philip.........	1809	K	1	35	Rupp, Mary.............	1849	U	1	668
Roop, Christian........	1831	Q	1	102	Rupp, Nicholas.........	1818	U	1	159
Root, Christian........	1804	H	1	419	Rush, Christian........	1848	U	1	567
Root, Henry............	1797	J	1	225	Rush, Henry, Esq.......	1838	R	1	540
Rose, Joseph, Esq......	1779	C	1	576	Rush, Martha...........	1842	T	1	22
Ross, Adam.............	1749	J	1	211	Rusher, Henry..........	1793	J	1	218
Ross, George, Esq......	1832	Q	1	327	Rusher, Henry..........	1796	F	1	633
Ross, Col. George T....	1817	M	1	72	Rusing, Bernard........	1784	Y	2	534
Ross, Robert May.......	1849	U	1	701	Rusing, Henry..........	1841	S	1	456
Rost, George...........	1796	F	1	636	Russel, James.........	1761	B	1	382
Roth, Daniel...........	1841	S	1	419	Russel, Jane..........	1766	C	1	30
Roth, George...........	1783	J	1	218	Rut, Peter.............	1805	I	1	390
Roth, Henry............	1819	M	1	214	Ruth, Catharine.......	1847	U	1	258
Roth, Henry............	1823	N	1	322	Ruth, Elizabeth........	1826	O	1	571
Roth, Jacob............	1820	M	1	452	Ruth, Jonas...........	1844	T	1	477
Roth, John.............	1811	L	1	217	Rutherford, Thomas.....	1777	C	1	462
Roth, Ludwig...........	1819	U	1	278	Rutledge, Mathew.......	1749	A	1	173
Roth, Philip...........	1797	G	1	227	Rutt, Henry...........	1842	T	1	64
Roth, Philip...........	1824	O	1	246	Rutter, Catherine......	1843	T	1	314
Roth, Theobold.........	1799	G	1	545	Rutter, Conrad........	1737	A	1	29
Roud, Philip...........	1815	L	1	405	Rutter, George........	1807	I	1	405
Rouner, Anton..........	1799	G	1	600	Rutter, Henry.........	1811	K	1	320
Rouse, Thomas..........	1747	J	1	208	Rutter, Mary..........	1829	P	1	364
Row, Catharine.........	1849	U	1	710	Rutter, Nancy.........	1875	B	2	550
Row, Francis...........	1806	I	1	403	Rutter, Nathaniel......	1843	T	1	305
Rowland, Barbara.......	1816	M	1	69	S				
Rowland, Catharine.....	1819	M	1	216	Sadler, Christian.....	1779	C	1	587
Rowland, Jacob.........	1764	C	1	28	Sahler, Frederick.....	1756	Y	2	568
Rowland, John..........	1763	C	1	25	Sahm, George.........	1810	K	1	325
Rowland, Jonathan......	1807	I	1	407	Sahm, Jacob...........	1824	O	1	222
Royer, Abraham.........	1847	U	1	396	Salladay, Frederick...	1770	C	1	85
Royer, Barbara.........	1844	T	1	342	Saltzgerber, Andrew				
Royer, Benjamin........	1841	S	1	512	(in German).........	1769	Y	2	562
Royer, Christopher.....	1805	I	1	386	Saltzman, Francis.....	1787	Y	2	573
Royer, David..........	1833	Q	1	438	Sample, Hugh..........	1749	A	1	174
Royer, Emick..........	1769	C	1	39	Sample, James.........	1757	J	1	242
Royer, Ephraim........	1847	U	1	257	Sample, Nathaniel......	1849	U	1	770
Royer, John...........	1816	M	1	70	Sample, William.......	1795	I	1	424
Royer, Jonathan.......	1844	T	1	376	Sander, Jacob F.(Xander)	1827	P	1	46
Royer, Peter..........	1823	N	1	277	Sanders, Jacob(German)..	1797	Y	2	589
Royer, Philip.........	1804	Y	2	537	Sando, Barbara........	1838	R	1	444
Royer, Philip.........	1810	L	1	212	Sandoe, Jacob.........	1803	H	1	343
Royer, Sebastian......	1759	Y	2	518	Sapp, Messach.........	1811	K	1	347
Ruby, John(in German)...	1763	Y	2	517	Sauder, Crhistopher....	1806	X	2	14
Rudisill, Christina....	1820	M	1	410	Sauder, Daniel........	1802	H	1	171
Rudisill, George......	1850	U	1	954	Sauder, Henry........	1826	O	1	447
Rudisill, Michael.....	1829	P	1	374	Sauder, Jacob.........	1820	M	1	386
Rudisill, Philip.......	1755	B	1	112	Sauder, John, Sr(German)	1805	J	1	269
Rudisilly, Melchior....	1805	I	1	394	Sauder, John..........	1814	K	1	647
Rudy, Abraham.........	1776	Y	2	529	Sauders, Henry........	1772	C	1	261
Rudy, Charles.........	1845	T	1	543	Sauders, Isaac, Esq....	1781	D	1	197
Rudy, Daniel..........	1792	F	1	366	Sauer, Michael........	1821	N	1	192
Rudy, Daniel..........	1818	M	1	172	Sauer, Philip.........	1819	M	1	286
Rudy, Daniel..........	1846	U	1	207	Sauter, Cathrine......	1846	U	1	146
Rudy, Eunnich.........	1807	I	1	414	Sawer, Henry..........	1843	T	1	193
Rudy, Frederick.......	1849	U	1	695	Sawyer, William.......	1784	E	1	145
Rudy, John............	1816	M	1	69	Schaeffer, Peter......	1841	S	1	553
Rudy, John............	1846	U	1	233	Schaffer, Anna Maria....	1845	S	1	590
Ruhl, Christian........	1829	P	1	299	Schaffer, Philip......	1758	X	2	22
Ruhl, Rosinae.........	1853	V	1	362	Schaffner, Jacob......	1625	O	1	282
Rumberger, Christian....	1776	C	1	372	Schantz, Anna Maria.....	1798	Y	2	588

Name	Year	Bk.	Vol	Page	Name	Year	Bk.	Vol	Page
Schantz, Magdalena......	1794	F	1	518	Scott, Andrew...........	1795	G	1	340
Schauer, Christopher....	1836	R	1	244	Scott, James............	1765	C	1	59
Schauer, John...........	1843	T	1	181	Scott, James............	1817	M	1	88
Scheaffer, William......	1846	U	1	53	Scott, Jane.............	1810	K	1	328
Schenck, John, Sr......	1818	M	1	188	Scott, Jane.............	1841	S	1	393
Schenck, Michael.......	1804	H	1	441	Scott, Jennet...........	1796	G	1	225
Schinckel, Salome.......	1817	M	1	186	Scott, John.............	1748	J	1	232
Schitz, Christiana......	1849	U	1	747	Scott, John.............	1752	J	1	241
Schitz, Philip..........	1761	B	1	360	Scott, John.............	1807	J	1	297
Schlabach, Henry........	1793	F	1	478	Scott, John.............	1817	M	1	89
Schlabach, Rosina.......	1839	S	1	166	Scott, John.............	1843	T	1	189
Schlott, Leah...........	1847	U	1	419	Scott, Joseph...........	1746	A	1	123
Schminkey, Henry.......	1831	Q	1	29	Scott, Josiah..........	1766	C	1	60
Schmuck, John Jacob....	1825	O	1	404	Scott, Martha..........	1746	A	1	112
Schmuck, Magdalena.....	1822	N	1	124	Scott, Patrick.........	1782	D	1	224
Schneder, Jonathan.....	1823	O	1	33	Scott, Robert..........	1757	B	1	190
Schneder, Michael......	1831	Q	1	90	Scott, Robert..........	1816	M	1	83
Schneider, Abraham.....	1838	S	1	2	Scott, Samuel				
Schneider, Christian....	1824	O	1	243	(Little Britain)....	1777	C	1	467
Schneider, Henry.......	1767	C	1	74	Scott, Samuel (Rapho)...	1777	C	1	469
Schneider, Henry.......	1803	H	1	270	Scott, Thomas..........	1789	F	1	177
Schneider, John........	1793	Y	2	591	Scott, William.........	1743	A	1	78
Schneider, John........	1795	G	1	233	Scott, William.........	1746	A	1	119
Schneider, John, Sr.....	1829	P	1	356	Scott, William.........	1774	C	1	268
Schneider, Lorentz.....	1800	X	2	41	Scotten, Squire........	1839	S	1	161
Schneider, Michael.....	1804	H	1	444	Seegrist, Eve..........	1792	Y	2	580
Schneider, Peter........	1817	M	1	85	Sees, Barbara (German)..	1834	Y	2	583
Schneider, Philip......	1774	C	1	266	Sees, Elizabeth........	1832	Q	1	236
Schneider, Philip......	1799	G	1	564	Sees, Emanuel..........	1792	Y	2	578
Schneider, William.....	1790	F	1	199	Seger, George..........	1767	C	1	72
Schnell, Nicholas......	1749	A	1	181	Segner, Thomas.........	1794	J	1	420
Schnirer, Michael......	1824	O	1	216	Segrist, Bartholmew.....	1768	C	1	76
Schock, Abraham........	1822	N	1	120	Segrist, Solomon.......	1782	Y	2	575
Schock, Anna...........	1841	S	1	404	Seib, Francis..........	1763	C	1	51
Schock, John, Sr........	1829	P	1	310	Seidel, Cathrine.......	1839	S	1	105
Schoener, John.........	1802	H	1	185	Seidenspinner, Joseph...	1787	E	1	423
Schoenera, William.....	1827	P	1	103	Seig, Jacob............	1773	B	1	740
Schoenlein, Leonard.....	1808	X	2	6	Seigrist, Solomon......	1782	D	1	210
Scholds, Jacob.........	1760	B	1	316	Seitel, Valentine......	1784	D	1	428
Scholfield, Nathan C....	1849	U	1	677	Seitz, Cathrine........	1827	O	1	598
Scholtey, William......	1848	U	1	629	Seitz, George..........	1838	S	1	10
Schoner, Johannes......	1802	X	2	8	Seitz, George Christopher	1840	S	1	237
Schopf, Anna...........	1849	U	1	773	Seitz, Jacob...........	1822	X	2	28
Schreiner, Michael.....	1754	B	1	54	Seldomrich, George......	1821	M	1	510
Schriber, George........	1764	C	1	55	Seltenrich, George.....	1788	F	1	50
Schroeter, Ann Cathrine.	1835	R	1	93	Semple, John...........	1758	B	1	210
Schroeter, Carl Frederick	1821	N	1	20	Sener, John............	1814	K	1	601
Schropp, Christian.....	1827	O	1	607	Senger, Christian......	1796	G	1	230
Schuck, Adam...........	1832	Q	1	263	Sennet, Oliver, Sr......	1842	T	1	167
Schuemly, Jacob........	1772	C	1	255	Sensenich, Christian....	1847	U	1	435
Schuyler, Elizabeth.....	1845	T	1	570	Sensenich, John........	1819	M	1	244
Schwab, John...........	1781	D	1	195	Sensenig, Christian....	1753	X	2	44
Schwar, Elizabeth......	1847	U	1	363	Sensenig, Christian.....	1831	Q	1	18
Schwartz, Conrad.......	1820	M	1	392	Sensenig, Jacob........	1814	K	1	593
Schwartz, Elizabeth.....	1834	Q	1	490	Sensenig, Jacob........	1833	Q	1	423
Schwartz, George.......	1799	G	1	573	Sensenig, John.........	1826	O	1	585
Schwartz, Henry........	1846	U	1	80	Sensenig, Joshua.......	1826	O	1	493
Schwartz, John.........	1849	U	1	641	Sensenig, Michael......	1836	R	1	264
Schwartz, Nicholas.....	1839	S	1	112	Sensenigh, Michael				
Schwartz, Peter........	1779	Y	2	594	(German)............	1806	X	2	15
Schweigart, John.......	1779	Y	2	593	Sentart, John..........	1777	C	1	463
Schweigart, Peter(German)	1775	Y	2	557	Sentman, Michael.......	1839	S	1	182
Schweitzer, Andrew......	1771	Y	2	559	Sentzel, John..........	1823	N	1	303
Schweitzer, George.....	1804	H	1	484	Sergeant, Bartholomew...	1822	N	1	138
Schweitzer, John.......	1827	P	1	105	Sergeant, Jean.........	1820	M	1	360
Schweitzer, Stephen....	1804	H	1	415	Sergeson, Michael......	1841	S	1	502
Schwenly, Jacob........	1772	Y	2	559	Seyler, John...........	1782	D	1	220
Scott, Abraham..........	1775	C	1	276	Seyler, John...........	1784	E	1	11
Scott, Alexander.......	1777	C	1	468	Shaeffer, Abraham				
Scott, Alexander........	1787	E	1	408	(German)............	1804	X	2	9
Scott, Alexander........	1810	K	1	183	Shaeffer, John.........	1843	T	1	237
Scott, Alexander........	1831	Q	1	131	Shaeffer, Peter........	1848	U	1	535

Name	Year	Bk.	Vol	Page	Name	Year	Bk.	Vol	Page
Shaffer, Martin	1790	F	1	258	Sheffer, John	1843	T	1	264
Shaffner, Ann Mary	1833	Q	1	420	Sheibley, Henry	1818	M	1	92
Shaffner, Casper	1773	B	1	741	Sheibly, Casper	1775	C	1	380
Shaffner, Casper, Jr	1825	O	1	277	Sheibly, John	1797	F	1	414
Shaffner, Casper	1826	O	1	434	Sheirick, Nicholas	1832	Q	1	279
Shaffner, Philip	1837	R	1	387	Shelly, Abraham	1786	E	1	333
Shallenberger, George	1789	X	2	27	Shelly, Abraham	1844	T	1	474
Shallenberger, Jacob	1812	L	1	260	Shelly, Barbara(German)	1797	Y	2	586
Shallenberger, John	1813	K	1	399	Shelly, Christian	1760	J	1	244
Shallenberger, John	1814	K	1	598	Shelly, Christian	1788	Y	2	572
Shanck, Christian	1759	X	2	19	Shelly, Christian	1829	P	1	314
Shanck, Henry	1762	C	1	46	Shelly, Daniel	1844	T	1	484
Shank, Barbara	1785	E	1	229	Shelly, Eve Cathrine	1821	X	2	35
Shank, George	1777	C	1	472	Shelly, Jacob	1813	K	1	592
Shank, Jacob	1757	B	1	195	Shelly, Jacob	1839	S	1	108
Shank, John	1744	X	2	23	Shelly, Magdalena	1796	Y	2	587
Shank, Michael	1744	X	2	41	Shenck, Andrew	1826	O	1	559
Shank, Michael	1759	B	1	264	Shenck, Barbara	1822	N	1	224
Shank, Michael	1763	C	1	48	Shenck, Christian	1803	H	1	260
Shank, Michael	1848	U	1	566	Shenck, Christian, Sr	1826	O	1	478
Shannon, Thomas	1737	A	1	26	Shenck, Christian	1829	P	1	334
Shannon, William	1742	A	1	69	Shenck, Christian (German)	1831	X	2	20
Shanour, John	1756	B	1	122	Shenck, Christopher	1844	T	1	404
Shantz, Christian	1776	C	1	378	Shenck, Elizabeth	1838	R	1	451
Shantz, John	1776	C	1	378	Shenck, John	1803	H	1	356
Shapes, Chrisby	1748	X	2	48	Shenck, John	1826	O	1	595
Sharer, Abraham	1794	F	1	548	Shenck, John (E. Hempfield)	1835	R	1	161
Sharer, David	1840	S	1	268	Shenck, John (Martic)	1835	R	1	162
Sharer, Michael	1787	E	1	414	Shenck, Martin	1813	K	1	586
Sharmon, John	1795	G	1	369	Shenck, Rosina	1806	J	1	285
Sharp, Cathrine	1842	T	1	10	Shenk, Anna	1827	P	1	57
Sharp, Christian	1836	R	1	203	Shenk, Elizabeth (German)	1830	X	2	26
Sharp, Edward	1765	J	1	246	Shenk, Henry	1838	R	1	488
Sharp, Elizabeth	1833	Q	1	478	Shenk, John	1819	X	2	38
Sharp, Jacob	1824	O	1	158	Shenk, Magdalena	1824	O	1	166
Sharp, John	1832	Q	1	290	Shenk, Martin	1841	S	1	485
Sharp, John	1841	S	1	458	Shenk, Mary	1841	S	1	540
Sharp, Peter	1799	G	1	554	Shenk, Michael	1782	D	1	217
Sharp, Susanna	1842	T	1	103	Shenk, Michael	1790	F	1	229
Sharp, Thomas	1757	B	1	261	Shenk, Michael	1811	K	1	337
Sharp, Thomas	1782	D	1	244	Shennan, John	1731	A	1	4
Sharrer, George	1833	Q	1	398	Shepard, Solomon	1749	A	1	167
Shartle, Jacob	1767	C	1	71	Sherb, Adam	1835	R	1	132
Shartz, Barbara	1790	F	1	195	Sherb, Christopher	1807	J	1	304
Shau, Daniel	1778	C	1	492	Sherck, David	1769	X	2	41
Shau, David	1748	J	1	-	Sherck, Jacob	1788	Y	2	570
Shau, David	1833	Q	1	402	Sherck, John	1790	X	2	16
Shaub, Peter	1764	C	1	56	Sherck, John	1837	R	1	305
Shaum, Melchoir	1837	R	1	312	Sherck, Peter	1770	Y	2	561
Shaum, Philip	1815	L	1	415	Sherer, Henry	1835	R	1	90
Shaup, Barbara	1793	F	1	442	Sherer, Isabella	1825	O	1	339
Shaver, Henry	1757	X	2	10	Sherer, Joseph	1776	C	1	385
Shaw, Anthony	1744	A	1	86	Sherer, Michael	1777	C	1	387
Shaw, Samuel	1743	A	1	79	Sherk, Christian	1847	U	1	429
Shaw, Samuel	1778	C	1	577	Sherrer, David	1847	U	1	406
Sheaffer, Alexander	1786	E	1	337	Sherrer, John	1813	K	1	419
Sheaffer, Baltzer	1769	C	1	81	Shertz, John	1799	G	1	556
Sheaffer, Dorothea	1828	P	1	276	Shertz, John	1822	N	1	165
Sheaffer, Frederick	1802	J	1	254	Shertzer, Casper	1775	C	1	265
Sheaffer, George	1843	T	1	198	Shertzer, Jacob	1794	F	1	535
Sheaffer, Henry	1757	B	1	159	Shiber, Michael	1829	P	1	338
Sheaffer, Jacob	1805	J	1	272	Shick, Leonard	1801	H	1	113
Sheaffer, Jacob	1846	U	1	95	Shiffer, Henry	1812	L	1	256
Sheaffer, John	1819	M	1	228	Shiffer, Peter	1822	N	1	252
Sheaffer, John	1849	U	1	804	Shiler, Julianna	1789	F	1	52
Sheaffer, Julianna	1832	Q	1	145	Shill, George	1836	R	1	206
Sheaffer, Michael	1796	G	1	1	Shiller, John	1795	G	1	338
Sheaffer, Philip	1758	B	1	247	Shimp, Andrew	1839	S	1	150
Sheaffer, Samuel	1849	U	1	760	Shindel, George	1821	N	1	91
Sheaffer, Vonica	1844	T	1	344					
Shearer, Joseph	1776	C	1	385					
Shefel, John Ernst	1794	F	1	600					

Name	Year	Bk.	Vol	Page	Name	Year	Bk.	Vol	Page
Shindelman, Nicholas	1764	C	1	53	Shreiner, Charles	1832	Q	1	176
Shindle, Peter	1784	E	1	57	Shreiner, George Michael	1812	L	1	263
Shippen, Ann M	1847	U	1	366	Shreiner, John Sr.	1828	P	1	128
Shippen, Edward Esq	1781	D	1	202	Shreiner, John	1843	T	1	220
Shippen, Joseph	1810	K	1	165	Shreiner, John Adam	1744	A	1	94
Shippen, Robert	1841	S	1	382	Shreiner, Martin	1807	J	1	311
Shirick, John	1826	O	1	430	Shreiner, Martin	1826	O	1	517
Shire, Ann	1807	J	1	309	Shreiner, Mathias Andrew	1802	X	2	7
Shire, Conrad	1790	F	1	205	Shreiner, Michael	1827	P	1	504
Shirk, Barbara	1790	Y	2	571	Shreiner, Michael	1836	R	1	190
Shirk, David	1810	K	1	323	Shreiner, Philip	1791	F	1	279
Shirk, David	1830	P	1	478	Shreiner, Philip	1830	P	1	453
Shirk, Elizabeth	1826	O	1	470	Shreiner, Samuel	1840	S	1	316
Shirk, Henry	1836	R	1	286	Shreyer, Christian	1744	X	2	25
Shirk, Jacob	1823	F	1	65	Shrieber, John	1788	F	1	40
Shirk, John	1812	L	1	239	Shuck, Martin	1801	H	1	143
Shirk, Joseph	1770	C	1	89	Shuey, Daniel	1777	Y	2	553
Shirk, Joseph	1807	X	2	5	Shuey, Ludwig	1775	Y	2	557
Shirk, Joseph	1826	O	1	467	Shufflebottom, Josiah	1849	U	1	700
Shirk, Mary	1840	S	1	292	Shuhmacher, William	1848	U	1	631
Shirk, Peter	1812	L	1	224	Shuler, Jacob	1811	K	1	338
Shirk, Peter	1826	O	1	428	Shuler, Regina	1813	K	1	390
Shirk, Ulrich	1763	C	1	47	Shultz, Andrew	1789	F	1	167
Shirts, Christian	1783	D	1	383	Shultz, John	1803	H	1	386
Shirts, Jacob	1755	B	1	105	Shultz, John	1805	J	1	267
Shirts, John	1798	G	1	172	Shultze, Christian	1786	E	1	319
Shissler, Conrad	1821	X	2	35	Shumacher, Jacob, Jr	1833	Q	1	454
Shissler, Philip	1832	Q	1	238	Shumacher, Jacob	1836	R	1	278
Shits, George	1768	C	1	74	Shumacher, John(German)	1828	X	2	33
Shitz, Daniel	1803	H	1	297	Shuman, Cathrine	1826	O	1	597
Shitz, Dillman	1769	C	1	83	Shuman, George	1793	J	1	249
Shitz, Frederick	1820	X	2	38	Shup, George Adam	1822	N	1	238
Shitz, John	1790	F	1	227	Shute, John	1778	Y	2	593
Shitz, John	1840	S	1	326	Shwartz, Ann	1779	Y	2	582
Shitz, John	1847	U	1	287	Shwartz, John	1795	Y	2	540
Shitz, Magdalena	1789	F	1	172	Shweitzer, John	1815	L	1	417
Shlott, John	1789	X	2	24	Sides, George	1826	O	1	565
Shnebly, John	1753	B	1	39	Sides, Peter	1826	O	1	524
Shnyder, Christian	1795	I	1	425	Sidwell, Ann	1801	H	1	131
Shoak, Jacob	1782	D	1	214	Sidwell, Isaac	1793	F	1	516
Shober, Andrew	1805	J	1	270	Sidwell, John	1758	B	1	237
Shober, Rosina	1814	K	1	600	Sidwell, John	1810	K	1	322
Shock, Jacob	1818	M	1	191	Sidwell, Joseph	1816	M	1	95
Shoemaker, John	1843	T	1	247	Siegel, Adam	1809	K	1	50
Shoemaker, Peter	1773	C	1	257	Siegrist, Jacob	1781	D	1	199
Shoemaker, Philip	1791	Y	2	579	Siegrist, Jacob	1807	X	2	4
Shoemaker, Philip (German)	1796	Y	2	584	Siegrist, John	1824	O	1	103
Shoemaker, Philip	1796	Y	2	585	Siegrist, Michael	1752	X	2	22
Shoenborge, Ann Maria	1843	T	1	199	Siegrist, Michael	1800	H	1	22
Shoff, Barbara	1760	X	2	21	Siegrist, Michael	1826	O	1	484
Shoff, Frederick	1800	H	1	80	Siegrist, Michael	1836	R	1	272
Shoff, Henry	1804	J	1	256	Silknitter, Michael	1826	O	1	581
Shonaur, Jacob	1764	C	1	53	Simmons, Samuel	1747	J	1	230
Shonower, Ursula	1773	C	1	264	Simone, John Jacob	1789	F	1	173
Shop, Dietrich	1765	C	1	58	Simons, Joseph	1804	H	1	445
Shop, Elizabeth	1826	O	1	477	Simony, Eve	1805	J	1	275
Shopp, Henry	1831	Q	1	96	Simpson, John	1738	A	1	33
Short, John	1828	P	1	231	Simpson, Thomas	1761	B	1	383
Shotter, John	1776	C	1	381	Simpson, Thomas	1772	J	1	247
Shoufelberger, Philip	1759	B	1	283	Simpson, Thomas	1777	C	1	384
Shoup, Christopher	1769	C	1	77	Singer, Abraham	1842	T	1	69
Showalter, Barbara	1830	P	1	524	Singer, David	1827	P	1	124
Showalter, Christian	1799	G	1	552	Singer, Martin	1825	O	1	392
Showalter, Jacob	1809	K	1	38	Singer, Philip	1798	Y	2	582
Showalter, John	1792	F	1	385	Singhass, Casper	1809	K	1	42
Showalter, John	1838	R	1	456	Sink, Elizabeth	1842	T	1	138
Showalter, Joseph	1848	U	1	586	Sites, Peter	1793	F	1	440
Showalter, Samuel	1834	R	1	9	Skiles, Alexander	1779	C	1	581
Showawer, Abraham	1762	C	1	45	Skiles, Henry	1779	C	1	582
Shower, Rosina	1819	M	1	254	Skiles, John	1767	C	1	63
Shrantz, John	1812	L	1	265	Skyles, Henry	1749	-	-	-
					Skyles, Henry	1750	J	1	238

Name	Year	Bk.	Vol	Page	Name	Year	Bk.	Vol	Page
Slater, John	1831	Q	1	120	Smith, Theobold	1804	J	1	262
Slaymaker, Amos	1837	R	1	376	Smith, William	1748	Y	2	567
Slaymaker, Henry	1785	E	1	290	Smith, William	1788	F	1	63
Slaymaker, Henry	1844	T	1	415	Smith, William, Esq.	1806	J	1	282
Slaymaker, John	1796	F	1	389	Smith, William	1826	O	1	455
Slaymaker, John, Sr.	1831	Q	1	99	Smith, William	1835	R	1	144
Slaymaker, Lawrence	1748	A	1	164	Smoker, Christian	1782	D	1	238
Slaymaker, Mathias	1762	C	1	43	Smoker, John	1818	M	1	161
Slaymaker, Mathias	1804	I	1	450	Smout, Edward	1751	A	1	196
Slemons, Thomas	1765	C	1	57	Smuck, Jacob	1796	G	1	8
Slemons, Thomas	1792	F	1	335	Smutz, Abraham	1774	C	1	390
Slick, Jacob	1844	T	1	503	Smyth, Daniel	1781	D	1	207
Slighter, Thomas	1784	D	1	458	Snable, Jacob	1744	A	1	91
Sloan, James	1775	C	1	383	Snader, Benjamin	1838	S	1	69
Sloan, John	1741	A	1	58	Snavely, Henry	1845	T	1	596
Sloan, Samuel	1771	B	1	743	Snavely, Samuel	1827	P	1	119
Slough, Christian	1819	M	1	328	Sneader, Christian	1846	U	1	155
Slough, Jacob	1750	A	1	204	Sneally, John	1747	-	-	-
Smedly, Joseph	1812	L	1	248	Sneavly, John	1772	B	1	738
Smith, Abraham	1792	Y	2	580	Sneder, Christian	1793	F	1	425
Smith, Abraham	1843	T	1	282	Sneider, Jacob	1794	F	1	559
Smith, Alexander Landry	1818	M	1	160	Sneider, Jacob	1782	D	1	236
Smith, Alice	1772	B	1	737	Sneider, Peter	1765	C	1	58
Smith, Anna Maria	1807	J	1	299	Sneider, Peter	1780	D	1	189
Smith, Catherine	1756	X	2	15	Sneider, William	1825	O	1	311
Smith, Christian	1777	J	1	248	Snepper, George	1795	F	1	613
Smith, Christian	1812	L	1	258	Snevely, Casper	1764	E	1	147
Smith, Christian	1834	R	1	25	Snevely, Edmond	1767	C	1	67
Smith, Christopher	1806	J	1	292	Snevely, Jacob	1782	Y	2	596
Smith, Daniel	1815	L	1	414	Snevely, John	1747	X	2	21
Smith, Dewalt	1780	D	1	187	Snoddy, James	1760	B	1	325
Smith, Dorothea	1834	R	1	43	Snoddy, Jane	1746	J	1	230
Smith, Eleanor	1783	D	1	343	Snoddy, John	1736	A	1	22
Smith, Elizabeth	1843	T	1	236	Snodgrass, Alexander	1750	J	1	237
Smith, Ephraim	1813	K	1	590	Snodgrass, Hannah	1825	O	1	272
Smith, Esther	1843	T	1	336	Snodgrass, James	1750	J	1	236
Smith, George	1767	C	1	68	Snodgrass, James	1774	C	1	268
Smith, George	1806	M	1	217	Snodgrass, John	1792	F	1	338
Smith, George	1806	J	1	284	Snodgrass, Robert	1777	C	1	466
Smith, George	1830	P	1	534	Snodgrass, William	1793	F	1	432
Smith, Hannah	1816	M	1	81	Snodgrass, William	1809	K	1	125
Smith, Henry	1775	C	1	270	Snody, Mathew	1780	D	1	193
Smith, Henry	1783	D	1	422	Snowdy, William	1735	A	1	20
Smith, Henry	1825	O	1	313	Snyder, Anthony	1774	C	1	259
Smith, Isaac, Sr.	1833	Q	1	345	Snyder, Barbara	1825	O	1	353
Smith, Jacob, Sr.	1826	O	1	583	Snyder, Christian	1830	P	1	446
Smith, James	1739	A	1	34	Snyder, Christian	1842	T	1	137
Smith, James	1756	B	1	133	Snyder, Emich	1818	M	1	180
Smith, James, Esq.	1761	C	1	41	Snyder, George	1838	R	1	446
Smith, James	1775	C	1	275	Snyder, George	1842	T	1	165
Smith, John	1769	C	1	84	Snyder, Jacob	1844	T	1	402
Smith, John	1777	C	1	464	Snyder, Lorentz (German)	1806	J	1	283
Smith, John	1782	D	1	359	Snyder, Magdalena	1839	S	1	147
Smith, John	1801	H	1	146	Snyder, Mary	1843	T	1	260
Smith, John	1818	M	1	141	Snyder, Melchoir	1785	E	1	287
Smith, John	1826	O	1	511	Snyder, Peter	1826	O	1	426
Smith, John	1830	P	1	443	Soehner, Godlieb	1802	J	1	255
Smith, John	1834	R	1	5	Sohl, Henry	1804	X	2	9
Smith, John, Jr.	1844	T	1	407	Sollenberger, Abraham	1808	J	1	315
Smith, Joseph	1759	J	1	243	Sollinger, Christopher	1769	Y	2	562
Smith, Joseph	1825	O	1	401	Sommer, Leonard	1836	R	1	212
Smith, Magdalena	1832	Q	1	147	Songmaster, Ezekiel	1785	X	2	17
Smith, Margaret	1803	H	1	316	Souder, Barbara (German)	1804	Y	2	567
Smith, Martin	1828	P	1	193	Souder, Cathrine	1822	N	1	126
Smith, Mary	1819	M	1	298	Souder, John	1788	F	1	66
Smith, Mathias	1793	F	1	456	Souter, Rudy	1782	X	2	42
Smith, Peter	1756	B	1	155	Sowder, Jacob (German)	1737	J	1	229
Smith, Philip	1756	X	2	10	Sower, Henry	1799	G	1	579
Smith, Philip	1816	M	1	80	Sower, Joseph	1843	T	1	185
Smith, Robert	1757	B	1	156	Sowter, Ann	1795	I	1	424
Smith, Sampson	1781	D	1	206	Spade, George	1818	M	1	138
Smith, Samuel	1794	J	1	421	Spangler, Kathrine	1819	M	1	255

Name	Year	Bk.	Vol	Page	Name	Year	Bk.	Vol	Page
Spath, John	1820	M	1	432	Steaffe, Philip	1801	H	1	115
Spatts, Conrad	1849	U	1	691	Stearn, Valentine	1761	B	1	389
Spear, George	1846	U	1	183	Steel, Alexander	1756	B	1	132
Spear, Robert	1800	H	1	28	Steel, Elizabeth	1821	N	1	48
Speck, Bernard	1813	K	1	585	Steel, Francis	1807	J	1	307
Speck, Christopher	1814	K	1	596	Steel, Thomas	1746	A	1	127
Spence, John, Sr.	1835	R	1	168	Steel, William	1769	C	1	87
Spencer, Robert	1841	S	1	387	Steel, William	1780	D	1	185
Spendle, Peter	1849	U	1	660	Steele, Elizabeth	1826	O	1	567
Spera, John	1830	P	1	511	Steele, James	1756	B	1	129
Speth, William	1846	U	1	104	Steele, Mary	1815	L	1	530
Spickler, Margaret	1783	Y	2	595	Steele, Robert	1756	B	1	121
Spickler, Martin	1782	Y	2	573	Steele, Samuel	1825	O	1	271
Spickler, Martin	1796	G	1	57	Steele, William	1822	N	1	188
Spies, Philip	1827	X	2	47	Steer, Philip	1803	H	1	403
Spitler, John	1758	B	1	245	Steffe, George	1836	R	1	230
Spohnhour, Jacob	1807	J	1	300	Stegar, Adam	1785	E	1	296
Sponhaver, Jacob	1827	X	2	31	Stegel, Christian	1767	C	1	73
Sponn, Ulrich	1782	Y	2	598	Stehly, John	1776	Y	2	555
Sprecher, George	1783	D	1	246	Stehman, Jacob	1799	G	1	575
Sprecher, George	1848	U	1	518	Stehman, John	1845	U	1	31
Sprenkle, Michael	1748	A	1	154	Stehr, Henry	1782	Y	2	597
Spriegel, Maria(German)	1833	Y	2	581	Steigelman, George	1826	X	2	26
Sprigel, Jacob	1798	J	1	253	Steigelman, Jacob	1807	J	1	302
Springer, Jacob	1782	Y	2	576	Steigelman, Ludwig	1816	M	1	79
Springer, Philip	1774	C	1	256	Steigerwalt, Everhart	1807	J	1	305
Spuckler, Barbara	1811	K	1	342	Steigerwalt, Frederick	1827	P	1	26
Spycker, John	1762	C	1	44	Steigler, Jacob	1793	F	1	428
Stah, Jacob	1829	P	1	293	Stein, John	1750	X	2	44
Stahl, Ann Mary	1753	B	1	31	Stein, Robert	1769	C	1	86
Stahl, Elizabeth	1839	S	1	101	Steineke, Samuel	1819	X	2	39
Stahl, John	1833	Q	1	361	Steiner, Henry	1800	Y	2	566
Stahle, Jacob, Jr.	1811	K	1	345	Steiner, Henry	1828	P	1	219
Stahley, Christian	1809	K	1	62	Steiner, Jacob	1783	D	1	241
Stake, George R.	1815	L	1	529	Steiner, Joseph	1847	U	1	387
Stambach, Henry	1794	J	1	421	Steinman, Christian	1776	C	1	388
Stamper, John (German)	1745	X	2	40	Steinman, Christian F.				
Staple, Barbara	1849	U	1	774	(German)	1808	Y	2	599
Stare, John	1749	J	1	233	Steinman, John F.	1823	O	1	87
Starr, Moses	1786	E	1	383	Steinman, Magdalena	1817	M	1	88
Starret, Robert	1777	C	1	465	Steinmetz, Adam	1832	Q	1	255
Starret, Samuel	1776	C	1	382	Steinmetz, Charles	1833	Q	1	365
Stauffer, Abraham	1838	R	1	459	Steiss, Jacob	1805	J	1	269
Stauffer, Christian	1776	Y	2	555	Steitz, Peter	1842	T	1	159
Stauffer, Christian	1808	J	1	316	Steman, Anna	1821	N	1	97
Stauffer, Christian	1833	Q	1	482	Steman, Barbara	1835	R	1	94
Stauffer, Christian	1842	T	1	89	Steman, Christian	1785	X	2	18
Stauffer, Elizabeth	1811	K	1	340	Steman, Christian, Sr.	1844	T	1	445
Stauffer, Esther	1833	Q	1	468	Steman, John	1766	C	1	61
Stauffer, Feronica	1823	O	1	59	Steman, John	1792	F	1	378
Stauffer, Frederick	1828	P	1	247	Steman, John	1819	M	1	245
Stauffer, George	1832	Q	1	301	Steman, Mary	1814	K	1	608
Stauffer, Hannah	1847	U	1	256	Steman, Samuel	1797	J	1	252
Stauffer, Henry	1805	J	1	265	Steman, Tobias	1816	Q	1	139
Stauffer, Henry	1819	M	1	204	Steman, Tobias	1832	Q	1	139
Stauffer, Henry	1838	S	1	81	Stempel, Peter	1761	B	1	359
Stauffer, Henry	1845	T	1	558	Stepgen, Frederick	1742	A	1	76
Stauffer, Jacob					Stephen, Andrew	1770	C	1	88
(Lampeter)	1794	J1	1	416	Stephen, Ulrich	1760	Y	2	600
Stauffer, Jacob	1799	G	1	549	Stephens, Christopher	1830	P	1	508
Stauffer, Jacob	1816	M	1	85	Steply, John	1776	C	1	379
Stauffer, Jacob	1821	N	1	78	Steret, John	1748	A	1	146
Stauffer, Jacob	1833	Q	1	340	Stern, John	1809	K	1	37
Stauffer, John	1767	Y	2	565	Stern, John Michael	1753	X	2	21
Stauffer, John	1798	G	1	468	Sterret, Martha	1754	B	1	50
Stauffer, John	1812	L	1	241	Sterrett, James	1809	K	1	47
Stauffer, Matthias	1758	Y	2	568	Stertzer, Baltzer	1820	M	1	449
Stauffer, Peter, Jr.	1802	H	1	225	Stetler, Abraham	1760	B	1	333
Stauffer, Peter	1831	Q	1	113	Stettler, John	1782	D	1	233
Stauffer, Ulrich	1746	X	2	21	Stevenson, James	1768	C	1	78
Staug, Nicholas(German)	1763	-	-	-	Stevenson, Nathaniel	1778	C	1	513
Stayman, John	1785	E	1	255	Stewart, Andrew	1774	C	1	263

Name	Year	Bk.	Vol	Page	Name	Year	Bk.	Vol	Page
Stewart, George	1769	C	1	81	Stoutsenberger, John	1802	H	1	192
Stewart, James	1756	B	1	124	Stoutt, Jonathan	1839	S	1	151
Stewart, James	1783	D	1	398	Stoutzenberger, Isaac	1838	R	1	534
Stewart, John	1777	C	1	463	Stoutzenberger, Margaret	1830	P	1	507
Stewart, John	1809	K	1	130	Stover, John Casper	1779	C	1	584
Stewart, Robert	1754	B	1	59	Stowler, Ann	1811	K	1	343
Stewart, William	1748	A	1	150	Strain, Robert	1753	B	1	24
Steyman, Barbara	1798	G	1	465	Strain, Thomas	1780	D	1	192
Stibge, Jacob	1821	X	2	36	Strean, David	1783	D	1	365
Stibgen, Anna	1828	P	1	189	Strein, John Jacob	1831	X	2	32
Stillinger, Mary	1821	X	2	36	Streng, Mary E	1834	Q	1	502
Stits, George	1767	C	1	65	Strenge, Christian Esq.	1828	P	1	198
Stitzer, Susanna	1843	T	1	205	Streyn, John	1752	J	1	239
Stivers, Peter	1845	T	1	519	Strickler, Abraham	1821	M	1	517
Stober, George	1828	P	1	180	Strickler, Ann	1847	U	1	251
Stober, John	1817	M	1	87	Strickler, Barbara	1849	U	1	854
Stober, Philip	1845	U	1	487	Strickler, George	1791	F	1	289
Stock, Adam	1825	O	1	326	Strickler, Henry	1761	B	1	377
Stock, George	1832	Q	1	284	Strickler, Henry	1796	G	1	9
Stocksleger, Philip	1824	O	1	147	Strickler, Henry, Sr.	1830	P	1	488
Stockslegle, Alexander	1763	C	1	50	Strickler, Jacob	1812	L	1	227
Stockton, David	1752	J	1	-	Strickler, Jacob	1824	O	1	186
Stockton, George	1747	A	1	140	Strickler, Jacob	1848	U	1	469
Stockton, Isabella	1747	A	1	138	Strickler, John Sr	1832	Q	1	149
Stockton, Robert	1748	-	-	-	Strickler, Joseph	1813	K	1	588
Stoehn, Philip	1781	Y	2	594	Strickler, Sarah	1827	P	1	192
Stoehr, Philip	1781	D	1	201	Strickler, Ulrich	1804	J	1	258
Stoffer, David	1811	K	1	339	Stroh, Eve (German)	1832	Q	1	299
Stoft, Mary	1819	M	1	341	Strohl, Jacob	1830	P	1	519
Stohler, Frederick	1847	U	1	330	Strohl, Mary	1845	T	1	575
Stohler, Sebastian	1775	Y	2	556	Strohm, Henry	1834	R	1	17
Stoler, Rachel	1799	G	1	577	Strunk, Wymer	1793	Y	2	577
Stoll, Jacob	1822	N	1	168	Strunk, Wymer	1794	J	1	422
Stoll, Martin(In German)	1806	X	2	14	Stuart, George	1732	A	1	7
Stoltz, Jacob	1805	X	2	12	Stuart, John	1749	A	1	188
Stoltzfuss, Jacob	1810	K	1	173	Stuart, Rebecca	1749	J	1	234
Stone, Ludwig	1782	D	1	227	Stubbs, Daniel	1808	J	1	320
Stoneman, Joseph	1756	B	1	130	Stubbs, Priscilla	1831	Q	1	126
Stoneman, Tobias (Stehman)	1771	C	1	251	Stuckey, John	1786	X	2	23
Stoner, Abraham	1803	H	1	364	Stump, Christopher	1778	C	1	578
Stoner, Ann	1821	N	1	11	Stump, Elias	1792	F	1	410
Stoner, Cathrine	1785	E	1	261	Stump, John	1749	A	1	172
Stoner, Cathrine	1797	G	1	107	Sturgeon, Samuel	1750	J	1	235
Stoner, Christian	1758	B	1	271	Sturgis, Samuel	1845	T	1	529
Stoner, Christian	1816	M	1	82	Sturgiss, John Dr	1831	Q	1	313
Stoner, Elizabeth	1785	E	1	185	Stutenroth, Henry	1809	K	1	21
Stoner, Isaac	1847	U	1	237	Stutenroth, Susanna	1847	U	1	252
Stoner, Jacob	1806	J	1	277	Styer, Adam	1837	R	1	396
Stoner, Jacob	1832	Q	1	252	Sullenberger, Ann	1826	O	1	425
Stoner, Jacob	1845	U	1	46	Sullivan, Cornelius	1770	C	1	250
Stoner, John	1771	Y	2	560	Summer, Peter	1836	R	1	258
Stoner, John	1777	Y	2	592	Summers, Christian	1788	F	1	49
Stoner, Rudy	1769	Y	2	563	Summy, Christian	1847	U	1	284
Stoner, Rudy	1776	C	1	388	Summy, Henry	1783	D	1	364
Stoneroad, Thomas	1827	O	1	611	Summy, Jacob	1762	X	2	11
Stormfeltz, Conrad	1842	T	1	83	Summy, Jacob	1807	J	1	293
Stosz, Maria Barbara	1877	R	1	450	Summy, John	1812	L	1	251
Stoud, Henry	1784	E	1	154	Summy, Mary	1828	P	1	224
Stouffer, Christian	1784	E	1	71	Summy, Peter	1791	F	1	295
Stouffer, Daniel	1803	H	1	378	Summy, Peter	1836	R	1	196
Stouffer, Daniel	1823	O	1	97	Swab, George Michael	1758	B	1	239
Stouffer, Jacob	1768	Y	2	564	Swan, Alexander	1778	C	1	510
Stouffer, Jacob(Mt.Joy)	1794	J	1	419	Swan, James	1741	A	1	63
Stouffer, John	1799	G	1	568	Swan, William	1782	D	1	234
Stouffer, Margaret	1799	G	1	563	Swar, Elizabeth	1819	M	1	285
Stouffer, Peter	1787	E	1	454	Swar, John	1821	M	1	486
Stouffer, Susanna	1808	J	1	314	Swar, John	1823	X	2	30
Stout, David	1764	C	1	52	Swar, John	1830	P	1	518
Stouter, Kathrine	1796	G	1	69	Swar, John	1836	R	1	208
Stouter, Rudy	1782	D	1	226	Swartz, Ann	1799	G	1	553
Stoutsberger, Andrew	1760	B	1	301	Swartz, Henry C.	1844	T	1	435
					Swartz, Maria	1837	R	1	323

Name	Year	Bk.	Vol	Page	Name	Year	Bk.	Vol	Page
Swartz, Philip	1782	D	1	208	Thompson, Thomas	1770	C	1	98
Sweeney, Ambrose	1792	F	1	294	Thompson, William	1791	F	1	294
Sweigart, David Sr.	1841	S	1	400	Thompson, William Dr.	1839	S	1	170
Sweigart, Elizabeth	1816	M	1	78	Thornborough, Thomas	1759	B	1	289
Sweigart, George	1806	J	1	288	Thornbrough, Edward	1734	A	1	18
Sweigart, Jacob	1804	J	1	264	Thornbrow, Joseph	1820	U	1	363
Sweigart, Sebastian (German)	1808	Y	2	586	Thorwarth, Martin	1771	X	2	49
					Thuma, John	1819	U	1	321
Sweitzer, Henry	1800	H	1	25	Thume, John	1820	U	1	423
Sweitzer, John	1788	Y	2	569	Tippet, Mary	1829	P	1	323
Sweitzer, Ludwig	1832	Q	1	308	Todd, Hugh	1772	C	1	277
Swentzel, Frederick	1834	R	1	63	Todd, James	1783	D	1	389
Swigart, Abraham	1841	S	1	469	Tomlinson, William	1825	O	1	290
Swisher, John Sr.	1840	S	1	291	Toole, Durmis	1767	X	2	57
Swobe, Cathrine	1825	O	1	356	Torn, Francis	1774	X	2	51
Swobe, Henry	1808	J	1	322	Tosh, James	1750	I	1	433
Swope, Daniel	1822	N	1	111	Tosh, Jonathan	1750	I	1	434
Swope, Jacob	1811	K	1	331	Tovie, Conrad	1766	C	1	95
Sybert, Henry	1806	J	1	280	Townsend, John	1847	U	1	384
Syble, Conrad	1821	N	1	37	Trachsell, John	1780	D	1	249
Symons, Nicholas	1775	C	1	273	Traeger, Aaron	1848	U	1	523
Syrus, Matthew	1749	J	1	234	Traft, Martha	1830	P	1	460
Taggart, John	1836	R	1	186	Trainer, James	1821	N	1	115
Taggert, John Jr.	1833	Q	1	408	Trazer, Jacob	1816	L	1	607
Tait, Jane	1832	Q	1	162	Treber, Justis	1771	C	1	92
Taite, William	1749	A	1	187	Trego, Dorothy	1889	H	2	598
Talabach, Jacob	1771	J	1	328	Treickler, Elizabeth	1845	T	1	626
Tanger, Andrew	1823	O	1	14	Treish, Adam	1819	U	1	348
Tanneberg, David	1804	X	2	54	Treish, Leonard	1788	F	1	26
Tanner, Barbara	1820	M	1	455	Tremayne, Dr. John	1844	T	1	413
Tarbit, John	1762	C	1	91	Trexel, Abraham	1784	E	1	147
Tate, Adam	1833	Q	1	399	Trich, Charles	1811	K	1	348
Tate, William	1746	A	1	114	Trimble, Rose	1821	N	1	7
Taylor, Agnes	1775	C	1	278	Trimble, William	1812	K	1	350
Taylor, Barbara	1825	O	1	353	Trinkly, Christopher	1752	J	1	326
Taylor, David	1761	B	1	347	Trissler, John, Sr.	1843	T	1	319
Taylor, Isaac	1756	B	1	134	Troesher, Jacob	1824	X	2	56
Taylor, Jane	1764	C	1	279	Trouch, Helena	1849	U	1	807
Taylor, John	1777	C	1	478	Trout, Paul	1794	F	1	596
Taylor, William	1760	B	1	305	Troutman, George	1789	F	1	138
Taylor, William	1818	M	1	138	Troutman, Heronimus	1774	X	2	50
Teas, John	1750	I	1	433	Troutwine, Heronimus	1774	X	2	50
Temple, Elizabeth	1788	E	1	466	Troutwine, Philip	1850	U	1	943
Templeton, Andrew	1806	J	1	329	Truckamiller, Michael	1778	X	2	52
Tepley, Elizabeth	1808	J	1	331	Trump, John	1801	H	1	132
Teply, John	1803	H	1	281	Tryer, Andrew	1822	N	1	175
Tetteborne, Ludwig Henry.	1753	X	2	52	Tschautz, John	1776	X	2	50
Thatcher, Richard	1763	C	1	93	Tuckney, Henry	1785	E	1	285
Thoma, Ann Margaret	1824	O	1	123	Tunis, Jacob	1760	B	1	312
Thoman, John	1789	X	2	53	Turbett, Samuel	1796	G	1	17
Thomas, Adam	1762	X	2	49	Turner, David	1752	I	1	435
Thomas, Elizabeth	1823	N	1	263	Turner, Eve Marie	1832	Q	1	205
Thomas, John	1803	H	1	281	Turner, James	1777	C	1	477
Thomas, John	1834	R	1	45	Turner, John	1755	B	1	76
Thomas, Julianna	1815	L	1	606	Tweed, Agnes	1814	K	1	612
Thomas, Philip	1815	L	1	606	Tweed, James	1817	L	1	609
Thomas, Rebecca	1830	P	1	471	Tweed, Jesse	1842	T	1	105
Thomas, Regina	1783	D	1	251	Tweed, Robert	1767	C	1	96
Thomas, Salome(German)	1834	X	2	55	Tweed, William	1815	L	1	418
Thome, Ann Maria	1825	O	1	294	Ulrich, Adam	1781	D	1	253
Thome, David	1750	I	1	432	Ulrich, Elizabeth	1844	T	1	352
Thomen, Jacob	1770	X	2	48	Ulrich, John	1758	B	1	217
Thompson, Agnes	1802	H	1	154	Ulrich, Paul	1773	C	1	392
Thompson, Catherine	1845	U	1	29	Umberger, John	1779	C	1	588
Thompson, Hugh	1766	J	1	327	Umberger, Leonard	1766	C	1	101
Thompson, James	1799	G	1	581	Umble, Christian	1821	M	1	497
Thompson, James	1824	O	1	140	Umborn, Philip	1772	C	1	102
Thompson, John	1778	C	1	587	Upjohn, James	1841	S	1	570
Thompson, Mary	1841	T	1	3	Urban, John	1847	U	1	286
Thompson, Nathan	1813	K	1	610	Urban, Lewis	1850	U	1	816
Thompson, Robert Esq.	1764	C	1	94	Urban, Ludwig	1811	K	1	351
Thompson, Robert J.	1823	O	1	38	Ury, Frances	1767	X	2	58

Name	Year	Bk.	Vol	Page	Name	Year	Bk.	Vol	Page
Uttzman, John............	1764	C	1	99	Watson, Dr. John........	1843	T	1	324
Vance, John.............	1734	A	1	13	Watson, John............	1850	U	1	973
Vance, John.............	1754	B	1	38	Watson, Nathaniel.......	1818	M	1	170
Vanlear, Christopher....	1750	I	1	436	Watt, James.............	1804	H	1	436
Vannin, Hatil..........	1748	I	1	436	Watt, Margaret..........	1844	T	1	504
Vaughn, Jane..:........	1822	N	1	119	Way, Faithful...........	1812	K	1	371
Vernor, Benjamin........	1831	Q	1	114	Weaver, Adam............	1810	K	1	358
Vernor, John...........	1754	B	1	44	Weaver, Adam............	1847	U	1	450
Vinegar, Ann Maria.....	1810	K	1	362	Weaver, Barbara.........	1843	T	1	204
Vinegar, Christian......	1800	H	1	30	Weaver, Christian.......	1816	M	1	98
Vinegar, David.........	1802	H	1	196	Weaver, Christian.......	1823	N	1	302
Vogan, James............	1824	O	1	190	Weaver, Christian.......	1843	T	1	311
Vogan, John.............	1747	J	1	334	Weaver, Christopher.....	1788	F	1	10
Vogan, Margaret.........	1831	Q	1	27	Weaver, Conrad..........	1810	K	1	356
Vogan, Thomas...........	1811	K	1	354	Weaver, Elizabeth.......	1840	S	1	364
Voght, Christian........	1813	K	1	620	Weaver, George..........	1791	F	1	327
Voglesong, Catherine....	1850	U	1	981	Weaver, George..........	1818	M	1	104
Vondersaal, Abraham.....	1832	Q	1	198	Weaver, George..........	1845	T	1	531
Vondersaal, Henry.......	1823	N	1	273	Weaver, Henry...........	1745	A	1	97
Vonkennen, Baltzer.....	1776	X	2	58	Weaver, Henry...........	1787	E	1	442
Vonkennen, Catherine...	1804	I	1	437	Weaver, Henry...........	1826	O	1	463
Vonkennen, Jacob........	1843	T	1	328	Weaver, Jacob...........	1747	J	1	334
Wacker, Christian......	1779	C	1	591	Weaver, Jacob...........	1776	C	1	401
Waddle, John............	1752	A	1	201	Weaver, Jacob...........	1793	X	2	82
Waddle, Thomas..........	1756	B	1	138	Weaver, Jacob...........	1814	K	1	600
Wade, Charles..........	1817	M	1	99	Weaver, John............	1755	B	1	102
Wade, Daniel...........	1841	S	1	568	Weaver, John............	1773	C	1	401
Waechter, George........	1803	H	1	304	Weaver, John............	1802	H	1	229
Waggoner, George........	1819	M	1	256	Weaver, John, Sr.......	1832	Q	1	270
Waginer, Adam...........	1777	C	1	479	Weaver, John............	1848	U	1	486
Wagner, Elizabeth.......	1829	P	1	281	Weaver, Joseph..........	1844	T	1	371
Wagner, John............	1785	X	2	67	Weaver, Joseph L........	1846	U	1	63
Wagoner, Henry..........	1788	E	1	459	Weaver, Michael.:......	1837	R	1	358
Walborn, Christian.....	1769	J	1	348	Weaver, Samuel..........	1770	C	1	308
Walker, Andrew..........	1762	C	1	105	Weaver, Samuel..........	1782	-	-	-
Walker, Andrew..........	1822	N	1	173	Weaver, Samuel..........	1850	U	1	887
Walker, Asahel.........	1838	S	1	18	Webb, James............	1785	F	1	108
Walker, David..........	1834	Q	1	505	Weber, Christian.......	1820	M	1	389
Walker, Isaac...........	1770	C	1	397	Weber, Christian.......	1825	O	1	365
Walker, James..........	1753	B	1	3	Weber, Christian.......	1835	X	2	80
Walker, James..........	1784	E	1	117	Weber, Christian(German)	1835	R	1	172
Walker, James..........	1849	U	1	743	Weber, George..........	1799	G	1	588
Walker, John...........	1773	C	1	316	Weber, George..........	1825	O	1	292
Walker, John...........	1798	G	1	472	Weber, Henry...........	1827	P	1	56
Walker, Joseph.........	1802	H	1	226	Weber, Joseph..........	1769	C	1	306
Wallace, Charles........	1747	A	1	128	Weber, Peter (Weaver)...	1837	R	1	332
Wallace, Francis.......	1852	V	1	97	Webster, George.........	1846	U	1	82
Wallace, Hugh..........	1826	O	1	592	Webster, Joshua........	1834	Q	1	516
Wallace, James..........	1784	E	1	5	Webster, Rachel........	1808	J	1	380
Wallace, Robert........	1783	D	1	269	Wedertz, John Nicholas..	1757	X	2	96
Wallace, Robert........	1794	F	1	533	Weibright, Elizabeth....	1803	H	1	376
Waller, Henry..........	1757	B	1	183	Weick, George..........	1842	T	1	135
Walter, Baltzer........	1841	S	1	435	Weidel, John...........	1796	F	1	637
Walter, Gerhart........	1824	X	2	79	Weidler, Anna..........	1821	M	1	524
Walter, Henry..........	1755	B	1	92	Weidler, Elizabeth.....	1783	D	1	378
Walter, Henry..........	1768	X	2	77	Weidler, Elizabeth.....	1815	L	1	425
Walter, Jacob..........	1782	D	1	259	Weidler, John..........	1776	C	1	394
Walter, Jacob..........	1798	X	2	99	Weidler, Magdalena.....	1817	M	1	101
Walter, Joseph.........	1790	F	1	253	Weidler, Michael.......	1770	C	1	284
Wance, John (or Vance)..	1734	A	1	13	Weidler, Michael.......	1805	J	1	358
Wance, John (or Vance)..	1754	B	1	38	Weidler, Michael.......	1808	K	1	377
Wanner, John...........	1798	G	1	195	Weidley, Frederick.....	1773	C	1	395
Warden, George.........	1811	K	1	368	Weidman, Abraham.......	1779	C	1	594
Warden, George.........	1839	S	1	93	Weidman, Christian.....	1826	O	1	419
Warden, Joseph.........	1842	T	1	13	Weidman, Christopher....	1794	I	1	439
Warfel, George.........	1804	H	1	577	Weidman, George........	1835	R	1	129
Warfle, Margaret.......	1806	J	1	364	Weidman, Jacob.........	1845	T	1	607
Warnock, John..........	1792	F	1	381	Weidman, John..........	1790	F	1	251
Watson, Benjamin.......	1846	U	1	114	Weidman, J. Michael.....	1844	T	1	461
Watson, David.........	1801	H	1	120	Weidman, Michael.......	1768	C	1	301
Watson, David, Esq.....	1805	J	1	355	Weigand, Joanna........	1840	S	1	263
Watson, John...........	1757	B	1	153	Weiland, Christian.....	1794	J	1	353

Name	Year	Bk.	Vol	Page	Name	Year	Bk.	Vol	Page
Weiler, Andrew	1835	R	1	160	White, Jane	1786	E	1	314
Weiman, George	1788	X	2	91	White, John	1751	J	1	342
Weimer, Christopher	1816	M	1	98	White, Joseph	1763	C	1	280
Weinhold, Catherine	1850	U	1	823	White, Josiah	1753	B	1	17
Weinholt, Jacob	1771	X	2	72	White, Mary	1821	N	1	59
Weinholt, Nicholas	1792	X	2	83	White, Moses	1757	B	1	182
Weinholt, Peter	1848	U	1	561	White, Robert	1745	A	1	-
Weinland, John	1812	L	1	278	White, Thomas	1779	C	1	593
Weirich, George	1751	X	2	88	White, Thomas	1792	F	1	358
Weirick, Christian	1771	C	1	312	White, Thomas	1850	U	1	871
Weiss, George	1800	H	1	39	Whitehill, Elizabeth	1837	R	1	454
Weiss, Henry	1758	X	2	89	Whitehill, James	1766	C	1	290
Weit, Peter (White)	1849	U	1	703	Whitehill, John	1779	C	1	592
Weitzel, Deitrich	1765	X	2	69	Whitehill, John				
Weitzel, Henry	1776	C	1	399	Sanderson	1811	K	1	364
Weitzel, Jacob	1797	G	1	198	Whitehill, Margaret	1804	H	1	561
Weitzel, Martin	1784	E	1	83	Whitehill, Mary	1829	P	1	305
Weitzer, Margaret	1819	M	1	322	Whitehill, Robert	1817	M	1	104
Welcker, Valentine	1782	D	1	261	Whiteside, Abraham, Esq.	1797	G	1	189
Welde, Margaret	1822	N	1	151	Whiteside, Abraham	1821	M	1	489
Welfling, Henry	1805	H	1	647	Whiteside, Mary	1807	J	1	372
Welker, George	1842	T	1	71	Whiteside, Robert	1842	T	1	55
Wells, David	1764	C	1	281	Whiteside, Thomas	1808	J	1	363
Wells, Robert	1754	B	1	36	Whitseal, Charles	1767	C	1	291
Welsh, David	1843	T	1	197	Whitson, Thomas	1809	K	1	6
Welsh, James	1754	B	1	48	Wickersham, Elizah	1779	C	1	597
Welsh, James	1769	C	1	313	Widder, George	1795	G	1	345
Welsh, James	1800	H	1	31	Wieland, Henry	1842	T	1	107
Welsh, Jane	1784	E	1	3	Wieland, Michael	1814	K	1	633
Welsh, Margaret	1832	Q	1	190	Wiest, Christian	1815	L	1	422
Welsh, Philip	1804	X	2	95	Wiggins, John	1762	C	1	106
Welty, Henry	1765	X	2	71	Wike, Barbara	1840	S	1	305
Wenger, Abraham	1846	U	1	190	Wike, John	1740	A	1	44
Wenger, Abraham	1849	U	1	718	Wike, Joseph	1837	R	1	325
Wenger, Christian	1749	J	1	338	Wile, Peter	1806	J	1	366
Wenger, Christian	1817	M	1	100	Wiley, John	1761	B	1	351
Wenger, Christian	1823	N	1	269	Wilfington, Jacob	1753	B	1	20
Wenger, Christian	1840	S	1	306	Wilhelm, Adam	1824	O	1	200
Wenger, Eve	1790	X	2	94	Wilhelm, Catherine	1811	L	1	271
Wenger, Henry	1802	H	1	211	Wilhelm, Jacob	1775	J	1	350
Wenger, Henry	1823	O	1	84	Wilhelm, Jacob	1795	F	1	619
Wenger, Henry	1823	N	1	288	Wilhelm, Peter	1769	X	2	62
Wenger, John	1800	H	1	36	Wilkins, Peter	1748	J	1	334
Wenger, John	1838	S	1	14	Wilkins, Thomas	1746	J	1	333
Wenger, John	1845	T	1	573	Will, John	1812	L	1	276
Wenger, Joseph	1787	X	2	86	Will, John	1837	R	1	419
Wenger, Juliana	1836	R	1	287	Willey, Christian	1769	X	2	72
Wenger, Mary	1775	X	2	74	Williams, Charity	1826	O	1	417
Wenger, Michael	1793	I	1	438	Williams, Ezekiel	1849	U	1	789
Wenger, Steven	1786	X	2	84	Williams, James	1748	J	1	337
Wengert, Christian	1775	C	1	398	Williams, James	1764	C	1	292
Werfel, Peter, Jr.	1803	H	1	274	Williams, John	1846	U	1	84
Werner, Jacob	1791	X	2	97	Williams, Robert	1781	D	1	257
Werner, John(or Vernor)	1754	B	1	44	Williams, Samuel	1778	C	1	516
Werner, John William	1787	E	1	421	Williams, Sarah	1828	P	1	223
Werns, Conrad	1767	C	1	298	Williams, Thomas	1761	B	1	392
Werntz, Mary Elizabeth	1794	F	1	602	Williamson, Stuart	1814	K	1	638
Westenberger, Christian	1805	X	2	60	Willis, Joseph	1813	K	1	621
Westenberger, Christopher	1783	D	1	267	Wilson, Alexander	1760	B	1	315
Westenberger, Christopher	1805	I	1	442	Wilson, David	1739	A	1	35
Westheffer, Conrad	1804	X	6	68	Wilson, David	1766	C	1	289
Weyth, George	1847	U	1	289	Wilson, Elizabeth	1802	H	1	222
Wharry, John	1801	H	1	117	Wilson, Francis	1740	A	1	50
Wharry, Thomas	1788	E	1	468	Wilson, George	1750	J	1	340
Whitaker, George H.	1850	U	1	834	Wilson, James	1734	A	1	12
Whitaker, Mary	1776	C	1	395	Wilson, James	1744	A	1	91
Whitcraft, George	1810	K	1	183	Wilson, James	1767	C	1	293
Whitcraft, George	1826	O	1	558	Wilson, James	1796	G	1	84
White, Andrew	1771	C	1	310	Wilson, Jane	1808	J	1	379
White, Catherine	1821	M	1	504	Wilson, John	1738	A	1	33
White, Frederick					Wilson, John	1746	J	1	332
(or Wise)	1798	G	1	192	Wilson, John	1791	F	1	304

Name	Year	Bk.	Vol	Page	Name	Year	Bk.	Vol	Page
Wilson, John	1799	I	1	441	Witmer, Michael	1785	X	2	65
Wilson, John, Jr	1812	K	1	370	Witmer, Michael	1789	X	2	92
Wilson, John	1812	K	1	386	Witmer, Michael	1804	H	1	571
Wilson, Margaret	1783	D	1	361	Witmer, Peter	1792	F	1	370
Wilson, Mary	1805	I	1	443	Witmer, Peter	1810	L	1	266
Wilson, Moses	1781	D	1	255	Witmer, Sebastian	1782	X	2	60
Wilson, Nathaniel	1749	J	1	337	Witmeyer, Christian	1812	L	1	280
Wilson, Rebecca	1753	B	1	56	Witmyer, John	1840	S	1	238
Wilson, Robert	1824	O	1	234	Witter, Anna	1850	U	1	979
Wilson, Samuel	1798	G	1	560	Witter, John	1844	T	1	514
Wilson, Samuel	1800	G	1	560	Wittle, Michael	1841	S	1	534
Wilson, Thomas	1784	D	1	416	Wittmer, Oswald	1768	X	2	73
Winaur, Henry	1812	K	1	373	Witwer, John	1741	A	1	66
Windeck, Theobold	1761	B	1	387	Witwer, Mary	1845	U	1	44
Winegar, Ann Maria	1810	K	1	362	Witwer, Mary	1848	U	1	604
Winegar, Christian	1800	H	1	30	Witz, Frederick	1833	Q	1	349
Winegar, David	1802	H	1	196	Wogan, John	1747	J	1	334
Winehold, Michael	1850	U	1	906	Wogan, Thomas (Vogan)	1811	K	1	354
Wineland, Christian	1792	X	2	96	Wohlfart, George	1794	X	2	81
Wingert, John	1772	C	1	318	Wohlfart, Ludwig	1810	L	1	267
Winkelbeck, John	1767	C	1	297	Wohlgemuth, Christian	1813	K	1	624
Winour, John	1846	U	1	166	Woleslagel, John	1758	B	1	257
Winsh, Ulrick	1768	X	2	75	Woleslegel, Ann	1772	J	1	349
Winter, Christopher	1829	P	1	290	Woleslegel, Barbara	1777	C	1	393
Winterheimer, Jacob	1785	X	2	64	Wolf, Abraham	1768	A	1	207
Wise, George	1837	R	1	298	Wolf, Andrew	1781	X	2	61
Wise, Jacob	1839	S	1	189	Wolf, Bernard	1756	B	1	145
Wishon, Simon	1768	C	1	299	Wolf, Catherine	1833	Q	1	452
Wisler, Ann	1806	J	1	367	Wolf, Elias	1827	P	1	53
Wissler, Andrew	1804	H	1	569	Wolf, Elizabeth	1823	O	1	54
Wissler, Catherine	1800	H	1	33	Wolf, Henry	1822	N	1	122
Wissler, Christian	1795	F	1	627	Wolf, Henry	1826	O	1	532
Wissler, Christian	1827	P	1	27	Wolf, Jacob	1782	X	2	63
Wissler, David	1826	O	1	550	Wolf, Jacob	1832	Q	1	182
Wissler, Elizabeth	1816	M	1	97	Wolf, Jeremiah	1783	D	1	265
Wissler, Jacob	1789	F	1	149	Wolf, John	1842	T	1	67
Wissler, Jacob	1800	X	2	98	Wolf, Jonas	1754	X	2	95
Wissler, Jacob	1804	H	1	473	Wolf, Michael	1804	H	1	486
Wissler, Jacob	1848	U	1	520	Wolf, Nicholas	1771	X	2	75
Wissler, John	1745	A	1	106	Wolf, Regina	1789	F	1	91
Wissler, Michael	1848	U	1	596	Wolf, Samuel	1765	C	1	287
Wissler, Rudolph	1798	G	1	165	Wolfart, John	1750	X	2	88
Wissler, Samuel	1807	J	1	373	Wolfersberger, Frederick	1764	X	2	70
Wither, Augustine	1767	C	1	294	Wolfersberger, Frederick	1795	G	1	353
Withers, Elizabeth	1810	K	1	186	Wolff, Jeremias	1783	X	2	63
Withers, George	1829	P	1	325	Wolff, John	1848	U	1	489
Withers, George	1850	U	1	915	Wolfington, Eleanor	1795	G	1	370
Withers, Hannah	1826	O	1	501	Wolfskill, Henry	1788	F	1	32
Withers, Michael	1821	N	1	40	Wolgemuth, Abraham	1786	X	2	66
Withers, Phoebe	1839	S	1	207	Wolgemuth, Elizabeth	1794	I	1	439
Witman, Christopher	1770	C	1	307	Wollarton, Mary	1844	T	1	436
Witmer, Abraham	1783	D	1	266	Wollfart, Martin	1815	L	1	431
Witmer, Abraham	1818	M	1	150	Wondersaal, Abraham (or Vondersaal)	1832	Q	1	198
Witmer, Abraham	1836	R	1	269					
Witmer, Ann	1793	F	1	430	Wondersaal, Henry (Vandersaal)	1823	N	1	273
Witmer, Benjamin	1822	N	1	141					
Witmer, Benjamin	1849	U	1	663	Wood, Adam	1793	F	1	500
Witmer, Catherine	1828	P	1	268	Wood, Andrew	1756	B	1	136
Witmer, Christian	1777	X	2	75	Wood, George	1777	C	1	496
Witmer, Christian	1813	K	1	627	Wood, John	1770	C	1	309
Witmer, David, Sr	1835	R	1	147	Woods, Andrew	1761	B	1	376
Witmer, Feronica	1826	O	1	523	Woods, George	1747	A	1	138
Witmer, Jacob	1807	J	1	369	Woods, Margaret	1801	H	1	119
Witmer, Jacob	1811	K	1	365	Woods, Rev. Mathew	1785	E	1	178
Witmer, Jacob	1845	U	1	12	Woods, Nathan	1752	J	1	343
Witmer, Jacob	1849	U	1	664	Woods, Thomas	1790	F	1	243
Witmer, John	1782	X	2	78	Woolslegel, Barbara	1777	X	2	76
Witmer, John	1794	I	1	440	Work, Alexander	1749	A	1	169
Witmer, John	1841	S	1	537	Work, Andrew	1779	C	1	595
Witmer, Dr. John	1847	U	1	456	Work, James, Esq	1811	L	1	273
Witmer, Joseph	1844	T	1	397	Workman, Jacob	1848	U	1	507
Witmer, Michael(German)	1763	X	2	100	Workman, Samuel	1759	B	1	281

Name	Year	Bk.	Vol	Page	Name	Year	Bk.	Vol	Page
Worley, Caleb	1751	J	1	343	Zahm, Mathew	1844	T	1	518
Wormly, Elizabeth	1831	Q	1	42	Zanck, Henry	1801	H	1	121
Worrell, Elijah	1851	V	1	58	Zanck, Jacob	1816	M	1	107
Worst, George	1842	T	1	130	Zander, Jacob S.	1827	P	1	46
Worst, Peter	1822	N	1	130	Zandern, Anna Christina	1788	F	1	1
Wright, Elizabeth	1824	O	1	264	Zartman, Alexander	1762	C	1	44
Wright, George	1748	A	1	150	Zartman, Alexander, Sr.	1803	H	1	407
Wright, James	1764	C	1	286	Zartman, Barbara	1833	Q	1	404
Wright, James	1808	J	1	375	Zecker, Christian	1824	O	1	145
Wright, John	1808	J	1	381	Zegeheim, Mary	1830	P	1	502
Wright, John B.	1845	T	1	597	Zehmer, Anthony	1784	X	2	110
Wright, Joseph	1832	Q	1	269	Zehmer, Henry	1810	L	1	282
Wright, Mary	1815	L	1	428	Zehmer, Mary	1838	S	1	59
Wright, Susanna	1785	E	1	160	Zehmer, Sophia	1808	I	1	448
Wright, Thomas	1826	O	1	482	Zeigheim, Peter	1828	Q	1	316
Wyand, Magdalena	1815	L	1	420	Zeigler, Conrad	1832	X	2	112
Wyland, Peter	1759	X	2	89	Zeigler, George	1769	C	1	410
Wyrick, George	1751	J	1	343	Zeigler, George	1838	S	1	8
Yackie, Joseph	1847	U	1	260	Zeigler, Jacob(German)	1750	X	2	111
Yackle, Andrew	1836	K	1	288	Zeigler, Ludwig	1773	C	1	408
Yeager, Frederick	1850	U	1	845	Zeigler, Mary	1782	D	1	278
Yeager, Henry (German)	1748	-	-	-	Zeigler, William	1750	J	1	383
Yeates, John	1766	A	1	205	Zell, Adam	1777	C	1	480
Yeates, Jasper, Esq	1817	M	1	109	Zell, Adam	1836	R	1	256
Yeitz, Anthony	1781	D	1	117	Zell, Christopher	1828	P	1	135
Yentz, Jacob	1784	E	1	85	Zell, Jacob	1849	U	1	779
Yentzer, John	1834	R	1	59	Zeller, Andrew	1807	I	1	448
Yerletz, Mary	1813	K	1	637	Zeller, Jacob	1848	U	1	571
Yetter, Barbara	1833	Q	1	407	Zerbin, Jonathan	1791	F	1	313
Yetter, Martin	1804	H	1	537	Zercher, Christian	1835	R	1	134
Yetter, Peter	1781	D	1	274	Zercher, Jacob	1838	R	1	438
Yock, Martin	1776	C	1	405	Zerfass, Nicholas	1784	E	1	123
Yohn, Catherine Barbara	1827	P	1	75	Zerfass, Samuel	1773	X	2	114
Yorde, Peter (Jorde)	1765	B	1	589	Zimmerman, Adolph	1787	X	2	109
Yordy, Barbara	1821	N	1	72	Zimmerman, Anna	1816	M	1	108
Yordy, Christian	1818	M	1	192	Zimmerman, Anna	1846	U	1	167
Yordy, John	1766	X	2	101	Zimmerman, Anthony	1790	F	1	257
Yordy, Ulrich	1786	E	1	377	Zimmerman, Catherine	1783	E	1	294
Yost, Henry	1850	U	1	982	Zimmerman, Christian	1788	X	2	106
Yost, John	1827	P	1	64	Zimmerman, Christian	1826	O	1	494
Yost, Philip	1816	M	1	108	Zimmerman, Elizabeth	1764	X	2	112
Young, Alexander	1751	J	1	382	Zimmerman, Elizabeth	1822	N	1	215
Young, Christian	1800	H	1	40	Zimmerman, John	1777	X	2	113
Young, Daniel	1826	O	1	543	Zimmerman, John	1786	E	1	324
Young, Elizabeth	1828	X	2	103	Zimmerman, Leonhart	1841	S	1	475
Young, Frederick	1806	X	2	103	Zimmerman, Michael	1840	S	1	258
Young, Jacob	1797	G	1	258	Zimmerman, Peter	1790	X	2	104
Young, James	1747	A	1	142	Zimmerman, Susanna	1785	X	2	108
Young, John	1760	-	-	-	Zook, John	1842	T	1	163
Young, John	1775	C	1	407	Zorbach, John George	1836	T	1	246
Young, John	1805	I	1	446	Zuber, Daniel	1788	E	1	201
Young, John	1840	S	1	370	Zuck, Daniel	1836	R	1	263
Young, John	1844	T	1	490	Zudy, Jacob (German)	1750	X	2	112
Young, John Henry	1836	R	1	294	Zug, Christian	1829	P	1	401
Young, Marcus	1796	G	1	25	Zug, John	1822	N	1	139
Young, Margaret	1754	B	1	65	Zwally, Christian	1846	U	1	78
Young, Martha	1818	M	1	163	Zwecker, Margaret	1771	C	1	412
Young, Mathew	1774	C	1	406	Zwicker, Wendell	1749	-	-	-
Young, Mathias	1749	A	1	177					
Young, Mathias	1816	M	1	105					
Young, Reinhart(German)	1749	X	2	101					
Young, William(Leacock)	1761	B	1	379					
Young, William(Strasburg)	1762	C	1	321					
Young, William	1785	E	1	175					
Youngblood, Nicholas	1788	X	2	102					
Youts, Paul	1824	O	1	159					
Ysar, Jacob	1747	A	1	130					
Yundt, George	1770	C	1	404					
Yundt, John	1832	Q	1	219					
Yundt, Mary	1809	K	1	133					
Zahm, George	1810	K	1	325					
Zahm, Jacob	1824	O	1	222					

Name	Year	Bk.	Vol	Page	Name	Year	Bk.	Vol	Page
Arndt, Jacob, Jr.	1832	F	1	215	Balding, Richard	1835	H	1	33
Ash, Joseph	1799	-	-	-	Baldwin, Conrad	1830	E	1	190
Ash, Phinehas	1836	H	1	121	Baldwin, Dr. George	1827	D	1	61
Ashbridge, John	1772	-	-	-	Baldwin, Margaret	1843	L	1	114
Ashford, William	1747	-	-	-	Baldwin, William T.	1821	A	1	81
Ashton, Richard	1741	-	-	-	Ball, John	1743	-	-	-
Asper, Margaret	1830	E	1	206	Ballance, Rebecca	1783	-	-	-
Aspy, Josiah	1759	-	-	-	Balmer, Ann	1845	M	1	23
Asseyer, Sarah	1798	-	-	-	Balmer, Benjamin, Sr.	1842	K	1	296
Aston, Alexander	1743	-	-	-	Balmer, Christian, Jr.	1785	-	-	-
Aston, Joshua	1815	-	-	-	Balmer, Christian	1843	L	1	52
Aston, Joshua	1821	-	-	-	Balmer, Jacob	1823	B	1	3
Aswalt, William	1823	B	1	67	Balmer, Levi	1845	M	1	2
Atchinson, John	1789	-	-	-	Balspach, Peter	1748	-	-	-
Atkins, Thomas	1748	-	-	-	Bandon, William				
Atkinson, John C.	1848	N	1	6	(see Bender)	1825	C	1	14
Atkinson, Mahlen	1826	C	1	235	Banks, James	1790	-	-	-
Atkinson, Robert	1839	I	1	266	Barber, Alexander	1813	-	-	-
Atkinson, Robert	1847	M	1	393	Barber, Ann (Nancy)	1846	M	1	219
Atkinson, William	1826	C	1	222	Barber, James	1786	-	-	-
Atlee, Agustus William	1843	L	1	75	Barber, John	1759	-	-	-
Atlee, Samuel, Esq.	1787	-	-	-	Barber, John	1805	-	-	-
Atlee, Hon. William A.	1793	-	-	-	Barber, John	1806	-	-	-
Atlee, William P.	1815	-	-	-	Barber, John	1849	N	1	222
Aux, Jacob (Ochs)	1833	G	1	26	Barber, Nathaniel	1782	-	-	-
Auxer, Michael	1820	-	-	-	Barber, Mary	1812	-	-	-
Axe, John	1845	M	1	36	Barber, Robert	1749	-	-	-
Axer, Christopher	1803	-	-	-	Barber, Susanna	1827	D	1	45
Axer, Jacob	1824	B	1	198	Barber, Thomas	1805	-	-	-
Axer, Maria Barbara	1811	-	-	-	Barclay, Andrew	1769	-	-	-
Ayle, Jacob	1837	H	1	223	Barclay, William	1759	-	-	-
B					Barclet, Benjamin	1746	-	-	-
Bacher, Ann (Nancy)	1847	M	1	346	Barclet, John	1760	-	-	-
Bacher, Martin	1782	-	-	-	Bard, Ann Margaret	1796	-	-	-
Bachey, Elizabeth	1815	-	-	-	Bard, Daniel	1792	-	-	-
Bachman, Christian	1811	-	-	-	Bard, Emanuel	1849	N	1	248
Bachman, Christian	1826	C	1	218	Bard, Henry	1849	N	1	191
Bachman, Jacob	1849	N	1	226	Bard, John	1775	-	-	-
Bachman, John, Sr.	1833	G	1	115	Bard, John(or Bird)	1849	N	1	190
Bachman, John	1843	L	1	142	Bard, Margaret	1823	A	1	284
Bachman, Peter	1782	-	-	-	Bard, Martin	1834	G	1	174
Bachman, Peter	1839	I	-	286	Bard, Martin	1849	N	1	192
Backenstross, Andrew	1805	-	-	-	Bard, Michael	1837	H	1	276
Backwood, William	1733	-	-	-	Bare, Abraham	1836	H	1	167
Bader, Frederick	1798	-	-	-	Bare, David	1763	-	-	-
Baer, Abraham	1805	-	-	-	Bare, Henry	1773	-	-	-
Baer, Andrew	1797	-	-	-	Bare, Jacob	1759	-	-	-
Bahm, Adam	1814	-	-	-	Bare, Jacob	1787	-	-	-
Bahm, Barbara	1820	-	-	-	Bare, Joel	1829	E	1	34
Bailey, Alexander	1841	K	1	202	Bare, John	1779	-	-	-
Bailey, Jabes	1842	K	1	305	Bare, John	1782	-	-	-
Bailey, James	1799	-	-	-	Bare, John	1784	-	-	-
Bailey, James, Jr.	1813	-	-	-	Bare, Martin	1784	-	-	-
Bailey, James K.	1818	-	-	-	Bare, Martin	1838	I	1	117
Bailey, Thomas	1808	-	-	-	Bare, Martin	1843	L	1	140
Bair, Jacob	1849	N	1	188	Bare, Mathias	1797	-	-	-
Bair, Mary	1836	H	1	112	Bare, Rudy	1754	-	-	-
Baird, John, Esq.	1822	A	1	146	Bare, Ulrich	1750	-	-	-
Baird, John, Esq.	1829	E	1	77	Barge, Cathrine	1808	-	-	-
Bairman, William	1826	C	1	199	Barge, George	1776	-	-	-
Baker, Abraham	1845	M	1	16	Barge, George	1844	L	1	184
Baker, Frederick D.	1845	M	1	33	Bark, Jacob	1758	-	-	-
Baker, Jacob	1822	A	1	185	Barker, Henry	1813	-	-	-
Baker, Jacob	1823	A	1	273	Barkley, Andrew	1825	C	1	100
Baker, Jacob, Jr.	1823	B	1	27	Barkley, Steward	1827	D	1	20
Baker, John	1750	-	-	-	Barlow, Henry	1827	D	1	34
Baker, John	1825	C	1	65	Barnard, Joseph C.	1823	A	1	262
Baker, John	1839	I	1	232	Barnes, James	1802	-	-	-
Baker, Magdalena	1834	G	1	155	Barnes, James	1840	K	1	7
Baker, Martin	1804	-	-	-	Barnes, John	1855	H	1	38
Baker, Philip	1799	-	-	-	Barnes, William	1832	F	1	163
Baker, Philip	1842	K	1	224	Barnet, Anthony.	1737	-	-	-

Name	Year	Bk.	Vol	Page	Name	Year	Bk.	Vol	Page
Barnet, George	1827	D	1	146	Bear, Ann Maria	1843	L	1	66
Barnet, Henry	1828	D	1	270	Bear, Ann Maria	1844	L	1	277
Barnet, John	1734	-	-	-	Bear, George	1803	-	-	-
Barnet, Robert	1761	-	-	-	Bear, George	1823	B	1	94
Barnhard, Elizabeth	1847	M	1	359	Bear, George	1833	G	1	79
Barnwell, Jane	1847	M	1	414	Bear, Henry	1739	-	-	-
Barr, Barbara	1830	E	1	66	Bear, Henry	1834	G	1	248
Barr, Benjamin	1819	-	-	-	Bear, Henry	1837	H	1	233
Barr, Eve	1829	E	1	67	Bear, Henry K.	1846	M	1	99
Barr, George	1830	E	1	244	Bear, Jacob	1786	-	-	-
Barr, George	1833	G	1	51	Bear, Jacob	1797	-	-	-
Barr, Henry	1731	-	-	-	Bear, Jacob	1820	-	-	-
Barr, Jacob	1827	D	1	21	Bear, John	1799	-	-	-
Barr, Jacob	1834	G	1	254	Bear, John	1802	-	-	-
Barr, John	1785	-	-	-	Bear, John	1819	-	-	-
Barr, John	1830	E	1	226	Bear, John	1822	A	1	216
Barr, Martin	1826	D	1	12	Bear, John S.	1831	F	1	128
Barron, Daniel	1818	-	-	-	Bear, Julianna	1841	K	1	162
Barrow, Obediah	1794	-	-	-	Bear, Magdalena	1836	H	1	135
Bartges, Michael	1815	-	-	-	Bear, Martin	1771	-	-	-
Bartges, Michael	1820	-	-	-	Bear, Martin	1815	-	-	-
Bartholmen, Jacob	1806	-	-	-	Bear, Martin	1841	K	1	139
Bartle, Samuel	1816	-	-	-	Bear, Martin	1842	L	1	22
Bartleson, Isaac	1811	-	-	-	Bear, Mary	1839	I	1	237
Barton, David R.	1818	-	-	-	Bear, Michael	1741	-	-	-
Barton, John, Jr.	1844	L	1	228	Bear, Michael	1822	A	1	205
Barton, William	1815	-	-	-	Bear, Rosina	1787	-	-	-
Barton, William, Esq.	1822	A	1	231	Bear, Samuel	1785	-	-	-
Bartorpf, Hermanus	1760	-	-	-	Bear, Samuel	1788	-	-	-
Basken, Moses	1777	-	-	-	Bear, Samuel	1828	D	1	197
Baskins, Francis	1761	-	-	-	Bear, Ulrich	1839	I	1	180
Bassler, Daniel	1801	-	-	-	Bear, Ulrich	1846	M	1	204
Bassler, John	1815	-	-	-	Bear, Veronica	1838	I	1	51
Bassler, John	1839	I	1	271	Beatty, John	1749	-	-	-
Batdorf, Michael	1828	D	1	260	Beatty, Joseph	1823	B	1	70
Bateman, Daniel	1829	E	1	38	Beaver, John	1837	H	1	238
Bateman, George W.	1835	H	1	61	Beaver, John	1847	M	1	361
Bauchman, John	1849	N	1	239	Beble, Jacob	1782	-	-	-
Bauder, John	1784	-	-	-	Becher, Jacob	1783	-	-	-
Bauer, Andrew	1777	-	-	-	Becher, Nicholas	1791	-	-	-
Baughman, Felix	1785	-	-	-	Bechtel, Cathrine	1849	N	1	193
Baughman, Jacob	1800	-	-	-	Bechtel, Peter	1785	-	-	-
Baughman, John	1757	-	-	-	Bechtold, Anna Maria	1824	B	1	176
Baughman, John(Martic)	1757	-	-	-	Beck, Cathrine	1835	G	1	269
Baum, Magdalena	1844	L	1	227	Beck, George	1782	-	-	-
Bauman, Daniel	1821	A	1	70	Beck, George	1838	I	1	145
Bauman, Elizabeth	1847	M	1	236	Beck, Jacob	1774	-	-	-
Bauman, Esther	1847	M	1	240	Beck, Jacob	1829	E	1	136
Bauman, Samuel	1829	E	1	144	Beck, Jeremiah	1841	K	1	110
Baumgardner, Adam	1784	-	-	-	Beck, John Henry	1836	H	1	17
Baumgartin, Mathias	1779	-	-	-	Beck, Margaret	1816	-	-	-
Bausman, Michael	1777	-	-	-	Beck, Nicholas	1790	-	-	-
Baxter, James	1822	A	1	139	Beck, Nicholas(see Peck)	1833	G	1	130
Baxter, James	1843	L	1	46	Becker, Ann	1834	G	1	183
Bayley, Jacob	1797	-	-	-	Becker, Ann	1835	H	1	23
Bayley, John	1790	-	-	-	Becker, Arnold	1791	-	-	-
Bayley, Thomas	1807	-	-	-	Becker, Christopher	1776	-	-	-
Beakly, George	1734	-	-	-	Becker, Henry	1844	L	1	281
Bealer, Jacob	1849	-	-	305	Becker, Jacob	1803	-	-	-
Bealer, John	1831	F	1	120	Becker, John	1846	M	1	156
Bealls, John M.	1840	K	1	26	Becker, Valentine	1784	-	-	-
Beam, Adam	1800	-	-	-	Beckley, Mathias	1759	-	-	-
Beam, Ann	1826	C	1	245	Bedford, Gunning B.	1832	F	1	207
Beam, Christian	1826	C	1	244	Beecker, Susanna	1804	-	-	-
Beam, Jacob	1788	-	-	-	Beeker, John	1847	M	1	382
Beam, Jacob	1837	H	1	265	Beemsderfer, John	1814	-	-	-
Beam, John	1848	N	1	84	Been, Jane	1813	-	-	-
Bear, Abraham	1787	-	-	-	Beezer, John	1824	B	1	177
Bear, Abraham	1802	-	-	-	Behm, Adam	1819	-	-	-
Bear, Abraham	1824	C	1	2	Behm, Jacob	1847	M	1	301
Bear, Andrew	1805	-	-	-	Behmer, John	1839	I	1	284
Bear, Andrew L.	1848	N	1	111	Beidler, Jacob	1800	-	-	-

Name	Year	Bk.	Vol	Page	Name	Year	Bk.	Vol	Page
Beidler, John	1815	-	-	-	Bernhart, John	1779	-	-	-
Beigler, Henry	1821	-	-	-	Bernheuset, Martin	1778	-	-	-
Beiter, Andrew	1843	L	1	150	Berns, Ludwig	1758	-	-	-
Beitz, George	1849	N	1	306	Berringer, Cathrine	1790	-	-	-
Bell, Andrew	1762	-	-	-	Berst, Erasmus	1779	-	-	-
Bell, Joseph	1818	-	-	-	Besick, William	1730	-	-	-
Bell, Paterson	1834	G	1	181	Besore, Baltzer	1809	-	-	-
Bell, Robert	1806	-	-	-	Bethel, Samuel	1740	-	-	-
Bell, Thomas	1762	-	-	-	Bethel, Samuel	1775	-	-	-
Bell, Walter	1759	-	-	-	Bethel, Samuel	1819	-	-	-
Bell, Walter	1761	-	-	-	Bettle, Lydia	1764	-	-	-
Beltz, John	1838	I	1	100	Betz, Ann(see Petz)	1781	-	-	-
Bemis, Wilder	1809	-	-	-	Betz, Frederick	1760	-	-	-
Bender, Adam	1833	G	1	21	Betz, George	1826	C	1	209
Bender, Barbara	1771	-	-	-	Betz, Mathias	1785	-	-	-
Bender, Benjamin	1837	H	1	216	Betz, Michael	1766	-	-	-
Bender, Cathrine	1803	-	-	-	Betz, Michael, Sr.	1827	D	1	65
Bender, Diller	1847	M	1	402	Beyer, Ann	1841	K	1	114
Bender, Elizabeth	1845	L	1	307	Beyer, Ann	1841	K	1	128
Bender, Elizabeth	1848	N	1	44	Beyler, Ann	1829	E	1	51
Bender, George	1814	-	-	-	Bier, Elizabeth	1836	H	1	131
Bender, George	1829	E	1	157	Bigget, Randel	1772	-	-	-
Bender, James	1804	-	-	-	Biggs, Timothy	1735	-	-	-
Bender, John	1761	-	-	-	Bigham, John	1771	-	-	-
Bender, John	1808	-	-	-	Bing, Conrad	1800	-	-	-
Bender, John	1815	-	-	-	Binkley, Benjamin	1837	I	1	10
Bender, John	1828	D	1	182	Binkley, Christian	1805	-	-	-
Bender, John	1830	E	1	247	Binkley, David, Jr.	1821	A	1	107
Bender, John	1833	G	1	68	Binkley, David	1845	M	1	83
Bender, John L.	1838	I	1	102	Binkley, Elizabeth	1832	F	1	272
Bender, John William	1835	H	1	78	Binkley, Henry	1847	M	1	249
Bender, Leonard	1761	-	-	-	Binkley, Johnston	1813	-	-	-
Bender, Leonard	1814	-	-	-	Binkley, Louisa	1842	K	1	249
Bender, Ludwig	1779	-	-	-	Binkley, Mary	1833	G	1	47
Bender, Margaret	1783	-	-	-	Binkley, Susanna	1816	-	-	-
Bender, Margaret	1829	E	1	158	Binkly, John	1749	-	-	-
Benedict, Dietrich	1763	-	-	-	Bintzfill, John	1770	-	-	-
Benedict, George	1842	K	1	265	Bishop, John	1749	-	-	-
Benier, Adam	1763	-	-	-	Bishop, John	1803	-	-	-
Benninger, Stephen	1778	-	-	-	Bishop, John C.	1841	K	1	159
Benny, Anna	1811	-	-	-	Bishop, Peter	1820	-	-	-
Benson, George	1805	-	-	-	Bishop, William	1821	-	-	-
Bentz, Christian	1778	-	-	-	Bitner, Jacob	1834	G	1	263
Bentz, Conrad	1771	-	-	-	Bitner, Jacob	1848	N	1	101
Bentz, Mary	1821	A	1	5	Bitterman, Henry	1824	B	1	237
Bentz, Peter	1818	-	-	-	Bitterman, John	1814	-	-	-
Bentz, Polly	1834	G	1	141	Bitzer, Andrew	1826	C	1	221
Bentz, William	1825	C	1	69	Bitzer, Daniel	1844	L	1	263
Benybill, William	1759	-	-	-	Bitzer, Elizabeth	1829	E	1	45
Berg, Andrew	1832	F	1	213	Bitzer, John	1826	D	1	9
Berg, Barbara	1788	-	-	-	Bitzer, John, Sr.	1826	D	1	10
Berg, Cathrine	1844	L	1	290	Bitzer, Samuel	1829	E	1	46
Berg, Henry	1832	F	1	167	Bitzer, Solomon	1825	C	1	92
Berg, Jacob	1818	-	-	-	Bitzer, Solomon	1826	C	1	146
Berg, Jacob	1848	N	1	139	Bitzer, Solomon	1826	C	1	187
Berg, Maria	1845	M	1	5	Bitzer, Solomon	1826	D	1	11
Berg, Mary	1833	G	1	81	Bixler, Abraham, Sr.	1828	D	1	219
Berger, John	1792	-	-	-	Bixler, Cathrine	1828	D	1	210
Berger, Michael	1820	-	-	-	Bixler, Jacob	1831	F	1	4
Berger, Peter	1760	-	-	-	Bixler, Margaret	1837	H	1	268
Berger, Thomas	1751	-	-	-	Bixler, Michael	1738	-	-	-
Berglebach, George	1793	-	-	-	Black, Dublin	1813	-	-	-
Bergman, Baltzer	1831	F	1	131	Black, James	1781	-	-	-
Bergman, John	1822	A	1	131	Black, James	1848	N	1	109
Bergman, John	1822	A	1	145	Black, John	1799	-	-	-
Bergman, John	1835	H	1	27	Black, Joseph	1809	-	-	-
Bergner, Christian	1766	-	-	-	Black, Mary	1839	I	1	168
Bergolt, Isaac	1777	-	-	-	Black, Mathew	1748	-	-	-
Bergott, Michael	1825	C	1	135	Black, Moses	1768	-	-	-
Berkinbein, David	1831	F	1	68	Black, Robert	1746	-	-	-
Bernhard, Adam	1837	H	1	264	Black, Robert	1793	-	-	-
Bernhart, Eve	1782	-	-	-	Black, Thomas	1759	-	-	-

Name	Year	Bk.	Vol	Page	Name	Year	Bk.	Vol	Page
Blackall, John.........	1743	-	-	-	Born, Henry............	1814	-	-	-
Blackburn, Alexander....	1749	-	-	-	Bortold, Michael.......	1787	-	-	-
Blackburn, Stephen......	1830	E	1	261	Bosser, Rudy...........	1743	-	-	-
Blackburn, William......	1760	-	-	-	Bossler, Barbara.......	1830	E	1	194
Blair, Francis.........	1814	-	-	-	Bostler, Christian.....	1747	-	-	-
Blair, John............	1742	-	-	-	Bostler, Henry.........	1760	-	-	-
Blair, William.........	1748	-	-	-	Bott, Henry............	1781	-	-	-
Blair, William.........	1827	D	1	71	Bott, Henry............	1831	F	1	110
Blakeley, Robert.......	1746	-	-	-	Bott, John.............	1824	B	1	171
Blank, Peter...........	1848	N	1	50	Bott, Ulrich...........	1826	D	1	3
Blankert, Robert.......	1823	B	1	91	Bough,Susanna Margaret..	1796	-	-	-
Blantz,Barbara(Plantz)..	1833	G	1	20	Boulden, Eliza.........	1829	E	1	76
Blantz, Christopher.....	1754	-	-	-	Bowde, Thomas..........	1822	A	1	235
Blantz, John(Plantz)....	1797	-	-	-	Bowder, George.........	1785	-	-	-
Blantz, Mathias........	1797	-	-	-	Bower, George..........	1771	-	-	-
Blantz, Mathias........	1802	-	-	-	Bower, Jacob...........	1804	-	-	-
Blatner, Michael.......	1751	-	-	-	Bower, John............	1746	-	-	-
Blattenberger, John.....	1821	A	1	52	Bower, John............	1771	-	-	-
Blazer, Christian.......	1747	-	-	-	Bower, John............	1809	-	-	-
Bleacher, Jacob........	1835	H	1	53	Bower, John............	1848	N	1	76
Bleakley, Barry........	1806	-	-	-	Bower, Joseph..........	1821	-	-	-
Blecher, Andrew........	1782	-	-	-	Bower, Mary............	1822	A	1	136
Blecher, John..........	1785	-	-	-	Bower, Michael.........	1792	-	-	-
Bleem, Henry...........	1738	-	-	-	Bower, Sabina..........	1823	B	1	56
Blerow, Lion...........	1741	-	-	-	Bower, Samuel..........	1809	-	-	-
Blessrenner, George.....	1762	-	-	-	Bower, Thomas..........	1766	-	-	-
Blester, George........	1817	-	-	-	Bower, Valentine.......	1785	-	-	-
Blesterer, Margaret.....	1822	A	1	162	Bowers, John...........	1827	D	1	145
Bletcher, Henry........	1747	-	-	-	Bowers, Michael........	1847	M	1	372
Bletcher, Henry(Pletcher	1749	-	-	-	Bowman, Ann............	1807	-	-	-
Bletcher, Mandline					Bowman, Casper.........	1757	-	-	-
(see Pletcher)......	1747	-	-	-	Bowman, Daniel.........	1829	E	1	37
Bletz, Jacob...........	1641	K	1	196	Bowman, Daniel.........	1849	N	1	273
Blickenderfs, Jacob....	1779	-	-	-	Bowman, Emanuel........	1845	M	1	38
Bligher, William.......	1759	-	-	-	Bowman, Francis........	1831	F	1	41
Blister, Conrad					Bowman, Henry..........	1808	-	-	-
(see Plaisterer)....	1803	-	-	-	Bowman, Jacob..........	1745	-	-	-
Bloomshine, Henry......	1794	-	-	-	Bowman, Jacob..........	1849	N	1	270
Blover, John...........	1824	B	1	220	Bowman, John...........	1738	-	-	-
Blumhart, Jacob........	1779	-	-	-	Bowman, John...........	1749	-	-	-
Bodner, Ludwig.........	1747	-	-	-	Bowman, John...........	1760	-	-	-
Boehmer, Samuel........	1823	B	1	72	Bowman, John...........	1763	-	-	-
Boerstler, John........	1823	B	1	88	Bowman, John...........	1810	-	-	-
Boettner, John.........	1823	A	1	288	Bowman, John...........	1813	-	-	-
Boffemyer, David.......	1836	H	1	146	Bowman, John...........	1837	I	1	19
Boggs, Andrew..........	1785	-	-	-	Bowman, Joseph.........	1832	F	1	138
Boggs, Francis.........	1842	K	1	315	Bowman, Peter..........	1787	-	-	-
Boggs, Hugh............	1809	-	-	-	Bowman, Wendel.........	1735	-	-	-
Boggs, James...........	1753	-	-	-	Bower, Abraham.........	1843	L	1	152
Boggs, William.........	1744	-	-	-	Bowermaster, Jacob.....	1848	N	1	4
Bollender, Peter.......	1772	-	-	-	Bowmaster, Jacob.......	1847	M	1	355
Bollinger, Abraham.....	1814	-	-	-	Bowsman, Cathrine......	1784	-	-	-
Bollinger, Christian....	1753	-	-	-	Boyce, Robert..........	1834	G	1	195
Bollinger, Jacob.......	1762	-	-	-	Boyd, Albert...........	1793	-	-	-
Bollinger, Mary........	1834	G	1	233	Boyd, Andrew...........	1758	-	-	-
Bollinger, Rudy........	1767	-	-	-	Boyd, Archibald▼▼▼▼....	1792	-	-	-
Bombach, George........	1790	-	-	-	Boyd, Edward...........	1759	-	-	-
Bomberger, David.......	1805	-	-	-	Boyd, George...........	1762	-	-	-
Bomberger, Jacob.......	1828	D	1	211	Boyd, George...........	1836	H	1	182
Bomberger, John........	1841	K	1	124	Boyd, Hugh.............	1816	-	-	-
Bomberger, Joseph......	1811	-	-	-	Boyd, Isabella.........	1826	C	1	232
Bomberger, Joseph......	1846	M	1	213	Boyd, James............	1757	-	-	-
Bonghanan, Robert......	1748	-	-	-	Boyd, James............	1820	-	-	-
Bonn, Mathias..........	1793	-	-	-	Boyd, John.............	1747	-	-	-
Bony, John.............	1805	-	-	-	Boyd, John.............	1811	-	-	-
Boocher, Joseph........	1804	-	-	-	Boyd, John.............	1828	D	1	253
Booger, Henry..........	1802	-	-	-	Boyd, Joseph...........	1782	-	-	-
Book, Cathrine.........	1821	A	1	24	Boyd, Joseph...........	1791	-	-	-
Book, George...........	1842	L	1	20	Boyd, Joseph...........	1806	-	-	-
Book, Michael..........	1813	-	-	-	Boyd, Joseph...........	1846	M	1	189
Boreman, Christian.....	1803	-	-	-	Boyd, Mary.............	1830	E	1	266
Borkfield, Jacob.......	1826	C	1	169	Boyd, Mathew...........	1833	G	1	28

Name	Year	Bk.	Vol	Page	Name	Year	Bk.	Vol	Page
Boyd, Nicholas	1841	K	1	89	Breneman, Mary	1840	I	1	312
Boyd, Nicholas	1843	L	1	34	Breneman, Melchoir	1737	-	-	-
Boyd, Robert	1761	-	-	-	Breneman, Melchoir	1810	-	-	-
Boyd, Samuel	1801	-	-	-	Breneman, Melchoir	1819	-	-	-
Boyd, Stephen	1822	A	1	220	Breneman, Michael	1826	C	1	247
Boyd, Thomas	1777	-	-	-	Breneman, Patrick	1770	-	-	-
Boyd, William	1812	-	-	-	Breneman, Peter	1783	-	-	-
Boyer, Abraham	1849	N	1	300	Breneman, Stephen	1758	-	-	-
Boyer, Cathrine	1777	-	-	-	Breneman, Susanna	1794	-	-	-
Boyer, Henry	1825	C	1	18	Breneson, Valentine	1740	-	-	-
Boyer, John	1848	N	1	32	Brenhard, Abraham	1844	L	1	204
Boyer, Nicholas	1825	C	1	78	Brenisen, Adam	1816	-	-	-
Boyle, John	1764	-	-	-	Brenisen, Jacob	1778	-	-	-
Boyles, James	1814	-	-	-	Brenizer, Elizabeth	1844	L	1	199
Boys, Mary	1845	L	1	310	Brenn, John	1784	-	-	-
Boysh, Frederick	1774	-	-	-	Brenneman, Abraham	1821	-	-	-
Brackbill, John	1825	C	1	113	Brenneman, Ann	1800	-	-	-
Brackbill, Woolrich	1739	-	-	-	Brenneman, Christian	1820	-	-	-
Bradley, Alexander	1833	G	1	103	Brenneman, Christian	1842	K	1	274
Bradley, Edward	1820	-	-	-	Brenneman, Henry	1808	-	-	-
Bradley, Thomas	1816	-	-	-	Brenneman, Henry	1820	-	-	-
Brady, William	1814	-	-	-	Brenneman, Henry	1822	A	1	201
Bramson, Isabella	1811	-	-	-	Brenneman, Henry	1847	M	1	397
Brand, Christian	1816	-	-	-	Brenneman, John	1821	A	1	113
Brand, Christian	1831	F	1	45	Brenneman, Jonathan	1834	G	1	133
Brand, John	1783	-	-	-	Brenneman, Margaret	1821	A	1	4
Brand, Mary	1810	-	-	-	Brenner, Adam	1826	C	1	141
Brand, Peter	1800	-	-	-	Brenner, Barbara	1847	M	1	328
Brand, Samuel	1761	-	-	-	Brenner, Christiana	1846	M	1	127
Brandes, Henry	1814	-	-	-	Brenner, Christopher	1814	-	-	-
Brandon, John	1757	-	-	-	Brenner, Christopher	1848	M	1	433½
Brandt, Abraham	1838	I	1	138	Brenner, Daniel	1799	-	-	-
Brandt, Christian	1841	K	1	111	Brenner, Elizabeth	1822	A	1	219
Brandt, Jacob	1790	-	-	-	Brenner, Elizabeth	1839	I	1	206
Brandt, Jost	1777	-	-	-	Brenner, Frederick	1833	G	1	80
Brandt, Samuel	1812	-	-	-	Brenner, George	1822	A	1	147
Braught, John	1823	B	1	110	Brenner, George	1835	H	1	92
Brauhoeffer, John	1799	-	-	-	Brenner, George	1837	H	1	288
Brech, Adam	1778	-	-	-	Brenner, Gerhart	1824	B	1	147
Brecht, Elizabeth	1752	-	-	-	Brenner, Henry	1830	E	1	272
Brecht, John	1818	-	-	-	Brenner, Leonard	1770	-	-	-
Brecht, John, Sr	1847	M	1	410	Brenner, Philip	1803	-	-	-
Breckbill, Abraham	1775	-	-	-	Brenner, Philip	1826	C	1	167
Breckbill, Benedict	1754	-	-	-	Brenner, Philip	1841	K	1	116
Breckbill, Christian	1841	K	1	147	Bresser, Jacob	1784	-	-	-
Breckel, John George	1846	M	1	142	Bressler, Peter	1843	L	1	126
Breens, Ludwig	1758	-	-	-	Bretz, Anna Maria	1842	K	1	320
Brehm, Henry	1838	I	1	66	Bretz, Anthony	1770	-	-	-
Brehm, Peter	1795	-	-	-	Bretz, Michael	1821	A	1	87
Breining, Magdalina	1818	-	-	-	Brien, Edward H	1837	H	1	284
Breininger, John	1811	-	-	-	Brighton, Jacob	1848	M	1	449
Breisben, Dr. James	1806	-	-	-	Brinton, Joseph	1809	-	-	-
Bremmer, John	1796	-	-	-	Brinton, Moses,	1846	M	1	224
Bremmer, John	1840	K	1	23	Brintzel, Margaret	1826	C	1	286
Brendall, Marcus	1762	-	-	-	Brisben, Henry	1827	D	1	144
Brendle, George	1779	-	-	-	Britznis, George	1831	F	1	73
Breneisen, Conrad	1824	B	1	178	Britznis, Isaac	1819	-	-	-
Breneman, Abraham	1830	E	1	221	Brobst, Henry	1841	K	1	190
Breneman, Abraham, Sr	1847	M	1	420	Broch, John Peter	1831	F	1	95
Breneman,Dr.Abraham,Sr.	1848	M	1	428	Brocken, Cathrine	1823	B	1	95
Breneman,Dr.Abraham,Jr.	1848	M	1	430	Brogan, James	1844	L	1	236
Breneman, Adam	1779	-	-	-	Brogan, Mathias	1795	-	-	-
Breneman, Adam	1785	-	-	-	Brogen, John	1800	-	-	-
Breneman, Adam	1804	-	-	-	Bromberg, John	1759	-	-	-
Breneman, Adam	1847	M	1	256	Brooks, Thomas	1814	-	-	-
Breneman, Ann	1845	L	1	317	Brooks, William C	1824	B	1	183
Breneman, Christian	1814	-	-	-	Brosser,John(Prosser)	1829	E	1	97
Breneman, Christian	1846	M	1	131	Brossman, France	1749	-	-	-
Breneman, Feronica	1823	B	1	11	Brong, Peter	1817	-	-	-
Breneman, Jacob	1764	-	-	-	Brong, Peter	1835	H	1	17
Breneman, Jacob	1816	-	-	-	Brouch, Valentine	1784	-	-	-
Breneman, John, Esq	1810	-	-	-	Brouk, George	1733	-	-	-

Name	Year	Bk.	Vol	Page	Name	Year	Bk.	Vol	Page
Brown, Adam	1843	L	1	80	Brubaker, John, Jr.	1743	-	-	-
Brown, Albert G.	1858	I	1	62	Brubaker, John	1748	-	-	-
Brown, Caleb	1785	-	-	-	Brubaker, John	1760	-	-	-
Brown, Christian	1828	D	1	215	Brubaker, John	1768	-	-	-
Brown, Collin	1770	-	-	-	Brubaker, John	1800	-	-	-
Brown, Daniel	1819	-	-	-	Brubaker, John	1828	D	1	185
Brown, Daniel	1820	-	-	-	Brubaker, John	1840	K	1	47
Brown, George W.	1841	K	1	133	Brubaker, John Jacob,	1802	-	-	-
Brown, George, Sr.	1848	N	1	132	Brubaker, Maria	1845	M	1	15
Brown, Isaiah	1805	-	-	-	Brubaker, Michael	1831	F	1	98
Brown, Jacob	1829	E	1	162	Brubaker, Peter	1826	C	1	164
Brown, Jacob	1848	M	1	447	Brubaker, Philip	1824	B	1	145
Brown, James	1750	-	-	-	Brubeck, Bernet	1767	-	-	-
Brown, James	1752	-	-	-	Bruckhart, Jacob	1823	B	1	78
Brown, James	1764	-	-	-	Bruckhart, John	1843	L	1	82
Brown, James	1771	-	-	-	Bruckhoffer, John	1749	-	-	-
Brown, James	1776	-	-	-	Bruner, Ann	1847	M	1	258
Brown, James	1821	A	1	19	Bruner, Owen	1845	M	1	18
Brown, James	1849	N	1	295	Bruner, Peter	1834	G	1	232
Brown, Jean	1774	-	-	-	Brungard, George	1831	F	1	13
Brown, John	1747	-	-	-	Brunner, Cathrine	1847	M	1	327
Brown, John	1748	-	-	-	Brunner, Dr. Christian	1829	E	1	21
Brown, John	1773	-	-	-	Brunner, Jacob	1832	F	1	161
Brown, John	1785	-	-	-	Brunner, John, Sr.	1834	G	1	179
Brown, John	1816	-	-	-	Brussel, Philip	1805	-	-	-
Brown, Dr. John	1839	I	1	253	Brutensteen, Leonard	1748	-	-	-
Brown, John	1843	L	1	48	Bryan, Bryan O.	1822	A	1	236
Brown, Jonas	1827	D	1	119	Bryan, Edward	1817	-	-	-
Brown, Jonas	1844	L	1	235	Bryan, George	1838	I	1	158
Brown, Joseph	1772	-	-	-	Bryan, Mary	1779	-	-	-
Brown, Luke	1834	G	1	236	Bryan, William	1831	F	1	43
Brown, Maria	1845	L	1	324	Bryans, John	1743	-	-	-
Brown, Martin	1827	D	1	110	Brydengross, George	1749	-	-	-
Brown, Mary	1842	K	1	232	Bryn, Barnard	1768	-	-	-
Brown, Mary	1844	L	1	218	Buccannon, John	1801	-	-	-
Brown, Mary	1845	M	1	32	Buch, Christopher	1757	-	-	-
Brown, Moses	1847	M	1	370	Buch, Henry	1821	A	1	21
Brown, Mathew	1807	-	-	-	Buch, Isaac	1847	M	1	394
Brown, Messer	1826	C	1	233	Buch, John	1821	A	1	59
Brown, Patrick	1830	E	1	207	Buchanan, James	1747	-	-	-
Brown, Peter	1826	C	1	162	Buchanan, Thomas	1744	-	-	-
Brown, William	1749	-	-	-	Buchanan, William	1791	-	-	-
Brown, William	1828	E	1	4	Bucher, Cathrine	1849	N	1	183
Brubacher, Abraham	1819	-	-	-	Bucher, Christianna	1777	-	-	-
Brubacher, Ann	1843	L	1	30	Bucher, Conrad	1781	-	-	-
Brubacher, Anna	1833	G	1	94	Bucher, Elizabeth	1824	B	1	186
Brubacher, Christian	1843	L	1	122	Bucher, Elizabeth	1832	F	1	244
Brubacher, David	1825	C	1	7	Bucher, John	1810	-	-	-
Brubacher, Jacob	1834	G	1	163	Bucher, John	1815	-	-	-
Brubacher, Jacob	1843	L	1	28	Bucher, Martin	1813	-	-	-
Brubacher, John	1764	-	-	-	Bucher, Martin	1832	F	1	144
Brubacher, John	1828	D	1	262	Bucher, Nancy	1843	L	1	157
Brubacher, Samuel	1818	-	-	-	Buchmayer, Michael	1847	M	1	233
Brubacker, Christian	1833	G	1	72	Buchter, John	1830	E	1	175
Brubaker, Ann	1847	M	1	293	Buchter, Samuel	1827	D	1	27
Brubaker, Barbara	1840	K	1	28	Buck, Elizabeth	1845	M	1	75
Brubaker, Benjamin	1829	E	1	44	Buckalew, Amos	1818	-	-	-
Brubaker, Christian	1821	A	1	82	Buckius, John	1817	-	-	-
Brubaker, Christian	1822	A	1	168	Buckley, Thomas	1806	-	-	-
Brubaker, Christian	1824	C	1	48	Buckwalter, Cathrine	1809	-	-	-
Brubaker, Christian	1834	G	1	157	Buckwalter, David	1841	K	1	181
Brubaker, David	1846	M	1	144	Buckwalter, David	1847	M	1	323
Brubaker, Henry	1839	I	1	214	Buckwalter, Henry	1795	-	-	-
Brubaker, Henry	1840	I	1	310	Buckwalter, Henry	1828	D	1	257
Brubaker, Jacob	1752	-	-	-	Buckwalter, John	1832	F	1	261
Brubaker, Jacob	1766	-	-	-	Buckwalter, John	1833	G	1	107
Brubaker, Jacob	1779	-	-	-	Buckwalter, John	1838	I	1	44
Brubaker, Jacob	1793	-	-	-	Buckwalter, John M.	1840	K	1	7
Brubaker, Jacob	1813	-	-	-	Buckwalter, Magdalena	1819	-	-	-
Brubaker, Jacob	1825	C	1	97	Buckwalter, Martin	1842	K	1	256
Brubaker, Jacob	1834	G	1	140	Buehler, Jacob	1835	G	1	270
Brubaker, Jacob	1840	I	1	313	Buffenmayer, Henry	1847	M	1	321

Name	Year	Bk.	Vol	Page	Name	Year	Bk.	Vol	Page
Buffenmyer, John	1814	-	-	-	Caiter, Anna	1840	I	1	319
Bugh, George	1783	-	-	-	Caldwell, Andrew	1768	-	-	-
Buhman, Peter	1839	I	1	278	Caldwell, Andrew	1809	-	-	-
Bull, Levi G.	1842	L	3	3	Caldwell, Ann	1792	-	-	-
Bumberger, Christian	1785	-	-	-	Caldwell, David	1783	-	-	-
Bumside, John	1811	-	-	-	Caldwell, James A.	1845	M	1	65
Bunting, James	1834	G	1	152	Caldwell, John	1742	-	-	-
Bunting, William	1828	D	1	243	Caldwell, John	1777	-	-	-
Burbey, James	1776	-	-	-	Caldwell, John	1782	-	-	-
Burchell, William	1786	-	-	-	Caldwell, John	1812	-	-	-
Burg, John, Jr	1818	-	-	-	Caldwell, Margaret	1817	-	-	-
Burger, John	1768	-	-	-	Caldwell, Polly	1845	L	1	307
Burger, Michael	1737	-	-	-	Caldwell, Samuel	1838	I	1	77
Burges, Edward	1785	-	-	-	Caldwell, Sarah	1782	-	-	-
Burgher, Melchoir	1739	-	-	-	Caldwell, William	1746	-	-	-
Burgholder,Christopher H.	1804	-	-	-	Caldwell, William	1812	-	-	-
Burhman, Elizabeth	1839	I	1	279	Calhoun, James	1839	I	1	211
Burk, Richard	1802	-	-	-	Calhoun, Margaret	1830	E	1	176
Burk, Thomas	1827	D	1	63	Calhoun, Margaret	1831	F	1	21
Burk, Tobias	1736	-	-	-	Calhoun, Patrick	1743	-	-	-
Burket, Anna K.	1773	-	-	-	Calhoun, William	1746	-	-	-
Burkhard, Peter	1750	-	-	-	Calhoun, William	1838	I	1	124
Burkhart, Margaret	1813	-	-	-	Callaghan, John	1818	-	-	-
Burkholder, Abraham	1840	I	1	309	Callaugher, Peter	1808	-	-	-
Burkholder, Anna	1825	C	1	79	Cammeuer, Peter	1785	-	-	-
Burkholder, Christian	1766	-	-	-	Camp, Stephen S.	1845	M	1	31
Burkholder, Daniel	1836	H	1	184	Campbell, Andrew	1770	-	-	-
Burkholder, Frederick	1841	K	1	105	Campbell, Archibald	1738	-	-	-
Burkholder, John	1792	-	-	-	Campbell, Cathrine	1826	C	1	241
Burkholder, John	1824	B	1	150	Campbell, Ephriam	1835	H	1	127
Burkholder, John	1843	L	1	79	Campbell, George	1825	C	1	54
Burkman, Elizabeth	1834	G	1	230	Campbell, John	1748	-	-	-
Burkman, Thomas	1829	E	1	107	Campbell, John	1759	-	-	-
Burman, Irena	1836	H	1	194	Campbell, John	1776	-	-	-
Burn, Peter	1774	-	-	-	Campbell, John	1781	-	-	-
Burns, John	1792	-	-	-	Campbell, John	1784	-	-	-
Burns, Mary Ann	1848	N	1	12	Campbell, John	1824	B	1	149
Burns, Nicholas	1747	-	-	-	Campbell, Philip	1828	D	1	208
Burns, Thomas	1822	A	1	229	Campbell, Robert	1776	-	-	-
Burnside, William	1765	-	-	-	Campbell, Robert	1809	-	-	-
Burst, Martin	1765	-	-	-	Campbell, Walter	1823	B	1	75
Burst, Martin	1766	-	-	-	Candour, Joseph	1785	-	-	-
Burst, Michael	1741	-	-	-	Candour, Nickolas	1770	-	-	-
Burt, Andrew	1749	-	-	-	Cann, Peter	1808	-	-	-
Bush, Jacob	1745	-	-	-	Capis, Abraham	1829	E	1	25
Bush, Martin	1769	-	-	-	Capp, Feit	1785	-	-	-
Bushman, Cathrine	1797	-	-	-	Carlisle, James	1824	B	1	156
Bushman, Jacob	1825	C	1	101	Carmany, George	1830	E	1	241
Bushman, John	1798	-	-	-	Carmany, George	1832	G	1	11
Bushong, Jacob	1828	D	1	274	Carmichael, Joseph	1766	-	-	-
Bushong, John	1749	-	-	-	Carnathan, Joseph	1755	-	-	-
Busser, Elizabeth	1842	K	1	241	Carne, Abraham	1773	-	-	-
Butler, Ephriam	1783	-	-	-	Carolus, George	1813	-	-	-
Butz, Peter	1777	-	-	-	Carpenter, Dr. Abraham	1844	L	1	240
Buyers, Jane	1802	-	-	-	Carpenter, Appalonia	1792	-	-	-
Buyers, Robert A.	1816	-	-	-	Carpenter, Cathrine	1832	F	1	146
Buyers, Robert F.	1848	N	1	19	Carpenter, Charles	1844	L	1	253
Byer, John	1838	I	1	39	Carpenter, Christian	1839	I	1	181
Byerlin, John Christian	1827	D	1	138	Carpenter, Daniel	1764	-	-	-
Byers, Christian	1802	-	-	-	Carpenter, Daniel	1766	-	-	-
Byers, Daniel	1831	F	1	32	Carpenter, Daniel	1827	D	1	17
Byers, David	1743	-	-	-	Carpenter, Henry	1837	H	1	230
Byers, Feronica	1825	C	1	111	Carpenter, Henry	1848	N	1	80
Byers, Henry	1763	-	-	-	Carpenter, Jacob	1784	-	-	-
Byers, Jacob	1805	-	-	-	Carpenter, John	1843	L	1	100
Byers, John	1756	-	-	-	Carpenter, Dr. John S.	1821	A	1	62
Byers, Michael	1745	-	-	-	Carpenter, Levi	1847	M	1	231
Byers, Samuel	1737	-	-	-	Carpenter, Mary	1843	L	1	73
C					Carpenter, Massey G.	1826	C	1	276
Cachey, Samuel	1766	-	-	-	Carpenter, Nicholas	1739	-	-	-
Caffroth, Henry	1803	-	-	-	Carpenter, Rebecca	1833	G	1	42
Caig, Robert	1743	-	-	-	Carpenter, Salome	1827	D	1	96

Name	Year	Bk.	Vol	Page	Name	Year	Bk.	Vol	Page
Carpenter, Samuel, Esq..	1833	G	1	84	Christy, Henry	1749	-	-	-
Carr, Andrew	1766	-	-	-	Church, Mary	1839	I	1	287
Carrer, Casper	1748	-	-	-	Claman, Philip	1742	-	-	-
Carrigan, Patrick	1756	-	-	-	Clare, Frederick	1837	H	1	214
Carrigan, Patrick	1778	-	-	-	Clare, Samuel	1833	G	1	87
Carrigen, Andrew	1847	M	1	377	Clark, Daniel	1794	-	-	-
Carrish, George	1778	-	-	-	Clark, Edward	1833	G	1	38
Carrol, John	1820	-	-	-	Clark, Elizabeth	1828	D	1	159
Carron, Samuel	1760	-	-	-	Clark, James	1745	-	-	-
Carrothers, Robert	1834	G	1	134	Clark, James	1757	-	-	-
Carruth, Alexander	1739	-	-	-	Clark, James	1765	-	-	-
Carson, John	1777	-	-	-	Clark, James	1812	-	-	-
Carson, Mary	1825	C	1	74	Clark, John	1801	-	-	-
Carter, Jeremiah	1825	C	1	120	Clark, John	1832	F	1	222
Carter, Jerry	1837	H	1	250	Clark, Joseph	1845	M	1	26
Carter, John	1783	-	-	-	Clark, Margaret	1748	-	-	-
Carter, Mary	1822	A	1	165	Clark, Samuel	1837	H	1	278
Carter, William	1796	-	-	-	Clark, Sarah	1752	-	-	-
Carter, William C	1828	D	1	193	Clark, Sarah	1846	M	1	181
Carthy, John	1739	-	-	-	Clark, Thomas	1739	-	-	-
Caruthers, Robert	1747	-	-	-	Clark, William	1823	A	1	257
Carver, Gideon	1814	-	-	-	Claus, Jacob	1790	-	-	-
Casius, Peter	1777	-	-	-	Cleaver, Michael	1760	-	-	-
Caskey, James	1844	L	1	183	Cleeland, William	1823	B	1	31
Cassady, Cornelius	1742	-	-	-	Clements, John	1763	-	-	-
Cassel, Abraham	1776	-	-	-	Clements, John	1839	I	1	270
Cassel, Joseph	1780	-	-	-	Clemmons, Henry	1784	-	-	-
Cathey, Edward	1745	-	-	-	Clemmons, John	1800	-	-	-
Cauchey, Samuel	1787	-	-	-	Clemson, James	1741	-	-	-
Cautton, David	1744	-	-	-	Clemson, Sarah	1808	-	-	-
Cavet, Richard	1757	-	-	-	Clemson, Sarah	1816	-	-	-
Chamberlain, Joshua	1842	L	1	10	Clendenin, James	1829	E	1	112
Chamberlin, James	1749	-	-	-	Clendennin, David	1849	N	1	299
Chambers, James	1763	-	-	-	Clepper, Jacob	1815	-	-	-
Chambers, John	1781	-	-	-	Clepper, Jacob	1828	D	1	195
Chambers, Joseph	1748	-	-	-	Clepper, Joseph	1810	-	-	-
Chambers, Lydia	1831	F	1	25	Clepper, Mary	1848	M	1	425
Chambers, Randall	1748	-	-	-	Clepper, Nickolas	1832	F	1	219
Chambers, Robert	1733	-	-	-	Clerk, Robert	1741	-	-	-
Chambers, Robert	1746	-	-	-	Click, Hans Conrad	1760	-	-	-
Chambers, Robert	1815	-	-	-	Clime, Daniel	1826	C	1	268
Chambers, Samuel	1741	-	-	-	Cline, Elias	1849	N	1	286
Chambers, Stephen, Esq.	1831	F	1	24	Cline, Michael	1740	-	-	-
Chambers, Thomas	1764	-	-	-	Cling, Christian	1758	-	-	-
Chapman, Barbara	1835	H	1	110	Clouse, Elizabeth	1807	-	-	-
Charles, Christopher	1775	-	-	-	Clyne, Peter	1761	-	-	-
Charles, Henry	1758	-	-	-	Cobb, Cathrine	1841	K	1	91
Charles, Jacob, Jr	1833	G	1	102	Coble, Barbara	1841	K	1	138
Charles, Jane	1842	L	1	12	Coble, David	1790	-	-	-
Charles, John	1829	E	1	154	Coble, David	1841	K	1	137
Charles, Joseph	1814	-	-	-	Coble, Henry W.	1849	N	1	261
Charles, Simon	1760	-	-	-	Coble, Jacob & Maria	1774	-	-	-
Charlton, Francis	1799	-	-	-	Coble, John	1825	C	1	94
Charlton, Robert	1790	-	-	-	Coble, Mary Ann	1847	M	1	286
Chatters, James	1764	-	-	-	Coble, Michael, Sr	1825	A	1	271
Cherr, Cathrine	1823	B	1	40	Cochenauer, Elizabeth	1830	E	1	218
Cherry, George(Kersh)	1823	A	1	252	Cochenauer, Henry	1848	N	1	103
Cherry, Robert	1755	-	-	-	Cochenaur, John	1838	I	1	63
Cherry, William	1765	-	-	-	Cochenaur, Joseph	1817	-	-	-
Chesnut, Elizabeth	1806	-	-	-	Cochran, James	1804	-	-	-
Cheyney, Eliphas D.	1825	C	1	38	Cochran, John	1787	-	-	-
Chisnell, Eve	1826	C	1	227	Cochran, Samuel	1797	-	-	-
Chrisman, Powel	1846	M	1	206	Cochran, Samuel H.	1834	G	1	138
Christ, Christian	1828	D	1	229	Cochran, William	1774	-	-	-
Christ, Elizabeth	1840	K	1	64	Coelln, Claus	1832	F	1	197
Christ, Henry	1828	D	1	199	Coelln, Claus	1846	M	1	229
Christ, Jacob	1752	-	-	-	Coffman, Andrew	1744	-	-	-
Christ, Jacob	1848	N	1	27	Coffman, Isaac	1735	-	-	-
Christ, John	1818	-	-	-	Coffroad, Peter	1753	-	-	-
Christine, Cathrine	1822	A	1	167	Cohick, Daniel	1843	L	1	44
Christine, George	1819	-	-	-	Colden, Mathias	1820	-	-	-
Christy, Edward	1805	-	-	-	Cole, John	1791	-	-	-

Name	Year	Bk.	Vol	Page	Name	Year	Bk.	Vol	Page
Cole, Nickolas	1797	-	-	-	Copelan, Philip	1821	-	-	-
Coleman, Aaron	1823	A	1	275	Copenharer, Thomas	1761	-	-	-
Coleman, James, Esq	1851	F	1	122	Cornhass, John	1818	-	-	-
Coleman, John	1757	-	-	-	Cornish, Andrew	1734	-	-	-
Coleman, Robert	1846	M	1	103	Cornish, Andrew	1769	-	-	-
Coleman, Sarah H	1826	C	1	143	Correl, Magdalena	1826	C	1	253
Colmer, Daniel	1750	-	-	-	Correll, George	1818	-	-	-
Collins, Mary	1829	E	1	71	Correll, John	1793	-	-	-
Collins, Thomas	1840	I	1	301	Cortner, Francoise	1781	-	-	-
Colp, Adam, Jr	1834	G	1	161	Cosser, Jacob	1828	D	1	180
Colp, Adam	1834	G	1	162	Cotter, Thomas	1765	-	-	-
Colp, George	1830	E	1	214	Coulter, James	1795	-	-	-
Colter, David	1757	-	-	-	Coulter, William	1808	-	-	-
Colvin, David	1796	-	-	-	Counts, Henry	1770	-	-	-
Colvin, John Henry	1790	-	-	-	Cously, Constantine	1741	-	-	-
Comfort, Henry	1811	-	-	-	Covenowen, Joseph, Jr	1762	-	-	-
Comly, Peter	1844	L	1	185	Cover, Michael	1843	L	1	133
Commons, George	1807	-	-	-	Cowan, David	1758	-	-	-
Concklin, Samuel	1797	-	-	-	Cowan, George	1799	-	-	-
Conklin, Samuel	1833	G	1	105	Cowan, Joseph Clarkson	1842	L	1	6
Conlson, George	1838	I	1	64	Cowan, Thomas	1770	-	-	-
Conn, Henry	1848	N	1	86	Cowan, Thomas P	1833	G	1	57
Connelly, Ann	1821	A	1	83	Cox, Samuel	1842	L	1	8
Connelly, Patrick	1752	-	-	-	Cox, William	1828	D	1	235
Conner, Elizabeth	1813	-	-	-	Coyle, James	1817	-	-	-
Conner, George	1821	A	1	56	Coyle, James	1830	E	1	177
Conner, Patrick	1837	H	1	226	Coyle, Margaret	1823	B	1	118
Connihan, John	1803	-	-	-	Craig, Alexander	1754	-	-	-
Conningham, Janet	1822	A	1	129	Craig, George	1837	H	1	290
Conrad, Abraham	1841	K	1	173	Craig, John	1761	-	-	-
Conrad, Ann	1842	K	1	254	Craiger, George	1758	-	-	-
Conrad, George	1765	-	-	-	Craighead, Thomas	1739	-	-	-
Conrad, Jacob	1759	-	-	-	Cramer, John	1842	K	1	228
Conrad, Jacob	1771	-	-	-	Cramerer, Mathias	1772	-	-	-
Conrad, John	1794	-	-	-	Crawford, David	1773	-	-	-
Conrad, John	1801	-	-	-	Crawford, John	1748	-	-	-
Cook, John	1799	-	-	-	Crawford, John	1778	-	-	-
Cook, Joseph	1759	-	-	-	Crawford, Joseph	1807	-	-	-
Cook, William	1758	-	-	-	Crawford, Michael	1781	-	-	-
Cooke, David	1825	C	1	138	Crawford, Oliver	1748	-	-	-
Cooke, David	1829	E	1	48	Crawford, Samuel B	1832	F	1	203
Cooke, Samuel, Esq	1825	C	1	67	Creamer, Ann Maria	1834	G	1	143
Cookerly, Peter	1804	-	-	-	Creamer, Hans Adam	1732	-	-	-
Cookson, Charles	1752	-	-	-	Creamer, Jacob	1778	-	-	-
Cookson, Daniel	1741	-	-	-	Creamer, John	1828	D	1	167
Cookson, Daniel	1777	-	-	-	Creamer, John	1848	N	1	43
Cooper, George	1843	L	1	55	Creamer, Peter	1761	-	-	-
Cooper, Jacob	1753	-	-	-	Creigen, John	1831	F	1	69
Cooper, James	1749	-	-	-	Creighton, Thomas	1784	-	-	-
Cooper, James	1815	-	-	-	Cremer, Peter	1742	-	-	-
Cooper, James	1838	I	1	108	Creswell, Moses	1828	D	1	244
Cooper, James	1846	M	1	203	Crider, Daniel	1824	B	1	175
Cooper, James, Sr	1847	M	1	250	Crise, Henry C	1826	C	1	288
Cooper, James	1847	M	1	294	Criswell, William	1777	-	-	-
Cooper, Jane	1812	-	-	-	Croll, Nickolas	1834	G	1	167
Cooper, Jeremiah	1841	K	1	103	Cromwell, John	1834	G	1	197
Cooper, John	1758	-	-	-	Crope, Casper	1751	-	-	-
Cooper, John	1777	-	-	-	Cross, Christopher	1806	-	-	-
Cooper, John	1811	-	-	-	Crouse, John	1849	N	1	160
Cooper, John G	1845	M	1	67	Crow, Alexander	1814	-	-	-
Cooper, John George	1780	-	-	-	Crow, George	1816	-	-	-
Cooper, Mary	1832	F	1	137	Crow, Peter S	1846	M	1	100
Cooper, Mary	1839	I	1	275	Crowdon, Mary	1743	-	-	-
Cooper, Thomas	1752	-	-	-	Cryder, Elizabeth	1767	-	-	-
Cooper, Thomas	1832	F	1	149	Cryder, Francis	1750	-	-	-
Cooper, Valentine	1764	-	-	-	Cryder, Jacob	1755	-	-	-
Cooper, Wendel	1747	-	-	-	Cryder, Jacob	1758	-	-	-
Cooper, William	1820	-	-	-	Cryder, Jacob	1786	-	-	-
Cooper, William	1823	A	1	259	Cryder, Jacob	1802	-	-	-
Cooper, William	1842	K	1	318	Cryder, John	1785	-	-	-
Cooper, William	1846	M	1	154	Cryder, John	1801	-	-	-
Cope, John	1808	-	-	-	Cryst, John	1761	-	-	-

Name	Year	Bk.	Vol	Page	Name	Year	Bk.	Vol	Page
Culberson, Abigail	1823	A	1	278	Davidson, Samuel	1753	-	-	-
Culberson, Abigail	1827	D	1	40	Davies, John	1828	D	1	192
Culberson, Andrew	1746	-	-	-	Davies, Richard	1807	-	-	-
Culbert, Michael	1843	L	1	158	Davis, Benjamin T	1844	L	1	251
Culbertson, David	1837	H	1	225	Davis, Edward	1741	-	-	-
Cully, Mary	1835	H	1	195	Davis, Gabriel	1774	-	-	-
Cully, Thomas	1821	A	1	69	Davis, Gabriel	1801	-	-	-
Cully, William	1835	H	1	93	Davis, Isaac	1838	I	1	40
Cummings, Ann	1829	E	1	142	Davis, James	1741	-	-	-
Cummings, James, Jr	1825	C	1	131	Davis, James	1784	-	-	-
Cummings, James	1826	C	1	251	Davis, Jane	1754	-	-	-
Cummings, James, Jr	1827	D	1	52	Davis, Jane	1765	-	-	-
Cummings, Samuel	1785	-	-	-	Davis, John	1767	-	-	-
Cummings, Samuel	1828	D	1	174	Davis, John	1774	-	-	-
Cummins, John	1800	-	-	-	Davis, John	1814	-	-	-
Cummins, Jonathan	1824	B	1	141	Davis, John	1829	E	1	39
Cuncle, Elizabeth	1808	-	-	-	Davis, Joseph	1844	L	1	244
Cunkle, George	1803	-	-	-	Davis, Magdalena	1832	F	1	257
Cunkle, John	1804	-	-	-	Davis, Thomas	1820	-	-	-
Cunkle, John	1840	I	1	302	Davis, Thomas R	1825	C	1	82
Cunkle, Leonard	1778	-	-	-	Deague, Peter	1823	B	1	23
Cunkle, William, Sr	1831	F	1	132	Deal, Michael	1738	-	-	-
Cunningham, James	1733	-	-	-	Deal, Michael	1739	-	-	-
Cunningham, James	1746	-	-	-	Deal, William	1741	-	-	-
Cunningham, James	1774	-	-	-	Dean, Benjamin F	1843	L	1	102
Cunningham, John	1760	-	-	-	Dean, Caleb	1819	-	-	-
Cunningham, John	1781	-	-	-	Dean, Philip	1799	-	-	-
Cunningham, John	1786	-	-	-	Dean, William	1773	-	-	-
Cunningham, John	1827	D	1	77	Deardorf, John	1839	I	1	292
Cunningham, Joseph	1748	-	-	-	Dearduff, Henry	1749	-	-	-
Cunningham, Joseph	1769	-	-	-	Debbalee, Rudolp h	1757	-	-	-
Cunningham, Robert	1800	-	-	-	Debro, Francis, Sr	1842	K	1	275
Cunningham, Dr. Robert	1806	-	-	-	Dedlo, John	1798	-	-	-
Curpman, Christian	1801	-	-	-	Deeds, Jacob	1826	C	1	189
Curran, Sarah	1824	B	1	165	Deeg, Mary Magdalena	1843	L	1	151
Currey, William	1841	K	1	179	Deel, Magdalena	1790	-	-	-
Curry, Adam	1788	-	-	-	Deem, Adam	1788	-	-	-
Curry, Mathew	1814	-	-	-	Deerwechter, George	1797	-	-	-
Curry, Robert S., Esq	1832	F	1	241	Deets, Jacob	1754	-	-	-
Custard, Tobias	1765	-	-	-	Dehanah, Frederick	1759	-	-	-
Cuthberson, Rev. John	1791	-	-	-	Dehn, Philip	1777	-	-	-
Cutler, Agnes	1825	C	1	76	Dehna, Henry	1840	K	1	56
Cutler, Benjamin	1794	-	-	-	Dehuff, Abraham	1821	A	1	8
Cutt, Jacob	1749	-	-	-	Dehuff, Mathias	1803	-	-	-
D					Deibler, Albrecht	1777	-	-	-
Dague, Adam	1830	E	1	174	Deil, Jacob	1784	-	-	-
Dale, Samuel	1813	-	-	-	Deimler, Elizabeth	1830	E	1	271
Dally, Bartholomew	1824	B	1	144	Deimler, Philip	1831	F	1	114
Dance, John	1836	H	1	116	Deiter, John	1781	-	-	-
Dance, John	1841	K	1	172	Dellet, Henry	1785	-	-	-
Dane, Samuel	1746	-	-	-	Dellet, John, Sr	1845	M	1	91
Danes, John	1828	D	1	248	Dempsey, David	1828	D	1	277
Daniel, William	1828	D	1	247	Dempsey, David	1830	E	1	254
Danneberg, David	1804	-	-	-	Demsey, Isabella	1830	E	1	253
Danner, Adam	1841	K	1	149	Demsey, James	1748	-	-	-
Danner, Alexander	1768	-	-	-	Demuth, Christopher	1831	F	1	23
Danner, Cathrine	1817	-	-	-	Demuth, John	1822	A	1	186
Danner, Elizabeth	1841	K	1	150	Denaham, John	1795	-	-	-
Danner, Peter	1793	-	-	-	Dening, Henry, Esq	1800	-	-	-
Danner, Samuel	1823	B	1	129	Denker, John Julius	1784	-	-	-
Danner, Sophia	1825	C	1	26	Denlinger, Abraham	1785	-	-	-
Danney, George	1816	-	-	-	Denlinger, Ann	1834	G	1	154
Dans, Mary B	1797	-	-	-	Denlinger, Christian	1806	-	-	-
Dare, Rev.Ellmaker K	1826	C	1	259	Denlinger, John	1792	-	-	-
Darlaston, John	1750	-	-	-	Denlinger, Joseph	1823	B	1	26
Daud, Philip	1736	-	-	-	Denlinger, Michael	1736	-	-	-
Daugherty, John	1825	C	1	44	Dennies, John	1773	-	-	-
Daugherty, Joseph	1830	E	1	217	Denning, John	1845	M	1	82
Daugherty, John	1848	N	1	220	Denning, Solomon	1814	-	-	-
David, Ebenezer	1778	-	-	-	Dennis, William	1779	-	-	-
Davidson, John	1771	-	-	-	Dentlinger, Henry	1776	-	-	-
Davidson, Nathaniel	1814	-	-	-	Depo, Philip	1751	-	-	-

Name	Year	Bk.	Vol	Page	Name	Year	Bk.	Vol	Page
Drunckenmiller, Michael.	1778	-	-	-	Eberly, Henry	1822	A	1	193
Drunkenbroad, George	1841	K	1	119	Eberly, John	1805	-	-	-
Dubree, Nathan	1828	D	1	230	Eberly, John	1830	E	1	165
Dubs, Jacob	1761	-	-	-	Eberly, Peter	1826	C	1	204
Dubs, John	1784	-	-	-	Eberly, Samuel	1826	C	1	274
Duchman, Christian	1815	-	-	-	Eberly, Veronica	1833	G	1	25
Duchman, George	1848	N	1	72	Eberman, John Sr	1835	H	1	1
Duchman, Jacob	1831	F	1	84	Eberman, Mary	1828	D	1	237
Duffey, Patrick	1751	-	-	-	Eberman, Philip	1836	H	1	205
Duffy, Hugh	1783	-	-	-	Ebersole, Anna	1823	A	1	264
Duffy, Thomas	1813	-	-	-	Ebersole, Benjamin Sr	1832	F	1	145
Duke, Cathrine	1822	A	1	179	Ebersole, Bentz	1750	-	-	-
Duke, George	1763	-	-	-	Ebersole, Christian	1757	-	-	-
Duke, Jacob	1826	C	1	178	Ebersole, Daniel	1799	-	-	-
Duke, Jacob	1826	C	1	283	Ebersole, Elizabeth	1806	-	-	-
Duke, Susanna	1826	C	1	197	Ebersole, Henry	1848	N	1	122
Duke, Thomas	1821	A	1	15	Ebersole, John	1813	-	-	-
Dullenbaum, Leonard	1785	-	-	-	Ebersole, John	1844	L	1	287
Dunbar, John	1745	-	-	-	Ebersole, John Jr	1848	M	1	456
Duncan, James	1758	-	-	-	Ebersole, Jost	1784	-	-	-
Duncan, John	1746	-	-	-	Ebersole, Magdalena	1841	K	1	171
Duncan, John	1784	-	-	-	Ebersole, Martin	1848	M	1	444
Duncan, Robert	1744	-	-	-	Ebersole, Nancy	1841	K	1	96
Duncan, William	1784	-	-	-	Ebert, Philip	1770	-	-	-
Dundore, Jacob	1810	-	-	-	Eby, Abraham	1832	G	1	10
Dunkan, Thomas	1756	-	-	-	Eby, Abraham	1834	G	1	242
Dunkin, John	1767	-	-	-	Eby, Christian	1803	-	-	-
Dunkle, John	1842	K	1	307	Eby, Christian	1824	B	1	212
Dunlap, Fanny	1842	K	1	253	Eby, Elizabeth	1830	E	1	201
Dunlap, James	1814	-	-	-	Eby, Elizabeth	1831	F	1	8
Dunlap, John	1843	L	1	84	Eby, Elizabeth	1847	M	1	295
Dummma, Henry	1820	-	-	-	Eby, George	1743	-	-	-
Dunn, John	1838	I	1	126	Eby, Jacob	1834	G	1	187
Dunning, George	1838	I	1	136	Eby, Jacob	1841	K	1	188
Dunshee, Thomas	1758	-	-	-	Eby, Jacob	1843	L	1	126
Dunwoody, John	1746	-	-	-	Eby, Jacob Sr	1846	M	1	277
Durno, John	1836	H	1	179	Eby, John	1744	-	-	-
Dutt, George	1830	E	1	170	Eby, John	1798	-	-	-
Dutt, George	1831	F	1	22	Eby, John	1843	L	1	38
Duzen, Jane	1837	H	1	227	Eby, John	1847	M	1	386
Dwyer, John A	1839	I	1	177	Eby, Martin	1767	-	-	-
E					Eby, Mary	1801	-	-	-
Eaby, Christian	1756	-	-	-	Eby, Peter	1845	L	1	327
Eaby, Jacob Sr	1842	K	1	225	Eby, Peter	1846	M	1	207
Eaby, John	1794	-	-	-	Eby, Samuel	1833	G	1	46
Eaby, Samuel	1833	G	1	101	Eccles, Samuel	1844	L	1	283
Eagan, Elizabeth	1836	H	1	213	Echternacht, Jacob	1837	H	1	250
Eagan, James	1834	G	1	211	Eckenrode, Christian	1806	-	-	-
Eagan, James Sr	1836	H	1	120	Eckenroth, Henry	1810	-	-	-
Eagan, Thomas, Jr	1839	I	1	272	Eckenroth, Simon	1828	D	1	164
Eagell, Leven	1803	-	-	-	Ecker, Barbara	1811	-	-	-
Eagle, George	1838	I	1	121	Eckert, George Esq	1829	E	1	65
Eagle, Henry B	1848	N	1	131	Eckert, George	1849	N	1	198
Eakenrode, Joseph	1784	-	-	-	Eckert, Jonas	1802	-	-	-
Eakenroth, Simon	1841	K	1	165	Eckert, Peter	1828	D	1	212
Eakin, Andrew	1749	-	-	-	Eckles, William	1847	M	1	398
Eakin, Richard	1749	-	-	-	Eckley, William	1812	-	-	-
Eakins, James	1765	-	-	-	Ecklin, James	1802	-	-	-
Earhart, Nicholas	1776	-	-	-	Eckman, Daniel Esq	1832	F	1	214
Earkins, Thomas	1765	-	-	-	Eckman, Elizabeth	1828	D	1	231
Earnst, William	1750	-	-	-	Eckman, Henry	1821	A	1	67
Easton, John	1833	G	1	59	Eckman, Henry	1837	H	1	234
Ebay, Jacob	1745	-	-	-	Eckman, John	1776	-	-	-
Eberhard, William G	1847	M	1	383	Eckman, John Esq	1804	-	-	-
Eberholtz, Joseph	1747	-	-	-	Eckman, John	1815	-	-	-
Eberle, Mary M	1839	I	1	235	Eckman, John	1838	I	1	70
Eberly, Abraham	1816	-	-	-	Eckman, John	1846	M	1	176
Eberly, Ann	1831	F	1	16	Eckman, Martin	1832	F	1	178
Eberly, Barbara	1784	-	-	-	Eckman, Martin	1838	I	1	107
Eberly, David	1816	-	-	-	Eckman, Nicholas	1830	E	1	205
Eberly, Elizabeth	1842	K	1	264	Eckman, Peter	1812	-	-	-
Eberly, Henry	1817	-	-	-	Eddle, John	1823	B	1	46

Name	Year	Bk.	Vol	Page	Name	Year	Bk.	Vol	Page
Edes, Samuel...............	1825	C	1	88	Epler, David............	1838	I	1	213
Edmiston, Martha........	1835	H	1	83	Epler, John............	1773	-	-	-
Edmondson, Archibald....	1747	-	-	-	Eppele, John............	1778	-	-	-
Edward, Evan.............	1749	-	-	-	Eppler, Ann.............	1805	-	-	-
Edwards, John............	1825	C	1	106	Erb, Cathrine...........	1845	L	1	312
Edwards, John............	1877	D	1	29	Erb, Christian..........	1823	A	1	254
Egley, Marks.............	1767	-	-	-	Erb, Christian..........	1842	K	1	312
Ehler, Martin............	1813	-	-	-	Erb, Isaac.............	1838	I	1	85
Ehrhard, Elizabeth......	1840	K	1	72	Erb, John..............	1825	C	1	139
Ehrishman, Melchoir.....	1740	-	-	-	Erb, Joseph............	1822	A	1	178
Ehrisman, Christian.....	1849	N	1	167	Erb, Joseph............	1834	G	1	139
Ehrman, Casper..........	1825	C	1	122	Erb, Judish............	1839	I	1	227
Ehrman, Christian.......	1825	C	1	127	Erb, Salome............	1838	I	1	41
Ehrman, Peter...........	1823	B	1	73	Erb, Samuel............	1818	-	-	-
Ehrman, Peter...........	1833	G	1	110	Erford, John...........	1816	-	-	-
Ehrman, Samuel..........	1834	G	1	215	Erhart, John...........	1837	H	1	281
Eibe, Michael...........	1753	-	-	-	Erisman, Abraham.......	1843	L	1	130
Eichelberger, Thomas....	1843	L	1	33	Erisman, Christian.....	1798	-	-	-
Eichelbery, George......	1746	-	-	-	Erisman, Daniel........	1838	I	1	142
Eichler, Abram..........	1846	M	1	124	Erisman, Daniel........	1838	I	1	143
Eichler, David..........	1822	A	1	175	Erisman, Jacob.........	1794	-	-	-
Eichley, Jacob..........	1846	M	1	199	Erisman, Jacob.........	1823	B	1	97
Eicholtz, Ann Maria.....	1828	D	1	221	Erisman, Jacob.........	1823	B	1	103
Eicholtz, Cathrine......	1832	F	1	204	Erisman, John..........	1745	-	-	-
Eicholtz, John..........	1849	N	1	335	Erivin, Samuel.........	1744	-	-	-
Eicholtz, Leonard.......	1817	-	-	-	Ernst, Cathrine........	1806	-	-	-
Eicholtz, Leonard.......	1828	E	1	15	Ernst, George..........	1769	-	-	-
Eicholtz, Margaret......	1795	-	-	-	Ernst, Henry...........	1820	-	-	-
Eicholtz, Susan.........	1843	L	1	77	Ernstberger, Henry.....	1754	-	-	-
Eipe, Jacob.............	1742	-	-	-	Ervens, Samuel.........	1822	A	1	232
Elder, David............	1764	-	-	-	Erving, James..........	1823	B	1	35
Elder, Preston B........	1840	I	1	299	Erwin, John............	1737	-	-	-
Elevlein, Frederick.....	1825	C	1	50	Erwin, Joseph..........	1748	-	-	-
Elevlin, John...........	1822	A	1	148	Esbenshade, John.......	1832	F	1	152
Ellenberger, Christian..	1758	-	-	-	Esbenshade, Peter......	1845	M	1	48
Ellenberger, Christian..	1773	-	-	-	Eshbach, Michael.......	1803	-	-	-
Ellenberger, Nickolas...	1761	-	-	-	Eshbach, Michael.......	1847	M	1	291
Elliot, Hannah..........	1809	-	-	-	Eshbaugher, Christian..	1766	-	-	-
Elliot, John............	1773	-	-	-	Eshleman, Abner........	1821	A	1	7
Elliot, John............	1820	-	-	-	Eshleman, Benjamin.....	1809	-	-	-
Elliott, Robert.........	1832	F	1	247	Eshleman, Benjamin.....	1828	D	1	158
Elliott, Thomas.........	1842	K	1	288	Eshleman, Benjamin.....	1830	E	1	243
Ellmaker, Anthony.......	1821	A	1	46	Eshleman, Benjamin.....	1835	H	1	58
Ellmaker, Elas..........	1758	-	-	-	Eshleman, Benemi.......	1847	M	1	409
Ellmaker, George........	1836	H	1	209	Eshleman, David........	1819	-	-	-
Ellmaker, Isaac.........	1830	E	1	257	Eshleman, David........	1832	F	1	187
Ellmaker, Leonard.......	1829	E	1	63	Eshleman, Elizabeth....	1814	-	-	-
Ellmaker, Leonard.......	1831	F	1	106	Eshleman, Henry........	1796	-	-	-
Ellmaker, Leonard.......	1833	G	1	123	Eshleman, Henry........	1812	-	-	-
Ellmaker, Mary..........	1823	B	1	17	Eshleman, Jacob........	1806	-	-	-
Ellmaker, Peter Esq.....	1798	-	-	-	Eshleman, Jacob........	1813	-	-	-
Elser, George...........	1849	N	1	145	Eshleman, Jacob........	1816	-	-	-
Embray, Moses...........	1748	-	-	-	Eshleman, Jacob........	1821	A	1	112
Emer, Philip............	1759	-	-	-	Eshleman, Jacob........	1825	C	1	61
Enck, John..............	1777	-	-	-	Eshleman, John Sr......	1801	-	-	-
Enck, John..............	1805	-	-	-	Eshleman, John.........	1807	-	-	-
Enck, Rebecca...........	1834	G	1	175	Eshleman, John Jr......	1849	N	1	158
Endress,					Eshleman, Leonard......	1769	-	-	-
Rev. Christian F. L.	1827	D	1	124	Eshleman, Michael......	1839	I	1	252
Engel, John.............	1836	H	1	199	Eshleman, Peter........	1804	-	-	-
England, Theophilus.....	1775	-	-	-	Eshleman, Peter........	1840	K	1	48
Engle, Ann..............	1764	-	-	-	Eshleman, Samuel.......	1843	L	1	107
Engle, John.............	1831	F	1	109	Eshleman, Samuel.......	1847	M	1	268
Engle, John F...........	1823	B	1	84	Espey, Margaret........	1830	E	1	206
Engle, Magdalena........	1824	B	1	184	Espy, John.............	1770	-	-	-
Engle, Peter............	1823	B	1	14	Esterley, William......	1838	I	1	137
Engle, Ulrich...........	1757	-	-	-	Etter, Anna............	1828	D	1	273
English, William........	1830	E	1	171	Etter, Daniel..........	1827	D	1	30
Enk, Barbara............	1823	B	1	106	Etter, John............	1773	-	-	-
Enk, Samuel.............	1849	N	1	210	Etter, John............	1821	-	-	-
Ensminger, Peter........	1739	-	-	-	Evans, Abner...........	1818	-	-	-
Eordan, Casper..........	1821	A	1	93	Evans, Caleb...........	1802	-	-	-

Name	Year	Bk.	Vol	Page	Name	Year	Bk.	Vol	Page
Evans, Caleb............	1817	-	-	-	Fawber, Bernard.........	1792	-	-	-
Evans, Caleb............	1845	L	1	298	Fawkes, Samuel..........	1817	-	-	-
Evans, Caleb............	1845	L	1	301	Fechtly, Henry..........	1819	-	-	-
Evans, David............	1801	-	-	-	Feder, Bernhard.........	1777	-	-	-
Evans, David............	1827	D	1	62	Feder, Henry, Jr........	1823	B	1	122
Evans, David............	1828	E	1	8	Fegan, George...........	1818	-	-	-
Evans, Edwards..........	1748	-	-	-	Fegan, John.............	1828	D	1	240
Evans, Evan.............	1765	-	-	-	Fegan, Samuel...........	1775	-	-	-
Evans, Evan.............	1792	-	-	-	Fehl, Andrew............	1827	D	1	31
Evans, Isaac............	1849	N	1	302	Fehl, George............	1828	D	1	279
Evans, James...........	1802	-	-	-	Fehl, Jacob, Jr.........	1828	D	1	238
Evans, James...........	1805	-	-	-	Feige, Christian........	1801	-	-	-
Evans, John............	1797	-	-	-	Felker, Frederick.......	1846	M	1	183
Evans, John............	1802	-	-	-	Felker, George(Velker)..	1828	D	1	163
Evans, John............	1828	D	1	284	Felker, Philip..........	1848	N	1	133
Evans, John............	1740	-	-	-	Fellenbaum, David.......	1611	-	-	-
Evans, John............	1844	L	1	295	Fellenberger, Henry.....	1847	M	1	364
Evans, John............	1848	N	1	90	Penichel, George........	1784	-	-	-
Evans, Joseph..........	1805	-	-	-	Fenstermacher, Henry....	1842	K	1	282
Evans, Joshua..........	1838	I	1	151	Fenstermacher, Jacob....	1840	K	1	43
Evans, Mary............	1798	-	-	-	Fenstermacher, Philip...	1829	E	1	72
Evans, Morgan..........	1823	B	1	111	Ferguson, Andrew........	1821	-	-	-
Evans, Nathan..........	1777	-	-	-	Ferguson, Hugh..........	1813	-	-	-
Evans, Robert..........	1782	-	-	-	Fernsler, Magdalena.....	1820	-	-	-
Evans, Robert..........	1832	F	1	141	Ferree, Conrad..........	1802	-	-	-
Evans, Samuel..........	1805	-	-	-	Ferree, David..........	1806	-	-	-
Evans, Samuel..........	1816	-	-	-	Ferree, David..........	1834	G	1	239
Evans, Susanna.........	1791	-	-	-	Ferree, David..........	1839	I	1	191
Evans, Thomas..........	1847	M	1	304	Ferree, Elisha, Sr......	1832	F	1	206
Evans, William.........	1744	-	-	-	Ferree, Isaac..........	1782	-	-	-
Evans, William.........	1772	-	-	-	Ferree, Israel.........	1821	-	-	-
Evans, William.........	1804	-	-	-	Ferree, Jacob..........	1782	-	-	-
Evans, William.........	1840	K	1	71	Ferree, John...........	1769	-	-	-
Evats, Jeremiah........	1746	-	-	-	Ferree, John...........	1808	-	-	-
Everly, Jacob..........	1810	-	-	-	Ferree, Joseph.........	1802	-	-	-
Evits, Conrad..........	1814	-	-	-	Ferree, Joseph.........	1814	-	-	-
Evits, William........	1808	-	-	-	Ferree, Philip.........	1796	-	-	-
Evy, Joseph............	1821	A	1	35	Ferree, Philip.........	1820	-	-	-
Ewalt, Ludwig..........	1807	-	-	-	Fesler, Leonard........	1773	-	-	-
Ewing, Alexander.......	1799	-	-	-	Pessler, Andrew........	1782	-	-	-
Ewing, Alexander.......	1844	L	1	267	Pessler, John..........	1787	-	-	-
Ewing, Mary............	1737	-	-	-	Fetter, George.........	1848	N	1	65
Ewing, Thomas..........	1741	-	-	-	Fetter, Jacob..........	1784	-	-	-
Ewing, William........	1814	-	-	-	Pierre, Daniel.........	1762	-	-	-
Eyeman, Anna...........	1794	-	-	-	Pierre, John...........	1736	-	-	-
Eyeman, Ulrich.........	1765	-	-	-	Fighter, Christian......	1733	-	-	-
Eyman, Christian.......	1834	G	1	217	Pinck, Philip, Sr.......	1826	C	1	159
Eyseck, Charles........	1746	-	-	-	Findley, Robert........	1803	-	-	-
Eysell, Jacob..........	1764	-	-	-	Finlay, Jonathan.......	1816	-	-	-
F					Finley, Thomas.........	1833	G	1	95
Faber, Frantz..........	1773	-	-	-	Finney, Edward.........	1849	N	1	303
Faber, Jacob...........	1763	-	-	-	Finney, Thomas.........	1778	-	-	-
Faddes, Isaiah.........	1814	-	-	-	Fire, Andrew...........	1735	-	-	-
Fairlamb, William......	1850	N	1	359	Pirestein, Jacob.......	1822	A	1	233
Faris, Robert..........	1748	-	-	-	Fishburn, Anthony......	1758	-	-	-
Farmer, Gregory........	1826	-	-	-	Fisher, Adam...........	1833	G	1	60
Farmer, Henry..........	1754	-	-	-	Fisher, Ann............	1817	-	-	-
Farquehar, Hugh........	1787	-	-	-	Fisher, Christopher.....	1821	A	1	27
Farr, William..........	1769	-	-	-	Fisher, Jacob..........	1820	-	-	-
Farren, Edward.........	1822	A	1	116	Fisher, Jacob..........	1832	F	1	212
Farren, William........	1831	F	1	10	Fisher, Jacob..........	1838	I	1	42
Farringer, Jacob.......	1804	-	-	-	Fisher, John...........	1739	-	-	-
Farry, Patrick.........	1827	D	1	100	Fisher, Michael........	1832	F	1	157
Fasnacht, Adam.........	1757	-	-	-	Fisher, Peter..........	1783	-	-	-
Fasnacht, Conrad.......	1799	-	-	-	Fisher, William.......	1752	-	-	-
Fasnacht, Elizabeth....	1812	-	-	-	Fisler, Jacob..........	1781	-	-	-
Fauer, John............	1737	-	-	-	Fisler, John...........	1826	C	1	155
Faust, George Frederick.	1818	-	-	-	Pissel, Frederick......	1792	-	-	-
Faust, Isaac...........	1847	M	1	269	Fitchorn, Philip.......	1828	D	1	203
Fautz, Martin..........	1821	A	1	22	Fite, Jacob............	1828	E	1	16
Fautz, Michael(Pfautz)..	1741	-	-	-	Fite, Peter............	1822	A	1	161
Fawber, Adam...........	1767	-	-	-	Fitzgerald, James.......	1757	-	-	-

Name	Year	Bk.	Vol	Page	Name	Year	Bk.	Vol	Page
Fitzgerald, John	1746	-	-	-	Fordney, William	1825	C	1	112
Fitzgerald, Mary	1772	-	-	-	Fordney, William	1827	D	1	16
Fixley, Ulrich	1791	-	-	-	Foreman, John	1850	N	1	341
Pleeman, Jacob	1761	-	-	-	Forney, Abraham	1821	-	-	-
Fleisman, John C	1812	-	-	-	Forney, Abraham	1831	F	1	38
Fleming, David A.	1850	O	1	53	Forney, Catherine	1836	H	1	177
Fleming, Isaac	1816	-	-	-	Forney, Peter	1747	-	-	-
Fleming, James	1777	-	-	-	Forney, William	1831	F	1	94
Fleming, James	1843	L	1	98	Porree, John	1786	-	-	-
Fleming, James	1844	L	1	178	Forree, John	1801	-	-	-
Fleming, John	1747	-	-	-	Forrest, Elizabeth	1820	-	-	-
Fletcher, John	1828	D	1	217	Forrey, George	1817	-	-	-
Flick, Christian	1826	C	1	206	Forrey, John	1802	-	-	-
Flick, Sarah	1828	D	1	254	Forrey, John	1843	L	1	145
Flick, William	1838	I	1	84	Forrey, John	1845	M	1	17
Flicker, Peter H.	1847	M	1	315	Forster, John	1757	-	-	-
Flickinger, Catherine	1812	-	-	-	Forster, William	1761	-	-	-
Flickinger, John	1821	A	1	17	Forsythe, John	1824	B	1	157
Flickinger, Joseph	1812	-	-	-	Fortnee, David	1796	-	-	-
Flickinger, Richard	1848	N	1	52	Foster, David	1762	-	-	-
Flinn, Dennis	1836	H	1	114	Foster, Eli	1830	E	1	208
Flinn, Henry	1748	-	-	-	Foster, John	1747	-	-	-
Flinn, Luke	1827	D	1	90	Foulk, John	1795	-	-	-
Flora, John	1781	-	-	-	Foulk, William	1844	L	1	255
Flory, Daniel	1792	-	-	-	Foulk, William	1847	M	1	311
Flory, Eve	1816	-	-	-	Foustenour, John	1801	-	-	-
Flowry, Joseph	1741	-	-	-	Foutz, Jacob	1800	-	-	-
Flubacker,Jacob (Brubacker)	1744	-	-	-	Fox, Abraham	1821	A	1	88
Flubacker,Jacob (Brubacker)	1821	A	1	95	Fox, Christian	1793	-	-	-
Flubacker, John (Brubacker)	1777	-	-	-	Fox, Christopher	1788	-	-	-
Flynn, Bernard	1847	M	1	376	Fox, Edward	1739	-	-	-
Foag, Conrad	1745	-	-	-	Fox, James	1748	-	-	-
Foelher, Catherine	1850	O	1	33	Fox, John	1752	-	-	-
Foesig, Jacob	1821	A	1	103	Fox, John	1786	-	-	-
Foesig, John	1829	E	1	79	Fox, Thomas	1814	-	-	-
Foesig, John	1836	H	1	109	Fraelich, Jacob	1842	K	1	299
Foesig, Margaret	1822	A	1	212	France, Christian	1739	-	-	-
Foesig, Philip	1823	B	1	59	Francis, John	1824	B	1	196
Foetzer, George (Pfoetzer)	1781	-	-	-	Franciscus, John	1838	I	1	30
Foght, Conrad (Voght)	1824	B	1	194	Franciscus, Margaret	1758	-	-	-
Fogle, Adam, Esq	1842	K	1	261	Franck, Jacob	1828	D	1	173
Fogle, Andrew	1769	-	-	-	Frank, Catherine	1839	I	1	233
Fogle, John	1786	-	-	-	Frank, David	1843	L	1	120
Folk, George	1772	-	-	-	Frank, George	1839	I	1	293
Folk, George	1834	G	1	159	Frank, John	1848	N	1	40
Folk, Peter	1744	-	-	-	Frank, John	1849	N	1	267
Folk, Peter	1756	-	-	-	Frank, Martin	1781	-	-	-
Foltz, Adam	1802	-	-	-	Frankford, Philip	1818	-	-	-
Foltz, Adam	1840	K	1	13	Frankfort, Peter	1842	K	1	309
Foltz, George	1827	-	-	-	Franklin, John	1827	D	1	51
Foltz, Henry	1785	-	-	-	Frantz, Andrew	1842	K	1	297
Foltz, John	1801	-	-	-	Frantz, Baltzer	1747	-	-	-
Foltz, Jacob	1803	-	-	-	Frantz, Catherine	1846	M	1	162
Fondersmith, George	1834	G	1	251	Frantz, Christian	1828	D	1	165
Fondersmith, Susanna	1832	F	1	179	Frantz, Daniel	1776	-	-	-
Fonell, Henry	1792	-	-	-	Frantz, David	1841	K	1	200
Forbes, Julianna	1832	F	1	253	Frantz, George	1739	-	-	-
Forbes, William	1804	-	-	-	Frantz, Jacob	1777	-	-	-
Ford, Thomas	1846	M	1	113	Frantz, Jacob	1850	N	1	343
Fordinee, John	1793	-	-	-	Frantz, John	1847	M	1	278
Fordney, Casper	1817	-	-	-	Frazer, William	1844	L	1	238
Fordney, Elizabeth Charlotte	1835	H	1	44	Frazier, John	1803	-	-	-
Fordney, Jacob, Esq.	1850	O	1	29	Frazier, Joseph	1741	-	-	-
Fordney, John, Jr.	1825	C	1	52	Frederick, Christian	1836	H	1	129
Fordney, Margaret	1822	A	1	128	Frederick, John	1784	-	-	-
Fordney, Margaret	1849	N	1	166	Frederick, Noah	1759	-	-	-
Fordney, Melchoir	1846	M	1	208	Frederick, Susanna	1803	-	-	-
					Freed, Abraham	1840	K	1	12
					Freeman, Clarkson D.	1843	L	1	98
					Freidley, John	1823	A	1	261
					Frelich, Jacob	1784	-	-	-
					French, John	1783	-	-	-

Name	Year	Bk.	Vol	Page
Frey, Adam	1844	L	1	211
Frey, Andrew	1750	-	-	-
Frey, Anna	1835	H	1	96
Frey, Catherine	1847	M	1	275
Frey, Christian	1793	-	-	-
Frey, Christiana	1832	F	1	159
Frey, Christopher	1784	-	-	-
Frey, Conrad	1770	-	-	-
Frey, Conrad	1828	D	1	249
Frey, Frederick	1831	F	1	79
Frey, Frederick	1832	F	1	220
Frey, George	1818	-	-	-
Frey, Henry	1823	B	1	64
Frey, Henry	1847	M	1	282
Frey, Jacob	1822	A	1	127
Frey, Jacob	1835	H	1	98
Frey, Jacob	1845	M	1	43
Frey, John	1846	M	1	146
Frey, Mary	1824	B	1	191
Frey, Peter	1823	A	1	253
Frey, Peter	1824	B	1	235
Frey, Samuel	1846	M	1	97
Freyer, George P.	1821	-	-	-
Freymeyer, Catherine	1838	I	1	144
Frick, Christian	1824	B	1	208
Frick, John	1760	-	-	-
Frick, Lewis	1834	G	1	210
Fricker, John George	1844	L	1	250
Pricks, Jacob	1743	-	-	-
Friday, Jacob	1832	G	1	10
Fridley, Alexander	1758	-	-	-
Frie, Henry	1739	-	-	-
Fritz, Anna	1828	D	1	206
Fritz, Jacob	1765	-	-	-
Fritz, Jacob	1807	-	-	-
Fritz, Jacob, Sr	1839	I	1	208
Fritz, John	1840	K	1	24
Fritz, Ludwig	1838	I	1	149
Froelich, Jacob	1826	C	1	270
Froelich, Samuel	1850	N	1	416
Fronce, Ann	1746	-	-	-
Fry, George	1840	K	1	3
Fry, George	1847	M	1	405
Fry, Henry	1746	-	-	-
Fry, Jacob	1771	-	-	-
Fry, John	1768	-	-	-
Fry, Martin	1739	-	-	-
Fry, Martin	1849	N	1	195
Fry, Tobias	1748	-	-	-
Frymeyer, Henry	1848	N	1	117
Frymeyer, Jacob	1848	N	1	104
Fuhrman, Frederick	1812	-	-	-
Fulk, Mary Magdalene	1802	-	-	-
Fullman, John	1749	-	-	-
Fullerton, Daniel	1774	-	-	-
Fullerton, Margaret	1788	-	-	-
Fullmer, John	1827	D	1	112
Fullmer, John	1833	G	1	109
Fulmer, John, Jr	1832	F	1	223
Fulton, Hugh	1820	-	-	-
Fulton, Robert	1774	-	-	-
Fulton, Thomas	1747	-	-	-
Fulton, Thomas	1748	-	-	-
Fulton, Thomas	1830	E	1	229
Fulton, Thomas	1851	N	1	80
Fulton, William	1741	-	-	-
Fulton, William	1818	-	-	-
Funck, Catherine	1823	A	1	267
Funck, Jacob	1838	I	1	153
Funck, John	1807	-	-	-
Funck, Magdalena	1825	C	1	35
Funck, Samuel	1813	-	-	-

Name	Year	Bk.	Vol	Page
Fundersmith, Esther	1813	-	-	-
Funk, Elizabeth	1849	N	1	249
Funk, John	1749	-	-	-
Funk, John	1755	-	-	-
Funk, Martin	1825	C	1	123
Funk, Martin	1838	I	1	140
Furgeson, Robert	1793	-	-	-
Furlow, George	1845	L	1	275
Furney, Robert	1738	-	-	-
Furniss, Thomas	1831	F	1	17
Furrey, Abraham	1802	-	-	-
Furrey, Edward	1850	N	1	458
G				
Gable, Henry	1792	-	-	-
Gable, Jacob	1824	B	1	189
Gable, William	1837	H	1	291
Galately, Alexander	1761	-	-	-
Galbraith, Bartram	1804	-	-	-
Galbraith, Dr. Bartram	1826	D	1	2
Galbraith, Bartram	1839	I	1	263
Galbraith, Elizabeth	1757	-	-	-
Galbreath, Robert	1738	-	-	-
Galbreath, Samuel S., Esq	1810	-	-	-
Galbreath, William B.	1840	K	1	18
Gale, Thomas	1760	-	-	-
Gall, George	1845	M	1	24
Gall, Henry	1826	D	1	6
Gall, Martin	1843	L	1	27
Gallacher, Ann	1819	-	-	-
Gallacher, Francis	1810	-	-	-
Gallacher, John	1746	-	-	-
Gallacher, Margaret	1840	K	1	9
Gallacher, Peter	1808	-	-	-
Gallacher, Philip	1806	-	-	-
Gallagher, George	1793	-	-	-
Gallard, James	1794	-	-	-
Gallery, John M.	1832	F	1	170
Galligan, James	1849	N	1	238
Galt, James	1773	-	-	-
Galt, James	1826	C	1	273
Galt, William	1842	K	1	235
Gamber, John	1850	N	1	396
Gamber, Rudolph	1785	-	-	-
Gamble, James	1795	-	-	-
Gamble, John	1758	-	-	-
Gambler, Jacob	1845	M	1	35
Gantz, Frederick	1825	C	1	-
Gantz, Magdalena	1778	-	-	-
Gantz, Philip	1816	-	-	-
Garbel, Ephriam B.	1771	-	-	-
Garber, Catherine	1771	-	-	-
Garber, Catherine	1841	K	1	85
Garber, Christian	1751	-	-	-
Garber, Christian	1827	D	1	139
Garber, Hans	1739	-	-	-
Garber, John	1768	-	-	-
Garber, John	1783	-	-	-
Garber, John	1784	-	-	-
Garber, John	1839	I	1	226
Garber, Michael	1769	-	-	-
Garber, Michael	1846	M	1	106
Garber, Samuel	1835	H	1	97
Gardner, Apolona	1812	-	-	-
Gardner, Christian	1825	C	1	33
Gardner, Daniel	1780	-	-	-
Gardner, George	1770	-	-	-
Gardner, John	1743	-	-	-
Gardner, John	1753	-	-	-
Gardner, Philip	1826	C	1	289
Gardner, Thomas	1753	-	-	-
Gardner, William	1755	-	-	-
Garman, Henry	1824	B	1	146

Name	Year	Bk.	Vol	Page	Name	Year	Bk.	Vol	Page
Garman, Jacob...........	1830	E	1	109	Getz, Peter.............	1810	-	-	-
Garrad, William.........	1825	C	1	66	Getz, Peter.............	1828	D	1	256
Garretson, John.........	1816	-	-	-	Getz, Samuel............	1826	C	1	239
Garretson, Sarah........	1818	-	-	-	Geyer, George..........	1847	M	1	369
Garrett, John..........	1767	-	-	-	Geyer, John Charles.....	1797	-	-	-
Garst, Jacob............	1821	A	1	78	Gibbeney, Isabelle......	1766	-	-	-
Gartner, Valentine......	1804	-	-	-	Gibble, Abraham.........	1842	K	1	222
Gaston, John............	1850	N	1	349	Gibble, Elizabeth......	1834	G	1	156
Gault, Mary.............	1842	K	1	301	Gibble, John............	1850	N	1	459
Gault, William.........	1838	I	1	46	Gibbler, John..........	1843	L	1	132
Gavel, John.............	1799	-	-	-	Gibboney, John.........	1759	-	-	-
Gear, John..............	1761	-	-	-	Gibboney, John.........	1767	-	-	-
Geesey, David(Keesey)..	1801	-	-	-	Gibbons, John..........	1757	-	-	-
Geesey, Jacob(Keesey)...	1749	-	-	-	Gibson, David..........	1748	-	-	-
Geesey, Joseph(Keesey)..	1828	E	1	2	Gibson, John...........	1794	-	-	-
Geesy, Henry(Keesey)....	1836	H	1	156	Gibson, John...........	1795	-	-	-
Gehler, Barbara.........	1795	-	-	-	Gibson, Thomas.........	1821	A	1	23
Gehr, David.............	1820	-	-	-	Gibson, William.......	1845	M	1	57
Geib, Daniel...........	1824	B	1	143	Gibson, William.......	1848	M	1	438
Geiger, Nicholas.......	1784	-	-	-	Giesey, Elizabeth......	1832	F	1	173
Geigley, Ann Maria.....	1848	M	1	434	Giesey, John(Keesey)...	1827	D	1	141
Geigley, Ann Maria......	1850	N	1	399	Gilbert, Jesse.........	1829	E	1	70
Geigley, William......	1835	G	1	267	Gilbert, John..........	1832	F	1	250
Geip, Henry............	1848	N	1	91	Gilbert, Robert........	1836	H	1	163
Geist, Daniel..........	1833	G	1	48	Gilbert, Sarah.........	1833	G	1	63
Geist, Simon...........	1820	-	-	-	Gilbert, Wendel........	1785	-	-	-
Geitner, Elizabeth.....	1825	C	1	128	Giles, Conrad..........	1766	-	-	-
Geitner, Elizabeth.....	1838	I	1	72	Gilkison, Agnes........	1771	-	-	-
Geitner, Salome........	1837	H	1	245	Gill, James............	1796	-	-	-
Gelbaugh, Frederick....	1813	-	-	-	Gillespie, Benjamin.....	1761	-	-	-
Geldmacher, Henry......	1841	K	1	107	Gillespy, James........	1816	-	-	-
Gentizer,Maximillian					Gillespy, Robert.......	1785	-	-	-
Fedite.............	1837	I	1	20	Gillgore, Alexander				
Gepford, John..........	1834	G	1	207	(Killgore)...........	1793	-	-	-
Gerber, Andrew.........	1832	F	1	201	Gilligher, Michael.....	1821	A	1	90
Gerber, Elizabeth......	1831	F	1	56	Gillis, Daniel.........	1803	-	-	-
Gerber, Jacob..........	1820	-	-	-	Gillman, Daniel........	1811	-	-	-
Gerber, Jacob..........	1821	A	1	38	Gillman, Nicholas......	1806	-	-	-
Gerber, Magdalena......	1825	C	1	36	Ginder, Jacob..........	1819	-	-	-
Gerber, Mary...........	1845	M	1	12	Gingerich, Elizabeth....	1783	-	-	-
Gerber, Peter..........	1792	-	-	-	Gingerich, John........	1772	-	-	-
Gerber, Peter..........	1826	C	1	181	Gingerich, Joseph......	1773	-	-	-
Gerber, Peter, Jr......	1834	G	1	213	Gingerich, Jost........	1776	-	-	-
Gerhart, John..........	1850	N	1	412	Gingery, John..........	1760	-	-	-
Gerhart, Valentine.....	1764	-	-	-	Gingrich, Barbara......	1784	-	-	-
German, Adam...........	1782	-	-	-	Gingrich, Christian....	1787	-	-	-
German, Barbara........	1817	-	-	-	Gingrich, David........	1806	-	-	-
German, Barbara........	1836	H	1	216	Gingrich, Jonas........	1845	L	1	305
German, George........	1805	-	-	-	Ginon, John............	1832	F	1	239
German, George........	1822	A	1	133	Ginter, Anthony........	1794	-	-	-
German, George........	1831	F	1	71	Gippel, Henry..........	1812	-	-	-
German, John...........	1814	-	-	-	Gipson, William........	1746	-	-	-
German, Leonard, Sr.....	1832	F	1	237	Girtie, Simon(Girty)....	1750	-	-	-
German, Leonard........	1849	N	1	163	Gish, Christian........	1797	-	-	-
Gerner, Jacob..........	1844	L	1	245	Gish, John.............	1783	-	-	-
Gerstweiler, Mary......	1826	C	1	258	Gish, John.............	1846	M	1	125
Gerver, Casper.........	1748	-	-	-	Gish, Mathias..........	1757	-	-	-
Gesell, William........	1748	-	-	-	Gitton, Peter..........	1747	-	-	-
Gesse, James(Keesey)....	1786	-	-	-	Givler, Peter..........	1828	D	1	166
Gessler, Mary..........	1833	G	1	81	Glasgow, James.........	1774	-	-	-
Getter, Michael........	1840	K	1	20	Glass, John............	1807	-	-	-
Getz, Ann..............	1822	A	1	217	Glassbrenner, Conrad....	1772	-	-	-
Getz, Catherine........	1820	-	-	-	Glasser, Elizabeth.....	1823	B	1	15
Getz, George..........	1838	I	1	89	Glasser, Elizabeth.....	1832	F	1	242
Getz, George..........	1849	N	1	268	Glasser, Frederick.....	1830	E	1	233
Getz, Henry............	1803	-	-	-	Glasser, George........	1823	B	1	49
Getz, Jacob............	1850	N	1	346	Glasser, Jacob.........	1819	-	-	-
Getz, John, Sr.........	1841	K	1	187	Glatz, Catherine......	1846	M	1	94
Getz, John.............	1850	N	1	364	Glatz, George.........	1806	-	-	-
Getz, Joseph...........	1848	N	1	56	Glazier, Frederick.....	1846	L	1	91
Getz, Leonard..........	1801	-	-	-	Gleisinger, Ludwig,.....	1764	-	-	-
Getz, Peter............	1752	-	-	-	Glen, Robert...........	1761	-	-	-

Name	Year	Bk.	Vol	Page	Name	Year	Bk.	Vol	Page
Glenn, Hugh	1784	-	-	-	Good, Peter	1745	-	-	-
Glenn, William	1819	-	-	-	Good, Peter	1783	-	-	-
Gless, Frederick	1789	-	-	-	Good, Peter	1807	-	-	-
Glick, Philip	1789	-	-	-	Good, Peter	1850	N	1	317
Gline, Daniel(Cline)	1826	C	1	268	Good, Roland	1847	M	1	416
Glotz, William	1847	M	1	422	Good, Susanna	1800	-	-	-
Glouninger, Philip	1848	M	1	440	Good, William, Jr.	1785	-	-	-
Gnodel, Jacob(Knoble)	1795	-	-	-	Gooddittle, Michael	1801	-	-	-
Gochenour, Abraham, Sr.	1825	C	1	57	Goodman, Jacob	1825	C	1	24
Gochenour, Abraham	1828	D	1	275	Goodman, Mary	1844	L	1	241
Gochenour, Ann	1830	E	1	222	Goodyear, Charlotte	1817	-	-	-
Gochenour, Christian	1752	-	-	-	Goodyear, William	1829	E	1	159
Gochenour, Christian	1804	-	-	-	Gordon, Copeland	1771	-	-	-
Gochenour, Elizabeth	1830	E	1	218	Gordon, William	1769	-	-	-
Gochenour, Henry	1787	-	-	-	Gorgas, Jacob	1798	-	-	-
Gochenour, Henry	1848	N	1	103	Gorgas, Susanne	1835	H	1	57
Gochenour, Jacob	1817	-	-	-	Gorman, Owen	1813	-	-	-
Gochenour, Jacob	1828	D	1	227	Gormley, John, Esq.	1829	E	1	140
Gochenour, Jacob	1832	F	1	158	Gorner, John	1832	G	1	3
Gochenour, John	1838	I	1	63	Gorner, Philip	1831	F	1	18
Gochenour, John	1850	N	1	319	Gorsuch, William	1838	I	1	68
Gochenour, Simon	1847	M	1	400	Goshert, Isaac	1849	N	1	181
Gochenour, Tobias	1819	-	-	-	Gossler, Ann Mary	1843	L	1	113
Gockley, Barbara	1850	N	1	410	Gossler, Catherine	1844	L	1	177
Gockley, Dietrich	1793	-	-	-	Gossler, Catherine	1848	N	1	49
Gockley, Henry	1829	E	1	128	Gossler, Christian	1738	-	-	-
Gockley, John	1821	-	-	-	Gossler, Frederick G.	1847	M	1	274
Gockley, Magdalena	1844	L	1	168	Gossler, George	1844	L	1	223
Gockley, Sarah	1848	N	1	89	Gossler, Jacob	1842	K	1	287
Godshall, John	1817	-	-	-	Gossler, Jacob	1844	L	1	220
Gohl, George	1754	-	-	-	Gossler, Philip	1843	L	1	156
Golden, Edward	1788	-	-	-	Grabill, John	1783	-	-	-
Goldenberger, John	1788	-	-	-	Grabinger, Henry	1826	C	1	166
Goldman, Conrad	1765	-	-	-	Graeff, Frederick	1804	-	-	-
Golly, Peter	1781	-	-	-	Graeff, George, Esq.	1824	B	1	148
Gonder, George	1838	I	-	116	Graeff, Jacob, Esq.	1818	-	-	-
Gonder, Peter	1768	-	-	-	Graeff, Jacob	1849	N	1	225
Gonter, Elizabeth	1846	M	1	202	Graeff, John	1804	-	-	-
Gonter, John	1847	M	1	305	Graeff, Mary	1837	H	1	240
Gonter, Kelian	1779	-	-	-	Graeff, Michael	1836	H	1	134
Gonter, Susanne	1844	L	1	192	Graeffe, Hans	1748	-	-	-
Gonter, William	1848	M	1	451	Graff, Abraham	1815	-	-	-
Gontner, Ann	1779	-	-	-	Graff, Abraham	1838	I	1	50
Gontnor, John	1798	-	-	-	Graff, Albright	1762	-	-	-
Gontner, Peter F.	1842	K	1	266	Graff, Catherine	1811	-	-	-
Gontner, Peter F.	1843	L	1	41	Graff, Christian	1754	-	-	-
Good, Abraham	1848	M	1	452	Graff, Conrad	1784	-	-	-
Good, Ann	1825	C	1	102	Graff, David	1848	N	1	115
Good, Barbara	1827	D	1	147	Graff, George	1785	-	-	-
Good, Christian	1782	-	-	-	Graff, Hans	1730	-	-	-
Good, Christian	1843	L	1	160	Graff, Henry	1822	A	1	141
Good, Christian	1850	N	1	418	Graff, Jacob	1815	-	-	-
Good, Daniel	1771	-	-	-	Graff, John	1758	-	-	-
Good, David	1827	D	1	36	Graff, John	1765	-	-	-
Good, David	1848	N	1	71	Graff, John	1813	-	-	-
Good, Feronica	1816	-	-	-	Graff, John	1838	I	1	56
Good, Henry	1793	-	-	-	Graff, Margaret (see Trissler)	1822	A	1	159
Good, Henry	1796	-	-	-	Graff, Martin	1759	-	-	-
Good, Henry	1844	L	1	190	Graff, Susanne	1831	F	1	11
Good, Israel	1849	N	1	275	Graffe, Hans Jacob	1749	-	-	-
Good, Jacob	1730	-	-	-	Graft, John	1819	-	-	-
Good, Jacob	1783	-	-	-	Grafton, Jane	1848	N	1	66
Good, Jacob	1817	-	-	-	Graham, Alexander	1746	-	-	-
Good, Jacob	1835	H	1	15	Graham, Arthur	1747	-	-	-
Good, Jacob	1844	L	1	186	Graham, Elizabeth	1828	D	1	232
Good, John	1801	-	-	-	Graham, James	1745	-	-	-
Good, John	1820	-	-	-	Graham, James	1826	D	1	4
Good, John	1826	C	1	230	Graham, John	1738	-	-	-
Good, John	1844	L	1	222	Graham, Robert	1812	-	-	-
Good, John	1850	N	1	315	Graham, Robert	1818	-	-	-
Good, Margaret	1807	-	-	-	Graham, Robert	1819	-	-	-
Good, Mary	1836	H	1	133					

Name	Year	Bk.	Vol	Page	Name	Year	Bk.	Vol	Page
Graham, Samuel	1769	-	-	-	Griffith, Samuel	1746	-	-	-
Graustaffe, Bernard	1748	-	-	-	Griffith, Samuel R.	1837	H	1	248
Graver, John	1848	N	1	79	Griffith, William	1761	-	-	-
Gray, Isaac	1781	-	-	-	Grill, Adam	1839	I	1	207
Gray, Jacob	1743	-	-	-	Grill, Rebecca	1826	C	1	185
Gray, Justus, Sr	1833	G	1	35	Grill, William	1848	N	1	48
Gray, Robert	1745	-	-	-	Grim, John	1814	-	-	-
Greaninger, Dorothea	1799	-	-	-	Grim, Leonard	1850	N	1	352
Grebill, Henry	1738	-	-	-	Grim, Martha	1840	K	1	11
Grebill, Henry	1831	F	1	39	Grimes, Joseph	1757	-	-	-
Grebill, John	1814	-	-	-	Grimler, Hannah	1814	-	-	-
Grebill, John	1849	N	1	241	Grimler, Henry	1814	-	-	-
Grebill, Sarah	1813	-	-	-	Grimler, Henry & Hannah	1814	-	-	-
Grebiner, Paul	1784	-	-	-	Grimler, Henry	1832	G	1	1
Grebinger, Mary	1828	D	1	187	Griner, Martin	1742	-	-	-
Green, Jacob	1838	I	1	132	Grise, Henry, Sr	1826	C	1	288
Green, John	1760	-	-	-	Grise, John	1780	-	-	-
Green, John	1831	F	1	126	Grist, William(Crist)	1849	N	1	164
Green, Joseph	1837	H	1	279	Gritter, Michael	1739	-	-	-
Green, Neil	1816	-	-	-	Groff, Abraham	1788	-	-	-
Green, Patrick	1809	-	-	-	Groff, Abraham	1809	-	-	-
Green, Walter	1845	M	1	9	Groff, Adam	1822	A	1	188
Greenawald, Henry	1835	H	1	64	Groff, Ann	1833	G	1	50
Greenewalt, Abraham	1840	K	1	80	Groff, Barbara	1784	-	-	-
Greenland, Mary	1815	-	-	-	Groff, Barbara	1801	-	-	-
Greenland, William	1823	B	1	31	Groff, Barbara	1831	F	1	47
Greer, Robert	1745	-	-	-	Groff, Barbara	1837	H	1	275
Greer, Samuel	1819	-	-	-	Groff, Christopher	1814	-	-	-
Greider, Benjamin	1815	-	-	-	Groff, David	1784	-	-	-
Greider, Daniel	1812	-	-	-	Groff, David, Jr	1826	C	1	195
Greider, Daniel	1820	-	-	-	Groff, David	1831	F	1	86
Greider, Elizabeth (Cryder)	1767	-	-	-	Groff, Elias	1849	N	1	236
Greider, Elizabeth	1839	I	1	273	Groff, George	1804	-	-	-
Greider, George(Kreiter)	1832	F	1	150	Groff, Jacob	1730	-	-	-
Greider, Henry	1767	-	-	-	Groff, Jacob	1767	-	-	-
Greider, Henry(Kreiter)	1821	A	1	34	Groff, Jacob	1826	C	1	215
Greider, Henry	1839	I	1	194	Groff, Jacob	1834	G	1	185
Greider, Jacob	1755	-	-	-	Groff, John	1834	G	1	204
Greider, Jacob	1758	-	-	-	Groff, John	1844	L	1	256
Greider, Jacob	1786	-	-	-	Groff, Joseph	1846	M	1	151
Greider, Jacob	1802	-	-	-	Groff, Maria	1801	-	-	-
Greider, Jacob	1819	-	-	-	Groff, Martin	1846	M	1	101
Greider, Jacob	1823	B	1	124	Groff, Peter	1849	N	1	184
Greider, Jacob	1829	E	1	153	Groff, Susanna	1846	M	1	165
Greider, John	1785	-	-	-	Groh, Baltzer	1803	-	-	-
Greider, John	1810	-	-	-	Groh, Johannes	1751	-	-	-
Greider, Michael G.	1796	-	-	-	Groh, John	1826	C	1	229
Greider, Samuel	1834	G	1	262	Groll, Nicholas(Kroll)	1834	G	1	167
Greider, Susanna	1833	G	1	128	Gromberger, Felix N.	1743	-	-	-
Greiner, Barbara	1824	B	1	159	Groner, Jacob	1808	-	-	-
Greiner, Barbara	1829	E	1	101	Grosh, Barbara	1793	-	-	-
Greiner, Dietrich	1781	-	-	-	Grosh, Daniel	1847	M	1	296
Greiner, Jacob	1794	-	-	-	Grosh, David	1849	N	1	157
Greiner, John	1828	D	1	161	Grosh, Feronica	1836	H	1	124
Greist, Jeremiah	1842	L	1	4	Grosh, Henry	1846	M	1	175
Greitter, George	1744	-	-	-	Gross, Andrew	1829	E	1	137
Greitter, Jacob	1744	-	-	-	Gross, Jacob	1778	-	-	-
Gress, Christian	1819	-	-	-	Gross, John	1787	-	-	-
Gress, John	1847	M	1	411	Gross, John	1847	M	1	375
Gress, John	1848	N	1	37	Gross, Julianna	1825	C	1	10
Grey, Peter(Kray)	1756	-	-	-	Gross, Julianna	1826	C	1	277
Greybill, Rudy	1800	-	-	-	Gross, Ludwig	1845	M	1	44
Grider, Daniel(Kreiter)	1824	B	1	175	Gross, Martin	1837	H	1	261
Grider, Francis	1750	-	-	-	Gross, Michael	1820	-	-	-
Grider, Jacob	1784	-	-	-	Gross, Wiant	1833	G	1	99
Grider, Michael	1830	E	1	231	Grossman, John	1831	F	1	117
Griffith, Christopher	1748	-	-	-	Grossman, Mary	1832	F	1	225
Griffith, Christopher	1790	-	-	-	Grove, Adam	1823	B	1	74
Griffith, Francis	1819	-	-	-	Grove, Ann	1806	-	-	-
Griffith, James	1822	A	1	206	Grove, Christian	1818	-	-	-
Griffith, John	1773	-	-	-	Grove, Daniel, Jr	1844	L	1	225
					Grove, David	1849	N	1	146

Name	Year	Bk.	Vol	Page	Name	Year	Bk.	Vol	Page
Grove, Elizabeth.......	1824	B	1	172	Hafeld, Godleib........	1824	B	1	199
Grove, Elizabeth.......	1825	C	1	99	Haffley, Rachel........	1825	C	1	39
Grove, George.........	1815	-	-	-	Hagan, Patrick........	1783	-	-	-
Grove, Henry...........	1836	H	1	123	Hageman, Jacob.........	1759	-	-	-
Grove, Henry...........	1838	I	1	58	Hageman, John Henry.....	1754	-	-	-
Grove, John..........	1760	-	-	-	Hageman, William........	1763	-	-	-
Grove, John...........	1831	F	1	118	Hagen, Daniel...........	1784	-	-	-
Grove, Joseph..........	1776	-	-	-	Hagens, William........	1839	I	1	267
Grove, Joseph..........	1786	-	-	-	Hager, John.............	1825	C	1	31
Grubb, Christian.......	1758	-	-	-	Hager, William, Sr......	1840	K	1	61
Grubb, George..........	1841	K	1	145	Hagerty, John...........	1741	-	-	-
Grubb, Henry..........	1788	-	-	-	Hagey, Henry............	1839	I	1	290
Grubb, Henry..........	1848	N	1	5	Haggen, Arthur.........	1774	-	-	-
Grubb, Henry B.,Esq.....	1823	B	1	4	Hagy, Henry............	1839	I	1	290
Grubb, Jacob........	1829	E	1	115	Hagy, Jacob.............	1758	-	-	-
Grube, Casper..........	1834	G	1	202	Hagy, Jacob.............	1830	E	1	186
Grube, George, Sr.......	1841	K	1	199	Hahn, Mary O............	1850	O	1	13
Grube, Peter........	1824	B	1	169	Hahn, Michael...........	1748	-	-	-
Gruber, Frederick.......	1776	-	-	-	Hahnlen, Lewis...........	1847	M	1	335
Grumbauff, George.......	1818	-	-	-	Haines, Daniel..........	1824	B	1	173
Grupe, John Henry.......	1816	-	-	-	Haines, Hanson..........	1840	L	1	207
Grush, John.............	1776	-	-	-	Haines, Henry...........	1750	-	-	-
Gryder, John..........	1763	-	-	-	Haines, Henry...........	1786	-	-	-
Gryder, John............	1788	-	-	-	Haines, Henry, Sr.......	1842	K	1	237
Gryder, Martin..........	1839	I	1	251	Haines, Jacob..........	1825	C	1	68
Gryter, Henry..........	1750	-	-	-	Haines, John............	1850	N	1	350
Gryter, Jacob..........	1742	-	-	-	Haines, Magdalena.......	1791	-	-	-
Gundaker, Elizabeth.....	1846	M	1	171	Haines, Reuben..........	1839	I	1	264
Gundaker, Michael.......	1815	-	-	-	Haines, Samuel..........	1850	N	1	423
Gundaker, Michael, Jr...	1829	E	1	113	Hair, Emanuel...........	1839	I	1	229
Gunkel, William, Sr.					Hair, Jacob John........	1815	-	-	-
(Kunkle)...........	1831	F	1	132	Halbach, Godleib........	1846	M	1	152
Gunkle, John...........	1782	-	-	-	Haldeman, Christian.....	1758	-	-	-
Gunter, Peter..........	1823	B	1	90	Haldeman, Christian.....	1830	E	1	183
Gunty, Peter...........	1758	-	-	-	Haldeman, Christian....	1841	K	1	83
Gurley, Martha.........	1812	-	-	-	Haldeman, Christopher,Jr	1829	E	1	133
Guth, Feronica(Good)....	1818	-	-	-	Haldeman, Jacob.........	1764	-	-	-
Guy, James.............	1743	-	-	-	Haldeman, Jacob........	1821	A	1	97
Guy, John.............	1734	-	-	-	Haldeman, Jacob........	1837	H	1	219
Guy, Joseph............	1780	-	-	-	Haldeman, John.........	1774	-	-	-
Guyer, Henry..........	1745	-	-	-	Haldeman, John B.......	1837	H	1	243
Guysinger, Adam.......	1804	-	-	-	Haldeman, Rudolph......	1843	L	1	93
Gwinn, Cornelius(Quinn).	1772	-	-	-	Haldeman, Samuel........	1841	K	1	108
Gwinn, Daniel(Quinn)....	1784	-	-	-	Halderman, Christian.....	1782	-	-	-
Gwinn, Michael(Quinn)...	1830	E	1	202	Hall, Ann C............	1847	M	1	299
H					Hall, David............	1814	-	-	-
Haag, John.............	1755	-	-	-	Hall, George...........	1815	-	-	-
Haas, John Conrad.......	1807	-	-	-	Hall, Henry............	1825	C	1	87
Haas, Sarah.............	1828	E	1	3	Hall, John.............	1807	-	-	-
Habecker, Barbara.......	1821	-	-	-	Hall, Mary.............	1821	A	1	57
Habecker, Christian....	1786	-	-	-	Hall, Peter............	1838	I	1	112
Habecker, Christian....	1834	G	1	150	Hall, Robert...........	1804	-	-	-
Habecker, Christian....	1850	O	1	41	Hallacher, Robert.......	1833	G	1	42
Habecker, Jacob........	1827	D	1	150	Haller, Nicholas........	1814	-	-	-
Habecker, Jacob K.......	1850	N	1	360	Halliburton, Lowden.....	1788	-	-	-
Habecker, John........	1782	-	-	-	Hallman, Peter.........	1844	L	1	191
Habecker, Mary..........	1842	K	1	272	Halman, Peter..........	1777	-	-	-
Hable, Christian........	1836	H	1	109	Hamaker, John..........	1848	M	1	458
Hackenberger, John....	1835	H	1	20	Hamaker, Mary...........	1821	A	1	89
Hacker, Adam.............	1782	-	-	-	Hambright, Adam........	1793	-	-	-
Hacker, Jacob..........	1847	M	1	283	Hambright, Frederick....	1847	M	1	242
Hackman, Abraham........	1846	M	1	222	Hambright, George......	1814	-	-	-
Hackman, David H.......	1842	K	1	316	Hambright, Hannah......	1848	N	1	41
Hackman, Elizabeth.....	1848	N	1	69	Hambright, Martin......	1807	-	-	-
Hackman, Henry..........	1777	-	-	-	Hamilton, Alexander.....	1781	-	-	-
Hackman, Jacob.........	1775	-	-	-	Hamilton, Andrew........	1820	-	-	-
Hackman, John..........	1754	-	-	-	Hamilton, Bernard......	1792	-	-	-
Hackman, John..........	1826	C	1	171	Hamilton, George.......	1821	A	1	79
Hackman, Mary..........	1837	I	1	8	Hamilton, Hugh.........	1804	-	-	-
Hackman, Melchoir.......	1818	-	-	-	Hamilton, James........	1822	A	1	228
Haden, Francis.........	1832	F	1	232	Hamilton, John.........	1739	-	-	-
Haeslet, Robert.........	1777	-	-	-	Hamilton, John.........	1804	-	-	-

Name	Year	Bk.	Vol	Page	Name	Year	Bk.	Vol	Page
Hamilton, John..........	1829	E	1	28	Harry, Catherine.......	1849	N	1	240
Hamilton, John..........	1838	I	1	35	Harsh, Jacob...........	1849	N	1	263
Hamilton, Joseph........	1826	C	1	151	Harsh, Martin..........	1832	F	1	243
Hamilton, Robert........	1808	-	-	-	Hart, Adam.............	1826	C	1	224
Hamilton, Robert........	1847	M	1	255	Hart, Ann..............	1825	C	1	32
Hamilton, William.......	1810	-	-	-	Hart, Ann..............	1833	G	1	62
Hamilton, William.......	1812	-	-	-	Hart, Ann Margaret.....	1850	N	1	318
Hamilton, William.......	1820	-	-	-	Hart, Benjamin.........	1837	I	1	12
Hamilton, William.......	1823	B	1	6	Hart, Frederick........	1850	N	1	407
Hamilton, William.......	1824	B	1	166	Hart, George...........	1818	-	-	-
Hand, Edward, Esq.......	1805	-	-	-	Hart, George...........	1839	I	1	269
Hand, General Edward....	1844	L	1	272	Hart, John.............	1811	-	-	-
Hanford, Dr. Sylvester..	1836	H	1	130	Hart, Margaret.........	1844	L	1	210
Hanlen, Lewis...........	1849	N	1	178	Hart, Sarah............	1827	D	1	103
Hann, John.............	1848	N	1	93	Hartappel, Rupertus....	1782	-	-	-
Hannah, Andrew..........	1759	-	-	-	Harter, John...........	1848	N	1	110
Hanne, George..........	1774	-	-	-	Harting, Sarah.........	1850	N	1	372
Hanne, James...........	1805	-	-	-	Hartley, Jacob.........	1829	E	1	117
Hannum, George.........	1830	E	1	211	Hartman, Ann...........	1846	M	1	177
Hantz, Philip..........	1767	-	-	-	Hartman, Barbara.......	1755	-	-	-
Hapbaker, Joseph........	1786	-	-	-	Hartman, Barbara.......	1812	-	-	-
Hardens, Joseph.........	1836	H	1	176	Hartman, Casper........	1746	-	-	-
Harding, Richard.......	1785	-	-	-	Hartman, Catherine.....	1760	-	-	-
Hare, Abraham(Herr).....	1758	-	-	-	Hartman, Christian.....	1822	A	1	242
Hare, Anna.............	1767	-	-	-	Hartman, Christian.....	1825	C	1	119
Hare, Barbara..........	1773	-	-	-	Hartman, Christian.....	1843	L	1	81
Hare, Elizabeth					Hartman, George........	1825	C	1	86
(late Kendrick).....	1789	-	-	-	Hartman, Jacob.........	1795	-	-	-
Hare, Emanuel..........	1741	-	-	-	Hartman, John..........	1831	F	1	51
Harkey, George.........	1824	B	1	135	Hartman, Joseph........	1838	I	1	45
Harkness, David........	1770	-	-	-	Hartman, Malinda E.....	1849	N	1	200
Harlan, Benjamin.......	1840	K	1	58	Hartman, Samuel........	1805	-	-	-
Harlan, Joseph.........	1801	-	-	-	Hartman, Theophilus....	1765	-	-	-
Harley, William........	1832	G	1	5	Hartman, Theopilis	1751	-	-	-
Harman, Daniel.........	1844	L	1	258	Harvey, James..........	1817	-	-	-
Harman, Samuel.........	1832	F	1	260	Harvey, Robert.........	1743	-	-	-
Harner, Nickolas.......	1835	H	1	63	Haskill, Samuel L......	1824	B	1	222
Harnish, David, Jr.....	1821	A	1	94	Haslet, John...........	1832	F	1	238
Harnish, Henry.........	1830	E	1	259	Hasselbach, Henry......	1845	M	1	63
Harnish, Jacob.........	1799	-	-	-	Hassler, Christian.....	1799	-	-	-
Harnish, Jacob.........	1825	C	1	98	Hassler, Daniel........	1847	M	1	261
Harnish, Jacob.........	1829	E	1	145	Hassler, John..........	1843	L	1	65
Harnish, John..........	1804	-	-	-	Hassler, Michael.......	1817	-	-	-
Harnish, John..........	1829	E	1	143	Hassler, Michael.......	1848	N	1	30
Harnish, John..........	1838	I	1	104	Hastings, Enoch........	1823	A	1	255
Harnish, John..........	1847	M	1	352	Hastings, John, Sr.....	1835	H	1	18
Harnish, Joseph........	1821	A	1	13	Hastings, John, Sr.....	1835	H	1	76
Harnish, Martin........	1744	-	-	-	Hastings, John, Sr.....	1836	H	1	212
Harnish, Martin........	1841	K	1	164	Hastings, Richard......	1739	-	-	-
Harnish, Michael.......	1769	-	-	-	Hastings, Sarah........	1823	A	1	56
Harnish, Nancy.........	1831	F	1	99	Hastings, Sarah........	1823	A	1	282
Harnish, Rudolph.......	1841	K	1	175	Hastings, Stephen......	1832	F	1	196
Harper, Nicholas.......	1759	-	-	-	Hastings, Thomas.......	1777	-	-	-
Harper, Thomas.........	1820	-	-	-	Hastings, William......	1834	G	1	170
Harper, William.......	1793	-	-	-	Hastings, William......	1834	G	1	261
Harr, John, Esq........	1823	A	1	272	Hathorn, Thomas........	1791	-	-	-
Harrah, Dr. Patrick.....	1816	-	-	-	Hathorn, William.......	1850	N	1	402
Harrar, Hannah.........	1849	N	1	292	Hats, John.............	1821	-	-	-
Harrar, Jesse..........	1849	N	1	187	Hatz, John.............	1847	M	1	351
Harrick, Daniel.......	1800	-	-	-	Hatz, Rosina...........	1817	-	-	-
Harris, Henry..........	1783	-	-	-	Hauenstein, George.....	1824	B	1	12
Harris, Jacob..........	1826	D	1	8	Haugy, John............	1798	-	-	-
Harris, John..........	1817	-	-	-	Haun, Peter............	1756	-	-	-
Harris, Minty..........	1833	G	1	53	Haup, Henry............	1743	-	-	-
Harris, Susanna........	1844	L	1	174	Hauspocker, George.....	1748	-	-	-
Harris, Thomas.........	1747	-	-	-	Haverling, Adam........	1782	-	-	-
Harris, Thomas.........	1829	E	1	42	Haverling, Godfried....	1766	-	-	-
Harris, William.......	1762	-	-	-	Haverstick, Michael....	1819	-	-	-
Harris, William.......	1768	-	-	-	Hawdorn, John..........	1741	-	-	-
Harris, William.......	1776	-	-	-	Hawkins, George........	1836	H	1	147
Harris, William.......	1834	G	1	203	Hawkins, John..........	1786	-	-	-
Harrison, Elizabeth.....	1819	-	-	-	Hawkins, Nathaniel.....	1827	D	1	151

Name	Year	Bk.	Vol	Page
Hay, Hough..............	1779	-	-	-
Hayes, Hannah...........	1847	M	1	280
Hayes, Moses............	1733	-	-	-
Hays, David.............	1805	-	-	-
Hays, Ellen.............	1839	I	1	245
Hays, Hugh..............	1836	H	1	139
Hays, James.............	1746	-	-	-
Hays, James.............	1805	-	-	-
Hays, John..............	1813	-	-	-
Hays, John, Jr.........	1813	-	-	-
Hays, John..............	1826	D	1	1
Hays, Patrick..........	1748	-	-	-
Hays, Robert...........	1781	-	-	-
Hays, William..........	1763	-	-	-
Heagy, John.............	1798	-	-	-
Heard, Stephen..........	1836	H	1	202
Hebel, John.............	1834	G	1	160
Heck, Charles...........	1839	I	1	199
Heck, Elizabeth........	1831	F	1	27
Heck, John.............	1821	A	1	6
Heck, Lewis.............	1818	-	-	-
Heck, Lewis.............	1831	F	1	28
Heck, William..........	1836	H	1	149
Hecker, Ludwig..........	1796	-	-	-
Heckman, Peter..........	1759	-	-	-
Hedger, Robert.........	1841	K	1	86
Heedwohl, John..........	1794	-	-	-
Heedwohl, Mary..........	1803	-	-	-
Hefle, Sophia...........	1836	H	1	186
Heft, George...........	1774	-	-	-
Heft, George...........	1784	-	-	-
Heft, George...........	1840	K	1	21
Heger(Christian)Casper..	1790	-	-	-
Heger, George...........	1792	-	-	-
Heger, Noah.............	1796	-	-	-
Heger, Salome...........	1782	-	-	-
Heger, Valentine.......	1793	-	-	-
Heidelbach, John........	1821	A	1	96
Heidelbaugh, Elizabeth..	1820	-	-	-
Heidelbaugh, John Jacob.	1823	B	1	107
Heidler, William.......	1826	C	1	210
Heighlands, William.....	1806	-	-	-
Heighold, Martin........	1780	-	-	-
Heil, Elizabeth........	1832	F	1	139
Heil, Frederick........	1782	-	-	-
Heil, Peter.............	1823	B	1	53
Heineman, John..........	1844	L	1	229
Heineman, Joseph.......	1830	E	1	237
Heiney, Jacob...........	1821	-	-	-
Heiney, Jacob, Sr......	1834	G	1	194
Heiney, John............	1824	B	1	140
Heintzelman, Peter, Esq.	1824	B	1	230
Heinzelman, Frederick...	1810	-	-	-
Heise, Emily B.L.......	1850	O	1	35
Heise, Nancy............	1838	I	1	65
Heise, Solomon..........	1784	-	-	-
Heiser, John...........	1824	B	1	168
Heisey, Anna............	1844	L	1	187
Heisey, Daniel..........	1823	B	1	65
Heisey, Elizabeth.......	1848	N	1	78
Heisey, Henry...........	1843	L	1	109
Heisey, Jacob...........	1825	C	1	140
Heisey, John............	1844	L	1	167
Heisey, Joseph..........	1843	L	1	111
Heisley, Conrad........	1788	-	-	-
Heiss, Jacob...........	1842	L	1	5
Heiss, Reigart..........	1773	-	-	-
Heistand, Henry........	1800	-	-	-
Heistand, Jacob........	1756	-	-	-
Heistand, Peter........	1846	M	1	159
Heistand, Peter, Sr.....	1846	M	1	201
Heitler, Christian......	1835	H	1	52
Heitler, Richard R......	1848	M	1	427
Heitzman, Mathias.......	1841	K	1	155
Held, George............	1767	-	-	-
Held, George Frederick..	1774	-	-	-
Heller, Catherine.......	1818	-	-	-
Heller, Emanuel.........	1814	-	-	-
Heller, Jacob, Jr......	1775	-	-	-
Helm, John..............	1749	-	-	-
Helm, John..............	1830	E	1	193
Helm, John, Jr..........	1831	F	1	42
Helm, Michael...........	1827	D	1	111
Helm, Michael...........	1830	E	1	256
Helman, John............	1823	B	1	55
Hemling, Casper.........	1815	-	-	-
Hemperill, Rudolph......	1763	-	-	-
Hendel, John............	1813	-	-	-
Henderson, Archibald,Esq	1799	-	-	-
Henderson, Barton.......	1823	B	1	82
Henderson, Dr. Daniel...	1847	M	1	413
Henderson, David........	1839	I	1	244
Henderson, Ebenezer.....	1805	-	-	-
Henderson, Elizabeth....	1838	I	1	93
Henderson, George.......	1838	I	1	37
Henderson, James........	1821	A	1	108
Henderson, John.........	1742	-	-	-
Henderson, Margaret.....	1832	F	1	255
Henderson, Mary A.......	1806	-	-	-
Henderson, Mathew.......	1824	B	1	139
Henderson, Mathew.......	1835	H	1	36
Henderson, Rachel.......	1807	-	-	-
Henderson, Samuel.......	1824	C	1	1
Henderson, Thomas, Jr...	1769	-	-	-
Henderson, Thomas.......	1788	-	-	-
Hendrick, Albert........	1732	-	-	-
Hendrick, George........	1775	-	-	-
Hendricks, James, Jr...	1730	-	-	-
Hendrickson, Okey, Esq..	1841	K	1	134
Hening, Jacob...........	1769	-	-	-
Henley, John............	1847	M	1	239
Henly, Catherine.......	1829	E	1	102
Henly, Jacob............	1822	A	1	126
Henly, Joseph..........	1822	A	1	124
Henneberger, Barbara....	1799	-	-	-
Henneberger, John.......	1752	-	-	-
Henneberger, Melchoir...	1767	-	-	-
Henry, Abraham..........	1807	-	-	-
Henry, Ann..............	1799	-	-	-
Henry, Benjamin W.......	1807	-	-	-
Henry, James............	1824	B	1	188
Henry, John.............	1777	-	-	-
Henry, Matthew..........	1810	-	-	-
Henry, Michael..........	1791	-	-	-
Henry, Patrick..........	1820	-	-	-
Henry, Patrick..........	1826	C	1	269
Henry, Peter............	1801	-	-	-
Henry, Richard..........	1799	-	-	-
Henry, Samuel...........	1816	-	-	-
Henry, William.........	1813	-	-	-
Hensel, Christopher.....	1846	M	1	133
Hensel, George..........	1825	C	1	17
Hensel, John............	1840	K	1	32
Henzelman, John.........	1804	-	-	-
Hepner, Godleib.........	1823	A	1	132
Herberger, John.........	1747	-	-	-
Herbolt, Paul...........	1750	-	-	-
Herbst, Peter...........	1847	M	1	326
Herclerode, Lawrence....	1804	-	-	-
Herford, Jane..........	1842	K	1	246
Hergelroth, Christian...	1826	C	1	149
Herman, John............	1750	-	-	-
Herman, John............	1781	-	-	-
Herner, Mathias.........	1741	-	-	-

Name	Year	Bk.	Vol	Page	Name	Year	Bk.	Vol	Page
Hernley, John............	1842	L	1	13	Hershey, Andrew.........	1840	I	1	300
Herold, George C.......	1749	-	-	-	Hershey, Anna..........	1833	G	1	94
Herr, Abraham..........	1799	-	-	-	Hershey, Benedict......	1762	-	-	-
Herr, Abraham..........	1805	-	-	-	Hershey, Benjamin......	1774	-	-	-
Herr, Abraham..........	1811	-	-	-	Hershey, Christian.....	1745	-	-	-
Herr, Abraham S........	1839	I	1	216	Hershey, Christian.....	1800	-	-	-
Herr, Adam..............	1831	F	1	89	Hershey, Christian.....	1827	D	1	74
Herr, Ann..............	1813	-	-	-	Hershey, Christian.....	1834	G	1	220
Herr, Anna.............	1825	C	1	63	Hershey, Christian.....	1845	M	1	46
Herr, Barbara..........	1846	M	1	114	Hershey, Elizabeth.....	1833	G	1	97
Herr, Benjamin.........	1825	C	1	62	Hershey, Esther........	1792	-	-	-
Herr, Benjamin.........	1834	G	1	169	Hershey, Henry.........	1838	I	1	94
Herr, Benjamin.........	1839	I	1	202	Hershey, Jacob.........	1755	-	-	-
Herr, Benjamin.........	1848	N	1	20	Hershey, John..........	1815	-	-	-
Herr, Catherine........	1830	E	1	248	Hershey, John..........	1831	F	1	70
Herr, Catherine........	1845	M	1	79	Hershey, John..........	1848	N	1	94
Herr, Catherine........	1850	O	1	30	Hershey, Joseph, Sr.....	1852	F	1	143
Herr, Christian........	1804	-	-	-	Hershey, Margaret......	1827	D	1	143
Herr, Christian........	1807	-	-	-	Hershey, Maria.........	1801	-	-	-
Herr, Christian........	1815	-	-	-	Hershey, Maria.........	1838	I	1	114
Herr, Christian........	1824	B	1	187	Hershey, Nancy.........	1849	N	1	177
Herr, Christian........	1834	G	1	260	Hershey, Peter.........	1822	A	1	135
Herr, Christian........	1846	M	1	110	Herter, Andrew.........	1757	-	-	-
Herr, Christian B......	1847	M	1	317	Herter, Elizabeth......	1826	C	1	219
Herr, Daniel...........	1816	-	-	-	Hertzler, Ann..........	1847	M	1	342
Herr, Daniel...........	1828	D	1	269	Hertzler, Barbara......	1832	F	1	264
Herr, David............	1849	M	1	145	Hertzler, Catherine.....	1846	M	1	138
Herr, Elizabeth........	1811	-	-	-	Hertzler, Jacob........	1848	M	1	436
Herr, Elizabeth........	1844	L	1	169	Hertzler, John.........	1804	-	-	-
Herr, Emanuel..........	1798	-	-	-	Hertzler, John.........	1837	H	1	241
Herr, Emanuel..........	1826	C	1	271	Herzog, Peter..........	1831	F	1	78
Herr, Eve..............	1844	L	1	232	Hess, Abraham..........	1820	-	-	-
Herr, Francis..........	1838	I	1	106	Hess, Abraham..........	1825	C	1	80
Herr, Henry............	1810	-	-	-	Hess, Abraham..........	1849	N	1	205
Herr, Jacob............	1801	-	-	-	Hess, Ann..............	1830	E	1	219
Herr, Jacob............	1819	-	-	-	Hess, Anna.............	1844	L	1	249
Herr, John.............	1825	C	1	8	Hess, Catherine........	1824	B	1	132
Herr, John, Sr.........	1827	D	1	43	Hess, Catherine........	1827	D	1	24
Herr, John.............	1831	F	1	44	Hess, Christian........	1842	L	1	1
Herr, John.............	1847	M	1	254	Hess, Christian........	1850	O	1	22
Herr, John.............	1848	N	1	102	Hess, Daniel...........	1840	K	1	33
Herr, Lydia............	1848	N	1	3	Hess, David............	1793	-	-	-
Herr, Magdalena........	1846	M	1	134	Hess, David............	1834	G	1	229
Herr, Maria............	1783	-	-	-	Hess, David............	1835	H	1	60
Herr, Martin...........	1821	-	-	-	Hess, David............	1839	I	1	289
Herr, Mary.............	1830	E	1	195	Hess, Esther...........	1836	H	1	171
Herr, Samuel...........	1837	H	1	217	Hess, George...........	1813	-	-	-
Herr, Samuel...........	1839	I	1	251	Hess, George...........	1837	H	1	242
Herr, Susanna..........	1831	F	1	5	Hess, Jacob............	1741	-	-	-
Herring, Thomas........	1747	-	-	-	Hess, Jacob............	1850	N	1	421
Hersh, Andrew..........	1808	-	-	-	Hess, John.............	1733	-	-	-
Hersh, George, Sr......	1842	K	1	317	Hess, John.............	1783	-	-	-
Hersh, Jacob...........	1835	H	1	2	Hess, John.............	1813	-	-	-
Hersh, Martin..........	1840	K	1	51	Hess, John.............	1823	A	1	279
Hersh, Peter...........	1835	H	1	77	Hess, John.............	1824	B	1	215
Hershberger, Abraham....	1828	D	1	170	Hess, John.............	1831	F	1	77
Hershberger, Barbara....	1821	A	1	91	Hess, John.............	1842	K	1	208
Hershberger, Jacob......	1801	-	-	-	Hess, John.............	1843	L	1	36
Hershberger, John......	1813	-	-	-	Hess, John, Jr.........	1844	L	1	230
Hershberger, Joseph.....	1770	-	-	-	Hess, Joshua...........	1832	F	1	186
Hershberger, Magdalena..	1772	-	-	-	Hess, Martin...........	1843	L	1	153
Hershberger, Magdalena..	1840	K	1	50	Hess, Mary.............	1837	I	1	16
Hershelroad, - ..	1746	-	-	-	Hess, Michael..........	1827	D	1	42
Hershelroadt, Joan E....	1752	-	-	-	Hess, Michael..........	1837	H	1	247
Hershelroth, Lorence...	1822	A	1	160	Hess, Philip...........	1813	-	-	-
Hersheroad, Catherine...	1776	-	-	-	Hess, Samuel...........	1821	-	-	-
Hershey, Abraham.......	1811	-	-	-	Hess, Veronica.........	1845	M	1	1
Hershey, Abraham, Sr...	1839	I	1	212	Hess, Veronica.........	1849	N	1	254
Hershey, Abraham.......	1844	L	1	176	Hessner, Adam..........	1789	-	-	-
Hershey, Abraham.......	1848	N	1	95	Hessner, Adam..........	1823	A	1	276
Hershey, Andrew........	1822	A	1	169	Hestenstein, Peter......	1829	E	1	93
Hershey, Andrew, Sr.....	1835	H	1	81	Hetzler, George.........	1783	-	-	-

Name	Year	Bk.	Vol	Page	Name	Year	Bk.	Vol	Page
Hetzler, George	1807	-	-	-	Hoerner, Andrew	1847	M	1	285
Hewes, Hannah	1819	-	-	-	Hoff, Margaret	1848	N	1	99
Hewes, Joseph	1841	K	1	177	Hoffellringer, Martin	1742	-	-	-
Heyne, Christopher	1781	-	-	-	Hoffer, Christian	1814	-	-	-
Hibble, Conrad(Hipple)..	1850	N	1	414	Hoffer, John	1765	-	-	-
Hibshman, Hannah	1823	B	1	66	Hoffer, Salome	1832	F	1	190
Hickman, Nickolas	1830	E	1	205	Hoffer, Samuel	1842	L	1	2
Hicks, Thomas	1802	-	-	-	Hoffert, Magdalena	1832	G	1	16
Hide, Benjamin	1800	-	-	-	Hoffman, Anna Maria	1767	-	-	-
Hiestand, Abraham	1772	-	-	-	Hoffman, Baltis	1804	-	-	-
Hiestand, Anna	1850	N	1	447	Hoffman, Christian	1821	A	1	101
Hiestand, Jacob	1847	M	1	417	Hoffman, Christian	1824	B	1	182
Hiestand, Peter	1820	-	-	-	Hoffman, Christian,Sr	1839	I	1	248
Higginbothom, Thomas	1733	-	-	-	Hoffman, Christopher	1823	B	1	121
Higgins, Alexander	1778	-	-	-	Hoffman, Daniel	1833	G	1	104
High, Elizabeth	1823	B	1	89	Hoffman, Elizabeth	1848	N	1	60
High, Elizabeth	1834	G	1	164	Hoffman, Esther	1848	N	1	118
High, John	1823	B	1	92	Hoffman, Frederick	1758	-	-	-
Hildebrand, Jacob	1798	-	-	-	Hoffman, George	1825	C	1	81
Hildebrand, Michael	1814	-	-	-	Hoffman, Henry	1755	-	-	-
Hill, Ann	1823	B	1	42	Hoffman, Henry	1799	-	-	-
Hill, Frederick	1821	A	1	31	Hoffman, Henry, Esq	1841	K	1	117
Hill, Gilbert	1850	O	1	11	Hoffman, Jacob	1784	-	-	-
Hill, Godleib	1821	-	-	-	Hoffman, Jacob	1821	A	1	92
Hill, John	1747	-	-	-	Hoffman, Jacob	1837	H	1	271
Hill, John	1841	K	1	87	Hoffman, Jacob	1842	K	1	248
Hill, Martha	1747	-	-	-	Hoffman, John	1817	-	-	-
Hill, Melchoir	1780	-	-	-	Hoffman, John	1829	E	1	139
Hill, Thomas	1815	-	-	-	Hoffman, John	1842	K	1	255
Hill, William	1783	-	-	-	Hoffman, John E.	1752	-	-	-
Hiller, Rudolph	1734	-	-	-	Hoffman, Michael	1752	-	-	-
Hilt, Philip	1824	B	1	181	Hoffman, Michael	1782	-	-	-
Hilton, Edward	1824	B	1	180	Hoffman, Philip	1750	-	-	-
Himbich, Anna Maria	1779	-	-	-	Hoffman, Philip	1831	F	1	130
Himes, Reese C	1849	N	1	227	Hoffman, Philip	1849	N	1	173
Hindman, John	1748	-	-	-	Hoffman, Samuel	1848	N	1	129
Hinkle, Barbara	1810	-	-	-	Hoffman, Sebastian	1821	-	-	-
Hinkle, Henry	1800	-	-	-	Hoffman, Valentine	1767	-	-	-
Hinkle, John	1839	I	1	246	Hoffman, Valentine	1801	-	-	-
Hinkle, William	1819	-	-	-	Hoge, John	1749	-	-	-
Hinkson, Robert	1749	-	-	-	Hogendobler, Nickolas	1768	-	-	-
Hipple, Henry	1804	-	-	-	Hogendobler, Susanna	1845	M	1	41
Hipple, Jacob	1828	D	1	179	Hogentogler, Elizabeth..	1823	B	1	48
Hipple, Mary M	1834	G	1	201	Hogentogler, Elizabeth..	1824	B	1	229
Hirsh, Catherine	1810	-	-	-	Hogentogler, John	1849	N	1	170
Hirsh, Jacob	1792	-	-	-	Hohn, Peter	1774	-	-	-
Hitz, Benjamin	1809	-	-	-	Hoke, Adam	1768	-	-	-
Hitz, Benjamin	1810	-	-	-	Hoke, Andrew	1762	-	-	-
Hoak, Catherine	1845	M	1	42	Hoke, Catherine	1820	-	-	-
Hoak, Henry	1814	-	-	-	Hoke, John	1840	K	1	59
Hoak, Jacob	1831	F	1	63	Holdiman, Peter	1731	-	-	-
Hoak, John	1844	M	1	53	Holdrie, Peter	1813	-	-	-
Hoak, John	1845	M	1	54	Holdry, George	1816	-	-	-
Hoak, Sarah	1847	M	1	263	Holl, Catherine	1830	E	1	191
Hoar, Adam	1739	-	-	-	Holl, Christopher	1760	-	-	-
Hoar, Isaac	1802	-	-	-	Holl, Elizabeth	1829	E	1	54
Hoar, Jonas	1841	K	1	193	Holl, Elizabeth	1830	E	1	169
Hoar, Jonathan	1850	N	1	452	Holl, Hannah	1844	L	1	213
Hoar, Joseph	1817	-	-	-	Holl, Isaac	1829	E	1	58
Hoar, Joshua	1833	F	1	18	Holl, John	1829	E	1	36
Hoar, Mary	1805	-	-	-	Holl, John, Jr	1829	E	1	53
Hoar, William	1847	M	1	399	Holl, Joseph	1786	-	-	-
Hobsh, Joseph	1788	-	-	-	Holl, Levi	1844	L	1	198
Hoch, Daniel	1815	-	-	-	Holl, Levi	1850	N	1	321
Hoch, George	1811	-	-	-	Holl, Nickolas	1777	-	-	-
Hoch, Martin	1804	-	-	-	Holland, Peter M	1846	M	1	132
Hocker, Frederick	1812	-	-	-	Hollinger, Barbara	1831	F	1	133
Hodding, Thomas	1819	-	-	-	Hollinger, Daniel	1775	-	-	-
Hoe, Catherine	1849	N	1	203	Hollinger, Daniel	1822	A	1	158
Hoeffer, William	1830	E	1	204	Hollinger, George, Esq.	1825	C	1	93
Hoellouer, Philip	1757	-	-	-	Hollinger, Mary	1846	M	1	216
Hoenix, John	1802	-	-	-	Hollinger, Thomas	1834	G	1	158

Name	Year	Bk.	Vol	Page	Name	Year	Bk.	Vol	Page
Holmes, Abraham.........	1778	-	-	-	Hostetter, Abraham......	1834	G	1	226
Holmes, William.........	1787	-	-	-	Hostetter, Abraham......	1836	H	1	201
Holsapple, Jacob........	1795	-	-	-	Hostetter, Abraham......	1838	I	1	109
Holson, Thomas..........	1815	-	-	-	Hostetter, Abraham......	1843	L	1	119
Holstower, Leonard......	1757	-	-	-	Hostetter, Ann..........	1817	-	-	-
Holtry, Samuel..........	1806	-	-	-	Hostetter, Jacob........	1789	-	-	-
Holtzapple, Leonard.....	1837	H	1	257	Hostetter, Jacob........	1814	-	-	-
Holtzbaum, Andrew.......	1763	-	-	-	Hostetter, Jacob........	1823	B	1	125
Holtzhauer, Frederick...	1795	-	-	-	Hostetter, Magdalena....	1844	L	1	284
Holtzward, John C.......	1823	B	1	117	Hostetter, Maria........	1832	F	1	195
Holzinger, Conrad, Sr...	1828	D	1	246	Hostetter, Oswald.......	1749	-	-	-
Homsher, David..........	1844	L	1	259	Hottenstein, Henry......	1831	F	1	54
Hoober, Jacob...........	1794	-	-	-	Hottenstein, John......	1813	-	-	-
Hoober, John............	1825	C	1	91	Hougendobler, John......	1839	I	1	259
Hoober, Ulrich..........	1757	-	-	-	Hough, Richard..........	1746	-	-	-
Hook, George............	1787	-	-	-	Houn, George............	1777	-	-	-
Hoover, Abraham.........	1828	D	1	268	Houseal, Lydia..........	1845	L	1	319
Hoover, Barbara.........	1810	-	-	-	Householder, Jacob......	1814	-	-	-
Hoover, Catherine.......	1843	L	1	115	Householder, Margaret...	1807	-	-	-
Hoover, Catherine.......	1845	L	1	308	Housekeeper, Joshua.....	1822	A	1	125
Hoover, Christian.......	1747	-	-	-	Housekeeper, Thomas.....	1782	-	-	-
Hoover, Christian.......	1804	-	-	-	Houser, Ann.............	1814	-	-	-
Hoover, David, Jr.......	1847	M	1	357	Houser, Barbara.........	1801	-	-	-
Hoover, Jacob...........	1809	-	-	-	Houser, Catherine.......	1798	-	-	-
Hoover, John............	1843	L	1	135	Houser, George.........	1837	H	1	270
Hoover, Joseph..........	1826	C	1	220	Houser, Jacob...........	1767	-	-	-
Hoover, Joseph..........	1834	G	1	224	Houser, Jacob...........	1793	-	-	-
Hoover, Joseph..........	1847	M	1	336	Houston, Horatio M......	1839	I	1	239
Hoover, Joseph..........	1848	N	1	83	Houston, James.........	1779	-	-	-
Hoover, Joseph..........	1850	N	1	437	Houston, James.........	1809	-	-	-
Hoover, Margaret........	1751	-	-	-	Houston, John...........	1809	-	-	-
Hoover, Mathias.........	1837	H	1	221	Houston, Samuel.........	1842	L	1	7
Hopkins, James, Esq.....	1834	G	1	219	Houtz, John.............	1834	G	1	244
Hopkins, John...........	1764	-	-	-	Hover, Christopher......	1777	-	-	-
Hopkins, John R.........	1817	-	-	-	Hoverter, Henry.........	1818	-	-	-
Hopkins, Sarah..........	1778	-	-	-	Howard, Henry...........	1791	-	-	-
Hopkins, Washington,Esq.	1833	G	1	73	Howard, William........	1765	-	-	-
Horn, Christian.........	1803	-	-	-	Howell, Daniel.........	1748	-	-	-
Horn, Frederick.........	1747	-	-	-	Howell, John............	1812	-	-	-
Horn, George............	1820	-	-	-	Howerter, George.......	1805	-	-	-
Horn, John..............	1814	-	-	-	Howett, James..........	1820	-	-	-
Horn, Michael...........	1781	-	-	-	Howry, Jacob...........	1803	-	-	-
Hornberger, Stephen.....	1781	-	-	-	Howry, John............	1737	-	-	-
Hornberger, Stephen.....	1816	-	-	-	Howry, John, Jr........	1791	-	-	-
Hornberger, Susanna.....	1842	K	1	289	Howry, John............	1811	-	-	-
Horncomb, Henry.........	1833	G	1	24	Howry, John, Jr........	1829	E	1	24
Horner, Joseph..........	1847	M	1	363	Howry, John............	1829	E	1	43
Horning, Anna...........	1752	-	-	-	Howser, Philip.........	1786	-	-	-
Horning, Elizabeth......	1778	-	-	-	Hoydler, Anthony.......	1742	-	-	-
Horning, Michael........	1814	-	-	-	Hoyer, John F..........	1748	-	-	-
Horning, Wendel.........	1776	-	-	-	Hoyle, Henry...........	1749	-	-	-
Horsh, George...........	1777	-	-	-	Hoyt, Robert...........	1805	-	-	-
Horsh, George...........	1783	-	-	-	Hoyt, Sarah............	1846	M	1	174
Horsh, Mary.............	1782	-	-	-	Huber, Abraham.........	1790	-	-	-
Horst, Christian.......	1818	-	-	-	Huber, Abraham(Strasburg	1812	-	-	-
Horst, Christian.......	1823	A	1	285	Huber, Abraham(Warwick).	1814	-	-	-
Horst, Christian.......	1831	F	1	112	Huber, Abraham.........	1816	-	-	-
Horst, David...........	1824	B	1	155	Huber, Ann.............	1841	K	1	167
Horst, John, Sr........	1828	D	1	239	Huber, Anna............	1813	-	-	-
Horst, John............	1837	H	1	256	Huber, Anna............	1832	F	1	194
Horst, Maria...........	1828	D	1	171	Huber, Barbara.........	1841	K	1	142
Horst, Martin..........	1781	-	-	-	Huber, Christian.......	1814	-	-	-
Horst, Mary............	1794	-	-	-	Huber, Christian.......	1818	-	-	-
Horst, Mary............	1842	K	1	311	Huber, Christian.......	1830	E	1	252
Horst, Michael.........	1835	G	1	273	Huber, Christian.......	1849	N	1	307
Horst, Michael.........	1839	I	1	186	Huber, David...........	1795	-	-	-
Horting, Christian.....	1802	-	-	-	Huber, David, Jr.......	1823	B	1	16
Horting, Margaret......	1810	-	-	-	Huber, David...........	1832	F	1	262
Horting, Sarah.........	1835	H	1	39	Huber, Frederick.......	1781	-	-	-
Hossler, Jacob.........	1810	-	-	-	Huber, George.........	1763	-	-	-
Hostetter, Abraham.....	1831	F	1	36	Huber, George.........	1789	-	-	-
Hostetter, Abraham.....	1834	G	1	153	Huber, George.........	1849	N	1	309

Name	Year	Bk.	Vol	Page	Name	Year	Bk.	Vol	Page
Huber, Henry	1830	F	1	1	Hunter, Henry	1733	-	-	-
Huber, Henry	1833	G	1	36	Hunter, John	1760	-	-	-
Huber, Jacob	1743	-	-	-	Hunter, Robert	1834	G	1	240
Huber, Jacob	1804	-	-	-	Hunter, William	1828	E	1	5
Huber, Jacob	1834	G	1	182	Hurrah, Christiana	1824	B	1	239
Huber, John, Jr	1784	-	-	-	Hursh, Jacob	1757	-	-	-
Huber, John	1810	-	-	-	Hurst, Henry	1840	I	1	308
Huber, John	1815	-	-	-	Huss, David	1809	-	-	-
Huber, John, Esq	1826	C	1	212	Huss, David	1830	E	1	168
Huber, John	1837	H	1	292	Huss, John	1841	K	1	158
Huber, John George	1749	-	-	-	Huston, John	1749	-	-	-
Huber, John Ulrich	1775	-	-	-	Huston, John, Esq	1829	E	1	35
Huber, Joseph	1805	-	-	-	Hutchinson, James, Jr	1784	-	-	-
Huber, Mary	1826	C	1	200	Hutchinson, John	1765	-	-	-
Huber, Mathias	1805	-	-	-	Hutchinson, Samuel	1760	-	-	-
Huber, Michael	1774	-	-	-	Hutten, Kersey	1836	H	1	137
Huber, Michael	1812	-	-	-	Hutten, Reuben	1845	M	1	77
Huber, Peter	1850	O	1	23	Hutton, Sarah	1839	I	1	221
Huber, Philip	1784	-	-	-	Huver, Henry	1777	-	-	-
Huber, Rosina	1825	C	1	132	Hyde, William	1748	-	-	-
Huber, Samuel	1796	-	-	-	Hyne, Herman	1748	-	-	-
Huber, Ulrich	1775	-	-	-	Hyse, Elizabeth(Heiss)	1775	-	-	-
Huber, Ulrich	1783	-	-	-	Hysinger, John	1843	L	1	117
Hubley, Adam	1811	-	-	-	Hytler, Christian	1762	-	-	-
Hubley, Bernard	1838	I	1	118	**I**				
Hubley, Frederick D	1828	D	1	258	Ienish, Christian	1841	K	1	127
Hubley, George	1781	-	-	-	Ietter, Michael	1841	K	1	204
Hubley, Jacob	1844	L	1	219	Ihling, Christopher	1824	B	1	234
Hubley, John, Esq	1821	A	1	26	Ihling, John	1828	D	1	201
Hubley, John, Esq	1824	B	1	197	Illig, George	1804	-	-	-
Hubley, John, Jr	1827	D	1	67	Illig, George, Esq	1830	E	1	227
Hubley, John	1848	N	1	113	Illing, Frederick	1800	-	-	-
Hubley, Joseph	1796	-	-	-	Iman, Ulrich	1765	-	-	-
Hubley, Mary	1829	E	1	161	Imble, Jacob	1737	-	-	-
Hudders, John	1833	G	1	92	Immel, Jacob	1801	-	-	-
Hudson, Alice	1821	A	1	51	Ingram, Archibold	1822	A	1	208
Hudson, George, Jr	1747	-	-	-	Innis, James	1778	-	-	-
Hudson, Margaret	1761	-	-	-	Innold, David	1826	C	1	168
Hudson, William	1754	-	-	-	Irwin, Alexander	1781	-	-	-
Hudson, William	1785	-	-	-	Irwin, David	1748	-	-	-
Huey, Ephriam	1747	-	-	-	Irwin, Ezekel	1804	-	-	-
Huey, Samuel	1759	-	-	-	Irwin, Henry	1815	-	-	-
Huffnagle, Michael	1844	L	1	246	Irwin, Isaac	1785	-	-	-
Hughes, Catherine	1841	K	1	95	Irwin, Isaac	1831	F	1	59
Hughes, Edward	1783	-	-	-	Irwin, Jesse	1827	D	1	49
Hughes, Evan	1760	-	-	-	Irwin, John	1742	-	-	-
Hughes, James	1761	-	-	-	Irwin, Mathew	1800	-	-	-
Hughes, James	1809	-	-	-	Irwin, Samuel	1822	A	1	232
Hughes, James	1816	-	-	-	Irwin, Samuel	1842	K	1	286
Hughes, John	1743	-	-	-	Irwyn, William	1738	-	-	-
Hugins, John	1739	-	-	-	Isaac, Charles	1746	-	-	-
Huhn, Nickolas	1843	L	1	74	**J**				
Hull, John	1752	-	-	-	Jackson, Ann	1850	N	1	337
Hull, Sophia	1797	-	-	-	Jackson, David	1811	-	-	-
Humer, Abraham	1806	-	-	-	Jackson, Edward	1802	-	-	-
Humes, John	1828	E	1	13	Jackson, Hugh	1839	I	1	236
Humes, Robert	1828	E	1	12	Jackson, John	1809	-	-	-
Humes, Thomas	1784	-	-	-	Jackson, Mary	1822	A	1	198
Hummel, Christian	1832	F	1	205	Jackson, M. Lamar	1848	N	1	134
Hummel, Michael	1792	-	-	-	Jackson, Samuel	1748	-	-	-
Hummer, Abram	1846	M	1	115	Jacobs, Coleman R	1835	G	1	70
Hummer, Jacob	1838	I	1	148	Jacobs, Edward	1832	F	1	230
Hummer, John	1847	M	1	381	Jacobs, Joseph	1793	-	-	-
Hummer, John F	1850	M	1	455	Jacobs, Samuel	1840	I	1	303
Hummer, Peter, Jr	1787	-	-	-	Jacobs, Samuel O	1836	H	1	126
Hunsaker, Samuel	1782	-	-	-	Jago, John	1790	-	-	-
Hunshberger, Abraham	1785	-	-	-	Jameson, Samuel	1772	-	-	-
Hunsicker, Samuel, Jr	1829	E	1	30	Jamison, John	1733	-	-	-
Hunt, Henry	1742	-	-	-	Jamison, John	1783	-	-	-
Hunt, John	1749	-	-	-	Jamison, John	1794	-	-	-
Hunt, Peter	1770	-	-	-	Jamison, Margaret	1842	K	1	268
Hunter, Alexander	1760	-	-	-	Jefferes, Isaiah	1821	A	1	115

Name	Year	Bk.	Vol	Page	Name	Year	Bk.	Vol	Page
Jefferies, Jacob D......	1835	H	1	87	Jones, William..........	1814	-	-	-
Jefferies, John........	1822	A	1	177	Jones, William..........	1850	N	1	440
Jefferies, Joseph......	1833	G	1	85	Jordan, Alexander.......	1758	-	-	-
Jefferies, Joseph......	1833	G	1	112	Jordan, Casper..........	1821	A	1	93
Jefferies, Mary........	1831	F	1	102	Jordan, Elis............	1802	-	-	-
Jeffries, Emma.........	1808	-	-	-	Jordon, John............	1815	-	-	-
Jegger, Henry..........	1748	-	-	-	Joseph, Martin..........	1747	-	-	-
Jenish, Christian......	1841	K	1	127	Judin, Eve Barbara......	1775	-	-	-
Jenkins, David.........	1816	-	-	-	Judy, Jacob (Tshudy)....	1811	-	-	-
Jenkins, David.........	1850	N	1	404	Judy, Michael (Tshudy)..	1832	F	1	193
Jenkins, Elizabeth.....	1825	C	1	45	Judye, Robert...........	1751	-	-	-
Jenkins, George........	1836	H	1	211	Jutz, Anthony...........	1781	-	-	-
Jenkins, Isaac.........	1782	-	-	-	**K**				
Jenkins, John.........	1787	-	-	-	Kaffman, Abraham.......	1826	C	1	175
Jenkins, Robert.......	1848	N	1	107	Kaffroad, Henry........	1814	-	-	-
Jenkins, Ruth..........	1794	-	-	-	Kaffroth, Peter........	1753	-	-	-
Jenkins, Thomas.......	1824	B	1	158	Kafroth, George........	1849	N	1	244
Jenkins, William......	1834	G	1	247	Kafroth, Henry				
Jervis, Joseph.........	1752	-	-	-	(see Cuffroth).......	1803	-	-	-
Jetter, Michael........	1841	K	1	204	Kagense, Michael........	1829	E	1	110
Jingles, James........	1749	-	-	-	Kalkleser, John Henry...	1748	-	-	-
Joab, Jacob............	1745	-	-	-	Kameally, Christopher...	1798	-	-	-
Job, Jeremiah..........	1769	-	-	-	Kammerer, Mathias.......	1772	-	-	-
Johns, Abraham.........	1829	E	1	126	Kann, Peter.............	1808	-	-	-
Johns, Abraham.........	1848	N	1	62	Kapp, Anthony...........	1825	C	1	71
Johns, Catherine......	1827	D	1	129	Kapp, Feit..............	1785	-	-	-
Johns, Christian......	1741	-	-	-	Kappes, Christiana......	1793	-	-	-
Johns, Daniel..........	1837	H	1	224	Kappis, Abraham.........	1829	E	1	25
Johns, David...........	1850	N	1	406	Kauffman, Abraham.......	1822	A	1	166
Johns, John Sr.........	1831	F	1	55	Kauffman, Adam..........	1827	D	1	113
Johns, John...........	1848	N	1	54	Kauffman, Adam..........	1829	E	1	120
Johns, Levi............	1831	F	1	123	Kauffman, Andrew				
Johns, Mary............	1830	E	1	265	(See Coffman).......	1744	-	-	-
Johns, Peter...........	1837	I	1	22	Kauffman, Andrew.......	1795	-	-	-
Johnson, Barbara.......	1830	E	1	232	Kauffman, Andrew.......	1821	A	1	63
Johnson, Catherine.....	1846	M	1	122	Kauffman, Andrew.......	1828	D	1	261
Johnson, Daniel........	1847	M	1	307	Kauffman, Andrew.......	1837	H	1	253
Johnson, Elizabeth.....	1803	-	-	-	Kauffman, Andrew B.....	1847	M	1	246
Johnson, Guy...........	1831	F	1	97	Kauffman, Andrew M.....	1838	I	1	122
Johnson, Hannah........	1844	L	1	261	Kauffman, Catharine.....	1796	-	-	-
Johnson, James.........	1734	-	-	-	Kauffman, Christian.....	1817	-	-	-
Johnson, John..........	1804	-	-	-	Kauffman, Christian.....	1828	D	1	198
Johnson, John.........	1836	H	1	160	Kauffman, David.........	1793	-	-	-
Johnson, John N.......	1842	K	1	260	Kauffman, David.........	1815	-	-	-
Johnson, Mark..........	1816	-	-	-	Kauffman, David.........	1839	I	1	227
Johnson, Michael R.....	1835	H	1	34	Kauffman, David.........	1846	M	1	111
Johnson, Patrick.......	1756	-	-	-	Kauffman, David.........	1847	M	1	385
Johnson, Richard.......	1827	D	1	84	Kauffman, Elizabeth.....	1835	H	1	90
Johnson, Samuel A......	1839	I	1	285	Kauffman, Elizabeth.....	1845	L	1	321
Johnston, Francis......	1850	N	1	370	Kauffman, Feronica......	1829	E	1	130
Johnston, Gain.........	1761	-	-	-	Kauffman, Henry.........	1785	-	-	-
Johnston, James........	1817	-	-	-	Kauffman, Henry.........	1847	M	1	366
Johnston, Michael......	1783	-	-	-	Kauffman, Jacob.........	1776	-	-	-
Johnston, Samuel.......	1846	M	1	121	Kauffman, Jacob.........	1822	A	1	234
Johnston, Dr. Samuel A..	1846	M	1	117	Kauffman, Jacob.........	1838	I	1	43
Johnston, Thomas.......	1850	N	1	373	Kauffman, Jacob.........	1847	M	1	237
Jones, Asa.............	1849	N	1	169	Kauffman, John..........	1777	-	-	-
Jones, Caleb...........	1826	C	1	147	Kauffman, John..........	1802	-	-	-
Jones, Caleb...........	1827	D	1	25	Kauffman, John..........	1804	-	-	-
Jones, David...........	1762	-	-	-	Kauffman, John..........	1812	-	-	-
Jones, Isaac...........	1810	-	-	-	Kauffman, John..........	1822	A	1	163
Jones, Jacob...........	1840	K	1	49	Kauffman, John Jr......	1825	C	1	22
Jones, Jacob...........	1846	M	1	143	Kauffman, John..........	1829	E	1	108
Jones, James...........	1828	D	1	250	Kauffman, John..........	1833	G	1	88
Jones, Jennet..........	1758	-	-	-	Kauffman, John..........	1839	I	1	288
Jones, John...........	1785	-	-	-	Kauffman, John..........	1844	L	1	243
Jones, John...........	1814	-	-	-	Kauffman, John..........	1845	M	1	7
Jones, John W..........	1842	K	1	293	Kauffman, John..........	1846	M	1	150
Jones, Mary Ann........	1849	N	1	186	Kauffman, John..........	1847	M	1	362
Jones, Polly..........	1838	I	1	98	Kauffman, Joseph........	1811	-	-	-
Jones, Robert..........	1785	-	-	-	Kauffman, Joseph........	1824	B	1	190
Jones, William.........	1748	-	-	-	Kauffman, Mary Ann......	1837	I	1	28

Name	Year	Bk.	Vol	Page	Name	Year	Bk.	Vol	Page
Kauffman, Michael	1825	C	1	107	Kendig, Abraham	1850	N	1	310
Kauffman, Dr. Michael	1839	I	1	228	Kendig, Alice	1823	B	1	58
Kauffman, Samuel	1806	-	-	-	Kendig, Catharine	1824	B	1	238
Kauffman, Stephen	1849	N	1	197	Kendig, Christian	1807	-	-	-
Kaufroth, Leah	1843	L	1	60	Kendig, Christian	1827	D	1	23
Kautz, John	1846	M	1	116	Kendig, David	1828	D	1	177
Kautz, Philip	1818	-	-	-	Kendig, Elizabeth	1828	D	1	286
Kean, Daniel	1848	N	1	73	Kendig, Esther	1835	H	1	51
Kearns, William	1756	-	-	-	Kendig, Fanny	1845	M	1	84
Keck, Charles	1781	-	-	-	Kendig, Fanny	1845	M	1	93
Keebler, George	1751	-	-	-	Kendig, George	1824	B	1	134
Keecher, Jacob	1785	-	-	-	Kendig, George	1850	N	1	409
Keefe, James	1805	-	-	-	Kendig, Henry	1772	-	-	-
Keel, George	1849	N	1	213	Kendig, Henry	1809	-	-	-
Keemer, James	1818	-	-	-	Kendig, Henry	1818	-	-	-
Keener, John	1759	-	-	-	Kendig, Henry	1823	B	1	104
Keener, Peter	1757	-	-	-	Kendig, Henry	1827	D	1	22
Keener, Philip	1785	-	-	-	Kendig, Henry	1849	N	1	155
Keeports, Christian	1825	C	1	110	Kendig, Hettie	1836	H	1	180
Keeports, Daniel	1847	M	1	314	Kendig, John	1771	-	-	-
Keeports, Joseph	1836	H	1	105	Kendig, John	1806	-	-	-
Keese, James	1786	-	-	-	Kendig, John	1810	-	-	-
Keesey, Joseph	1828	E	1	2	Kendig, John	1822	A	1	240
Keff, Owen	1761	-	-	-	Kendig, John	1837	I	1	23
Kegereise, Jacob	1829	E	1	82	Kendig, John	1837	I	1	25
Keggerise, Michael	1792	-	-	-	Kendig, John	1837	I	1	26
Kehler, Andrew	1815	-	-	-	Kendig, John	1844	L	1	242
Kehler, Mary E.	1812	-	-	-	Kendig, John	1849	N	1	250
Keifer, Elizabeth	1847	M	1	292	Kendig, Martin	1822	A	1	202
Keiffer, Moses	1847	M	1	288	Kendig, Martin	1828	D	1	209
Keigler, John	1823	A	1	289	Kendig, Martin	1834	G	1	235
Keimer, James	1821	A	1	105	Kendig, Martin	1846	M	1	139
Keis, Peter	1750	-	-	-	Kendig, Martin	1849	N	1	172
Keiser, John	1818	-	-	-	Kendig, Mary	1830	E	1	239
Keiser, Michael	1817	-	-	-	Kendig, Michael	1843	L	1	92
Keiser, Ulrich	1805	-	-	-	Kendig, Susan	1847	M	1	302
Keiss, Andrew	1802	-	-	-	Kendrick, Christian	1765	-	-	-
Keiss, Jacob A	1821	A	1	68	Kendrick, Elizabeth	1789	-	-	-
Keith, Balthaser	1842	K	1	279	Kendrick, Henry	1787	-	-	-
Kelin, Abraham	1800	-	-	-	Kendrick, John	1822	A	1	137
Kelker, Rudolph	1812	-	-	-	Kendrick, Martin	1783	-	-	-
Keller, Christian	1850	N	1	438	Keneagy, Henry	1848	M	1	445
Keller, Frederick	1771	-	-	-	Kenigmacher, Dr. Jacob	1839	I	1	256
Keller, George	1794	-	-	-	Kenin, Romin	1760	-	-	-
Keller, Godleib	1801	-	-	-	Kennedy, Ann	1790	-	-	-
Keller, John	1752	-	-	-	Kennedy, James	1767	-	-	-
Keller, John	1825	C	1	83	Kennedy, John	1781	-	-	-
Keller, John	1828	D	1	204	Kennedy, John	1816	-	-	-
Keller, John	1850	N	1	403	Kennedy, Sarah	1784	-	-	-
Keller, Magdalena	1825	C	1	115	Kennedy, William	1782	-	-	-
Keller, Martin	1772	-	-	-	Kenney, James	1804	-	-	-
Keller, Mary	1828	D	1	205	Kenny, John	1812	-	-	-
Keller, Peter	1824	B	1	136	Kensel, Mauris	1840	K	1	78
Kelly, Andrew	1760	-	-	-	Kenworthy, Joshua	1746	-	-	-
Kelly, Dennis	1849	N	1	211	Kepfert, George	1743	-	-	-
Kelly, Edward	1786	-	-	-	Keppele, Henry	1811	-	-	-
Kelly, Edward	1829	E	1	148	Keppelee, John	1804	-	-	-
Kelly, Elizabeth	1798	-	-	-	Kepple, John	1826	D	1	7
Kelly, John	1758	-	-	-	Kepplinger, Jacob	1811	-	-	-
Kelly, Michael	1826	C	1	213	Kepplinger, Leonard	1838	I	1	97
Kelly, Patrick	1799	-	-	-	Kerber, Casper	1748	-	-	-
Kelly, Thomas	1800	-	-	-	Kergher, Feronica	1788	-	-	-
Kelly, William	1777	-	-	-	Kerhart, Valentine	1764	-	-	-
Kelly, William	1794	-	-	-	Kerll, John	1767	-	-	-
Kelly, William	1824	B	1	206	Kern, Barbara	1813	-	-	-
Kelton, John	1762	-	-	-	Kern, Barbara	1849	N	1	207
Kemberling, John	1766	-	-	-	Kern, Christopher	1804	-	-	-
Kemerer, Elizabeth	1820	-	-	-	Kern, David	1824	C	1	5
Kemerer, Peter	1837	I	1	1	Kern, Henry	1845	L	1	315
Kemper, Dietrich W.	1840	K	1	63	Kerns, Eli	1848	N	1	64
Kemper, John	1816	-	-	-	Kerns, Jacob	1825	C	1	129
Kempf, Vernon	1833	G	1	113	Kerns, Margaret	1810	-	-	-

Name	Year	Bk.	Vol	Page	Name	Year	Bk.	Vol	Page
Kerr, George	1734	-	-	-	Kinsey, Daniel	1821	A	1	73
Kerr, John	1778	-	-	-	Kinsh, Joseph	1834	G	1	165
Kerr, William	1783	-	-	-	Kinsler, David	1766	-	-	-
Kerr, William	1815	-	-	-	Kintzer, Jacob	1810	-	-	-
Kerr, William	1821	A	1	47	Kintzinger, Abraham	1749	-	-	-
Kesell, William	1748	-	-	-	Kintzinger, Daniel	1785	-	-	-
Kessler, John	1850	N	1	357	Kintzley, Rudy	1752	-	-	-
Kessler, Mary	1833	G	1	81	Kinzer, George	1834	G	1	255
Kettle, Peter	1766	-	-	-	Kinzer, William P.	1846	M	1	169
Key, William	1749	-	-	-	Kipp, George Sr	1826	C	1	175
Kiesey, Elizabeth	1832	F	1	173	Kirchenman, Mary	1824	B	1	203
Kiesy, Jacob	1749	-	-	-	Kirk, Andrew	1746	-	-	-
Kile, Joseph	1804	-	-	-	Kirk, Jacob	1743	-	-	-
Kilhefer, Christian	1784	-	-	-	Kirk, Jacob	1820	-	-	-
Kilheffer, Henry	1826	C	1	207	Kirkpatrick, Archibald	1814	-	-	-
Kilheffer, John	1826	C	1	256	Kirkpatrick, John	1814	-	-	-
Kilheffer, Maria	1834	G	1	166	Kirkpatrick, Samuel	1744	-	-	-
Kilhefler, John	1822	A	1	191	Kirkpatrick, William	1836	H	1	169
Kilhover, Henry	1763	-	-	-	Kish, John	1783	-	-	-
Killgore, Alexander	1793	-	-	-	Kissel, Henry	1766	-	-	-
Killhefer, Elizabeth	1794	-	-	-	Kissinger, Andrew	1760	-	-	-
Killhefer, Peter	1821	-	-	-	Kissinger, Jacob	1802	-	-	-
Killheffer, Christian	1847	M	1	230	Kissinger, Mary	1831	F	1	127
Killian, Abraham	1828	D	1	282	Kissinger, Philip	1781	-	-	-
Killian, Charles	1826	C	1	243	Kistler, John	1778	-	-	-
Killian, Christian	1738	-	-	-	Kitch, Michael	1741	-	-	-
Killian, Curtis	1839	I	1	265	Kitzmiller, Jacob	1748	-	-	-
Killian, Elizabeth	1822	A	1	189	Kizer, John	1849	N	1	285
Killian, Jacob	1839	I	1	254	Klantz, Thomas	1782	-	-	-
Killian, John	1784	-	-	-	Klap, Henry	1847	M	1	266
Killian, John	1824	B	1	207	Klare, Frederick	1836	H	1	214
Killian, Susan	1846	M	1	95	Klare, John	1843	L	1	162
Killough, John	1820	-	-	-	Klare, Samuel	1833	G	1	87
Killough, Samuel	1836	H	1	181	Kleim, George	1810	-	-	-
Kilpatrick, Alexander	1828	E	1	9	Klein, John	1788	-	-	-
Kilpatrick, Margaret M.	1845	L	1	304	Klein, John D.	1784	-	-	-
Kimble, John S.	1848	N	1	138	Klein, Michael	1781	-	-	-
Kimble, William	1849	N	1	162	Klein, Peter	1784	-	-	-
Kimmel, Adam	1778	-	-	-	Kleisinger, Ludwig	1764	-	-	-
Kimmel, Ann	1850	N	1	344	Kleiss, Elizabeth	1826	C	1	169
Kimmel, Eve	1783	-	-	-	Kleiss, John	1812	-	-	-
Kimmel, Jacob Jr	1814	-	-	-	Kleiss, John	1836	H	1	140
Kimmel, Valentine	1768	-	-	-	Kleiss, Margaret	1821	A	1	1
Kinch, Jacob Jr	1834	G	1	264	Kleiss, Philip	1806	-	-	-
Kindig, Daniel	1848	M	1	426	Kleman, John Adam	1770	-	-	-
Kindig, Henry	1736	-	-	-	Klepper, Nicholas	1832	F	1	219
Kindig, Jacob	1735	-	-	-	Klick, Hans Conrad				
King, Ann	1805	-	-	-	(see Click)	1760	-	-	-
King, Catharine	1839	I	1	241	Klicken, Susanna	1766	-	-	-
King, David	1840	I	1	304	Kline, Anthony	1819	-	-	-
King, Frederick	1793	-	-	-	Kline, Henry	1782	-	-	-
King, George	1834	G	1	216	Kline, Henry	1821	A	1	49
King, George	1842	K	1	214	Kline, Jacob	1813	-	-	-
King, George	1842	K	1	217	Kline, Jacob	1826	C	1	172
King, Henry	1745	-	-	-	Kline, Jacob	1827	D	1	125
King, Jacob	1775	-	-	-	Kline, Jacob	1836	H	1	142
King, James	1796	-	-	-	Kline, John	1817	-	-	-
King, James	1824	B	1	236	Kline, John	1826	C	1	284
King, James	1825	C	1	56	Kline, Leman	1803	-	-	-
King, Michael	1770	-	-	-	Kline, Mary	1829	E	1	111
King, Dr. Ruben	1821	A	1	72	Kline, Michael				
King, Samuel	1833	G	1	66	(see Cline)	1740	-	-	-
Kingrich, Elizabeth	1783	-	-	-	Kline, Michael	1805	-	-	-
Kinhead, John	1832	F	1	265	Kline, Peter(see Clyne)	1761	-	-	-
Kinkead, Samuel	1832	F	1	266	Kline, Peter	1808	-	-	-
Kinner, John	1748	-	-	-	Kline, Peter	1823	B	1	61
Kinports, Daniel	1782	-	-	-	Kline, Susan	1846	M	1	137
Kinports, Daniel	1802	-	-	-	Kline, William	1777	-	-	-
Kinports, Daniel	1808	-	-	-	Kline, William H.	1839	I	1	176
Kinports, David	1805	-	-	-	Klinefellin, John	1755	-	-	-
Kinports, Nicholas	1800	-	-	-	Kling, Christian				
Kinsey, Catherine	1821	A	1	74	(see Cling)	1758	-	-	-

Name	Year	Bk.	Vol	Page
Kling, Christopher......	1785	-	-	-
Kling, John.............	1847	M	1	330
Kling, John.............	1847	M	1	333
Klingelhafler, Michael..	1822	A	1	130
Klug, Ann Caroline......	1837	I	1	4
Klug, Christopher.......	1836	H	1	187
Klug, Henry.............	1821	A	1	102
Klugh, Charles..........	1782	-	-	-
Klugh, Godfried........	1825	C	1	129
Klyne, Lydia...........	1836	H	1	196
Klyne, Marcus..........	1756	-	-	-
Kneisley, Abraham......	1822	A	1	154
Kneisley, Christian....	1835	H	1	55
Kneisley, Jacob				
(See Nicely)........	1749	-	-	-
Knessley, George.......	1814	-	-	-
Knight, Ann............	1847	M	1	259
Knight, Henry..........	1832	F	1	166
Knight, Henry..........	1845	M	1	30
Knight, Thomas.........	1826	C	1	154
Knigmacher, Abraham....	1825	C	1	116
Knigmacher, Benjamin...	1850	N	1	451
Kninsbitt, Christopher..	1793	-	-	-
Knob, Susanna..........	1830	E	1	242
Knodel, James..........	1795	-	-	-
Knoll, Henry Jr........	1822	A	1	200
Knoll, Henry...........	1829	E	1	135
Knop, Eve..............	1821	A	1	16
Knox, James............	1820	-	-	-
Knox, Martha...........	1832	F	1	221
Knox, Mary.............	1814	-	-	-
Knox, Mary.............	1816	-	-	-
Knox, Robert...........	1848	M	1	441
Knox, William..........	1812	-	-	-
Knull, Gertrude........	1748	-	-	-
Knup, John.............	1782	-	-	-
Kobach, Conrad.........	1780	-	-	-
Koch, John George......	1765	-	-	-
Koch, Michael..........	1767	-	-	-
Koehler, Jacob.........	1807	-	-	-
Koelln, Claus..........	1832	F	1	197
Koenig, Conrad.........	1836	H	1	151
Koenig, John...........	1837	I	1	3
Koenig, Margaret.......	1816	-	-	-
Koerper, Godleib.......	1843	L	1	31
Kohl, Nicholas.........	1797	-	-	-
Kohr, Michael..........	1784	-	-	-
Kolb, Andrew...........	1850	N	1	443
Kolb, George...........	1830	E	1	214
Kolp, Adam Jr..........	1834	G	1	161
Kolp, Adam.............	1834	G	1	162
Kolp, Christian........	1827	D	1	55
Kolp, Peter............	1807	-	-	-
Konklin, Samuel........	1833	G	1	105
Kopp, Christena........	1841	K	1	97
Kornhaus, Jacob........	1842	K	1	259
Korrel, Magdalena......	1826	C	1	243
Koser, Jacob...........	1828	D	1	180
Koutz, George..........	1821	-	-	-
Kozer, David...........	1849	N	1	282
Krafroth, Susanna......	1849	N	1	215
Krass, Peter...........	1848	N	1	128
Kraus, Jacob...........	1842	K	1	245
Krause, John...........	1844	L	1	193
Kreamer, John				
(See Creamer).......	1828	D	1	167
Kreamer, Peter				
(See Creamer).......	1742	-	-	-
Kreamer, Peter.........	1784	-	-	-
Kreamer, Sarah.........	1849	N	1	235
Kreamer, William.......	1850	N	1	325
Krebill, John..........	1814	-	-	-

Name	Year	Bk.	Vol	Page
Krebs, Christian........	1749	-	-	-
Krebs, George...........	1782	-	-	-
Krebsin, Frena.........	1744	-	-	-
Kreemer, John..........	1808	-	-	-
Kreibill, Henry........	1831	F	1	39
Kreider, Christian.....	1847	M	1	272
Kreider, Daniel				
(See Crider).......	1824	B	1	175
Kreider, Elizabeth.....	1837	H	1	260
Kreider, George........	1832	F	1	150
Kreider, George........	1849	N	1	298
Kreider, Henry.........	1821	A	1	34
Kreider, Jacob.........	1845	M	1	29
Kreider, Jacob.........	1849	N	1	212
Kreider, John..........	1794	-	-	-
Kreider, John..........	1808	-	-	-
Kreider, Michael.......	1841	K	1	112
Kreider, Tobias........	1847	M	1	379
Kreiner, John..........	1828	D	1	161
Kreiser, Philip........	1804	-	-	-
Kreiter, Barbara.......	1845	L	1	326
Kreiter, Peter A.......	1819	-	-	-
Kremer, Ann Marie......	1834	G	1	143
Kremer, Hans Adam......	1732	-	-	-
Kremer, Jacob..........	1779	-	-	-
Kremer, Jacob..........	1847	M	1	371
Kresh, George				
(See Cheney).......	1823	A	1	252
Krey, Peter............	1756	-	-	-
Krider, Michael........	1830	E	1	231
Kriner, Jacob..........	1794	-	-	-
Krise, Henry Sr.				
(See Crise)........	1826	C	1	288
Krisley, Anthony				
(See Crimer).......	1733	-	-	-
Kroll, Daniel..........	1798	-	-	-
Kroll, Nicholas........	1834	G	1	167
Krouse, John...........	1849	N	1	218
Krug, Henry............	1848	N	1	106
Krutzer, Ann...........	1817	-	-	-
Kugle, John............	1850	N	1	379
Kuhn, Adam Esq.........	1780	-	-	-
Kuhn, Frederick........	1816	-	-	-
Kuhn, Frederick........	1835	G	1	266
Kuhn, Dr. John.........	1811	-	-	-
Kummer, John G.........	1846	M	1	179
Kummerer, Christian....	1826	C	1	194
Kummerer, Peter........	1785	-	-	-
Kunkle, Henry..........	1841	K	1	125
Kunkle, John...........	1841	K	1	126
Kunkle, John...........	1848	N	1	74
Kunkle, William Sr.....	1831	F	1	132
Kuntz, Ada.............	1771	-	-	-
Kuntz, Francis.........	1786	-	-	-
Kuntz, George..........	1781	-	-	-
Kuntz, Henry				
(See Counts)........	1770	-	-	-
Kuntz, John............	1807	-	-	-
Kuntz, John............	1810	-	-	-
Kuntz, Margaret........	1801	-	-	-
Kuntz, Michael.........	1750	-	-	-
Kuntz, Peter...........	1791	-	-	-
Kuntz, Peter...........	1793	-	-	-
Kuntz, Philip..........	1764	-	-	-
Kuntz, William.........	1826	C	1	246
Kupper, John George.....	1780	-	-	-
Kurner, Thomas.........	1801	-	-	-
Kurpman, Christian.....	1801	-	-	-
Kurtz, Abram...........	1846	M	1	161
Kurtz, Catharine.......	1834	G	1	132
Kurtz, Conrad..........	1836	H	1	157
Kurtz, Conrad..........	1843	L	1	154

Name	Year	Bk.	Vol	Page	Name	Year	Bk.	Vol	Page
Kurtz, Daniel	1840	K	1	31	Laughery, James	1821	A	1	99
Kurtz, David	1815	-	-	-	Lauman, Elizabeth	1810	-	-	-
Kurtz, Jacob	1816	-	-	-	Lauman, Ludwig	1821	A	1	86
Kurtz, Jacob	1832	F	1	154	Lauman, Ludwig	1830	E	1	212
Kurtz, Jacob	1848	N	1	98	Lauman, Ludwig	1833	G	1	71
Kurtz, John	1831	F	1	154	Lauman, Martin	1824	B	1	177
Kurtz, John	1849	N	1	218	Lausser, John	1778	-	-	-
Kurtz, Martha	1836	H	1	111	Laverty, John	1755	-	-	-
Kurtz, Thomas	1785	-	-	-	Lawler, Andrew	1747	-	-	-
Kuster, Michael	1831	F	1	129	Lawrence, Peter	1757	-	-	-
Kyle, James	1735	-	-	-	Lawrentz, Henry	1834	G	1	257
Kyle, John	1759	-	-	-	Lawshey, Jacob	1848	N	1	9
L					Layer, Frederick	1838	I	1	159
Laber, Hans Vendle	1749	-	-	-	Lazarus, Peter	1793	-	-	-
Laber, Margaret	1761	-	-	-	Leachy, John, Sr	1832	F	1	174
Laber, Michael	1777	-	-	-	Lead, Allen	1847	U	1	238
Lahn, Jacob	1801	-	-	-	Lead, George	1833	G	1	32
Lahr, Christian	1791	-	-	-	Lead, George	1838	I	1	125
Lahr, George	1847	M	1	338	Lead, Israel	1839	I	1	188
Lambach, Christian	1785	-	-	-	Lead, Susanna	1847	M	1	388
Lambert, John	1827	D	1	94	Leader, Lewis, Jr	1842	K	1	292
Lambert, John	1838	I	1	90	Leady, John	1839	I	1	260
Lambert, Mary	1842	L	1	24	Leafsell, Christian	1748	-	-	-
Lamberton, Magdalena Eva	1840	K	1	17	Leaman, Abraham	1839	I	1	210
Lambron, Clarkson	1847	M	1	284	Leaman, Catharine	1848	N	1	34
Lamp, Henry	1841	K	1	166	Leaman, Elizabeth	1758	-	-	-
Land, Felix, Sr	1739	-	-	-	Leaman, Elizabeth	1828	E	1	14
Lander, Charles R	1832	F	1	198	Leaman, John, Sr	1790	-	-	-
Landers, George	1849	N	1	144	Leaman, John	1793	-	-	-
Landes, Abraham	1790	-	-	-	Leaman, John	1823	B	1	7
Landis, Abraham	1843	L	1	123	Leaser, Frederick	1766	-	-	-
Landis, Anna	1845	U	1	92	Leaser, Joseph	1841	K	1	109
Landis, Anna	1846	U	1	118	Lebazius, James	1827	D	1	87
Landis, Barbara	1828	D	1	242	Leber, George	1834	G	1	191
Landis, Benjamin	1824	B	1	228	Lechey, John Von	1751	-	-	-
Landis, Benjamin	1829	E	1	116	Lechler, John	1822	A	1	248
Landis, Benjamin	1849	N	1	308	Leckey, John	1832	F	1	245
Landis, Daniel	1823	B	1	71	Lecky, Thomas	1812	-	-	-
Landis, Elizabeth	1833	G	1	97	Ledlie, William	1777	-	-	-
Landis, Hannah	1850	N	1	311	Lee, John	1762	-	-	-
Landis, Henry	1791	-	-	-	Lee, Robert	1756	-	-	-
Landis, Henry	1836	H	1	128	Lee, William	1749	-	-	-
Landis, Jacob	1730	-	-	-	Lee, William	1771	-	-	-
Landis, Jacob	1835	H	1	4	Leech, Francis	1776	-	-	-
Landis, John	1756	-	-	-	Leech, George	1798	-	-	-
Landis, John	1823	B	1	44	Leech, Robert	1769	-	-	-
Landis, Magdalena	1839	I	1	162	Leek, John	1838	I	1	76
Landis, Maria	1839	I	1	274	Leelan, John	1746	-	-	-
Lane, Abraham	1828	D	1	264	Leen, Henry	1827	D	1	54
Lane, Cornelius	1780	-	-	-	Leevon, Daniel	1769	-	-	-
Lane, Peter	1776	-	-	-	Leferer, Mary	1817	-	-	-
Lanius, Elizabeth	1831	F	1	58	Leferer, Mary	1833	G	1	96
Lanker, George	1829	E	1	69	Leferer, Dr. Peter	1844	L	1	237
Lantz, Amos	1850	N	1	368	Leferer, Philip	1766	-	-	-
Lantz, John	1828	D	1	207	Lefever, Daniel	1814	-	-	-
Lapp, Franey	1845	M	1	80	Lefever, Isaac	1783	-	-	-
Lapp, George	1806	-	-	-	Lefever, Jacob	1826	C	1	255
Lapp, George	1843	L	1	97	Lefever, John	1795	-	-	-
Lapp, Isaac	1819	-	-	-	Lefever, Joseph	1835	H	1	19
Lapp, John	1832	F	1	216	Lefever, Mary	1783	-	-	-
Larshey, Mary	1835	H	1	62	Lefever, Samuel	1813	-	-	-
Lash, Philip	1793	-	-	-	Lefevre, Abraham	1735	-	-	-
Lashe, Philip	1793	-	-	-	Lefevre, Adam	1814	-	-	-
Latchem, Isaiah	1840	K	1	6	Leffler, John	1834	G	1	241
Latchem, Susan	1846	M	1	120	Legner, Abaloney	1776	-	-	-
Latta, James	1802	-	-	-	Lehman, George	1816	-	-	-
Latta, Robert	1784	-	-	-	Lehman, Peter	1843	L	1	128
Laudenslager, Albright	1848	N	1	92	Lehr, Jacob	1830	E	1	181
Laudermilk, Jacob	1770	-	-	-	Lehr, Peter	1786	-	-	-
Lauer, Niccoll	1749	-	-	-	Leib, Christian	1842	K	1	276
Laughead, James	1794	-	-	-	Leib, Christian	1843	L	1	61
Laughead, William	1799	-	-	-	Leib, Christian, Jr	1843	L	1	61

Name	Year	Bk.	Vol	Page	Name	Year	Bk.	Vol	Page
Leib, John, Sr.	1830	E	1	172	Lindemuth, Peter	1830	E	1	255
Leibley, John	1809	-	-	-	Lindemuth, Peter	1832	F	1	156
Leibrick, John	1785	-	-	-	Linder, Daniel	1805	-	-	-
Leibrick, John	1804	-	-	-	Linder, John	1806	-	-	-
Leibrick, Nichols	1788	-	-	-	Linder, Margaret	1806	-	-	-
Leid, Henry	1798	-	-	-	Lindersmith, Jacob	1792	-	-	-
Leidig, John	1784	-	-	-	Lindy, Jacob	1835	H	1	43
Leighh, Jacob	1748	-	-	-	Line, Abraham	1811	-	-	-
Lein, Jacob	1762	-	-	-	Line, Christian	1795	-	-	-
Leiss, Susanna	1809	-	-	-	Line, David	1814	-	-	-
Leister, Thomas	1850	N	1	374	Line, Jacob	1815	-	-	-
Leler, Jacob	1838	I	1	91	Line, John	1794	-	-	-
Lelm, Elizabeth	1873	-	-	-	Line, Peter	1818	-	-	-
Leman, Ann	1742	-	-	-	Lines, John	1845	M	1	6
Leman, Anna Maria	1793	-	-	-	Lingefelder, Daniel	1819	-	-	-
Leman, Christian	1744	-	-	-	Lingenfield, John	1768	-	-	-
Leman, Elizabeth	1759	-	-	-	Lingerfield, John	1756	-	-	-
Leman, George	1793	-	-	-	Lingerfield, Michael	1827	D	1	76
Leman, Isaac	1774	-	-	-	Lingston, John	1836	H	1	155
Leman, Isaac	1814	-	-	-	Linngston, Jane	1838	I	1	161
Leman, Jacob	1855	H	1	89	Linngston, William, Jr.	1841	K	1	193
Leman, Peter	1748	-	-	-	Lintner, John	1778	-	-	-
Leman, William, Jr.	1772	-	-	-	Lintner, John	1840	K	1	41
Lemont, Archibald	1770	-	-	-	Lipp, Christopher	1842	K	1	273
Lenhart, Magdalena	1850	N	1	417	Lips, Jacob	1783	-	-	-
Lenhart, Philip	1841	K	1	84	Litle, Andrew	1756	-	-	-
Lenis, George W	1849	N	1	175	Litle, Andrew	1786	-	-	-
Lentz, Jacob	1772	-	-	-	Litle, Nathaniel	1778	-	-	-
Leonard, George	1847	M	1	395	Little, Joseph	1788	-	-	-
Leonard, Luke	1815	-	-	-	Lloyd, Absolam	1820	-	-	-
LeRoi, Abraham	1763	-	-	-	Lloyd, David	1814	-	-	-
LeRue, Henry	1783	-	-	-	Lloyd, George	1847	M	1	264
LeRue, Jonas	1760	-	-	-	Lloyd, William	1808	-	-	-
Lesher, Barbara	1812	-	-	-	Lloyd, William	1829	E	1	81
Lesher, Mary	1784	-	-	-	Locher, Henry	1836	H	1	108
Lesher, Sebastian	1759	-	-	-	Lock, John	1744	-	-	-
Lether, Frederick	1746	-	-	-	Lockard, Charles	1817	-	-	-
Leviston, Henry	1753	-	-	-	Lockard, Charles	1826	C	1	264
Leviston, Mary Sarah	1751	-	-	-	Lockard, John	1814	-	-	-
Leviston, William	1749	-	-	-	Lockard, John	1830	E	1	224
Lewis, David	1748	-	-	-	Lockart, Elizabeth	1838	I	1	130
Leybolt, Nicholas	1812	-	-	-	Lockhart, Andrew	1803	-	-	-
Leysi, George	1763	-	-	-	Loeser, Jacob	1793	-	-	-
Lichtenberger, Jacob	1840	K	1	54	Loeser, Mathias	1766	-	-	-
Lichty, Ann	1826	C	1	148	Loeser, Nicholas	1822	A	1	155
Lichty, Ann	1845	L	1	300	Logan, James	1747	-	-	-
Lichty, Christian	1835	H	1	12	Logan, John	1799	-	-	-
Lichty, Henry	1820	-	-	-	Logan, Patrick	1822	A	1	199
Lichty, Peter	1807	-	-	-	Logue, Patrick	1817	-	-	-
Lickty, David	1838	I	1	67	Logue, Robert	1805	-	-	-
Lied, Peter	1829	E	1	47	Lombach, Philip	1774	-	-	-
Light, Ann	1846	U	1	198	Loney, Benjamin	1847	M	1	423
Light, Daniel	1819	-	-	-	Long, Abraham	1801	-	-	-
Light, David	1799	-	-	-	Long, Abraham	1847	U	1	238
Light, Jacob	1751	-	-	-	Long, Abraham, Sr.	1849	N	1	301
Light, Joseph	1733	-	-	-	Long, Abraham K.	1843	L	1	43
Light, Lewis	1831	F	1	6	Long, Christian	1767	-	-	-
Lightner, Adam	1798	-	-	-	Long, Elizabeth	1805	-	-	-
Lightner, George	1779	-	-	-	Long, Elizabeth	1808	-	-	-
Lightner, Isaac F.	1842	K	1	321	Long, Elizabeth	1823	B	1	80
Lightner, John, Esq.	1848	N	1	45	Long, Emanuel	1849	N	1	151
Lightner, Leah	1842	K	1	278	Long, Frederick	1815	-	-	-
Lightner, Leah	1847	M	1	341	Long, George	1843	L	1	59
Lightner, Maria	1832	T	1	185	Long, Herman	1772	-	-	-
Lightner, Maria	1849	N	1	156	Long, Herman	1804	-	-	-
Lightner, Nathaniel F.	1847	M	1	344	Long, Hugh	1814	-	-	-
Lile, Elizabeth	1787	-	-	-	Long, Isaac	1803	-	-	-
Lindaman, John	1847	M	1	421	Long, James	1819	-	-	-
Lindasmush, George, Sr.	1826	C	1	231	Long, James	1845	L	1	306
Lindeberger, George	1794	-	-	-	Long, John	1744	-	-	-
Lindemuth, John	1836	H	1	138	Long, John	1747	-	-	-
Lindemuth, Peter	1830	E	1	250	Long, John	1753	-	-	-

Name	Year	Bk.	Vol	Page	Name	Year	Bk.	Vol	Page
Long, John	1772	-	-	-	Lutes, Andrew	1786	-	-	-
Long, John	1781	-	-	-	Luther, Christian	1832	F	1	217
Long, John	1783	-	-	-	Lutman, Everhard	1766	-	-	-
Long, John	1832	F	1	271	Lutz, David	1829	E	1	49
Long, John	1835	H	1	22	Lutz, Elizabeth	1794	-	-	-
Long, John	1843	L	1	163	Lutz, Elizabeth	1826	D	1	5
Long, John	1849	N	1	209	Lutz, Eve	1805	-	-	-
Long, Jonas	1841	K	1	157	Lutz, Eve	1838	I	1	150
Long, Joseph	1794	-	-	-	Lutz, George	1797	-	-	-
Long, Leonard	1758	-	-	-	Lutz, Henry	1827	D	1	93
Long, Magdalina	1805	-	-	-	Lutz, John	1816	-	-	-
Long, Mathias	1774	-	-	-	Lutz, John	1827	D	1	127
Long, Michael	1802	-	-	-	Lutz, John	1832	F	1	211
Long, Robert	1747	-	-	-	Lutz, John	1836	H	1	168
Longacre, John	1752	-	-	-	Lutz, Margaret	1801	-	-	-
Longanecker, Daniel	1762	-	-	-	Lutz, Martin	1777	-	-	-
Longenecker, Daniel	1804	-	-	-	Lutz, Mary	1835	H	1	82
Longenecker, David	1810	-	-	-	Lutz, Nicholas	1821	A	1	53
Longenecker, David	1842	K	1	221	Lutz, Peter	1807	v	-	-
Longenecker, Feronica	1823	B	1	11	Lutz, Stephens	1797	-	-	-
Longenecker, Jacob	1825	C	1	89	Lutz, William	1829	E	1	91
Longenecker, Jacob	1834	G	1	209	Lyman, Margaret	1786	-	-	-
Longenecker, John	1798	-	-	-	Lynch, James	1812	-	-	-
Longenecker, John	1833	G	9	49	Lynch, Jane	1830	E	1	182
Longenecker, Peter	1806	-	-	-	Lyne, Barbara	1846	M	1	127
Longenecker, Peter	1848	M	1	429	Lyne, Henry	1762	-	-	-
Longenecker, Dr.Samuel	1808	-	-	-	Lyne, John	1764	-	-	-
Longenecker, Solomon	1812	-	-	-	Lyon, James	1749	-	-	-
Longenecker, Susanna	1826	C	1	263	Lyon, John	1760	-	-	-
Longerke, Frederick H.A.	1823	B	1	116	Lyon, Joseph	1768	-	-	-
Longhead, Robert	1823	B	1	33	Lyon, Thomas	1832	F	1	172
Longinacher, Christian	1749	-	-	-	Lyon, Thomas, Sr	1832	F	1	177
Longnecker, Catharine	1836	H	1	178	Lytle, Andrew	1808	-	-	-
Lorah, George	1850	N	1	442	Lytle, Archibald	1815	-	-	-
Lorentz, Catherine	1799	-	-	-	Lytle, James	1849	N	1	230
Lorentz, Frantz Peter	1795	-	-	-	Lytle, Robert	1827	D	1	149
Losh, Stephen	1766	-	-	-	Lytle, William	1798	-	-	-
Loshbaugh, Herman	1775	-	-	-	Lytle, William	1823	B	1	108
Losk, Thomas	1757	-	-	-	**Mc**				
Lotshau, Joseph	1775	-	-	-	McAfee, Daniel	1793	-	-	-
Lou, James	1847	M	1	279	McAnespey, Archibald	1843	L	1	94
Lou, Joseph	1838	I	1	123	McBride, Thomas	1747	-	-	-
Loudon, James	1760	-	-	-	McCafferty, Margaret	1848	N	1	15
Lougherty, Samuel	1846	M	1	223	McCaffery, Patrick	1825	C	1	108
Lougherty, Samuel	1846	M	1	225	McCaffy, Robert	1828	D	1	267
Louks, John	1753	-	-	-	McCalla, Roger	1753	-	-	-
Louman, George	1744	-	-	-	McCallister, Margaret	1779	-	-	-
Love, James	1802	-	-	-	McCallister, Neal	1757	-	-	-
Love, Thomas	1824	B	1	137	McCamon, James	1743	-	-	-
Lovett, John	1823	B	1	37	McCamons, John	1748	-	-	-
Lovinder, Sandress	1843	L	1	125	McCan, Patrick	1826	C	1	156
Lowden, James	1744	-	-	-	McCann, Barnabas	1814	-	-	-
Lowden, Richard	1846	-	-	-	McCannis, Arthur	1734	-	-	-
Lowden, William	1741	-	-	-	McCardle, William	1829	E	1	151
Lowe, John	1748	-	-	-	McCarnant, William	1763	-	-	-
Lowe, Joshua	1748	-	-	-	McCartney, Andrew	1844	L	1	194
Lowry, James	1737	-	-	-	McCartney, Peter	1806	-	-	-
Lowry, James	1756	-	-	-	McCarty, David	1817	-	-	-
Lowry, John	1750	-	-	-	McCausland, George	1812	-	-	-
Lowry, John	1815	-	-	-	McCausland, William	1771	-	-	-
Lowry, John	1823	B	1	127	McCausland, William	1821	A	1	114
Lowry, Joseph	1781	-	-	-	McChesney, Robert	1826	C	1	287
Lowry, Sarah	1813	-	-	-	McChesney, William	1825	C	1	21
Lowry, Sarah	1816	-	-	-	McClain, Catharine	1841	K	1	98
Loy, Ludwig	1775	-	-	-	McClaskey, Bernard	1802	-	-	-
Luchman, Casper	1744	-	-	-	McClausland, Maxwell	1821	A	1	106
Luck, Catherine	1847	M	1	289½	McClean, Hugh	1750	-	-	-
Luckey, Andrew	1739	-	-	-	McClelland, Margaret	1825	C	1	51
Ludwig, Conrad	1807	-	-	-	McClelland, Robert	1812	-	-	-
Luft, John	1792	-	-	-	McClelland, William	1773	-	-	-
Luphold, John	1843	L	1	53	McClemery, Patrick	1749	-	-	-
Luppin, John	1845	L	1	297	McClenachan, William	1753	-	-	-

Name	Year	Bk.	Vol	Page	Name	Year	Bk.	Vol	Page
McClenacher, Ann	1832	F	1	263	McFaddin, Daniel	1800	-	-	-
McClery, Finley	1752	-	-	-	McFannel, David	1802	-	-	-
McClintock, Robert	1773	-	-	-	McFarland, Robert	1751	-	-	-
McCloskey, Charles	1813	-	-	-	McFarquhar, Rev. Colin	1824	B	1	202
McCloskey, Michael	1809	-	-	-	McFarquhar, Colin	1829	E	1	40
McCloskey, Richard	1846	M	1	217	McFarson, Alexander	1748	-	-	-
McCloud, Alexander	1813	-	-	-	McFeague, Darby	1821	-	-	-
McCloy, Mary	1833	G	1	47	McFeague, Peter	1833	G	1	37
McCluer, John	1747	-	-	-	McFeeley, Robert	1755	-	-	-
McClun, Thomas	1746	-	-	-	McFerson, Martha	1762	-	-	-
McClung, Charles	1814	-	-	-	McGarr, Roger	1825	C	1	58
McClung, Palmer	1773	-	-	-	McGee, John	1748	-	-	-
McClure, Charles	1758	-	-	-	McGee, Samuel	1749	-	-	-
McClure, Samuel	1773	-	-	-	McGlogen, Michael	1822	A	1	250
McClure, Thomas	1747	-	-	-	McGowan, Patrick	1835	H	1	59
McClure, William	1827	D	1	59	McGrann, Bernard	1793	-	-	-
McClure, William	1849	N	1	245	McGrann, Elizabeth	1844	L	1	292
McColl, Dennis	1805	-	-	-	McGrann, Mathew	1845	M	1	78
McCollon, Charles	1813	-	-	-	McGuigan, Francis	1848	N	1	33
McCollough, William	1807	-	-	-	McGuigan, Michael	1830	E	1	184
McCollum, Richard	1811	-	-	-	McGuign, Patrick	1820	-	-	-
McConeld, Robert	1775	-	-	-	McGuines, Margaret	1814	-	-	-
McConnel, Edward	1736	-	-	-	McGuire, Samuel	1826	C	1	262
McConnel, Robert	1747	-	-	-	McHarry, Samuel	1843	L	1	89
McConnel, Samuel	1773	-	-	-	McHugh, Andrew	1836	H	1	113
McConnel, Samuel	1816	-	-	-	McIlvaine, Alexander	1803	-	-	-
McConnel, Thomas	1744	-	-	-	McIlvaine, Mary	1800	-	-	-
McConnell, Daniel	1749	-	-	-	McIlvaine, Moses	1760	-	-	-
McConnell, William	1748	-	-	-	McIntire, Alexander	1803	-	-	-
McConnell, William	1790	-	-	-	McIntire, Andrew	1831	F	1	92
McConohay, John	1748	-	-	-	McIntyre, Mary	1804	-	-	-
McCord, David	1758	-	-	-	McKean, Elizabeth	1822	A	1	150
McCord, Richard	1832	G	1	9	McKean, William	1812	-	-	-
McCord, William	1739	-	-	-	McKee, Samuel	1850	O	1	40
McCormick, Dennis	1767	-	-	-	McKennet, Daniel	1745	-	-	-
McCormick, George W.	1817	-	-	-	McKillips, Samuel	1818	-	-	-
McCoubry, William	1773	-	-	-	McKin, Elizabeth	1838	I	1	152
McCouch, Robert	1832	F	1	210	McKinney, Abraham	1831	F	1	103
McCowan, Margaret	1758	-	-	-	McKinney, George	1833	G	1	30
McCowan, Robert	1846	M	1	220	McKinney, Samuel	1843	L	1	54
McCoy, Alexander	1786	-	-	-	McKinsey, Alexander	1818	-	-	-
McCoy, Daniel	1831	F	1	76	McKinsey, Patrick	1748	-	-	-
McCoy, George	1802	-	-	-	McKissick, Mary	1849	N	1	312
McCoy, James	1743	-	-	-	McKnaight, Andrew	1775	-	-	-
McCoy, John	1731	-	-	-	McKneely, William, Jr.	1771	-	-	-
McCoy, Margaret	1818	-	-	-	McKneely, William	1780	-	-	-
McCoy, William	1793	-	-	-	McKnight, John	1746	-	-	-
McCracken, Elizabeth	1829	E	1	156	McKnight, Samuel	1772	-	-	-
McCrea, Patrick	1822	A	1	171	McKnight, William	1847	M	1	353
McCreary, Margaret	1849	N	1	228	McLaughlin, Andrew	1817	-	-	-
McCreary, Samuel	1784	-	-	-	McLaughlin, Isaac	1823	B	1	123
McCullough, Alexander	1760	-	-	-	McLenegan, Elijah	1844	L	1	179
McCullough, Alexander	1821	A	1	29	McLenegan, Samuel	1831	F	1	12
McCullough, Margaret	1774	-	-	-	McLowell, Margaret	1844	L	1	274
McCullough, Patrick	1750	-	-	-	McLucas, Patrick	1746	-	-	-
McCullough, William	1828	D	1	190	McMachen, Alexander	1807	-	-	-
McCullough, William	1832	F	1	227	McMahon, Henry	1738	-	-	-
McCullough, William	1837	I	1	9	McMannus, Charles	1748	-	-	-
McCumsey, Mathias	1836	H	1	188	McManus, Bernard	1809	-	-	-
McDaniel, Aaron	1747	-	-	-	McManus, Charles	1749	-	-	-
McDaniel, Francis	1760	-	-	-	McMicael, Richard	1773	-	-	-
McDermott, William	1821	A	1	85	McMin, William	1761	-	-	-
McDonald, Catharine	1802	-	-	-	McMinn, Isaac	1848	N	1	63
McDonald, Durnan	1832	F	1	176	McMullen, Hugh	1742	-	-	-
McDonald, Randall	1778	-	-	-	McNaughton, Mary	1814	-	-	-
McDonough, Mathew	1818	-	-	-	McNeal, Archibald	1800	-	-	-
McDonough, Peter	1840	K	1	38	McNeal, Daniel	1761	-	-	-
McElary, Miles	1761	-	-	-	McNeal, Hugh	1747	-	-	-
McElhadden, Samuel	1784	-	-	-	McNeal, John	1736	-	-	-
McElheny, Martin	1813	-	-	-	McNeal, Neal	1800	-	-	-
McFadden, Alexander	1793	-	-	-	McNeal, Neal	1846	M	1	123
McFadden, Andrew B.	1841	K	1	104	McNeely, David, Sr.	1850	N	1	368

Name	Year	Bk.	Vol	Page	Name	Year	Bk.	Vol	Page
McNeil, Robert..........	1774	-	-	-	Martin, Christian.......	1804	-	-	-
McNeill, Samuel.........	1819	-	-	-	Martin, Christian.......	1806	-	-	-
McPaul, George.........	1816	-	-	-	Martin, Christian.......	1828	D	1	278
McPeak, Robert.........	1793	-	-	-	Martin, Daniel.........	1832	F	1	209
McPherson, Rebecca H....	1850	O	1	24	Martin, David.........	1741	-	-	-
McTeer, William........	1748	-	-	-	Martin, David..........	1836	H	1	117
McVey, Daniel..........	1801	-	-	-	Martin, David H........	1850	N	1	329
McVitte, Alice.........	1848	N	1	35	Martin, Elizabeth.......	1830	E	1	188
McVity, Cromwell........	1789	-	-	-	Martin, Francis.........	1840	K	1	1
McWilliams, Hugh........	1743	-	-	-	Martin, George..........	1797	-	-	-
M					Martin, George..........	1821	-	-	-
Maberry, Jeremiah.......	1808	-	-	-	Martin, George..........	1850	O	1	48
Macdonald, Oliver.......	1843	L	1	110	Martin, Henry...........	1827	D	1	50
Mackamore, Robert.......	1734	-	-	-	Martin, Henry...........	1829	E	1	64
Mackey, Abraham.........	1760	-	-	-	Martin, Henry...........	1848	M	1	435
Mackey, James..........	1804	-	-	-	Martin, Isaac..........	1834	G	1	190
Mackey, Joseph..........	1804	-	-	-	Martin, Jacob..........	1809	-	-	-
Mackey, Margaret.......	1826	C	1	174	Martin, Jacob..........	1841	K	1	99
Mackey, Richard........	1811	-	-	-	Martin, James..........	1739	-	-	-
Mackey, Robert.........	1746	-	-	-	Martin, James..........	1785	-	-	-
Mackey, Thomas.........	1799	-	-	-	Martin, John...........	1747	-	-	-
Mackley, Jacob.........	1825	C	1	77	Martin, John...........	1757	-	-	-
Mackley, Melchior......	1822	A	1	215	Martin, John...........	1760	-	-	-
Madden, William........	1850	N	1	384	Martin, John...........	1824	B	1	221
Magee, Thomas..........	1820	-	-	-	Martin, John...........	1844	L	1	279
Maggadagert, James......	1777	-	-	-	Martin, John...........	1847	M	1	339
Magull, Sophia.........	1848	N	1	53	Martin, John Justis....	1845	M	1	34
Mahaffy, Robert........	1808	-	-	-	Martin, Joseph.........	1813	-	-	-
Mahan, Mary............	1850	O	1	6	Martin, Magdalena.......	1772	-	-	-
Mainzer, John..........	1821	A	1	76	Martin, Magdalina.......	1842	K	1	216
Maize, James..........	1810	-	-	-	Martin, Margaret.......	1832	F	1	231
Malone, Dennis.........	1832	F	1	234	Martin, Martin Jr.......	1803	-	-	-
Manderbaugh, Henry......	1825	C	1	114	Martin, Martin.........	1842	K	1	302
Manderbaugh, Henry.....	1827	D	1	48	Martin, Michael Jr......	1823	B	1	93
Maney, Patrick.........	1834	G	1	246	Martin, Moses..........	1739	-	-	-
Manigoe, John Jacob.....	1807	-	-	-	Martin, Moses..........	1828	D	1	265
Mann, Bernard..........	1823	A	1	286	Martin, Nancy..........	1850	N	1	361
Mann, Sarah............	1832	F	1	224	Martin, Peter..........	1745	-	-	-
Mann, William..........	1768	-	-	-	Martin, Robert.........	1835	H	1	86
Manning, Fanny..........	1849	N	1	281	Martin, Samuel.........	1796	-	-	-
Manning, Pernica.......	1814	-	-	-	Martin, Samuel.........	1842	K	1	300
Manning, Joseph........	1850	N	1	339	Martin, Samuel.........	1844	L	1	203
Manoe, Robert..........	1743	-	-	-	Martin, Samuel.........	1845	M	1	49
Marafftry, Daniel......	1838	I	1	131	Martin, Susanna.........	1803	-	-	-
Marck, Henry...........	1775	-	-	-	Martin, Susanna.........	1835	H	1	14
Margell, John..........	1761	-	-	-	Martin, Thomas.........	1739	-	-	-
Maria, Bernard.........	1841	K	1	178	Martin, William........	1841	K	1	123
Markley, Dr. Charles....	1829	E	1	87	Martzall, Catharine.....	1817	-	-	-
Markley, Christian.....	1823	B	1	113	Martzall, Christian.....	1811	-	-	-
Markley, George........	1849	N	1	202	Martzall, John.........	1806	-	-	-
Markley, Jacob..........	1829	E	1	52	Martzall, John.........	1827	D	1	148
Markley, John..........	1836	H	1	191	Martzall, Magdalena.....	1814	-	-	-
Marks, Nicholas........	1832	F	1	268	Martzall, Philip........	1827	D	1	120
Marlkley, George........	1828	E	1	1	Martzall, Samuel........	1819	-	-	-
Marlsley, Eve..........	1809	-	-	-	Mason, William.........	1822	A	1	187
Marple, David..........	1850	O	1	7	Master, Henry..........	1845	M	1	39
Marple, Harriet........	1846	M	1	218	Master, John...........	1832	F	1	258
Marquedant, Lorentz.....	1783	-	-	-	Masterson, Edward......	1827	D	1	19
Marsden, Henry.........	1776	-	-	-	Mathay, Christopher.....	1783	-	-	-
Marsh, Hollingsworth....	1809	-	-	-	Mathews, James.........	1741	-	-	-
Marsh, Sarah...........	1785	-	-	-	Mathews, Samuel........	1748	-	-	-
Marshall, Caleb........	1829	E	1	155	Mathiot, David.........	1850	N	1	390
Marshall, Patrick......	1778	-	-	-	Mathiot, Jacob.........	1846	M	1	136
Marshall, Tarirus......	1820	-	-	-	Mathiot, Jacob.........	1849	N	1	242
Mart, Mathias..........	1757	-	-	-	Mathiot, John..........	1802	-	-	-
Martin, Alexander......	1777	-	-	-	Mathiot, John Sr.......	1828	D	1	178
Martin, Ann............	1842	K	1	294	Mathiot, John..........	1843	L	1	45
Martin, Anna...........	1843	L	1	39	Mathiot, John..........	1848	M	1	443
Martin, Baltzer........	1835	G	1	256	Mathiot, Joseph........	1826	C	1	158
Martin, Barbara........	1846	M	1	215	Matter, Adam...........	1850	N	1	283
Martin, Catharine......	1805	-	-	-	Matter, George.........	1796	-	-	-
Martin, Catharine......	1823	B	1	21	Matthew, John..........	1778	-	-	-

Name	Year	Bk.	Vol	Page	Name	Year	Bk.	Vol	Page
Mauderbaugh, John	1777	-	-	-	Mengle, Maria	1842	K	1	284
Mauke, Philip	1747	-	-	-	Menoch, Robert C	1841	K	1	143
Maurer, Baltzer	1850	N	1	332	Mentzer, Jacob	1835	G	1	271
Maurer, Jacob	1830	E	1	267	Mentzer, Peter	1834	G	1	171
Maurer, Peter	1848	N	1	46	Mercer, Caleb	1775	-	-	-
Maxwell, Abby Ann	1840	K	1	36	Mercer, Caleb	1825	C	1	15
Maxwell, Abigal	1850	O	1	20	Merckle, George	1799	-	-	-
Maxwell, Ann Mary	1850	O	1	91	Mering, Henry	1823	B	1	39
Maxwell, John	1785	-	-	-	Merrow, James	1775	-	-	-
Maxwell, John	1826	C	1	214	Merrow, Peter	1813	-	-	-
Maxwell, John	1830	E	1	223	Meser, John	1740	-	-	-
Maxwell, Robert	1832	F	1	235	Meshar, Christian	1748	-	-	-
Maxwell, Robert Esq	1847	M	1	343	Meshey, Anna	1842	K	1	298
Maxwell, William S	1849	N	1	247	Messenger, Martin	1829	E	1	33
May, Catharine	1787	-	-	-	Messenkohl, Adam	1802	-	-	-
Mayer, Christian	1842	K	1	231	Messenkop, George	1845	L	1	325
Mayer, Conrad	1835	H	1	7	Messenkop, Henry	1826	C	1	260
Mayer, George Louis	1837	H	1	258	Messenkop, Philip	1828	D	1	276
Mayer, Jacob	1812	-	-	-	Messenkope, John	1810	-	-	-
Mayer, Jacob	1822	A	1	227	Messeran, Joshea	1821	A	1	100
Mayer, John	1822	A	1	121	Messersmith, Nicholas	1762	-	-	-
Mayer, Maria	1845	M	1	13	Messner, Barbara	1774	-	-	-
Mayer, Samuel	1814	-	-	-	Messner, Catharine	1850	N	1	398
Mayers, Samuel	1814	-	-	-	Messner, Christian	1827	D	1	158
Mayes, James	1733	-	-	-	Messner, Christian	1836	H	1	102
Mays, Catharine	1829	E	1	57	Messner, Philip	1836	H	1	115
Meban, John	1799	-	-	-	Messner, Simon	1850	N	1	428
Meburry, Jeremiah	1806	-	-	-	Meteer, John	1817	-	-	-
Mecartney, Philip	1846	M	1	204	Metz, Christian	1827	D	1	101
Meck, Jacob	1846	M	1	147	Metz, Ludwig	1757	-	-	-
Meckley, Jacob	1783	-	-	-	Metzger, Adam	1850	N	1	340
Meckley, William H	1845	M	1	20	Metzger, Adam	1850	N	1	366
Meecke, Michael	1840	K	1	27	Metzger, Frederick	1843	L	1	68
Megesick, James	1765	-	-	-	Metzger, Henry	1850	O	1	4
Meguire, Thomas	1841	K	1	182	Metzger, Jacob J	1835	H	1	6
Mehaffey, Ann	1843	L	1	147	Metzger, Michael	1845	D	1	314
Mehaffy, John Jr	1819	-	-	-	Metzger, Philip	1772	-	-	-
Mehring, Ann	1841	K	1	151	Metzger, Tobias	1785	-	-	-
Meickle, Samuel	1840	K	1	52	Metzler, Abraham	1818	-	-	-
Meier, George	1745	-	-	-	Metzler, Christian	1833	G	1	41
Meily, Jacob	1844	L	1	181	Metzler, John	1806	-	-	-
Meiskey, Benjamine	1793	-	-	-	Metzler, Martin	1807	-	-	-
Meister, Henry	1844	L	1	200	Metzler, Valentine	1783	-	-	-
Meixel, Andrew	1740	-	-	-	Meyer, Barbara	1804	-	-	-
Meixel, Jacob Jr	1818	-	-	-	Meyer, Christian	1802	-	-	-
Meixel, Juliana	1825	C	1	19	Meyer, David	1791	-	-	-
Meixel, Julianna	1805	-	-	-	Meyer, Frederick	1802	-	-	-
Meixel, Martin Jr	1822	A	1	221	Meyer, George	1749	-	-	-
Meixel, Martin	1825	C	1	40	Meyer, Jacob	1807	-	-	-
Meixel, Susanna	1835	H	1	48	Meyer, Jacob	1821	A	1	42
Meldrum, John	1836	H	1	170	Meyer, Jacob	1822	A	1	241
Melinger, Maria	1832	G	1	4	Meyer, John	1777	-	-	-
Meller, Adam	1764	-	-	-	Meyer, John	1786	-	-	-
Melligan, Dennis	1773	-	-	-	Meyer, John	1798	-	-	-
Mellinger, Benedict	1802	-	-	-	Meyer, John	1807	-	-	-
Mellinger, Catharine	1848	N	1	15	Meyer, John	1810	-	-	-
Mellinger, Jacob	1777	-	-	-	Meyer, John	1826	C	1	177
Mellinger, Jacob	1830	E	1	249	Meyer, John	1829	E	1	146
Mellinger, John	1831	F	1	111	Meyer, Martin	1826	C	1	265
Mellinger, John	1834	G	1	136	Meyer, Mary	1818	-	-	-
Mellinger, John	1837	I	1	18	Meyer, Mary	1823	B	1	9
Mellinger, John	1844	L	1	265	Meyer, Mary	1833	G	1	52
Mellinger, Joseph	1841	K	1	205	Meyer, Philip	1809	-	-	-
Mellinger, Michael	1849	N	1	259	Meyer, Samuel	1755	-	-	-
Mellinger, Samuel	1830	E	1	273	Meyers, Jacob	1842	K	1	238
Mellinger, William Sr	1847	M	1	390	Michael, Everhard	1778	-	-	-
Meloney, John	1829	E	1	41	Michael, Jacob	1840	K	1	81
Meloney, William	1816	-	-	-	Michael, William	1776	-	-	-
Meloy, Daniel	1807	-	-	-	Mickley, Jacob	1744	-	-	-
Meney, Barbara	1846	M	1	148	Middleton, George	1747	-	-	-
Mengel, George	1790	-	-	-	Middleton, John	1740	-	-	-
Mengle, Jacob	1847	M	1	290	Middleton, Robert	1731	-	-	-

Name	Year	Bk.	Vol	Page	Name	Year	Bk.	Vol	Page
Middleton, William......	1748	-	-	-	Miller, Jacob..........	1842	K	1	258
Middleton, William......	1831	F	1	31	Miller, Jacob..........	1846	M	1	214
Middletown, Mary.......	1747	-	-	-	Miller, James..........	1746	-	-	-
Milchrack, George.......	1803	-	-	-	Miller, James..........	1778	-	-	-
Mildrum, Henry..........	1811	-	-	-	Miller, James..........	1803	-	-	-
Miles, George..........	1824	B	1	204	Miller, James..........	1808	-	-	-
Miles, Sarah...........	1799	-	-	-	Miller, John..........	1745	-	-	-
Miles, Thomas..........	1747	-	-	-	Miller, John..........	1772	-	-	-
Miley, Henry...........	1805	-	-	-	Miller, John..........	1776	-	-	-
Miley, Samuel..........	1740	-	-	-	Miller, John..........	1793	-	-	-
Miller, Abraham........	1773	-	-	-	Miller, John..........	1801	-	-	-
Miller, Abraham Jr.....	1827	D	1	97	Miller, John Jr......	1801	-	-	-
Miller, Abraham Sr.....	1829	E	1	22	Miller, John..........	1812	-	-	-
Miller, Adam...........	1748	-	-	-	Miller, John..........	1815	-	-	-
Miller, Adam Esq.......	1831	F	1	107	Miller, John..........	1819	-	-	-
Miller, Adam...........	1847	M	1	347	Miller, John (miller)...	1840	K	1	53
Miller, Agness.........	1825	C	1	76	Miller, John D.........	1841	K	1	152
Miller, Alexander......	1767	-	-	-	Miller, Joseph.........	1799	-	-	-
Miller, Andrew.........	1754	-	-	-	Miller, Dr. J. W.......	1845	L	1	313
Miller, Andrew.........	1810	-	-	-	Miller, Dr. J. Whitmer.	1843	L	1	57
Miller, Andrew.........	1838	I	1	80	Miller, Leonard........	1766	-	-	-
Miller, Ann............	1842	K	1	290	Miller, Leonard........	1807	-	-	-
Miller, Ann............	1842	K	1	291	Miller, Margaret.......	1782	-	-	-
Miller, Anna...........	1791	-	-	-	Miller, Margaret.......	1818	-	-	-
Miller, Archibald......	1826	C	1	238	Miller, Margaret.......	1819	-	-	-
Miller, Barbara........	1850	N	1	405	Miller, Maria..........	1746	-	-	-
Miller, Benjamine......	1797	-	-	-	Miller, Maria..........	1845	M	1	13
Miller, Benjamin......	1824	B	1	233	Miller, Martin.........	1743	-	-	-
Miller, Benjamin Sr....	1830	E	1	262	Miller, Martin.........	1828	D	1	266
Miller, Benjamin......	1844	L	1	248	Miller, Martin.........	1832	F	1	200
Miller, Brue...........	1740	-	-	-	Miller, Martin.........	1842	K	1	233
Miller, Catharine......	1838	I	1	157	Miller, Martin.........	1848	N	1	31
Miller, Catharine......	1841	K	1	120	Miller, Mary..........	1825	C	1	30
Miller, Catharine......	1846	M	1	190	Miller, Michael........	1739	-	-	-
Miller, Christian......	1790	-	-	-	Miller, Michael........	1774	-	-	-
Miller, Daniel.........	1822	A	1	225	Miller, Michael........	1828	D	1	189
Miller, Daniel.........	1836	H	1	197	Miller, Nicholas.......	1762	-	-	-
Miller, David..........	1813	-	-	-	Miller, Nicholas.......	1778	-	-	-
Miller, David..........	1827	D	1	18	Miller, Nicholas.......	1798	-	-	-
Miller, Elizabeth......	1749	-	-	-	Miller, Peter.........	1765	-	-	-
Miller, Elizabeth......	1793	-	-	-	Miller, Peter.........	1781	-	-	-
Miller, Elizabeth......	1824	B	1	161	Miller, Peter.........	1797	-	-	-
Miller, Elizabeth......	1842	K	1	239	Miller, Peter.........	1814	-	-	-
Miller, Ernst..........	1806	-	-	-	Miller, Peter.........	1821	A	1	58
Miller, Feronica.......	1778	-	-	-	Miller, Peter.........	1830	E	1	164
Miller, Frederick......	1806	-	-	-	Miller, Peter.........	1836	H	1	204
Miller, Frederick......	1840	I	1	297	Miller, Philip........	1802	-	-	-
Miller, George........	1761	-	-	-	Miller, Rachel........	1847	M	1	358
Miller, George........	1770	-	-	-	Miller, Rebecca........	1842	K	1	218
Miller, George........	1806	-	-	-	Miller, Rebecca........	1849	N	1	265
Miller, George........	1841	K	1	174	Miller, Robert........	1822	A	1	156
Miller, George........	1845	M	1	66	Miller, Rudolph.......	1831	F	1	15
Miller, George........	1850	N	1	430	Miller, Rudolph.......	1837	I	1	243
Miller, George M.......	1841	K	1	180	Miller, Rudolph.......	1845	M	1	73
Miller, Godfried......	1827	D	1	37	Miller, Samuel.........	1783	-	-	-
Miller, Hannah.........	1831	F	1	80	Miller, Samuel.........	1818	-	-	-
Miller, Hans Adam......	1760	-	-	-	Miller, Samuel.........	1838	I	1	71
Miller, Henry.........	1817	-	-	-	Miller, Samuel.........	1839	I	1	204
Miller, Henry, Jr.....	1835	H	1	54	Miller, Samuel.........	1847	M	1	340
Miller, Henry M........	1848	M	1	457	Miller, Sebastian......	1843	L	1	136
Miller, Jacob..........	1737	-	-	-	Miller, Stuart........	1825	C	1	34
Miller, Jacob..........	1740	-	-	-	Miller, Thomas........	1733	-	-	-
Miller, Jacob..........	1757	-	-	-	Miller, Tobias........	1834	G	1	180
Miller, Jacob..........	1758	-	-	-	Miller, Tobius........	1843	L	1	105
Miller, Jacob..........	1776	-	-	-	Miller, Tolly.........	1746	-	-	-
Miller, Jacob..........	1782	-	-	-	Miller, Ulrich........	1814	-	-	-
Miller, Jacob..........	1811	-	-	-	Miller, Valentine......	1771	-	-	-
Miller, Jacob..........	1813	-	-	-	Miller, Warrick.......	1814	-	-	-
Miller, Jacob..........	1823	B	1	52	Miller, William.......	1826	C	1	196
Miller, Jacob..........	1824	B	1	226	Miller, William.......	1839	I	1	203
Miller, Jacob..........	1828	E	1	7	Miller, William........	1850	O	1	19
Miller, Jacob..........	1838	I	1	139	Mills, Benjamin........	1804	-	-	-

Name	Year	Bk.	Vol	Page	Name	Year	Bk.	Vol	Page
Mills, William	1828	D	1	184	Moore, John	1837	H	1	235
Milroy, Henry	1769	-	-	-	Moore, John	1838	I	1	36
Miney, Elizabeth	1836	H	1	141	Moore, Louisa	1822	A	1	170
Mingel, Catharine	1814	-	-	-	Moore, Mary	1768	-	-	-
Mingle, Francis	1822	A	1	195	Moore, Mary	1847	M	1	298
Mingle, Francis	1828	D	1	185	Moore, Moses	1835	G	1	274
Minnea, John	1801	-	-	-	Moore, Moses	1847	M	1	245
Minor, Peter F.	1832	F	1	229	Moore, Richard	1841	K	1	146
Minor, Sheldon	1827	D	1	135	Moore, Richard	1848	N	1	125
Minor, Sherman	1801	-	-	-	Moore, Robert (miller)	1823	A	1	277
Mishey, Jacob	1850	N	1	322	Moore, Dr. Robert	1833	G	1	19
Mishey, John	1821	A	1	60	Moore, Salina	1826	C	1	145
Mishler, Woolrick	1759	-	-	-	Moore, Samuel B	1634	G	1	231
Miskey, John	1805	-	-	-	Moore, Thomas	1834	G	1	227
Mitchel, Elizabeth	1734	-	-	-	Moore, William	1747	-	-	-
Mitchel, James	1843	L	1	144	Moore, William	1815	-	-	-
Mitchell, Ann	1822	A	1	184	Moore, William	1816	-	-	-
Mitchell, Hannah	1751	-	-	-	Moore, Zacharia	1760	-	-	-
Mitchell, John	1790	-	-	-	Moore, Zacharia	1803	-	-	-
Mitchell, John	1827	D	1	46	Moore, Zacharia	1829	E	1	114
Mixell, Ann Mary	1748	-	-	-	Moore, Zacharia	1847	M	1	408
Modderwell, Samuel	1831	F	1	90	Moorehead, Mary	1848	N	1	57
Mohl, Christopher	1817	-	-	-	Morgan, David	1788	-	-	-
Mohler, Henry	1845	M	1	69	Morgan, James	1770	-	-	-
Mohler, Mary	1837	I	1	6	Morgan, John	1747	-	-	-
Mohler, Mary Ann	1849	N	1	182	Morgan, Joseph S	1850	N	1	334
Mohler, Samuel Esq	1827	D	1	151	Morgan, Morgan	1807	-	-	-
Moll, John	1754	-	-	-	Morgan, Thomas	1732	-	-	-
Mollyneux, Edward	1746	-	-	-	Morgan, William	1748	-	-	-
Monahan, Hugh	1843	L	1	40	Morgan, William	1802	-	-	-
Mondorf, John	1801	-	-	-	Morgan, William	1850	N	1	366
Money, Thomas	1800	-	-	-	Morgronder, Adams	1778	-	-	-
Montandon, Henry L.	1802	-	-	-	Morris, Charles	1810	-	-	-
Montelnis, Marcis	1831	F	1	2	Morris, Henry	1810	-	-	-
Montgomery, Agnes	1744	-	-	-	Morris, John	1832	F	1	151
Montgomery, Archibald	1774	-	-	-	Morrison, Eleanor	1826	C	1	240
Montgomery, David Esq	1826	C	1	236	Morrison, James	1811	-	-	-
Montgomery, Humphrey	1753	-	-	-	Morrison, Jane	1829	E	1	104
Montgomery, John	1822	A	1	245	Morrison, John	1741	-	-	-
Montgomery, Robert	1765	-	-	-	Morrison, Joseph	1840	I	1	294
Montgomery, Sarah	1784	-	-	-	Morrison, Robert	1805	-	-	-
Montgomery, William	1816	-	-	-	Morrison, Samuel	1747	-	-	-
Montgomery, William Esq.	1826	C	1	170	Morrison, Samuel	1849	N	1	266
Moody, Robert	1736	-	-	-	Morrow, John	1760	-	-	-
Mooney, Daniel	1795	-	-	-	Morrow, John	1822	A	1	239
Mooney, George	1829	E	1	138	Morry, Elizabeth	1804	-	-	-
Mooney, Joseph	1823	B	1	38	Morry, Henry	1825	C	1	13
Mooney, Peter	1777	-	-	-	Morton, David	1768	-	-	-
Moore, Adam	1787	-	-	-	Morton, James	1822	A	1	120
Moore, Adam	1808	-	-	-	Mosely, Peter	1833	G	1	100
Moore, Andrew	1828	D	1	245	Moseman, Christian	1755	-	-	-
Moore, Ann	1847	M	1	243	Moser, Adam	1769	-	-	-
Moore, Ann	1847	M	1	289	Mosey, Christian	1827	D	1	75
Moore, Daniel	1822	A	1	210	Mosher, Jeremiah	1830	E	1	228
Moore, David	1775	-	-	-	Mosher, William	1823	B	1	50
Moore, Eliza	1746	-	-	-	Mosser, Jacob	1760	-	-	-
Moore, Ephraim	1821	A	1	14	Mosser, Jacob	1800	-	-	-
Moore, Garvin	1758	-	-	-	Mosser, Magdalena	1810	-	-	-
Moore, George	1773	-	-	-	Moulton, John N.	1821	-	-	-
Moore, Dr. George	1809	-	-	-	Mourer, Elizabeth	1841	K	1	132
Moore, George	1837	H	1	262	Mouse, Barnard	1766	-	-	-
Moore, George	1850	N	1	429	Mowrer, Christiana	1850	N	1	351
Moore, Henry	1830	E	1	167	Mowrer, George	1759	-	-	-
Moore, Jacob	1848	N	1	51	Mowrer, Henry	1767	-	-	-
Moore, James	1755	-	-	-	Mowrer, Jacob	1800	-	-	-
Moore, James	1809	-	-	-	Mowrer, Martin	1771	-	-	-
Moore, James	1813	-	-	-	Moyel, Jacob	1735	-	-	-
Moore, James	1814	-	-	-	Moyer, Frederick	1842	K	1	319
Moore, Jane	1839	I	I	240	Moyer, Henry	1775	-	-	-
Moore, John	1752	-	-	-	Moyer, Margaret	1789	-	-	-
Moore, John	1781	-	-	-	Moyer, Michael	1785	-	-	-
Moore, John	1832	F	1	269	Muckle, Benjamin	1812	-	-	-

Name	Year	Bk.	Vol	Page	Name	Year	Bk.	Vol	Page
Muckle, Eve	1850	O	1	39	Musser, George	1806	-	-	-
Muecke, Christian	1843	L	1	116	Musser, Hans Adam Jr	1759	-	-	-
Muhlenberg, Frederick A.	1801	-	-	-	Musser, Henry	1804	-	-	-
Muhlenberg, Frederick A.	1844	L	1	278	Musser, Henry	1808	-	-	-
Muldoon, Edward	1825	C	1	103	Musser, Henry	1823	A	1	274
Mulgren, Francis	1848	N	1	23	Musser, Henry (tailor)	1830	E	1	180
Mulhollin, Joseph	1840	K	1	39	Musser, Henry	1846	M	1	98
Mulholne, James	1784	-	-	-	Musser, Henry	1847	M	1	349
Mull, Barbara	1844	L	1	188	Musser, Jacob	1782	-	-	-
Mull, Barbara	1845	M	1	52	Musser, Jacob	1817	-	-	-
Mullen, Arslill	1747	-	-	-	Musser, Jacob	1825	C	1	6
Mullin, John	1839	I	1	190	Musser, Jacob	1832	F	1	140
Muma, Henry	1843	L	1	118	Musser, John	1804	-	-	-
Mumma, Abraham	1826	C	1	248	Musser, John	1827	D	1	38
Mumma, Abraham	1830	E	1	246	Musser, Magdalena	1840	K	1	30
Mumma, Ann	1847	M	1	310	Musser, Dr. Martin	1849	N	1	262
Mumma, Christian	1754	-	-	-	Musser, Mary	1828	D	1	263
Mumma, Christian	1797	-	-	-	Musser, Mary	1849	N	1	149
Mumma, Frederick	1822	A	1	142	Musser, Nicholas	1783	-	-	-
Mumma, Lawrence	1752	-	-	-	Musser, Peter	1782	-	-	-
Mumma, Leonard	1770	-	-	-	Musser, Peter	1848	N	1	59
Mumma, Peter	1785	-	-	-	Musser, Samuel	1838	I	1	71
Mummer, Jacob	1748	-	-	-	Musser, William	1803	-	-	-
Mundorf, Christian	1825	C	1	15	Mussleman, Ann	1834	G	1	178
Munshauer, Henry Sr	1834	G	1	145	Mussleman, John	1799	-	-	-
Munshauer, Henry Sr	1834	G	1	149	Mussleman, Mary	1837	I	1	7
Murphy, Charles	1747	-	-	-	Myer, Abraham	1771	-	-	-
Murphy, Daniel	1746	-	-	-	Myer, Abraham	1780	-	-	-
Murphy, Daniel	1747	-	-	-	Myer, Christian	1804	-	-	-
Murphy, John	1847	M	1	270	Myer, Christopher	1762	-	-	-
Murphy, Jonothan	1848	M	1	446	Myer, George	1757	-	-	-
Murphy, Michael	1840	K	1	25	Myer, Hans	1756	-	-	-
Murray, Absolom	1824	D	1	57	Myer, Henry	1769	-	-	-
Murray, Edward	1849	N	1	260	Myer, Henry	1781	-	-	-
Murray, Felix	1832	F	1	208	Myer, Isaac	1770	-	-	-
Murray, John	1833	G	1	91	Myer, Jacob	1743	-	-	-
Murray, John	1847	M	1	380	Myer, Jacob	1788	-	-	-
Murray, John	1847	M	1	387	Myer, Jacob	1796	-	-	-
Murray, Joseph	1805	-	-	-	Myer, John	1766	-	-	-
Murray, Joseph	1849	N	1	206	Myer, Judy	1787	-	-	-
Murray, Rachael	1816	-	-	-	Myer, Lawrence	1855	-	-	-
Murray, Susanna	1798	-	-	-	Myer, Magdalena	1838	I	1	53
Murray, Susanna	1807	-	-	-	Myer, Michael	1751	-	-	-
Murray, Susanna	1813	-	-	-	Myer, Michael	1775	-	-	-
Murron, Francis	1788	-	-	-	Myer, Michael	1778	-	-	-
Murry, John	1846	M	1	104	Myer, Michael	1802	-	-	-
Murry, Robert	1733	-	-	-	Myer, Rudolph	1818	-	-	-
Musgetness, John	1792	-	-	-	Myer, Socrates	1837	I	1	5
Musgrave, John	1753	-	-	-	Myer, Valentine	1796	-	-	-
Musgrove, John	1750	-	-	-	Myers, Ann	1833	G	1	40
Musketnuss, Adam	1821	A	1	43	Myers, Ann Elizabeth	1826	C	1	272
Musselman, Christian	1734	-	-	-	Myers, Barbara	1843	L	1	138
Musselman, Christian	1816	-	-	-	Myers, Christian	1833	G	1	41
Musselman, Christian	1832	F	1	191	Myers, Dewalt	1776	-	-	-
Musselman, David	1829	E	1	100	Myers, Esther	1829	E	1	68
Musselman, David	1848	N	1	1	Myers, Frederick	1826	C	1	280
Musselman, Henry	1752	-	-	-	Myers, Hans	1752	-	-	-
Musselman, Jacob	1814	-	-	-	Myers, Henry	1849	N	1	176
Musselman, Jacob	1819	-	-	-	Myers, Isaac	1837	H	1	269
Musselman, Jacob	1822	A	1	122	Myers, Jacob	1840	K	1	77
Musselman, Jacob	1828	D	1	223	Myers, Jacob	1848	N	1	137
Musselman, Jacob	1840	K	1	45	Myers, John	1787	-	-	-
Musselman, John	1832	F	1	135	Myers, John	1827	D	1	98
Musselman, John	1849	N	1	216	Myers, John	1831	F	1	62
Musselman, Peter	1828	D	1	255	Myers, John	1841	K	1	100
Musselman, Salome	1766	-	-	-	Myers, Louisa	1838	I	1	52
Musselman, Susan	1846	M	1	212	Myers, Louisa	1847	M	1	354
Musser, Benjamin	1824	B	1	170	Myers, Martin	1741	-	-	-
Musser, Catharine	1843	L	1	58	Myers, Michael	1776	-	-	-
Musser, Christian	1741	-	-	-	Myers, William	1839	I	1	218
Musser, Christian	1755	-	-	-	Myler, Martin	1751	-	-	-
Musser, Elizabeth	1826	C	1	219	Mylin, Christian	1839	I	1	193

Name	Year	Bk.	Vol	Page	Name	Year	Bk.	Vol	Page
Mylin, Christian	1844	L	1	289	Newcomer, Christian	1814	-	-	-
Mylin, Daniel	1842	K	1	213	Newcomer, Jacob	1759	-	-	-
Mylin, Elizabeth	1848	M	1	448	Newcomer, John	1732	-	-	-
Mylin, Jacob	1837	H	1	215	Newcomer, John	1788	-	-	-
Mylin, Martin	1839	I	1	238	Newcomer, John	1826	C	1	203
N					Newlin, Thomas	1840	-	-	-
Naftsiger, Ulrich	1754	-	-	-	Newman, Catharine	1826	C	1	142
Nagel, John	1818	-	-	-	Newman, Daniel	1787	-	-	-
Nagle, Charles	1832	F	1	136	Newman, David	1775	-	-	-
Nagle, Henry	1846	M	1	172	Newman, John	1850	N	1	367
Nagle, John	1813	-	-	-	Newman, Seit	1777	-	-	-
Nagle, John George	1789	-	-	-	Newschwander, Christian	1847	M	1	253
Nagle, Joseph	1808	-	-	-	Newswanger, Christian	1769	-	-	-
Nagle, Margaret	1768	-	-	-	Newswanger, Christian	1846	M	1	135
Nagle, Margaret	1850	N	1	453	Newswanger, Emanuel	1805	-	-	-
Nauman, Frederick	1818	-	-	-	Newswanger, Jacob	1835	H	1	80
Nauman, Godleib	1803	-	-	-	Newswanger, Joseph	1819	-	-	-
Nauman, John	1791	-	-	-	Newswanger, Woolrich	1751	-	-	-
Nauman, John	1836	H	1	203	Ney, Henry	1784	-	-	-
Neagly, Jacob	1791	-	-	-	Ney, Joseph	1784	-	-	-
Neal, McNeal	1846	M	1	123	Nicholson, Samuel	1757	-	-	-
Neare, John	1759	-	-	-	Nickey, John	1788	-	-	-
Nease, Michael	1761	-	-	-	Niedy, Abraham	1752	-	-	-
Nease, Philip	1830	E	1	269	Nippling, Michael	1765	-	-	-
Nebbett, John	1748	-	-	-	Nissley, Christian,Jr	1822	A	1	196
Neeper, James	1844	L	1	171	Nissley, Christian	1847	M	1	418
Neff, Ann	1793	-	-	-	Nissley, Henry, Sr	1849	N	1	152
Neff, Benjamin	1828	D	1	226	Nissley, John	1800	-	-	-
Neff, Catharine	1828	D	1	280	Nissley, John	1837	H	1	251
Neff, Catharine	1845	M	1	64	Nissley, John	1849	N	1	279
Neff, Christian	1799	-	-	-	Nissley, Martin	1779	-	-	-
Neff, Christian	1821	A	1	30	Nissley, Martin	1838	I	1	33
Neff, Daniel	1763	-	-	-	Nissley, Mary	1801	-	-	-
Neff, Daniel	1787	-	-	-	Nissly, Jacob	1749	-	-	-
Neff, Elizabeth	1800	-	-	-	Nixdorf, John	1802	-	-	-
Neff, Francis	1739	-	-	-	Nixon, John	1821	A	1	61
Neff, Henry	1745	-	-	-	Nixon, William	1824	B	1	205
Neff, Henry	1845	M	1	59	Noble, Andrew	1769	-	-	-
Neff, Jacob K	1845	M	1	11	Noble, John	1775	-	-	-
Neff, John	1788	-	-	-	Noble, Margaret	1840	I	1	317
Neff, Magdalena	1820	-	-	-	Noecker, John Diel	1757	-	-	-
Neff, Nancy	1850	N	1	420	Noll, Henry, Jr	1822	A	1	200
Negele, Leonhart	1771	-	-	-	Nolt, David	1846	M	1	163
Negley, Catharine	1817	-	-	-	Nolt, Elizabeth	1836	H	1	125
Neidich, Michael	1830	E	1	264	Nolt, John	1825	C	1	75
Neil, John	1784	-	-	-	Nolt, Joseph	1848	N	1	121
Neil, William	1813	-	-	-	Nolt, Magdalena	1833	G	1	118
Neiman, John	1850	N	1	320	Nolt, Nancy	1846	M	1	196
Neiman, Margaret	1835	H	1	37	Norbeck, Catharine	1818	-	-	-
Neiman, Margaret	1839	I	1	165	North, William L	1834	G	1	250
Neimeier, John	1849	N	1	204	Northamer, John	1818	-	-	-
Neimeyer, Mary	1848	N	1	10	Nuden, Thomas	1781	-	-	-
Neisley, John	1823	B	1	77	Nugent, James	1838	I	1	81
Neisley, Martin	1833	G	1	116	Null, Jacob	1849	N	1	196
Neissley, Christian	1849	N	1	271	**O**				
Nelch, Abraham	1767	-	-	-	Ober, Henry	1838	I	1	61
Nelson, James	1832	F	1	188	Ober, Henry	1839	I	1	195
Nelson, Margaret	1754	-	-	-	Ober, Henry	1843	L	1	96
Nelson, Margaret	1779	-	-	-	Ober, Margaret	1841	K	1	94
Nelson, Robert	1831	F	1	125	Oberholtz, Jacob	1806	-	-	-
Nelson, Thomas	1759	-	-	-	Oberholtzer, Jacob	1812	-	-	-
Nelson, Thomas	1803	-	-	-	Oberholtzer, John	1801	-	-	-
Nerius, John	1802	-	-	-	Oberlin, Adam	1780	-	-	-
Nestleroth, Christian	1813	-	-	-	Oberlin, Ann	1819	-	-	-
Nestleroth, John	1822	A	1	138	Oberlin, Henry	1804	-	-	-
Netz, Sebastian	1753	-	-	-	Oberlin, Jacob	1793	-	-	-
Netzler, Casper	1767	-	-	-	Oberlin, Jacob	1822	A	1	164
Neuycomet, John	1782	-	-	-	Oblinger, Barbara	1803	-	-	-
Newcomar, John	1755	-	-	-	OBrian, Michael	1797	-	-	-
Newcomer, Ann	1842	K	1	236	OBrian, Thomas	1839	I	1	258
Newcomer, Christian	1786	-	-	-	OBryan, Bryan	1822	A	1	236
Newcomer, Christian	1798	-	-	-	OBryan, Elizabeth	1747	-	-	-

Name	Year	Bk.	Vol	Page	Name	Year	Bk.	Vol	Page
OBryan, Neal	1747	-	-	-	Patterson, John	1825	C	1	20
Ochs, Jacob	1833	G	1	26	Patterson, Joseph	1785	-	-	-
OConner, James	1816	-	-	-	Patterson, Margaret	1811	-	-	-
Odenwald, George	1814	-	-	-	Patterson, Mary	1837	H	1	229
Offner, Mathias	1784	-	-	-	Patterson, Robert	1848	N	1	82
Offner, Samuel C	1821	A	1	84	Patterson, Samuel	1758	-	-	-
Ogeltree, John	1741	-	-	-	Patterson, William	1785	-	-	-
Ohmit, Jacob, Sr	1833	G	1	98	Patterson, William	1796	-	-	-
Old, Davis	1805	-	-	-	Patterson, William	1806	-	-	-
Oldweiler, Frederick	1800	-	-	-	Pattin, James	1739	-	-	-
Oldweiler, Frederick	1832	F	1	165	Pattin, John	1741	-	-	-
Oldweiler, George	1790	-	-	-	Patton, Cunningham	1825	C	1	85
Oliver, Joseph	1743	-	-	-	Patton, Hugh	1770	-	-	-
ONeal, Daniel	1826	C	1	176	Patton, Jane	1834	G	1	205
ONeal, James	1786	-	-	-	Patton, Jane	1834	G	1	218
ONeal, Owen	1730	-	-	-	Patton, Jennett	1790	-	-	-
Orendorff, Herman	1777	-	-	-	Patton, Jennett	1839	I	1	183
Orendorff, John	1850	N	1	375	Patton, John	1758	-	-	-
Ori, John	1829	E	1	149	Patton, John	1769	-	-	-
Orr, James	1756	-	-	-	Patton, Joseph	1769	-	-	-
Oster, Henry	1838	I	1	130	Patton, Margaret	1849	N	1	277
Oswald, William	1823	B	1	67	Patton, Robert	1745	-	-	-
Otenkirk, David	1816	-	-	-	Patton, Thomas H	1844	L	1	208
Ott, George	1845	M	1	70	Patton, William	1771	-	-	-
Otto, John	1824	B	1	138	Paul, John George	1840	K	1	16
Otto, Margaret	1802	-	-	-	Paulees, Elizabeth	1808	-	-	-
Otto, Ulrich	1784	-	-	-	Pauling, Elizabeth	1788	-	-	-
Ourn, Elizabeth	1821	A	1	50	Pearson, David	1740	-	-	-
Overholtz, Samuel	1748	-	-	-	Pearson, Samuel	1847	M	1	365
Overholtzer, Abraham	1835	H	1	9	Peart, Benjamin	1837	I	1	21
Overholtzer, Jacob	1755	-	-	-	Peart, Thomas	1831	F	1	29
Overholtzer, Martin	1767	-	-	-	Peck, ,	1822	A	1	204
Owen, Jonathan, Sr	1801	-	-	-	Peck, Catharine	1835	G	1	269
Owen, Jonathan	1845	M	1	58	Peck, John	1812	-	-	-
Owen, Lydia	1827	D	1	80	Peck, Nicholas	1833	G	1	130
Owen, Lydia	1829	E	1	121	Peck, Samuel	1837	H	1	227
Owens, Theoplsis	1749	-	-	-	Pedan, Mary	1825	C	1	96
P					Pedan, Sarah	1831	F	1	100
Paden, John	1849	O	1	44	Pedan, Sarah	1831	F	1	101
Painter, Philip	1802	-	-	-	Peden, John	1821	-	-	-
Palmer, Michael	1773	-	-	-	Peden, Samuel S	1819	-	-	-
Palmer, Philip Adam	1761	-	-	-	Peeble, Jacob	1782	-	-	-
Palmn, Jacob	1823	B	1	3	Peeper, Abraham	1810	-	-	-
Pannabecker, Daniel	1825	C	1	117	Pegan, Andreas	1830	E	1	258
Pant, John	1754	-	-	-	Peidegaiffer, Nicholas	1741	-	-	-
Pantz, Ernst	1830	E	1	192	Peifer, John	1830	E	1	230
Park, James	1826	C	1	237	Peifer, Joseph	1846	M	1	145
Park, John	1848	N	1	67	Peifer, Maria	1847	M	1	267
Park, Samuel	1739	-	-	-	Peifer, Martin	1831	F	1	37
Park, Samuel	1740	-	-	-	Peiffer, Jacob	1785	-	-	-
Parker, Joseph	1823	B	1	62	Peirce, Marris	1836	H	1	101
Parker, Joseph	1849	N	1	392	Pemiler, Michael	1763	-	-	-
Parker, Robert	1820	-	-	-	Penery, Robert	1765	-	-	-
Parker, Robert	1823	B	1	60	Penett, Charles Lewis				
Parks, Margaret	1751	-	-	-	Mathew	1795	-	-	-
Parks, William	1749	-	-	-	Pennell, William W	1848	M	1	453
Parr, William	1786	-	-	-	Pennice, David	1760	-	-	-
Parry, Seneca	1848	N	1	100	Penninger, Peter	1821	A	1	64
Parsons, William	1833	G	1	82	Pennock, Catharine	1815	-	-	-
Passmore, John	1823	B	1	57	Pennock, Jacob	1811	-	-	-
Passmore, John, Esq	1827	D	1	136	Pennock, Jacob	1821	A	1	31
Patomer, Frederick	1752	-	-	-	Pennock, William	1847	M	1	374
Patrick, Hugh	1778	-	-	-	Penny, Joseph	1835	H	1	8
Patterson, Andrew	1733	-	-	-	Peoples, James	1820	-	-	-
Patterson, Arthur	1764	-	-	-	Peoples, Samuel	1752	-	-	-
Patterson, Clements	1805	-	-	-	Peppel, Peter	1765	-	-	-
Patterson, David	1742	-	-	-	Perrin, Thomas	1746	-	-	-
Patterson, Eliza L	1831	F	1	93	Peter, George	1838	I	1	59
Patterson, Elizabeth	1830	E	1	240	Peter, Michael	1806	-	-	-
Patterson, James	1825	C	1	104	Peter, Valentine	1824	B	1	151
Patterson, John	1785	-	-	-	Peterman, Henry	1824	B	1	237
Patterson, John	1798	-	-	-	Peterman, Jacob	1769	-	-	-

Name	Year	Bk.	Vol	Page	Name	Year	Bk.	Vol	Page
Peterman, Jacob	1834	G	1	249	Porter, William	1810	-	-	-
Peterman, Joachim	1842	K	1	263	Porterfield, David	1768	-	-	-
Peterman, Joseph	1848	M	1	431	Potter, Joshua	1823	B	1	83
Peters, Conrad	1827	D	1	137	Potter, Samuel	1828	D	1	200
Peters, Elias	1783	-	-	-	Potter, Thomas	1795	-	-	-
Peters, Jacob	1795	-	-	-	Potts, James	1755	-	-	-
Peters, John	1805	-	-	-	Potts, Joseph	1826	C	1	279
Peters, John	1826	C	1	285	Potts, Samuel	1829	E	1	80
Peters, Leonard	1817	-	-	-	Powel, George	1802	-	-	-
Petersheim, Christian	1831	F	1	48	Powel, Mary	1767	-	-	-
Peterson, Catharine R.	1844	L	1	221	Powers, John	1827	D	1	69
Petry, George	1767	-	-	-	Powers, Robert	1849	N	1	387
Petticoffer, Isaac	1818	-	-	-	Pownall, Maria	1843	L	1	121
Petticoffer, John, Sr.	1834	G	1	177	Prasser, Thomas	1849	N	1	168
Petticoffer, John	1845	M	1	10	Prater, Anthony	1750	-	-	-
Petticoffer, John	1848	N	1	85	Praton, Anthony	1746	-	-	-
Petz, Ann	1781	-	-	-	Preelinger, Mary	1749	-	-	-
Peusch, John	1844	L	1	286	Prees, David	1774	-	-	-
Pfeiffer, Mary	1848	N	1	29	Preese, David	1745	-	-	-
Pfoetzer, George	1781	-	-	-	Preinisholtz, Elizabeth	1781	-	-	-
Pfouts, Jacob	1800	-	-	-	Prenniman, Stephen	1758	-	-	-
Pfoutz, Martin	1821	A	1	22	Price, John	1849	N	1	333
Pfund, John Adam	1847	M	1	350	Price, Joseph	1827	D	1	95
Philips, Charles S.	1849	N	1	254	Price, Joseph	1831	F	1	40
Philips, John	1817	-	-	-	Price, Samuel	1750	-	-	-
Philips, William	1757	-	-	-	Price, Samuel	1760	-	-	-
Phillips, Henry	1849	N	1	214	Price, Dr. William	1829	E	1	89
Phillips, William	1749	-	-	-	Price, William P.	1839	I	1	175
Phite, Jacob	1828	E	1	16	Pricker, Henry	1838	I	1	60
Phite, Peter	1822	A	1	161	Pritzins, George	1831	F	1	73
Phyfer, Martin	1823	B	1	115	Prong, Peter	1835	H	1	17
Pickel, George	1849	N	1	413	Prosser, John	1829	E	1	97
Pickel, Peter	1821	A	1	44	Pruitzel, Margaret	1826	C	1	286
Piersol, Catharine	1825	C	1	105	Pudigater, Ann Barbara	1746	-	-	-
Piersol, Isaac	1825	-	-	-	Punch, Hans Michael	1754	-	-	-
Piersol, Jacueus	1804	-	-	-	Purviance, James	1748	-	-	-
Pillman, Christian	1749	-	-	-	Purviance, John	1749	-	-	-
Pinkerton, David	1803	-	-	-	Pyfer, Martin	1752	-	-	-
Pinkerton, Henry	1837	H	1	286	Pyle, Isaac	1849	N	1	328
Pinkerton, Henry	1837	H	1	287	Pyle, John	1840	I	1	298
Pinkerton, John	1787	-	-	-	Pyle, John	1842	K	1	262
Pinkerton, John, Sr.	1832	F	1	202	**Q**				
Pinkerton, Thomas	1783	-	-	-	Quickle, Philip	1749	-	-	-
Plaisterer, Conrad	1803	-	-	-	Quickley, Patrick	1783	-	-	-
Plank, John	1844	L	1	276	Quigle, Philip	1749	-	-	-
Plantz, Barbara	1833	G	1	20	Quin, Cornelius	1772	-	-	-
Plantz, Christopher	1754	-	-	-	Quinn, Daniel	1784	-	-	-
Plantz, John	1797	-	-	-	Quinn, Michael	1830	E	1	202
Plantz, Mathias	1797	-	-	-	Quinn, Michael	1835	H	1	72
Plantz, Mathias	1802	-	-	-	**R**				
Plasterer, Margaret	1822	A	1	162	Raeder, John	1778	-	-	-
Platt, Thomas	1841	K	1	118	Ragy, Peter	1767	-	-	-
Platt, William	1801	-	-	-	Rahm, Melchoir	1783	-	-	-
Please, Jesse	1825	C	1	137	Raiser, Mary	1805	-	-	-
Pleis, Jacob	1765	-	-	-	Raiser, Michael	1838	I	1	29
Pletcher, Henry	1749	-	-	-	Ralson, Paul	1838	I	1	74
Pletcher, Mandlin	1747	-	-	-	Ralston, Joseph	1812	-	-	-
Plunk, Samuel	1844	L	1	271	Ralston, Paul	1813	-	-	-
Plunkett, Robert	1823	B	1	91	Ralston, Paul, Jr.	1829	E	1	78
Poh, Wendel	1768	-	-	-	Rambacher, David	1776	-	-	-
Poicht, Jacob	1806	-	-	-	Rambo, Susan	1730	-	-	-
Poicht, Jacob	1831	F	1	96	Ramsay, Nathaniel	1820	-	-	-
Pontz, Michael	1741	-	-	-	Ramsbottom, Samuel	1741	-	-	-
Pool, Abraham	1791	-	-	-	Ramsey, Alexander	1831	F	1	65
Poolman, Christopher	1774	-	-	-	Ramsey, Elizabeth	1817	-	-	-
Poor, William	1826	C	1	226	Ramsey, David	1780	-	-	-
Poorman, George	1739	-	-	-	Ramsey, Isaac	1847	M	1	406
Poorman, George	1743	-	-	-	Ramsey, Michael	1771	-	-	-
Pope, Richard	1746	-	-	-	Ramsey, Robert	1778	-	-	-
Porter, James	1798	-	-	-	Ramsey, Robert	1789	-	-	-
Porter, John	1765	-	-	-	Ramsey, William	1737	-	-	-
Porter, Thomas	1777	-	-	-	Ramsey, William	1784	-	-	-

Name	Year	Bk.	Vol	Page	Name	Year	Bk.	Vol	Page
Ramsey, William.........	1803	-	-	-	Reese, William.........	1839	I	1	283
Ranck, Abraham.........	1831	F	1	105	Reeser, Christian......	1818	-	-	-
Ranck, Barbara.........	1783	-	-	-	Reeser, Christian......	1849	N	1	252
Ranck, Caroline.......	1848	N	1	81	Reesler, Samuel........	1838	I	1	147
Ranck, Elizabeth......	1842	K	1	303	Reesor, John..........	1850	N	1	326
Ranck, Jacob..........	1814	-	-	-	Reganass, John J.......	1850	N	1	395
Ranck, John...........	1848	N	1	87	Regar, Jacob...........	1825	C	1	41
Ranck, Lewis..........	1832	F	1	147	Regnas, Jacob..........	1752	-	-	-
Ranck, Magdalena......	1815	-	-	-	Reib, Joseph...........	1842	K	1	209
Ranck, Michael........	1778	-	-	-	Reichenbach, Edward G...	1823	B	1	63
Ranck, Michael........	1826	C	1	266	Reichurin, Henry.......	1824	B	1	213
Ranck, Philip.........	1784	-	-	-	Reid, John.............	1796	-	-	-
Randall, Jesse L......	1831	F	1	35	Reidabaugh, John, Sr....	1833	G	1	67
Ranger, James.........	1839	I	1	250	Reidle, Yost...........	1802	-	-	-
Rank, Isaac...........	1826	C	1	182	Reidlinger, John, Sr...	1825	C	1	27
Ranken, John..........	1770	-	-	-	Reidlinger, John, Sr...	1825	C	1	28
Rankin, James.........	1830	E	1	251	Reidlinger, Margaret....	1825	C	1	29
Rankin, John..........	1748	-	-	-	Reier, Samuel..........	1763	-	-	-
Ranlein, George.......	1784	-	-	-	Reiff, Abraham.........	1818	-	-	-
Ranshall, Simon.......	1793	-	-	-	Reiff, Jacob...........	1821	-	-	-
Rapp, Jacob...........	1844	L	1	247	Reiff, Jacob...........	1827	D	1	123
Rascon, William.......	1797	-	-	-	Reiff, Susanna.........	1847	M	1	412
Rathacker, John.......	1783	-	-	-	Reigart, Ann...........	1829	E	1	55
Rathfon, Catharine....	1804	-	-	-	Reigart, Christian.....	1824	B	1	160
Rathfon, Elizabeth....	1850	N	1	411	Reigart, Daniel.......	1831	F	1	19
Rathfon, Jacob, Sr....	1829	E	1	106	Reigart, Henry.........	1821	A	1	98
Rathfon, Jacob........	1839	I	1	230	Reigart, Michael......	1841	K	1	92
Rathfon, John.........	1832	F	1	228	Reigart, Philip W......	1833	G	1	106
Rathfon, Joseph.......	1821	A	1	80	Reiger, Ann...........	1813	-	-	-
Rathfon, Michael......	1823	A	1	249	Reiger, Jacob, Esq.....	1793	-	-	-
Rathmacher, Christian...	1831	F	1	74	Reily, John...........	1826	C	1	180
Rathvon, George.......	1799	-	-	-	Reily, Lewis..........	1812	-	-	-
Ratten, William, Sr...	1846	M	1	195	Reily, William B......	1850	N	1	422
Rauch, Barbara........	1827	D	1	66	Reimer, Jacob.........	1812	-	-	-
Raub, Jacob...........	1815	-	-	-	Reinert, Catharine....	1831	F	1	83
Raub, Jacob...........	1832	F	1	226	Reinert, Frederick.....	1819	-	-	-
Raub, Jonas...........	1848	N	1	47	Reinhard, Frederick....	1755	-	-	-
Rauch, John M.........	1777	-	-	-	Reinhart, Charles......	1804	-	-	-
Rauls, Philip.........	1840	K	1	8	Reinhart, Charles.....	1805	-	-	-
Rawlins, Dr. Morgan...	1832	F	1	171	Reinhart, Christian....	1819	-	-	-
Razer, Adam...........	1739	-	-	-	Reinhart, Christopher...	1847	M	1	403
Razor, Adam...........	1739	-	-	-	Reinhart, Daniel.......	1805	-	-	-
Rea, Charles..........	1739	-	-	-	Reinhart, Jacob........	1805	-	-	-
Rea, James............	1788	-	-	-	Reinhart, Michael......	1827	D	1	128
Read, James...........	1802	-	-	-	Reinhart, Michael......	1829	E	1	60
Read, John............	1753	-	-	-	Reinhold, John.........	1844	L	1	288
Read, Thomas..........	1781	-	-	-	Reinick, Christian.....	1785	-	-	-
Read, Thomas M., Esq...	1820	-	-	-	Reinke, Abraham........	1833	G	1	43
Reaff, John...........	1807	-	-	-	Reis, Samuel..........	1822	A	1	211
Ream, Henry...........	1840	K	1	57	Reiss, Henry..........	1814	-	-	-
Ream, Jacob...........	1802	-	-	-	Reist, Abraham H.......	1847	M	1	265
Ream, John............	1792	-	-	-	Reist, Ann............	1843	L	1	141
Ream, John............	1803	-	-	-	Reist, Jacob..........	1750	-	-	-
Ream, Juliana.........	1824	B	1	185	Reist, John...........	1817	-	-	-
Reasor, Mathias.......	1771	-	-	-	Reist, John, Esq.......	1821	A	1	3
Reasor, Peter.........	1823	B	1	8	Reitz, John...........	1813	-	-	-
Reddick, John.........	1842	L	1	14	Reitzel, Jacob........	1826	C	1	257
Redsecker, George.....	1788	-	-	-	Reitzel, John, Esq.....	1826	C	1	254
Reece, Peter..........	1828	E	1	6	Reitzel, Peter........	1804	-	-	-
Reed, James...........	1768	-	-	-	Reitzel, Philip.......	1848	N	1	25
Reed, John............	1770	-	-	-	Remley, Anna M........	1802	-	-	-
Reed, Peter...........	1850	N	1	342	Remly, Elizabeth......	1832	F	1	148
Reed, William........	1786	-	-	-	Remly, George.........	1839	I	1	219
Rees, David..........	1791	-	-	-	Remly, John...........	1803	-	-	-
Rees, Leonard........	1784	-	-	-	Renich, William......	1741	-	-	-
Rees, Peter..........	1811	-	-	-	Renick, Henry........	1771	-	-	-
Reese, Benjamin......	1845	M	1	76	Rennaman, John.......	1746	-	-	-
Reese, Catharine.....	1830	E	1	209	Renner, George B.....	1762	-	-	-
Reese, David.........	1829	E	1	31	Rennick, George.....	1737	-	-	-
Reese, George........	1846	M	1	186	Rennick, Mary.......	1747	-	-	-
Reese, Jacob.........	1828	D	1	222	Resch, Peter........	1785	-	-	-
Reese, Peter.........	1824	B	1	164	Resh, Jacob.........	1731	-	-	-

Name	Year	Bk.	Vol	Page	Name	Year	Bk.	Vol	Page
Resh, Jacob	1810	-	-	-	Rippith, Hugh	1772	-	-	-
Resh, John	1782	-	-	-	Rippith, James	1744	-	-	-
Resh, John	1824	C	1	3	Risdel, Mary	1850	N	1	354
Resh, John	1827	D	1	154	Risdell, Jennett	1841	K	1	82
Resh, Mary	1807	-	-	-	Risht, Peter	1743	-	-	-
Resh, Mary	1849	N	1	231	Risk, Robert	1846	M	1	205
Resh, Peter	1759	-	-	-	Rissel, Jacob	1829	E	1	75
Resh, Peter	1787	-	-	-	Risser, Catharine	1787	-	-	-
Ressler, George	1841	K	1	161	Risser, Elizabeth	1845	M	1	8
Rettig, George	1784	-	-	-	Risser, Peter	1840	K	1	74
Retzer, George	1815	-	-	-	Rit, Ferdinant	1775	-	-	-
Retzer, George	1829	E	1	119	Ritchey, William	1841	K	1	140
Reudy, Conrad	1744	-	-	-	Rittenhouse, Charles	1826	C	1	193
Reynbold, William	1739	-	-	-	Ritter, Conrad	1769	-	-	-
Reyner, Michael	1822	A	1	143	Ritter, Joseph	1770	-	-	-
Reynolds, Isaac	1834	G	1	199	Ritter, Tobias	1763	-	-	-
Reynolds, Isreal	1835	H	1	24	Ritz, Simon	1823	B	1	34
Reynolds, Jacob	1822	A	1	173	Ritz, Soloman	1790	-	-	-
Reynolds, Jacob	1822	A	1	174	Ritze, Charles F.	1825	C	1	118
Reynolds, Jacob	1827	D	1	89	Rixecker, Frederick	1835	H	1	56
Reynolds, Manuel	1825	C	1	11	Road, Andrew	1811	-	-	-
Reynolds, Reuben	1823	B	1	41	Road, George	1827	D	1	132
Reynolds, Reuben	1834	G	1	192	Road, Joseph	1790	-	-	-
Rhea, William	1800	-	-	-	Road, William	1815	-	-	-
Rhine, Stephen	1833	G	1	129	Roadaker, John	1849	N	1	274
Rhoads, Adam	1844	L	1	206	Roads, Samuel	1836	H	1	164
Rhoads, Joseph	1828	D	1	169	Robb, John	1799	-	-	-
Riblet, Abraham	1777	-	-	-	Robb, Sarah	1762	-	-	-
Riblet, Peter	1777	-	-	-	Roberk, Mary	1823	B	1	17
Rice, Michael	1770	-	-	-	Roberts, Daniel	1835	G	1	265
Rice, Peter	1829	E	1	18	Roberts, Thomas	1822	A	1	119
Rice, Peter	1842	K	1	270	Roberts, Thomas	1833	G	1	120
Rich, John	1756	-	-	-	Robeson, Joseph	1742	-	-	-
Richard, Bernard	1748	-	-	-	Robeson, Samuel L.	1836	H	1	136
Richard, Elizabeth	1749	-	-	-	Robinson, Agnes	1823	B	1	100
Richard, John	1750	-	-	-	Robinson, Andrew	1798	-	-	-
Richards, Isaac	1835	H	1	29	Robinson, Elizabeth	1847	M	1	248
Richardson, John	1798	-	-	-	Robinson, Ephraim	1839	I	1	261
Richardson, Lawrence	1748	-	-	-	Robinson, George	1822	A	1	246
Richardson, Samuel	1767	-	-	-	Robinson, George	1825	B	1	109
Richardson, William	1809	-	-	-	Robinson, Hugh	1729	-	-	-
Richey, William	1784	-	-	-	Robinson, Hugh	1831	F	1	72
Richtshit, Andrew	1749	-	-	-	Robinson, James	1757	-	-	-
Richwine, Joseph	1835	H	1	94	Robinson, James	1823	B	1	102
Rickert, Daniel	1834	G	1	214	Robinson, John	1801	-	-	-
Ricksecker, Rachael	1839	I	1	257	Robinson, John, Sr.	1827	D	1	130
Riddle, John	1827	D	1	92	Robinson, John	1834	G	1	148
Riddle, John	1846	M	1	209	Robinson, Robert	1848	N	1	21
Ridebach, Nicholas	1791	-	-	-	Robinson, Rosanna	1812	-	-	-
Rider, Michael	1812	-	-	-	Robinson, Samuel	1759	-	-	-
Riegar, Jacob	1796	-	-	-	Robinson, Thomas	1768	-	-	-
Riegel, Henry	1827	D	1	64	Robinson, Thomas, Esq.	1797	-	-	-
Riegel, John	1796	-	-	-	Robinson, Thomas	1803	-	-	-
Rieger, Jacob	1821	-	-	-	Robinson, William	1756	-	-	-
Riezer, John	1811	-	-	-	Rock, Jacob	1824	B	1	218
Rife, Henry	1751	-	-	-	Rock, Peter	1814	-	-	-
Rife, Susanna	1822	A	1	140	Rock, William	1784	-	-	-
Rigel, Simon	1750	-	-	-	Rockey, George, Sr.	1843	L	1	101
Rigler, Henry	1814	-	-	-	Rockey, Henry	1796	-	-	-
Rine, George	1799	-	-	-	Rockey, John	1842	K	1	285
Rine, John	1801	-	-	-	Rockey, Leonard	1810	-	-	-
Rine, Michael	1782	-	-	-	Rockey, Mary E.	1844	L	1	273
Rine, Peter	1813	-	-	-	Rodebach, Christian	1742	-	-	-
Rinear, William	1839	I	1	282	Rodgers, William	1759	-	-	-
Ringland, John	1842	K	1	229	Rodney, Margaret	1807	-	-	-
Ringwalt, Barbara	1806	-	-	-	Roehrer, Ludwig	1846	M	1	109
Ringwalt, Jacob	1838	I	1	83	Roeting, William	1850	N	1	449
Ringwalt, Mary	1831	F	1	57	Rogers, Andrew	1782	-	-	-
Ringwalt, Sarah B.	1825	C	1	60	Rogers, Hannah	1840	K	1	70
Rip, Christian	1808	-	-	-	Rogers, Hugh	1758	-	-	-
Ripp, Hugh	1749	-	-	-	Rogers, Levi	1832	F	1	192
Rippey, Hugh	1763	-	-	-	Rogers, Samuel	1773	-	-	-

Name	Year	Bk.	Vol	Page	Name	Year	Bk.	Vol	Page
Rohrbach, Christian.....	1787	-	-	-	Royer, Joseph..........	1847	M	1	419
Rohrer, Abraham.........	1833	G	1	114	Royer, Maria..........	1830	E	1	199
Rohrer, Ann.............	1835	H	1	69	Royer, Sebastian.......	1759	-	-	-
Rohrer, Barbara........	1847	M	1	345	Rubb, Jacob............	1778	-	-	-
Rohrer, Christian......	1804	-	-	-	Rubey, Ann B...........	1765	-	-	-
Rohrer, Christian......	1825	C	1	73	Rubin, Anthony........	1791	-	-	-
Rohrer, Christian......	1837	I	1	24	Rubin, David..........	1794	-	-	-
Rohrer, Christian......	1838	I	1	57	Ruby, Johannes........	1763	-	-	-
Rohrer, Christian......	1843	L	1	51	Ruch, Elizabeth........	1799	-	-	-
Rohrer, David..........	1830	E	1	270	Ruch, John.............	1839	I	1	185
Rohrer, Feronica.......	1832	F	1	189	Rudenbaugh, William.....	1829	E	1	84
Rohrer, John...........	1782	-	-	-	Rudisill, Jacob........	1826	C	1	228
Rohrer, John...........	1793	-	-	-	Rudisill, Michael J.....	1843	L	1	148
Rohrer, John...........	1828	D	1	194	Rudisill, Sophia.......	1841	K	1	198
Rohrer, John...........	1840	I	1	318	Rudisill, Susanna.......	1768	-	-	-
Rohrer, Margaret.......	1821	A	1	1	Rudolph, John F........	1825	C	1	53
Rohrer, Martin.........	1813	-	-	-	Rudy, Andrew..........	1834	G	1	193
Rohrer, Mary...........	1829	E	1	127	Rudy, Daniel...........	1847	M	1	308
Roland, Elizabeth......	1821	A	1	37	Rudy, Elizabeth........	1835	H	1	46
Roland, Elizabeth......	1845	M	1	4	Rudy, Frederick.......	1767	-	-	-
Roland, George.........	1813	-	-	-	Rudy, George..........	1820	-	-	-
Roland, George.........	1850	N	1	324	Rudy, Henry...........	1792	-	-	-
Roland, Jacob..........	1836	H	1	210	Rudy, Henry...........	1818	-	-	-
Roland, John...........	1830	E	1	220	Rudy, Henry...........	1850	N	1	323
Roland, Molly..........	1799	-	-	-	Rudy, John............	1842	L	1	17
Roland, Susanna........	1816	-	-	-	Rudy, John............	1846	M	1	119
Rolson, Samuel.........	1838	I	1	136	Rudy, Sebastian........	1754	-	-	-
Romich, Susanna........	1848	N	1	38	Ruhl, Barbara.........	1846	M	1	112
Roney, Ann.............	1835	H	1	75	Ruhl, George..........	1811	-	-	-
Ronk, Samuel, Jr.......	1810	-	-	-	Ruhl, George..........	1832	F	1	164
Roop, Jacob............	1795	-	-	-	Rumel, Elizabeth.......	1840	I	1	314
Roop, Nancy............	1848	N	1	123	Rumel, Felix..........	1828	D	1	220
Roop, Nicholas.........	1849	N	1	180	Rumel, Valentine......	1826	C	1	281
Root, Christian........	1826	C	1	188	Rummel, Frederick......	1822	A	1	123
Root, Christian........	1833	G	1	33	Rummel, Peter..........	1797	-	-	-
Root, Dorothea.........	1811	-	-	-	Rummel, Valentine......	1814	-	-	-
Root, Elizabeth........	1821	A	1	9	Rup, Jacob.............	1756	-	-	-
Rorer, Jacob...........	1759	-	-	-	Rupley, John...........	1834	G	1	147
Rosbrough, John........	1770	-	-	-	Rupp, Catharine.......	1835	H	1	88
Rose, Daniel...........	1776	-	-	-	Rupp, Elizabeth........	1823	B	1	32
Rosenbaum, Anthony......	1774	-	-	-	Rupp, Maria...........	1823	B	1	1
Rosenfelder, John......	1809	-	-	-	Rupp, Nancy...........	1847	M	1	392
Rosh, Catharine........	1774	-	-	-	Rush, Henry...........	1754	-	-	-
Rosinberger, Peter......	1756	-	-	-	Rush, John............	1800	-	-	-
Ross, Francis..........	1748	-	-	-	Rush, John............	1831	F	1	104
Ross, George, Esq.......	1832	G	1	7	Rush, Martha..........	1833	G	1	64
Ross, John.............	1759	-	-	-	Rush, Mathias.........	1773	-	-	-
Ross, Joseph...........	1808	-	-	-	Rusing, Sophia........	1844	L	1	216
Ross, Robert...........	1740	-	-	-	Russel, Catharine......	1820	-	-	-
Ross, Samuel...........	1771	-	-	-	Russel, James.........	1832	F	1	181
Ross, Sophia...........	1814	-	-	-	Russel, John..........	1840	K	1	73
Ross, William B........	1828	D	1	175	Russel, William.......	1840	I	1	316
Roth, Elizabeth........	1778	-	-	-	Rust, Mathias.........	1811	-	-	-
Roth, George..........	1782	-	-	-	Ruth, Adam L..........	1848	N	1	136
Roth, George..........	1823	B	1	5	Ruth, Francis.........	1808	-	-	-
Roth, Henry...........	1815	-	-	-	Ruth, Henry...........	1827	D	1	78
Roth, John............	1810	-	-	-	Ruth, Isaac...........	1822	A	1	151
Roth, Julianna.........	1829	E	1	122	Ruth, Peter, Sr.......	1836	H	1	107
Roup, Peter...........	1793	-	-	-	Ruth, Peter...........	1843	L	1	37
Row, Catharine........	1813	-	-	-	Rutt, Christian.......	1850	N	1	355
Row, George...........	1841	K	1	135	Rutt, Jacob...........	1732	-	-	-
Row, Peter............	1797	-	-	-	Rutt, Jacob...........	1742	-	-	-
Rowan, Stewart.........	1777	-	-	-	Rutt, Jacob, Sr.......	1833	G	1	22
Rowen, Andrew.........	1768	-	-	-	Rutt, Jacob...........	1842	K	1	247
Rowland, Abraham........	1775	-	-	-	Rutt, John............	1805	-	-	-
Rowland, Jacob.........	1790	-	-	-	Rutter, Adam..........	1810	-	-	-
Rowland, Joseph........	1782	-	-	-	Rutter, Daniel........	1820	-	-	-
Royer, Ann M..........	1841	K	1	129	Rutter, Elizabeth......	1829	E	1	26
Royer, Benjamin.......	1828	D	1	160	Rutter, Henry.........	1850	N	1	462
Royer, Christian......	1839	I	1	215	Rutter, Jacob.........	1845	M	1	14
Royer, Henry..........	1767	-	-	-	Rutter, James.........	1828	D	1	218
Royer, Joseph..........	1843	L	1	134	Rutter, John..........	1817	-	-	-

Name	Year	Bk.	Vol	Page	Name	Year	Bk.	Vol	Page
Rutter, John............	1825	C	1	37	Schudry, Francis W......	1835	H	1	10
Rutter, Joseph..........	1808	-	-	-	Schwalge, John..........	1818	-	-	-
Rutter, Joseph..........	1839	I	1	242	Schwallie, David........	1793	-	-	-
S					Schwar, Martin..........	1847	M	1	262
Sable, Adam.............	1794	-	-	-	Schwartz, Henry, Jr.....	1825	C	1	84
Sadler, Christian.......	1779	-	-	-	Schwartz, Jacob.........	1829	E	1	86
Sahler, Frederick.......	1757	-	-	-	Schweitzer, Barbara	1843	L	1	99
Sahm, Benjamin..........	1841	K	1	184	Schwenck, John..........	1828	D	1	225
Sahm, George............	1833	G	1	127	Scot, Arthur............	1762	-	-	-
Sahm, Henry.............	1836	H	1	165	Scott, Eleanor..........	1797	-	-	-
Sahm, John..............	1823	B	1	99	Scott, Elizabeth........	1841	K	1	131
Sahm, Margaret..........	1848	N	1	68	Scott, Francis A........	1825	C	1	25
Saiger, Henry...........	1814	-	-	-	Scott, James............	1746	-	-	-
Sailor, Margaret........	1850	N	1	394	Scott, Jane.............	1841	K	1	88
Sallow, Magdalena.......	1849	N	1	284	Scot, John.............	1736	-	-	-
Sample, Catharine.......	1829	E	1	99	Scott, John............	1750	-	-	-
Sample, David...........	1841	K	1	169	Scott, John............	1766	-	-	-
Sample, Nathaniel W.....	1834	G	1	198	Scott, John............	1796	-	-	-
Sander, Barbara.........	1826	C	1	184	Scott, John............	1822	A	1	183
Sander, George.........	1805	-	-	-	Scott, John............	1842	K	1	313
Sander, Jacob...........	1842	K	1	304	Scott, John............	1842	L	1	9
Sanders, Catharine......	1839	I	1	225	Scott, Samuel...........	1757	-	-	-
Sanders, John...........	1818	-	-	-	Scott, Sarah............	1807	-	-	-
Sanderson, Francis......	1782	-	-	-	Scott, Thomas...........	1746	-	-	-
Sandoe, David...........	1829	E	1	94	Scott, William..........	1746	-	-	-
Sandoe, George..........	1824	B	1	133	Scott, William..........	1777	-	-	-
Sanseny, Christian......	1761	-	-	-	Scott, William..........	1830	E	1	234
Sauer, Michael..........	1823	B	1	126	Seabach, Nancy..........	1850	O	1	45
Saunders, Jacob.........	1837	I	1	15	Seachrist, Michael......	1844	L	1	231
Sauser, Christian.......	1804	-	-	-	Seadauler, Ann..........	1850	O	1	21
Sausman, Henry, Sr......	1802	-	-	-	Seaner, Godleib.........	1799	-	-	-
Sausman, Henry..........	1807	-	-	-	Sedwell, Hugh...........	1749	-	-	-
Savage, Edward..........	1815	-	-	-	Seebrooks, William......	1824	E	1	183
Savage, John............	1832	G	1	12	Seen, Jacob.............	1777	-	-	-
Saveroy, George S.......	1849	N	1	185	Seeright, William.......	1772	-	-	-
Savery, George S.......	1849	N	1	232	Sees, Jacob.............	1812	-	-	-
Sawyer, William........	1784	-	-	-	Seese, Baltzer..........	1765	-	-	-
Saylor, Rachel..........	1841	K	1	194	Seever, Barbara.........	1823	B	1	130
Schalbach, Elizabeth....	1845	M	1	86	Segar, Frederick........	1773	-	-	-
Scheibley, Elizabeth....	1845	M	1	22	Seibert, Henry..........	1845	M	1	28
Scheing, Jacob..........	1832	F	1	183	Seigrist, Christian.....	1845	L	1	323
Scheing, Jacob..........	1832	F	1	184	Seigrist, Jacob.........	1810	-	-	-
Schemley, Jacob.........	1772	-	-	-	Seiler, Nicholas........	1749	-	-	-
Schirk, Jacob(or Schock)	1828	D	1	179	Seiler, Ulrich..........	1740	-	-	-
Schiveinhart, John.....	1829	E	1	83	Seitz, Abraham..........	1814	-	-	-
Schlebach, Elizabeth....	1827	D	1	72	Seitz, Catharine........	1827	D	1	13
Schlebach, Jacob........	1829	E	1	92	Seitz, Catharine........	1827	D	1	14
Schlebaugh, George......	1823	A	1	263	Seitz, Daniel...........	1833	G	1	27
Schloat, Michael........	1845	M	1	51	Seitz, John.............	1848	M	1	455
Schlott, John...........	1848	N	1	28	Seldomridge, Jacob......	1823	A	1	251
Schmalina, George.......	1850	N	1	377	Seldomridge, John.......	1849	U	1	165
Schmuck, Jacob..........	1822	A	1	182	Sellers, Albina........	1823	B	1	86
Schmucker, Jacob........	1850	U	1	433	Sellers, David.........	1821	A	1	72
Schneader, Christian,Sr.	1829	E	1	56	Sellers, Ephraim.......	1824	B	1	217
Schneader, Daniel W.....	1841	K	1	102	Sellers, Sarah.........	1823	B	1	85
Schneder, Catharine....	1832	F	1	162	Seltemrick, Andrew.....	1760	-	-	-
Schneder, Elizabeth.....	1826	C	1	282	Semple, John...........	1754	-	-	-
Schneder, Jacob........	1823	B	1	69	Sener, Jacob...........	1797	-	-	-
Schneerer, John........	1829	E	1	90	Sengerwalt, Andrew.....	1823	B	1	10
Schnell, Leonard........	1784	-	-	-	Senseman, Jacob........	1776	-	-	-
Schnerer, George........	1849	N	1	174	Senseman, Margaret.....	1794	-	-	-
Schock, Anna............	1848	M	1	437	Senseman, Michael......	1831	F	I	124
Schock, Henry...........	1836	H	1	144	Sensenich, Barbara.....	1815	-	-	-
Schop, Christian........	1845	M	1	72	Sensenig, Anna.........	1844	L	1	201
Schop, Susanna..........	1846	M	1	158	Sensenig, John.........	1829	E	1	105
Schott, Henry...........	1839	I	1	249	Sensenig, Michael......	1845	M	1	50
Schreiner, John.........	1819	-	-	-	Sensenigh, Jacob.......	1769	-	-	-
Schriber, Adam..........	1750	-	-	-	Sensenigh, Jacob.......	1803	-	-	-
Schriner, Catharine.....	1792	-	-	-	Sensenigh, Michael.....	1773	-	-	-
Schriver, John..........	1765	-	-	-	Sensenman, John........	1819	-	-	-
Schryer, Adam...........	1768	-	-	-	Sensiman, Jophet.......	1758	-	-	-
Schudy, John............	1835	H	1	91	Senzill, Anna..........	1794	-	-	-

Name	Year	Bk.	Vol	Page	Name	Year	Bk.	Vol	Page
Sergeant, Bartholomew...	1823	B	1	25	Shaub, Henry............	1838	I	1	92
Sexton, Eleanor........	1819	-	-	-	Shaub, Jacob............	1832	F	1	169
Seyman, Christopher.....	1798	-	-	-	Shaub, John.............	1819	-	-	-
Shaack, Michael........	1758	-	-	-	Shaub, John.............	1840	I	1	321
Shade, Henry...........	1794	-	-	-	Shaub, John.............	1848	N	1	70
Shade, William P........	1815	-	-	-	Shaub, Martin...........	1847	M	1	312
Shaeffer, Anthony.......	1812	-	-	-	Shauf, Abraham..........	1817	-	-	-
Shaeffer, Emanuel.......	1838	I	1	156	Shaum, Benjamin.........	1814	-	-	-
Shaeffer, Jacob.........	1804	-	-	-	Shaup, Christian........	1804	-	-	-
Shaeffer, Jacob.........	1831	F	1	81	Shaup, Henry............	1791	-	-	-
Shaeffer, Jacob.........	1833	G	1	61	Shaver, Isaac...........	1749	-	-	-
Shaeffer, Jacob.........	1845	M	1	56	Shaver, Paul............	1747	-	-	-
Shaeffer, John.........	1815	-	-	-	Shaw, Alexander.........	1785	-	-	-
Shaeffer, John..........	1822	A	1	226	Shaw, William...........	1826	C	1	261
Shaeffer, Henry, Sr.....	1835	H	1	30	Shay, Daniel............	1792	-	-	-
Shaeffer, Magdalena.....	1843	L	1	26	Sheaff, John............	1839	I	1	179
Shaeffer, Magdalena.....	1850	N	1	460	Sheaff, Joseph..........	1827	D	1	26
Shaeffer, Martin.......	1820	-	-	-	Sheaffer, Adam..........	1842	K	1	314
Shaeffer, Martin.......	1835	H	1	31	Sheaffer, Cyrus.........	1829	E	1	124
Shaeffer, Michael......	1801	-	-	-	Sheaffer, Esther........	1816	-	-	-
Shaeffer, William......	1809	-	-	-	Sheaffer, Henry.........	1822	A	1	218
Shaffer, Henry.........	1757	-	-	-	Sheaffer, Isaac.........	1842	K	1	277
Shaffer, Jacob.........	1760	-	-	-	Sheaffer, Jacob.........	1832	F	1	180
Shalck, William........	1850	N	1	347	Sheaffer, John..........	1820	-	-	-
Shallenberger, Christian	1814	-	-	-	Sheaffer, John..........	1823	B	1	76
Shallenberger, Henry....	1834	G	1	252	Sheaffer, John..........	1849	U	1	253
Shallenberger, Jacob....	1777	-	-	-	Sheaffer, Martin........	1821	A	1	110
Shallenberger, Jacob....	1806	-	-	-	Sheaffer, Rebecca.......	1836	H	1	46
Shallenberger, John.....	1751	-	-	-	Sheaffer, Samuel........	1840	I	1	295
Shallenberger, John.....	1784	-	-	-	Sheaffer, Samuel........	1849	N	1	179
Shallenberger, John.....	1792	-	-	-	Shearer, Jacob..........	1840	K	1	44
Shallenberger, John.....	1839	I	1	200	Shearer, John...........	1792	-	-	-
Shallenberger, Magdalena	1814	-	-	-	Sheeler, Rosina.........	1844	L	1	252
Shaller, Jacob.........	1832	F	1	218	Sheeli, John............	1739	-	-	-
Shally, Daniel.........	1757	-	-	-	Sheelor, Ludwig.........	1789	-	-	-
Shally, Jacob..........	1752	-	-	-	Sheely, Dr. Jacob.......	1848	N	1	7
Shally, Jacob..........	1760	-	-	-	Shefel, John Ernst......	1794	-	-	-
Shallyberger, George....	1756	-	-	-	Sheffer, Baltzer........	1785	-	-	-
Shanaur, Christian......	1769	-	-	-	Sheffer, Henry..........	1782	-	-	-
Shank, George..........	1800	-	-	-	Sheffer, Isaac..........	1767	-	-	-
Shank, Jacob..........	1736	-	-	-	Sheibler, Magdalena.....	1778	-	-	-
Shank, Jacob..........	1760	-	-	-	Sheip, Henry............	1783	-	-	-
Shank, John............	1744	-	-	-	Sheirich, Henry.........	1833	G	1	124
Shank, John............	1752	-	-	-	Sheleberger, Martin.....	1760	-	-	-
Shank, Michael.........	1744	-	-	-	Shell, Martin...........	1774	-	-	-
Shank, Michael.........	1775	-	-	-	Sheller, John...........	1781	-	-	-
Shank, Susanna.........	1836	H	1	190	Shelly, Baltzer.........	1784	-	-	-
Shannon, James.........	1740	-	-	-	Shenck, Barbara.........	1824	B	1	232
Shannon, James.........	1806	-	-	-	Shenck, Christian.......	1804	-	-	-
Shannon, John, Sr.......	1766	-	-	-	Shenck, Christian.......	1834	G	1	196
Shanour, John.........	1746	-	-	-	Shenck, Jacob...........	1833	G	1	90
Shantz, John..........	1747	-	-	-	Shenck, Jacob...........	1833	G	1	126
Shantz, Christian......	1752	-	-	-	Shenck, John............	1783	-	-	-
Shantz, Jacob..........	1782	-	-	-	Shenck, John............	1805	-	-	-
Shantz, John..........	1790	-	-	-	Shenck, John............	1813	-	-	-
Shapes, Chrisby........	1748	-	-	-	Shenck, John............	1820	-	-	-
Sharer, Jacob..........	1748	-	-	-	Shenck, John, Jr........	1826	C	1	208
Sharer, John..........	1757	-	-	-	Shenck, John H..........	1841	K	1	121
Sharer, John...........	1843	L	1	159	Shenck, John S..........	1839	I	1	255
Sharp, Christian.......	1837	I	1	2	Shenck, Magdalena.......	1833	G	1	29
Sharp, George..........	1850	O	1	49	Shenck, Maria...........	1813	-	-	-
Sharp, Isaac..........	1783	-	-	-	Shenck, Michael.........	1815	-	-	-
Sharp, Margaret........	1848	N	1	58	Shenck, Susanna.........	1827	D	1	142
Sharp, Moses..........	1821	A	1	10	Shenk, Abraham..........	1841	K	1	115
Shartzer, Jacob........	1790	-	-	-	Shenk, Anna.............	1842	K	1	283
Shau, Barbara..........	1823	B	1	20	Shenk, Benjamin.........	1847	M	1	273
Shaub, Abraham........	1822	A	1	223	Shenk, Christian........	1824	B	1	163
Shaub, Barbara........	1834	G	1	206	Shenk, David............	1841	K	1	154
Shaub, Barbara........	1846	M	1	141	Shenk, Elizabeth........	1835	H	1	70
Shaub, Christian.......	1837	H	1	228	Shenk, Jacob, Sr........	1841	K	1	191
Shaub, Esther..........	1843	L	1	29	Shenk, Jacob............	1842	K	1	280
Shaub, Henry...........	1822	A	1	224	Shenk, John.............	1815	-	-	-

Name	Year	Bk.	Vol	Page	Name	Year	Bk.	Vol	Page
Shenk, John.............	1819	-	-	-	Shitz, John.............	1761	-	-	-
Shenk, John.............	1835	H	1	79	Shitz, Rudolph..........	1767	-	-	-
Shenk, Michael..........	1838	I	1	95	Shneel, Christian.......	1784	-	-	-
Shenk, Michael..........	1849	N	1	221	Shneider, Ann Maria.....	1810	-	-	-
Sheonefeld, Mary........	1823	A	1	258	Shnierer, Catharine.....	1828	D	1	236
Shepler, Elizabeth......	1843	L	1	160	Shoaff, Abraham.........	1829	E	1	74
Shepley, George.........	1786	-	-	-	Shober, William.........	1814	-	-	-
Sherb, Adam.............	1835	H	1	41	Shock, Mary.............	1775	-	-	-
Sherck, Joseph..........	1831	F	1	134	Shock, Sebastian........	1839	I	1	276
Sherer, Benjamin M......	1844	L	1	166	Shock, William..........	1798	-	-	-
Sherer, John...........	1802	-	-	-	Shoe, Catharine.........	1823	B	1	40
Sherer, John...........	1827	D	1	105	Shoe, John.............	1850	U	1	397
Sherer, Mary............	1743	-	-	-	Shoemaker, Adam.........	1793	-	-	-
Sherer, Mary............	1815	-	-	-	Shoemaker, Elizabeth....	1823	A	1	287
Sherer, Samuel..........	1806	-	-	-	Shoemaker, Frederick J..	1768	-	-	-
Sherer, Samuel..........	1808	-	-	-	Shoemaker, Henry........	1750	-	-	-
Sherer, Samuel..........	1827	D	1	116	Shoemaker, Jacob........	1764	-	-	-
Sherick, Anthony........	1801	-	-	-	Shoemaker, Jacob........	1839	I	1	231
Sherick, David..........	1783	-	-	-	Shoemaker, William......	1811	-	-	-
Sherk, Anna.............	1828	E	1	11	Shoff, Barbara..........	1828	D	1	213
Sherk, Catharine........	1827	D	1	85	Shoff, Frederick........	1843	L	1	63
Sherk, Henry............	1826	C	1	161	Shoff, Henry............	1830	E	1	185
Sherk, Jacob............	1825	C	1	132	Shoff, John.............	1813	-	-	-
Sherk, John.............	1839	I	1	170	Shoffelbottom, Joshua...	1807	-	-	-
Sherk, Samuel...........	1830	E	1	238	Shoffstall, Adam........	1836	H	1	192
Sherman, Hans Peter.....	1751	-	-	-	Sholl, Christian........	1830	E	1	236
Sherp, Christopher, Jr..	1789	-	-	-	Shollenberger, Abraham..	1815	-	-	-
Sherp, Emanuel..........	1842	K	1	243	Shoot, John.............	1778	-	-	-
Sherp, John.............	1842	K	1	242	Shop, John..............	1753	-	-	-
Sherp, Susanna..........	1842	K	1	244	Shope, Henry............	1762	-	-	-
Sherts, Jacob...........	1830	E	1	198	Shopf, John.............	1815	-	-	-
Sherts, Joseph..........	1848	N	1	116	Shopp, Francis..........	1814	-	-	-
Shertz, Elizabeth.......	1848	N	1	75	Shopperd, William.......	1801	-	-	-
Shertz, Jacob...........	1815	-	-	-	Shore, Henry............	1835	H	1	47
Shertz, Jacob...........	1834	G	1	188	Shore, Henry............	1844	L	1	224
Shertzer, Christian.....	1843	L	1	90	Shore, Henry............	1847	M	1	332
Shertzer, Mary..........	1834	G	1	223	Shorock, Henry..........	1748	-	-	-
Shertzer, Stephen.......	1777	-	-	-	Shorts, Martin..........	1850	O	1	17
Shickley, George........	1831	F	1	33	Shott, Frederick........	1784	-	-	-
Shiles, Herman..........	1803	-	-	-	Shouck, Christopher.....	1826	C	1	152
Shimp, Andrew...........	1802	-	-	-	Shoup, John.............	1783	-	-	-
Shimp, David............	1830	E	1	179	Shoup, Stophel..........	1781	-	-	-
Shimp, Jacob............	1793	-	-	-	Shoup, Susanna..........	1770	-	-	-
Shimp, Jacob............	1828	D	1	196	Shouse, George.........	1744	-	-	-
Shimp, Jacob............	1846	M	1	193	Showalter, Abraham......	1833	G	1	121
Shimp, Mathias..........	1777	-	-	-	Showalter, Henry........	1823	B	1	120
Shimp, Mathias..........	1799	-	-	-	Showalter, Jacob........	1794	-	-	-
Shindel, Elizabeth......	1840	K	1	40	Showalter, Jacob........	1829	E	1	152
Shindle, Michael........	1777	-	-	-	Showalter, Jane.........	1820	-	-	-
Shindle, Michael........	1818	-	-	-	Showalter, John.........	1836	H	1	200
Shipe, Henry............	1792	-	-	-	Shoy, Susanna...........	1793	-	-	-
Shippen, Beale B........	1834	G	1	208	Shraeter, Martin........	1761	-	-	-
Shirck, Ann.............	1837	H	1	244	Shreiner, Barbara.......	1822	A	1	172
Shirck, Catharine.......	1848	M	1	432	Shreiner, John..........	1848	N	1	16
Shireman, Jacob.........	1800	-	-	-	Shreiner, Michael, Jr...	1827	D	1	91
Shirk, Casper...........	1770	-	-	-	Shreiner, Rachel........	1844	L	1	257
Shirk, Catharine.......	1843	L	1	83	Shreiver, Frederick....	1826	C	1	192
Shirk, Elizabeth........	1828	E	1	17	Shreiver, John..........	1823	B	1	43
Shirk, Jacob............	1839	I	1	209	Shriever, John..........	1832	G	1	2
Shirk, Jacob............	1844	L	1	189	Shriver, Christian......	1832	F	1	182
Shirk, John.............	1832	F	1	142	Shroat, Samuel..........	1825	C	1	130
Shirk, John.............	1839	I	1	189	Shroll, Christian.......	1814	-	-	-
Shirk, John S...........	1846	M	1	178	Shugart, Zachary........	1739	-	-	-
Shirk, John S...........	1849	U	1	194	Shuler, Samuel..........	1805	-	-	-
Shirk, Michael..........	1757	-	-	-	Shullenberger, Andrew...	1831	F	1	7
Shirk, Michael..........	1827	D	1	56	Shultz, Casper..........	1749	-	-	-
Shirk, Nancy............	1836	H	1	122	Shultz, Henry...........	1822	A	1	207
Shirk, Samuel...........	1842	K	1	250	Shultz, John............	1845	M	1	81
Shirky, Arthur..........	1801	-	-	-	Shultz, Samuel..........	1822	A	1	243
Shirky, James...........	1796	-	-	-	Shultz, Valentine.......	1745	-	-	-
Shitz, Frederick........	1804	-	-	-	Shumacher, Frederick....	1831	F	1	85
Shitz, Frederick........	1807	-	-	-	Shumacher, John.........	1828	D	1	283

Name	Year	Bk.	Vol	Page	Name	Year	Bk.	Vol	Page
Shuman, Christian	1849	N	1	154	Slick, Barbara	1848	N	1	135
Shuman, Frederick	1812	-	-	-	Slick, Jacob, Sr	1840	I	1	315
Shuman, George	1850	N	1	316	Slick, Jacob	1844	L	1	197
Shuman, Henry	1760	-	-	-	Sloan, James	1778	-	-	-
Shuman, Jacob	1837	H	1	249	Slote, Samuel	1849	N	1	288
Shup, Jacob	1849	U	1	171	Slough, Elizabeth	1850	O	1	37
Shup, John	1757	-	-	-	Slough, Col. Jacob	1838	I	1	48
Shup, Nicholas	1806	-	-	-	Sloughter, Jacob	1797	-	-	-
Shupp, George	1780	-	-	-	Slutt, William	1818	-	-	-
Shurk, Jacob	1744	-	-	-	Small, Henry	1746	-	-	-
Shuster, John	1800	-	-	-	Small, James	1748	-	-	-
Shute, Andrew, Sr	1829	E	1	23	Smallwood, William	1816	-	-	-
Shute, Susanna	1847	M	1	356	Smallwood, William	1820	-	-	-
Shute, William	1839	I	1	164	Smeltz, Clemence	1822	A	1	209
Shutter, John	1843	L	1	35	Smeltz, Jacob	1828	D	1	228
Shutter, Joseph	1838	I	1	133	Smeltz, John	1810	-	-	-
Shyack, Jacob	1737	-	-	-	Smetzel, Andrew	1768	-	-	-
Shyer, Nicholas	1758	-	-	-	Smilen, George	1780	-	-	-
Sides, Catharine	1833	G	1	31	Smink, John	1746	-	-	-
Sides, Daniel	1804	-	-	-	Smiser, George	1748	-	-	-
Sides, Jacob	1805	-	-	-	Smith, Andrew	1747	-	-	-
Sides, Jacob	1814	-	-	-	Smith, Ann	1848	N	1	36
Sides, John	1823	B	1	47	Smith, Benjamin	1845	M	1	85
Sides, Samuel	1815	-	-	-	Smith, Bernard	1793	-	-	-
Sidwell, Ann	1806	-	-	-	Smith, Casper	1812	-	-	-
Siechrist, Jacob	1839	I	1	184	Smith, Chester C	1805	-	-	-
Siechrist, Magdalena	1824	B	1	154	Smith, Christian	1789	-	-	-
Siegrist, Jacob	1784	-	-	-	Smith, Christian	1812	-	-	-
Siegrist, John, Jr	1814	-	-	-	Smith, Christian	1824	B	1	219
Siegrist, Mary	1829	E	1	147	Smith, Christian	1845	M	1	19
Silknitter, Michael	1827	D	1	88	Smith, Daniel	1762	-	-	-
Simcoe, Joseph	1800	-	-	-	Smith, David	1807	-	-	-
Simmons, Joseph	1845	L	1	299	Smith, David	1849	N	1	175
Simmons, Robert	1846	M	1	191	Smith, Edward	1824	B	1	193
Simmonton, Theophlis	1750	-	-	-	Smith, Elizabeth	1827	D	1	115
Simon, Joseph	1842	K	1	308	Smith, Elizabeth	1836	H	1	70
Simpson, Elizabeth	1783	-	-	-	Smith, Elizabeth	1843	L	1	88
Simpson, John	1819	-	-	-	Smith, Elizabeth(Ohio)	1847	M	1	303
Simpson, John	1850	U	1	456	Smith, Francis	1785	-	-	-
Simpson, Samuel	1768	-	-	-	Smith, George	1775	-	-	-
Sinclair, Maria	1843	L	1	50	Smith, Hannah	1834	G	1	222
Singer, Christian	1807	-	-	-	Smith, Henry	1802	-	-	-
Singer, Elizabeth	1800	-	-	-	Smith, Henry Messner	1748	-	-	-
Singer, John	1821	A	1	390	Smith, Jacob	1796	-	-	-
Singer, Mary	1824	B	1	216	Smith, Jacob	1801	-	-	-
Singer, Simon	1761	-	-	-	Smith, Jacob	1818	-	-	-
Singleton, John	1821	A	1	54	Smith, Jacob	1819	-	-	-
Sink, Henry	1814	-	-	-	Smith, Jacob	1836	H	1	152
Sinnissy, Richard	1807	-	-	-	Smith, James	1749	-	-	-
Siple, Simon S	1836	H	1	193	Smith, John	1770	-	-	-
Sitz, John	1809	-	-	-	Smith, John	1813	-	-	-
Siverney, James	1833	G	1	111	Smith, John	1814	-	-	-
Skiles, Herman	1792	-	-	-	Smith, John	1826	C	1	217
Skiles, Rosanna	1789	-	-	-	Smith, John	1827	D	1	106
Skyles, William	1762	-	-	-	Smith, John	1827	D	1	157
Slabach, John	1818	-	-	-	Smith, John	1838	I	1	73
Slack, Abraham	1838	I	1	99	Smith, John	1845	M	1	21
Slack, John	1838	I	1	69	Smith, John	1845	M	1	74
Slager, George	1816	-	-	-	Smith, John, Sr	1848	N	1	114
Slaymaker, Amos	1831	F	1	82	Smith, John	1848	N	1	119
Slaymaker, Daniel	1799	-	-	-	Smith, John(baker)	1849	U	1	258
Slaymaker, Elizabeth	1837	I	1	13	Smith, Joseph	1802	-	-	-
Slaymaker, Elizabeth	1842	K	1	226	Smith, Joseph	1829	E	1	123
Slaymaker, James H	1849	U	1	141	Smith, Justina	1843	L	1	72
Slaymaker, Jasper, Esq.	1827	D	1	104	Smith, Leander	1820	-	-	-
Slaymaker, Mathias	1797	-	-	-	Smith, Martin	1803	-	-	-
Slaymaker, Samuel	1830	E	1	213	Smith, Martin	1828	D	1	181
Slaymaker, William, Esq.	1826	C	1	163	Smith, Mary	1819	-	-	-
Slaymaker, William M.	1828	D	1	191	Smith, Nicholas	1759	-	-	-
Slaymaker, William M.	1837	I	1	14	Smith, Rachel	1749	-	-	-
Slaymaker, William M.	1838	I	1	49	Smith, Rev. Robert	1793	-	-	-
Slence, Jacob	1741	-	-	-	Smith, Salome	1803	-	-	-

Name	Year	Bk.	Vol	Page	Name	Year	Bk.	Vol	Page
Smith, Samuel...........	1734	-	-	-	Sollenberger, John......	1847	M	1	296
Smith, Samuel...........	1743	-	-	-	Sommers, Elizabeth......	1842	K	1	210
Smith, Samuel...........	1748	-	-	-	Sommers, Leonard........	1841	K	1	203
Smith, Samuel...........	1794	-	-	-	Souder, Casper..........	1816	-	-	-
Smith, Samuel...........	1823	B	1	105	Souder, George..........	1768	-	-	-
Smith, Samuel W.........	1820	-	-	-	Souder, Jacob...........	1733	-	-	-
Smith, Sarah............	1825	C	1	64	Souter, John W..........	1812	-	-	-
Smith, Strachen........	1747	-	-	-	Sowder, Henry...........	1773	-	-	-
Smith, William.........	1830	E	1	173	Sower, Christopher......	1801	-	-	-
Smith, William.........	1834	G	1	225	Sower, William..........	1755	-	-	-
Smith, William P.......	1850	O	1	28	Spahn, Henry............	1846	M	1	128
Smitzer, John..........	1788	-	-	-	Spaid, Susanna..........	1842	L	1	18
Smoze, John.............	1746	-	-	-	Spangler, Augustus D....	1850	N	1	304
Smutz, John.............	1777	-	-	-	Spangler, John..........	1806	-	-	-
Snably, Jacob...........	1744	-	-	-	Spangler, John..........	1841	K	1	201
Snavely, Casper........	1784	-	-	-	Spangler, Matilda......	1848	N	1	108
Snavely, Henry.........	1773	-	-	-	Spangler, William A.....	1849	N	1	257
Snavely, Henry.........	1840	K	1	79	Spear, John.............	1816	-	-	-
Sneader, Isaac.........	1844	L	1	262	Spear, Robert...........	1850	N	1	369
Sneader, Jacob.........	1840	K	1	29	Spear, Sarah............	1850	O	1	47
Sneader, Samuel........	1850	O	1	32	Speck, Adam.............	1831	F	1	116
Sneathen, Reuben.......	1811	-	-	-	Speck, Sigman...........	1792	-	-	-
Snebely, Jacob.........	1741	-	-	-	Speer, John.............	1741	-	-	-
Sneider, George........	1784	-	-	-	Speihlman, George.......	1831	F	1	121
Sneider, Jacob.........	1759	-	-	-	Speihlman, Sarah........	1844	L	1	196
Sneider, John..........	1779	-	-	-	Spera, Jacob............	1817	-	-	-
Sneider, John..........	1826	C	1	183	Spera, Jacob............	1827	D	1	70
Sneider, Jost..........	1778	-	-	-	Spicer, Jeremiah.......	1752	-	-	-
Sneider, Simon.........	1784	-	-	-	Spickler, John, Sr.....	1834	G	1	259
Sneper, George.........	1795	-	-	-	Spickler, Mary..........	1818	-	-	-
Snepper, Christian.....	1793	-	-	-	Spickler, Mathias......	1761	-	-	-
Snerer, John...........	1805	-	-	-	Spiece, Conrad..........	1833	G	1	78
Snevely, Daniel........	1823	B	1	79	Spiece, Francis........	1828	D	1	285
Snevely, Jacob.........	1759	-	-	-	Spiehlman, Samuel......	1827	D	1	35
Snevely, John..........	1747	-	-	-	Spindler, Mathias......	1813	-	-	-
Snevely, John..........	1751	-	-	-	Spitler, John, Jr.....	1758	-	-	-
Snevely, John..........	1793	-	-	-	Spohnhaur, Jacob........	1808	-	-	-
Snevely, Thomas........	1734	-	-	-	Spohnhour, John........	1797	-	-	-
Snider, Charles........	1770	-	-	-	Sponhauer, Jacob........	1827	D	1	107
Snider, Sibilla........	1756	-	-	-	Spore, Herman..........	1795	-	-	-
Snoddy, John...........	1746	-	-	-	Sprats, John, Sr.......	1835	H	1	26
Snodgrass, Alexander....	1804	-	-	-	Sprecher, Jonathan.....	1848	N	1	11
Snodgrass, Alexander....	1815	-	-	-	Spriegel, Michael......	1814	-	-	-
Snodgrass, James.......	1800	-	-	-	Spring, Daniel.........	1814	-	-	-
Snodgrass, Rachel......	1804	-	-	-	Spring, Dewalt..........	1824	B	1	211
Snodgrass, William.....	1758	-	-	-	Spring, Jacob..........	1758	-	-	-
Snyder, Barbara........	1757	-	-	-	Spring, Samuel..........	1834	G	1	243
Snyder, Barbara........	1823	B	1	45	Spring, Samuel..........	1835	H	1	16
Snyder, Barbara........	1829	E	1	129	Springle, Michael......	1748	-	-	-
Snyder, Casper.........	1775	-	-	-	Springman, Daniel......	1754	-	-	-
Snyder, Christian......	1844	L	1	239	Sproat, John...........	1845	M	1	25
Snyder, Frederick......	1834	G	1	245	Sproul, James..........	1847	M	1	244
Snyder, George.........	1846	M	1	107	Sprout, Robert..........	1848	N	1	2
Snyder, Henry..........	1821	A	1	28	Sprout, Samuel.........	1747	-	-	-
Snyder, Henry..........	1839	I	1	166	Stable, Jacob, Jr......	1849	U	1	296
Snyder, Jacob..........	1774	-	-	-	Stackhouse, James......	1850	U	1	439
Snyder, Jacob..........	1792	-	-	-	Stacy, John.............	1845	M	1	3
Snyder, Jacob..........	1838	I	1	105	Stahl, Benjamin........	1822	A	1	247
Snyder, Jacob..........	1844	L	1	215	Stahl, Jacob...........	1804	-	-	-
Snyder, John...........	1760	-	-	-	Stahley, John..........	1833	G	1	39
Snyder, John...........	1819	-	-	-	Stake, Christian, Esq...	1799	-	-	-
Snyder, John, Jr.......	1836	H	1	132	Stakel, Ulrich.........	1739	-	-	-
Snyder, John...........	1841	K	1	101	Stall, John.............	1765	-	-	-
Snyder, John...........	1849	U	1	224	Stam, Nicholas.........	1760	-	-	-
Snyder, Leonard........	1807	-	-	-	Stambach, John.........	1808	-	-	-
Snyder, Lorentz........	1806	-	-	-	Stambach, Samuel.......	1814	-	-	-
Snyder, Magdalena......	1777	-	-	-	Stambaugh, Jacob.......	1831	F	1	34
Snyder, Maria Amelia....	1843	L	1	78	Stambrough, Samuel.....	1823	B	1	29
Snyder, Mathias........	1777	-	-	-	Stamm, Frederick.......	1839	I	1	262
Snyder, Susanna........	1839	I	1	169	Stamm, John.............	1832	F	1	270
Sohn, Michael..........	1778	-	-	-	Starck, John...........	1804	-	-	-
Sollenberger, John.....	1817	-	-	-	Stare, John.............	1749	-	-	-

Name	Year	Bk.	Vol	Page	Name	Year	Bk.	Vol	Page
Stark, Henry	1846	M	1	108	Stephen, George	1792	-	-	-
Stark, John	1845	M	1	90	Stephen, Martin	1766	-	-	-
Stark, Joseph	1820	-	-	-	Stephens, Francis	1735	-	-	-
Stark, Samuel	1832	G	1	8	Stephens, John	1744	-	-	-
Starrett, Nathaniel	1807	-	-	-	Stephens, John	1848	M	1	450
Stauffer, Abraham	1817	-	-	-	Stephens, Samuel	1747	-	-	-
Stauffer, Barbara	1847	M	1	322	Sterling, Thomas	1740	-	-	-
Stauffer, Christian	1747	-	-	-	Sterrett, Benjamin	1739	-	-	-
Stauffer, Christian	1827	D	1	39	Sterrett, William	1818	-	-	-
Stauffer, Daniel	1803	-	-	-	Stettler, Abraham	1805	-	-	-
Stauffer, Jacob	1802	-	-	-	Steven, Jacob	1763	-	-	-
Stauffer, Jacob	1832	F	1	249	Stevenson, David	1812	-	-	-
Stauffer, Jacob	1847	M	1	360	Stevenson, Margaret	1840	K	1	75
Stauffer, John	1748	-	-	-	Stevenson, Matthew	1808	-	-	-
Stauffer, John	1827	D	1	41	Stevenson, Samuel	1823	B	1	101
Stauffer, John	1849	U	1	256	Steward, James	1804	-	-	-
Stauffer, Maria	1848	M	1	454	Stewart, Adam	1846	M	1	168
Stauffer, Martin	1818	-	-	-	Stewart, Arthur	1747	-	-	-
Stauffer, Mary	1791	-	-	-	Stewart, James	1784	-	-	-
Stauffer, Mary	1828	D	1	216	Stewart, John	1780	-	-	-
Stauffer, William	1848	N	1	17	Stewart, John	1794	-	-	-
Staupher, Ulrich	1746	-	-	-	Stewart, John	1829	E	1	125
Stauter, Henry	1824	B	1	174	Stewart, John Joseph	1837	I	1	27
Stayman, John	1786	-	-	-	Stewart, Lazarus	1782	-	-	-
Stayman, Nancy	1785	-	-	-	Stewart, Robert	1783	-	-	-
Steady, William	1839	I	1	182	Stewart, Walter	1737	-	-	-
Steas, John Adam	1742	-	-	-	Steyer, Adams	1836	H	1	185
Stech, Christopher	1806	-	-	-	Stielwagon, Jacob	1840	I	1	320
Steck, Frederick	1777	-	-	-	Stighling, Barbara	1795	-	-	-
Stedman, Richard	1777	-	-	-	Stipe, Jacob	1820	-	-	-
Steehly, John	1786	-	-	-	Stipehen, Abraham	1805	-	-	-
Steel, Adam	1747	-	-	-	Stippens, Frederick	1742	-	-	-
Steel, Andrew	1756	-	-	-	St. John, Stephen	1831	F	1	75
Steel, David	1739	-	-	-	Stober, Jacob	1830	E	1	197
Steel, James	1814	-	-	-	Stock, Jacob	1828	D	1	234
Steel, James	1848	N	1	55	Stocksleger, Catharine	1823	B	1	40
Steele, John J.	1834	G	1	186	Stoffert, Christopher	1762	-	-	-
Steele, William	1822	A	1	190	Stofft, Jacob	1798	-	-	-
Steelman, John Hans	1749	-	-	-	Stohl, Adam	1805	-	-	-
Steemer, Anthony	1788	-	-	-	Stohler, Frederick	1815	-	-	-
Steer, John	1758	-	-	-	Stohler, Magdalena	1806	-	-	-
Steffy, Christian	1815	-	-	-	Stoler, Adam	1819	-	-	-
Steffy, Jacob	1824	B	1	198	Stoler, Catharine	1834	G	1	176
Steffy, Susanna	1844	L	1	205	Stoler, Jacob	1837	I	1	11
Stehman, Henry	1820	-	-	-	Stoler, Samuel	1845	M	1	88
Stehman, Jacob	1837	H	1	231	Stoler, Samuel	1850	O	1	18
Steiffel, Andrew	1850	N	1	432	Stone, Elizabeth	1765	-	-	-
Steigel, Henry	1802	-	-	-	Stone, Elizabeth Jun	1765	-	-	-
Steigelman, Jacob	1817	-	-	-	Stone, Frederick	1743	-	-	-
Steiger, Regina	1817	-	-	-	Stone, George	1783	-	-	-
Steigler, Daniel	1826	C	1	223	Stone, Jacob	1797	-	-	-
Stein, John	1750	-	-	-	Stone, Jacob	1834	G	1	151
Stein, Peter	1749	-	-	-	Stone, James	1842	L	1	25
Steiner, Christian	1783	-	-	-	Stone, John	1785	-	-	-
Steiner, Christopher	1794	-	-	-	Stone, Leonard	1785	-	-	-
Steinheiser, Sarah	1847	M	1	415	Stoneman, Christian	1752	-	-	-
Steinman, Christian F.	1838	I	1	113	Stoneman, Joseph	1758	-	-	-
Steinman, Conrad	1782	-	-	-	Stoneman, Peter	1748	-	-	-
Steinman, Sybilla M.	1831	F	1	115	Stoner, Abraham	1741	-	-	-
Steinmetz, Adam	1838	I	1	86	Stoner, Abraham	1797	-	-	-
Steltz, Nancy	1843	L	1	124	Stoner, Ann	1825	C	1	121
Steman, Abraham	1805	-	-	-	Stoner, Barbara	1811	-	-	-
Steman, Henry	1793	-	-	-	Stoner, Christian	1760	-	-	-
Steman, Jacob	1838	I	1	75	Stoner, Christian	1770	-	-	-
Steman, John	1813	-	-	-	Stoner, Christian	1801	-	-	-
Steman, John	1827	D	1	126	Stoner, Christian	1818	-	-	-
Steman, John	1829	E	1	88	Stoner, Christian	1832	F	1	259
Steman, John	1840	K	1	46	Stoner, Christian	1835	H	1	65
Steman, Rudolph	1826	C	1	201	Stoner, Christian	1844	L	1	296
Steman, Samuel	1795	-	-	-	Stoner, Christian	1850	N	1	382
Stentz, Sophia	1842	K	1	310	Stoner, David	1806	-	-	-
Stephen, Dorothy	1785	-	-	-	Stoner, Elizabeth	1785	-	-	-

Name	Year	Bk.	Vol	Page	Name	Year	Bk.	Vol	Page
Stoner, George.........	1823	A	1	260	Strickler, George.......	1758	-	-	-
Stoner, Henry..........	1812	-	-	-	Strickler, Henry H......	1841	K	1	153
Stoner, Henry..........	1823	B	1	22	Strickler, Jacob.......	1833	G	1	75
Stoner, Henry..........	1840	K	1	5	Strickler, Rosanna......	1624	B	1	214
Stoner, Henry..........	1842	K	1	257	Strickler, Wilhelm......	1767	-	-	-
Stoner, Jacob..........	1752	-	-	-	Stroh, Eve.............	1832	F	1	256
Stoner, Jacob..........	1782	-	-	-	Stroh, Nicholas........	1812	-	-	-
Stoner, Jacob..........	1844	L	1	164	Strohm, Mary...........	1843	L	1	155
Stoner, John..........	1750	-	-	-	Strome, John...........	1769	-	-	-
Stoner, John..........	1773	-	-	-	Stuart, Archibald......	1777	-	-	-
Stoner, John..........	1793	-	-	-	Stuart, Jean...........	1773	-	-	-
Stoner, John..........	1819	-	-	-	Stuart, John...........	1762	-	-	-
Stoner, John..........	1846	M	1	169	Stuart, John...........	1778	-	-	-
Stoner, John..........	1849	U	1	189	Stubbs, Daniel.........	1820	-	-	-
Stoner, John K.........	1844	L	1	280	Stubbs, Daniel.........	1848	N	1	130
Stoner, Joseph.........	1824	C	1	4	Studenroth, John.......	1820	-	-	-
Stoner, Mary...........	1746	-	-	-	Stump, Frederick.......	1802	-	-	-
Stoner, Michael........	1810	-	-	-	Stump, John...........	1813	-	-	-
Stoner, Susan..........	1850	N	1	381	Sturgis, Dr. John......	1833	G	1	54
Stoneroad, George......	1842	L	1	23	Stutenroth, Henry......	1847	M	1	257
Stoneroad, John........	1776	-	-	-	Styer, Frederick......	1840	K	1	69
Stoneroad, Susanna.....	1833	G	1	58	Sugar, Henry..........	1785	-	-	-
Stork, Elizabeth.......	1823	B	1	15	Suit, Jacob...........	1734	-	-	-
Stouffer, Ann(see Becker	1835	H	1	23	Sullivan, Catharine....	1787	-	-	-
Stouffer, Ann..........	1844	L	1	173	Sultzman, Francis......	1787	-	-	-
Stouffer, Anna.........	1792	-	-	-	Summerville, Andrew....	1822	A	1	192
Stouffer, Daniel.......	1777	-	-	-	Summy, Barbara........	1842	K	1	220
Stouffer, Elizabeth....	1837	H	1	255	Summy, Christian......	1843	L	1	149
Stouffer, Jacob........	1775	-	-	-	Summy, Henry..........	1845	M	1	62
Stouffer, Jacob........	1805	-	-	-	Summy, Henry M........	1842	K	1	281
Stouffer, Jacob........	1844	L	1	260	Summy, Jacob..........	1849	U	1	287
Stouffer, John........	1797	-	-	-	Summy, John, Jr.......	1828	D	1	202
Stouffer, Jonas........	1842	K	1	227	Summy, John...........	1835	H	1	40
Stouffer, Mathias......	1805	-	-	-	Summy, John...........	1842	K	1	219
Stouffer, Sophia.......	1835	H	1	35	Summy, Margaret........	1826	C	1	267
Stouffer, Vincent......	1748	-	-	-	Summy, Mary...........	1828	D	1	224
Stoughton, Augustus....	1832	G	1	15	Summy, Sirus..........	1842	K	1	234
Stousberger, Barbara....	1822	A	1	283	Sunday, Jacob.........	1825	C	1	46
Stousberger, Jacob.....	1805	-	-	-	Suter, John, Sr.......	1829	E	1	50
Stout, Charles.........	1742	-	-	-	Suter, John...........	1835	G	1	272
Stout, Samuel..........	1733	-	-	-	Sutton, James.........	1827	D	1	91
Stout, Samuel..........	1807	-	-	-	Swar, Agnes...........	1766	-	-	-
Stoute, David..........	1764	-	-	-	Swar, Christian.......	1844	L	1	233
Stoutsberger, Christian.	1785	-	-	-	Swar, Peter...........	1748	-	-	-
Stoutselberger, John....	1817	-	-	-	Swarr, Rudolph........	1850	N	1	444
Stoutsenberger, Isaac...	1838	I	1	87	Swartz, John..........	1838	I	1	101
Stoutzenberger, David...	1821	-	-	-	Swartz, Mary..........	1809	-	-	-
Stoutzenberger, John....	1815	-	-	-	Swartz, Nicholas......	1838	I	1	111
Stoutzenberger, Sarah...	1829	E	1	27	Swartzman, Andrew......	1771	-	-	-
Stouzenberger, Barbara..	1824	B	1	162	Swayne, Edward........	1815	-	-	-
Stoven, John..........	1839	I	1	196	Swayne, Edward........	1834	G	1	238
Stover, Anna...........	1820	-	-	-	Swecker, Wendil.......	1760	-	-	-
Stover, George........	1781	-	-	-	Sweeney, Edward.......	1802	-	-	-
Stover, George........	1849	N	1	217	Sweig, Michael........	1786	-	-	-
Stover, Henry..........	1796	-	-	-	Sweigart, Eve.........	1830	E	1	268
Stover, Jacob..........	1850	U	1	434	Sweigart, Felix.......	1826	C	1	186
Stover, Valentine......	1741	-	-	-	Sweigart, Martin......	1836	H	1	198
Stoy, Gustavus.........	1816	-	-	-	Sweigart, Martin......	1838	I	1	115
Strain, John..........	1768	-	-	-	Sweighart, Nicholas...	1775	-	-	-
Strawbridge, Robert.....	1846	M	1	188	Sweinhart, Susan.......	1847	M	1	281
Streble, Michael.......	1771	-	-	-	Sweitzer, Andrew......	1771	-	-	-
Streeper, Israel.......	1825	C	1	55	Swentzel, Henry.......	1812	-	-	-
Streeper, William......	1846	M	1	180	Swisher, Henry, Jr....	1839	I	1	217
Streim, John Adam......	1823	B	1	13	Swisher, Henry........	1840	K	1	42
Strein, Ferdinand......	1822	A	1	222	Switzer, Margaret.....	1819	-	-	-
Stremeler, Daniel......	1786	-	-	-	Swoeler, John.........	1782	-	-	-
Strenge, Christian, Esq.	1834	G	1	142	Swope, George........	1816	-	-	-
Strenge, Jacob........	1835	H	1	21	Swope, George........	1843	L	1	32
Strickler, Abraham.....	1830	E	1	187	Swope, John...........	1754	-	-	-
Strickler, Catharine...	1824	B	1	153	Swope, Mary...........	1826	C	1	153
Strickler, Christian...	1846	M	1	157	Syble, Conrad.........	1823	A	1	266
Strickler, Elizabeth...	1761	-	-	-					

Name	Year	Bk.	Vol	Page	Name	Year	Bk.	Vol	Page
T					Thuma, John.............	1846	M	1	185
Tallabach, Jacob........	1771	-	-	-	Tice, Elizabeth C.......	1791	-	-	-
Tamany, James..........	1835	H	1	66	Tice, Mathias..........	1748	-	-	-
Tanger, Hannah.........	1821	-	-	-	Tillman, William.......	1832	G	1	14
Tanger, John...........	1830	E	1	275	Tilt, John.............	1791	-	-	-
Tangert, Catharine.....	1827	D	1	122	Title, John............	1747	-	-	-
Tanner, John...........	1760	-	-	-	Title, John............	1751	-	-	-
Tanner, Jonas..........	1740	-	-	-	Titwiler, Jacob........	1784	-	-	-
Tapely, John...........	1803	-	-	-	Toat, Henry............	1819	-	-	-
Tate, Adam.............	1833	G	1	65	Toey, Simon............	1777	-	-	-
Tate, Joseph...........	1774	-	-	-	Tolan, James...........	1738	-	-	-
Tate, William.........	1847	M	1	318	Toland, William........	1782	-	-	-
Taupy, Christian.......	1815	-	-	-	Tole, Sebastian........	1745	-	-	-
Taylor, Aaron..........	1816	-	-	-	Tooty, Martin..........	1768	-	-	-
Taylor, Ann............	1749	-	-	-	Towsend, William.......	1845	M	1	40
Taylor, Edward.........	1792	-	-	-	Towson, Isaac..........	1831	-	-	-
Taylor, Egbert.........	1812	-	-	-	Trainer, Daniel........	1836	H	1	159
Taylor, Elizabeth......	1820	-	-	-	Trainer, James........	1818	-	-	-
Taylor, Jacob..........	1823	B	1	98	Trauker, Baltzer.......	1827	D	1	121
Taylor, James..........	1741	-	-	-	Traxell, John..........	1775	-	-	-
Taylor, James..........	1800	-	-	-	Trease, James..........	1779	-	-	-
Taylor, John...........	1733	-	-	-	Treber, Dorothea.......	1772	-	-	-
Taylor, John...........	1734	-	-	-	Treby, John............	1739	-	-	-
Taylor, John...........	1761	-	-	-	Treflinger, John.......	1761	-	-	-
Taylor, John...........	1813	-	-	-	Treish, Magdalena......	1828	D	1	214
Taylor, Mary...........	1816	-	-	-	Treish, Margaretta.....	1793	-	-	-
Taylor, Peter..........	1809	-	-	-	Treish, Michael........	1823	B	1	131
Taylor, Peter..........	1814	-	-	-	Trench, Benjamin.......	1832	F	1	175
Taylor, Robert.........	1760	-	-	-	Trimble, Archibald.....	1814	-	-	-
Taylor, Samuel.........	1840	-	-	-	Trimble, William.......	1848	N	1	105
Taylor, Sarah..........	1844	L	1	282	Trinkley, Christopher...	1752	-	-	-
Taylor, Thomas.........	1827	D	1	76	Tripple, Catharine.....	1846	M	1	210
Taylor, William.......	1849	N	1	159	Trissler, Margaret.....	1822	A	1	159
Teague, Peter..........	1823	B	1	23	Trissler, Susanna......	1798	-	-	-
Teas, John.............	1814	-	-	-	Tritch, Jacob..........	1801	-	-	-
Teesy, Moses...........	1747	-	-	-	Tritsh, Adam...........	1827	D	1	133
Teets, Jacob...........	1754	-	-	-	Trout, Magdalena.......	1760	-	-	-
Temple, William.......	1805	-	-	-	Trout, Philip..........	1760	-	-	-
Templin, Richard.......	1813	-	-	-	Trovinger, Peter.......	1750	-	-	-
Teply, Frena...........	1760	-	-	-	Truckamiller, Michael...	1778	-	-	-
Thoma, Dorst...........	1772	-	-	-	Trump, John............	1834	G	1	146
Thomas, Adam...........	1842	L	1	16	Tryer, Andrew..........	1829	E	1	160
Thomas, Eli H..........	1830	E	1	178	Tryer, John............	1828	D	1	241
Thomas, Jacob..........	1790	-	-	-	Tshudy, Jacob..........	1811	-	-	-
Thomas, Jacob..........	1799	-	-	-	Tshudy, John...........	1835	H	1	91
Thomas, John...........	1801	-	-	-	Tshudy, Michael........	1832	F	1	193
Thomas, John, Sr.......	1830	E	1	274	Tucker, Samuel.........	1748	-	-	-
Thomas, Martin.........	1842	L	1	19	Tuffts, Thomas.........	1788	-	-	-
Thomas, Robert.........	1835	H	1	28	Tullebaun, Leonard.....	1785	-	-	-
Thomas, Thomas.........	1828	D	1	186	Tully, James...........	1828	D	1	172
Thompson, Duncan.......	1767	-	-	-	Tunkin, John...........	1767	-	-	-
Thompson, Emma.........	1847	M	1	319	Turner, Ambrose........	1779	-	-	-
Thompson, Hugh.........	1770	-	-	-	Turner, Margaret.......	1842	K	1	230
Thompson, Jacob........	1844	L	1	180	Tuttle, Abigail........	1814	-	-	-
Thompson, James.......	1842	K	1	267	Tweed, Barbara.........	1849	N	1	223
Thompson, John........	1828	D	1	188	Tweed, Christiana......	1777	-	-	-
Thompson, Mary.........	1780	-	-	-	Tysinger, Peter........	1809	-	-	-
Thompson, Mary........	1842	K	1	207	Tysinger, Peter........	1816	-	-	-
Thompson, Robert.......	1779	-	-	-	**U**				
Thompson, Robert.......	1790	-	-	-	Uhland, Adam...........	1752	-	-	-
Thompson, Temple.......	1767	-	-	-	Uland, Mathias.........	1751	-	-	-
Thompson, William......	1791	-	-	-	Ullman, Frederick......	1760	-	-	-
Thompson, William......	1807	-	-	-	Ulland, Mary E.........	1754	-	-	-
Thompson, Dr. William...	1843	L	1	67	Ulrich, Adam...........	1786	-	-	-
Thornborough, Caleb.....	1803	-	-	-	Upmyer, Lawrence.......	1755	-	-	-
Thornborough, Joseph....	1730	-	-	-	Urban, Jacob...........	1839	I	1	220
Thornborough, Joseph....	1820	-	-	-	Urban, Lewis...........	1829	E	1	62
Thorne, Mary...........	1773	-	-	-	Urich, Christian.......	1779	-	-	-
Thorne, William.......	1760	-	-	-	Urich, Henry..........	1827	D	1	152
Thudy, Francis W.......	1835	H	1	10	Urich, John...........	1776	-	-	-
Thuma, Catharine.......	1846	M	1	160	Urich, Joseph..........	1747	-	-	-
Thuma, Henry..........	1820	-	-	-	Urich, Michael.........	1760	-	-	-

Name	Year	Bk.	Vol	Page	Name	Year	Bk.	Vol	Page
Urich, William.........	1847	L	1	384	Walker, James..........	1777	-	-	-
Usner, Adam.............	1818	-	-	-	Walker, James..........	1789	-	-	-
Usner, John.............	1792	-	-	-	Walker, James..........	1795	-	-	-
V					Walker, James..........	1850	O	1	5
Vanbleck, Henry........	1809	-	-	-	Walker, John...........	1791	-	-	-
Vance, Alexander.......	1751	-	-	-	Walker, Martha.........	1791	-	-	-
Vance, John............	1734	-	-	-	Walker, Mary...........	1818	-	-	-
Vance, John............	1748	-	-	-	Wall, John.............	1738	-	-	-
Vancourt, Daniel.......	1799	-	-	-	Wallace, Adam..........	1738	-	-	-
Vancourt, Lewis J.A....	1777	-	-	-	Wallace, Elias.........	1798	-	-	-
Vander, Peter..........	1814	-	-	-	Wallace, Hugh..........	1835	H	1	25
Vandine, Samuel........	1758	-	-	-	Wallace, Joseph H.,Esq..	1827	D	1	28
Vankennon, Baltzer.....	1836	H	1	161	Wallace, Robert........	1833	G	1	131
VanPatten, Dr. P.S.....	1848	N	1	88	Wallace, William.......	1754	-	-	-
Varley, Sophia.........	1838	I	1	96	Wallace, William.......	1766	-	-	-
Varns, Maria...........	1849	N	1	208	Waller, Peter..........	1809	-	-	-
Veasey, Thomas.........	1844	L	1	209	Wallick, Mathias.......	1806	-	-	-
Velker, George........	1828	D	1	163	Wallis, Robert.........	1745	-	-	-
Venditz, Magdalena.....	1825	E	1	43	Walter, Casper.........	1734	-	-	-
Vernor, Casper.........	1822	A	1	134	Walter, Catherine......	1790	-	-	-
Vernor, David..........	1743	-	-	-	Walter, David..........	1842	L	1	62
Vernor, James..........	1736	-	-	-	Walter, Jacob..........	1803	-	-	-
Vessel, Isaac..........	1764	-	-	-	Walter, John...........	1788	-	-	-
Vincent, Patrick.......	1838	I	1	31	Walter, John...........	1826	C	1	250
Vingard, Jacob.........	1757	-	-	-	Walter, John...........	1827	D	1	15
Virhultz, Cornelius....	1740	-	-	-	Walter, John M.........	1837	H	1	272
Vise, Peter............	1824	B	1	224	Walter, Peter..........	1816	-	-	-
Vogan, James...........	1848	N	1	8	Walter, Peter..........	1817	-	-	-
Vogan, Thomas..........	1811	-	-	-	Walter, Peter..........	1818	-	-	-
Vogelmuth, Feronica....	1821	A	1	75	Walter, Walcot.........	1815	-	-	-
Vogelson, Jacob........	1778	-	-	-	Walter, Walcot.........	1823	A	1	268
Vogelsong, Jacob.......	1842	K	1	252	Walton, Isaac..........	1818	-	-	-
Vogelsong, Jacob.......	1844	L	1	293	Walty, Christian.......	1749	-	-	-
Voght, Conrad..........	1824	B	1	194	Wampler, Peter.........	1749	-	-	-
Voight, John F.........	1829	E	1	61	Wan, Jacob.............	1822	A	1	153
Voight, John F.........	1836	H	1	143	Wanner, Magdalena......	1830	E	1	263
Vondersmith, Susanna....	1832	F	1	179	Wanner, Tobias.........	1807	-	-	-
VonKennon, Mary........	1804	-	-	-	Wanner, Tobias.........	1847	M	1	331
VonKennon, Michael.....	1831	F	1	87	Ward, Philip..........	1749	-	-	-
VonLachy, John.........	1751	-	-	-	Warden, Elizabeth......	1849	N	1	291
Vonneida, Jacob........	1835	G	1	3	Warden, James..........	1814	-	-	-
Vonneida, Philip.......	1847	L	1	325	Warden, Robert.........	1838	I	1	47
Voorhis, E. Charlotte...	1843	L	1	108	Warfel, Adam...........	1826	C	1	202
Voorhis, Michael C.....	1839	I	1	205	Warfel, B. A...........	1842	L	1	131
W					Warfel, George........	1833	G	1	45
Wachter, Catherine.....	1807	-	-	-	Warfel, Jacob..........	1811	-	-	-
Wachter, Frederick.....	1818	-	-	-	Warfel, Jacob..........	1848	N	1	124
Waddell, David.........	1746	-	-	-	Warfel, John...........	1846	M	1	194
Wade, Maria............	1847	M	1	373	Warner, George........	1752	-	-	-
Wade, Susanna..........	1839	I	1	189	Washon, David..........	1760	-	-	-
Waechter, John.........	1814	-	-	-	Watinger, John D.......	1827	D	1	53
Waggoner, Andrew.......	1738	-	-	-	Watson, David..........	1828	D	1	281
Waggoner, Elizabeth....	1792	-	-	-	Watson, Eliza..........	1837	H	1	280
Waggoner, Jacob........	1760	-	-	-	Watson, John...........	1805	-	-	-
Waggoner, Michael......	1771	-	-	-	Watson, Nathaniel......	1827	D	1	153
Wagner, Eliza..........	1832	F	1	267	Watson, Samuel P.......	1819	-	-	-
Wagner, Frederick......	1822	A	1	203	Watt, Alexander........	1758	-	-	-
Wagner, Jacob..........	1781	-	-	-	Watt, Samuel...........	1785	-	-	-
Wagner, Jacob..........	1835	H	1	67	Watts, Samuel..........	1799	-	-	-
Wagner, Sarah..........	1844	L	1	294	Wattson, Ann...........	1758	-	-	-
Wagoner, Casper........	1816	-	-	-	Way, Michael...........	1839	I	1	223
Wagoner, Susanna.......	1849	N	1	201	Wealand, George........	1816	-	-	-
Wahab, Edward..........	1801	-	-	-	Wealand, John..........	1847	M	1	300
Wahnshaff, Henry.......	1794	-	-	-	Weaver, Ann M..........	1821	A	1	104
Walk, Martin...........	1756	-	-	-	Weaver, Catherine......	1782	-	-	-
Walk, Samuel...........	1824	B	1	167	Weaver, Christian......	1774	-	-	-
Walker, David..........	1752	-	-	-	Weaver, Christopher....	1815	-	-	-
Walker, George........	1828	D	1	163	Weaver, Benjamin.......	1817	-	-	-
Walker, Isaac..........	1811	-	-	-	Weaver, Daniel.........	1848	N	1	42
Walker, Isaac..........	1847	M	1	334	Weaver, David..........	1844	L	1	195
Walker, Henry..........	1766	-	-	-	Weaver, David..........	1849	N	1	147
Walker, James..........	1766	-	-	-	Weaver, Frederick......	1822	A	1	180

Name	Year	Bk.	Vol	Page	Name	Year	Bk.	Vol	Page
Weaver, George	1782	-	-	-	Weidman, Christopher	1826	C	1	205
Weaver, George	1832	F	1	236	Weidman, Elizabeth	1848	N	1	14
Weaver, George	1835	H	1	50	Weidman, Eve	1830	E	1	216
Weaver, Henry	1774	-	-	-	Weidman, George	1845	L	1	311
Weaver, Henry	1816	-	-	-	Weidman, Jacob	1803	-	-	-
Weaver, Henry	1845	L	1	309	Weidman, Jacob	1815	-	-	-
Weaver, Henry	1848	N	1	24	Weidman, John, Sr.	1843	L	1	139
Weaver, Isaac	1820	-	-	-	Weidman, John	1849	N	1	276
Weaver, Jacob	1774	-	-	-	Weidman, Magdalena	1836	H	1	145
Weaver, Jacob	1818	-	-	-	Weidman, Martin	1803	-	-	-
Weaver, Jacob	1845	M	1	68	Weidman, Mathias	1743	-	-	-
Weaver, Jacob	1846	M	1	155	Weidman, Rudolph	1769	-	-	-
Weaver, Jacob	1847	M	1	324	Weidman, Samuel	1840	K	1	15
Weaver, John	1772	-	-	-	Weidner, Polly	1848	N	1	39
Weaver, John	1818	-	-	-	Weil, Andrew	1765	-	-	-
Weaver, John	1821	A	1	71	Weiland, Anna	1830	E	1	196
Weaver, John	1823	B	1	81	Weiler, Andrew	1817	-	-	-
Weaver, John	1832	F	1	246	Weilling, John	1837	I	1	17
Weaver, John	1838	I	1	120	Weiman, Conrad	1841	K	1	93
Weaver, John	1843	L	1	47	Weimel, Joseph	1838	I	1	155
Weaver, John	1844	L	1	264	Wein, George	1834	G	1	253
Weaver, John	1847	M	1	368	Wein, John	1845	L	1	322
Weaver, John	1847	M	1	391	Weingardner, Nicholas	1768	-	-	-
Weaver, John	1849	N	1	237	Weinhold, George	1846	M	1	101
Weaver, John	1850	O	1	10	Weinhold, Michael	1827	D	1	155
Weaver, Jonathan	1849	N	1	289	Weinhold, Philip	1823	B	1	96
Weaver, Joseph	1824	B	1	209	Weinhold, William	1845	M	1	89
Weaver, Margaret	1823	B	1	19	Weinholt, Jacob	1771	-	-	-
Weaver, Rosina	1824	B	1	125	Weirich, George	1751	-	-	-
Weaver, Samuel	1825	C	1	23	Weise, Joseph	1830	E	1	260
Weaver, Samuel	1840	K	1	62	Weise, Peter	1824	B	1	224
Weaver, Ulrich	1759	-	-	-	Weisehopf, Peter	1771	-	-	-
Weaver, William	1759	-	-	-	Weiss, Henry	1758	-	-	-
Weaver, William	1846	M	1	153	Weiss, Margaret	1812	-	-	-
Webb, Ann	1822	A	1	244	Weith, Henry	1849	N	1	294
Webb, Ezekiel	1843	L	1	87	Weitzel, George	1843	L	1	143
Webb, Frederick	1831	F	1	108	Weitzel, Paul	1797	-	-	-
Webb, James	1785	-	-	-	Weldy, Daniel	1797	-	-	-
Webb, James	1794	-	-	-	Welker, Matilda	1838	I	1	32
Webb, Jonathan	1826	C	1	225	Weller, Barbara	1828	D	1	162
Webb, Jonathan	1828	D	1	272	Weller, Henry	1847	M	1	260
Webb, Jonathan	1832	G	1	13	Weller, John	1758	-	-	-
Webb, Joseph A.	1828	D	1	271	Weller, John	1767	-	-	-
Weber, George	1825	C	1	42	Wells, William H.	1832	F	1	199
Webster, George	1846	M	1	173	Welsh, Ann	1847	M	1	337
Webster, Isaac	1823	B	1	36	Welsh, William	1742	-	-	-
Webster, Joseph	1843	L	1	112	Welty, Anthony	1785	-	-	-
Webster, Nathan	1804	-	-	-	Wenck, Felix	1756	-	-	-
Webster, Rachel	1808	-	-	-	Wenditz, Christian	1829	E	1	59
Webster, Sarah	1847	M	1	407	Wenditz, Magdalena	1825	C	1	43
Webster, William	1808	-	-	-	Wenditz, Magdalena	1832	G	1	16
Wechter, Elizabeth	1849	N	1	153	Wenger, Abraham	1844	L	1	266
Wechter, John	1838	I	1	79	Wenger, Christian	1772	-	-	-
Wederholt, Charles	1766	-	-	-	Wenger, Eve	1790	-	-	-
Ween, George	1788	-	-	-	Wenger, Jacob	1820	-	-	-
Weer, James	1784	-	-	-	Wenger, John	1794	-	-	-
Weibright, Martin	1774	-	-	-	Wenger, Joseph, Jr.	1817	-	-	-
Weick, John A.	1841	K	1	90	Wenger, Michael	1787	-	-	-
Weidel, Christian	1810	-	-	-	Wenger, Michael	1793	-	-	-
Weidel, Frederick	1811	-	-	-	Wenger, Michael	1801	-	-	-
Weidenbach, Henry	1739	-	-	-	Wenger, Michael	1847	M	1	316
Weidler, Elizabeth	1834	G	1	135	Wenger, Veronica	1841	K	1	183
Weidler, Elizabeth	1844	L	1	270	Wentling, George	1848	N	1	97
Weidler, Elizabeth	1849	N	1	148	Wentling, Mary	1850	N	1	371
Weidler, George, Sr.	1833	G	1	44	Wentz, Thomas	1829	E	1	98
Weidler, Jacob	1811	-	-	-	Werfel, John	1794	-	-	-
Weidler, John	1811	-	-	-	Werfel, Melchoir	1755	-	-	-
Weidler, Magdalena	1817	-	-	-	Werfel, Peter	1802	-	-	-
Weidley, Ann M.	1820	-	-	-	Werking, Catherine	1834	G	1	172
Weidley, Ann M.	1823	B	1	119	Werner, Casper	1822	A	1	134
Weidley, John	1812	-	-	-	Werns, George	1778	-	-	-
Weidman, Barbara	1828	D	1	252	Werntz, Barbara	1771	-	-	-

Name	Year	Bk.	Vol	Page	Name	Year	Bk.	Vol	Page
Werntz, Jacob	1838	I	1	119	Wilfington, John	1757	-	-	-
Wert, Benjamin F.	1806	-	-	-	Wilhelm, Jacob	1777	-	-	-
Wertz, Frederick	1793	-	-	-	Wilkin, John	1741	-	-	-
Wertz, Ludwig	1775	-	-	-	Wilkins, Robert	1765	-	-	-
Weshhoffer, Catherine	1814	-	-	-	Wilkins, Thomas	1747	-	-	-
Wessel, Isaac	1764	-	-	-	Wilkins, Thomas	1763	-	-	-
West, William	1814	-	-	-	Wilkins, William	1734	-	-	-
Westheffer, Jacob	1800	-	-	-	Wilkins, William	1760	-	-	-
Westley, Mary	1824	B	1	200	Will, Conrad	1823	A	1	270
Weymer, Casper	1789	-	-	-	Will, Daniel	1846	M	1	24
Weyrich, George	1765	-	-	-	Will, George	1835	H	1	99
Weyse, Jacob	1752	-	-	-	Willard, Jacob	1758	-	-	-
Wheelen, Phoebe	1819	-	-	-	Willenbrick, Henry	1817	-	-	-
Wheeler, Samuel	1823	B	1	54	Williams, Abraham	1752	-	-	-
Whipper, Benjamin	1822	A	1	197	Williams, Charles	1762	-	-	-
Whisler, George	1841	K	1	189	Williams, George	1845	L	1	329
Whisler, Henry	1755	-	-	-	Williams, James	1774	-	-	-
Whitcraft, George	1838	I	1	129	Williams, James	1814	-	-	-
White, Andrew	1747	-	-	-	Williams, John	1746	-	-	-
White, Christian	1747	-	-	-	Williams, John	1748	-	-	-
White, Dorothea	1828	D	1	233	Williams, John	1806	-	-	-
White, George	1818	-	-	-	Williams, Joshua	1808	-	-	-
White, Henry	1835	H	1	32	Williams, Lilley	1790	-	-	-
White, Hugh	1741	-	-	-	Williams, Margaret	1759	-	-	-
White, John	1745	-	-	-	Williams, Minshall	1799	-	-	-
White, John, Jr	1829	E	1	85	Williams, Peter	1846	M	1	140
White, Julianna	1807	-	-	-	Williams, Richard	1744	-	-	-
White, Ludwig	1848	M	1	439	Williams, Robert	1794	-	-	-
White, Margaret	1747	-	-	-	Williams, Thomas C.	1840	K	1	2
White, Robert	1746	-	-	-	Williams, William	1803	-	-	-
White, Samuel	1820	-	-	-	Williamson, John	1847	M	1	401
Whitecraft, George	1810	-	-	-	Willis, George	1808	-	-	-
Whitehill, George G.	1833	G	1	77	Willis, John	1795	-	-	-
Whitehill, James	1758	-	-	-	Willis, William	1736	-	-	-
Whitehill, James, Esq.	1826	C	1	160	Wilson, Abraham	1745	-	-	-
Whitehill, John	1779	-	-	-	Wilson, Adam	1758	-	-	-
Whitehill, John	1806	-	-	-	Wilson, Alexander	1816	-	-	-
Whitehill, William	1793	-	-	-	Wilson, Catherine	1789	-	-	-
Whitehill, William C.	1841	K	1	106	Wilson, David	1739	-	-	-
Whitely, Michael	1784	-	-	-	Wilson, Elizabeth	1813	-	-	-
Whiteman, John	1805	-	-	-	Wilson, Elisha	1834	G	1	212
Whitesecker, Frederick G.	1802	-	-	-	Wilson, James	1800	-	-	-
Whiteside, George	1747	-	-	-	Wilson, Jane	1808	-	-	-
Whiteside, Henry	1804	-	-	-	Wilson, Jane	1838	I	1	24
Whiteside, James	1804	-	-	-	Wilson, John	1738	-	-	-
Whiteside, James	1825	C	1	9	Wilson, John	1748	-	-	-
Whiteside, John	1830	E	1	235	Wilson, John	1754	-	-	-
Whiteside, Mary H.	1847	M	1	348	Wilson, John	1825	C	1	95
Whiteside, Thomas	1805	-	-	-	Wilson, John, Sr.	1842	K	1	212
Whiteside, Williams	1793	-	-	-	Wilson, John	1846	M	1	192
Whitestick, Michael	1809	-	-	-	Wilson, Joseph	1769	-	-	-
Whitmer, Jacob	1774	-	-	-	Wilson, Martha	1849	N	1	243
Whitmore, George	1804	-	-	-	Wilson, Mary	1796	-	-	-
Wicker, Philip	1835	H	1	85	Wilson, Morris, Esq.	1826	C	1	291
Wickerlin, Paul	1760	-	-	-	Wilson, Nathaniel	1749	-	-	-
Wicks, Edward	1840	K	1	65	Wilson, Robert	1743	-	-	-
Wide, John	1815	-	-	-	Wilson, Samuel	1773	-	-	-
Widele, Elizabeth	1782	-	-	-	Wilson, Thomas	1743	-	-	-
Wider, Michael	1788	-	-	-	Wilson, William	1738	-	-	-
Widler, Abraham	1848	N	1	140	Wilson, William	1786	-	-	-
Wieland, Margaret	1815	-	-	-	Wilt, Dewalt	1784	-	-	-
Wien, John	1833	G	1	86	Wilton, William	1739	-	-	-
Wike, Barbara	1839	I	1	268	Wimer, Michael	1831	F	1	60
Wike, George, Sr.	1806	-	-	-	Windbigler, Henry	1833	G	1	122
Wike, George, Sr.	1832	F	1	160	Winecourt, Joseph	1769	-	-	-
Wike, Jacob	1833	G	1	88	Wineland, Maria	1821	A	1	36
Wike, Joseph	1837	H	1	254	Winneman, Thomas	1837	H	1	259
Wiker, Susanna	1823	B	1	28	Winnenow, Abraham	1841	K	1	156
Wilans, John G.	1802	-	-	-	Winour, George	1848	N	1	26
Wilde, Margaret	1822	A	1	152	Winter, Jacob	1827	D	1	134
Wile, George	1834	G	1	173	Winter, John	1847	M	1	329
Wiley, Thomas	1741	-	-	-	Winterbower, Sebastian	1746	-	-	-

Name	Year	Bk.	Vol	Page	Name	Year	Bk.	Vol	Page
Winterkeimer, Jacob	1785	-	-	-	Wolf, Daniel	1794	-	-	-
Winters, George	1844	L	1	254	Wolf, Daniel	1811	-	-	-
Wise, Andrew	1845	M	1	71	Wolf, Elizabeth	1771	-	-	-
Wise, Christopher	1831	F	1	91	Wolf, George	1743	-	-	-
Wise, Frederick	1800	-	-	-	Wolf, George M.	1748	-	-	-
Wise, Jacob	1749	-	-	-	Wolf, Hans B.	1748	-	-	-
Wise, John	1764	-	-	-	Wolf, Henry	1819	-	-	-
Wise, Margaret	1827	D	1	118	Wolf, Henry	1824	B	1	227
Wisher, Thomas	1815	-	-	-	Wolf, Jacob	1777	-	-	-
Wissler, Jacob	1846	M	1	200	Wolf, Jacob	1823	B	1	128
Wissler, Jacob	1849	N	1	251	Wolf, Jacob, Sr	1827	D	1	81
Wissler, John	1822	A	1	149	Wolf, Jacob, Sr	1827	D	1	114
Withers, Pianna	1844	L	1	165	Wolf, Jacob	1831	F	1	53
Withers, George	1814	-	-	-	Wolf, John	1847	M	1	271
Withers, Jacob	1824	B	1	223	Wolf, Joseph	1806	-	-	-
Withers, Jacob	1827	D	1	102	Wolf, Peter	1742	-	-	-
Withers, Jacob	1829	E	1	96	Wolf, Samuel	1812	-	-	-
Withers, John	1813	-	-	-	Wolfe, John B.	1748	-	-	-
Withers, Joseph	1818	-	-	-	Wolfenberger, John	1803	-	-	-
Withers, Mary C.	1844	L	1	226	Wolfhart, Margaret	1822	A	1	181
Witman, Barbara	1774	-	-	-	Wolfly, George	1826	C	1	144
Witmer, Abraham	1832	F	1	248	Wolfy, John, Esq.	1822	A	1	214
Witmer, Ann	1822	A	1	157	Wolgemuth, Feronica	1821	A	1	75
Witmer, Benjamin	1822	A	1	144	Wolslegal, Frederick	1772	-	-	-
Witmer, Benjamin	1836	H	1	175	Wolver, Philip	1823	A	1	267
Witmer, Catherine	1807	-	-	-	Wonderly, Joseph	1849	N	1	161
Witmer, Christian	1804	-	-	-	Wood, James	1847	M	1	235
Witmer, Christian	1837	H	1	237	Wood, John	1839	I	1	167
Witmer, Conrad	1810	-	-	-	Wood, Thomas	1813	-	-	-
Witmer, Daniel	1817	-	-	-	Woodcraft, Reuben	1848	N	1	120
Witmer, Daniel	1830	E	1	163	Woods, David	1818	-	-	-
Witmer, Daniel	1831	F	1	49	Woods, David	1822	A	1	118
Witmer, Daniel	1832	G	1	6	Woods, Perry	1825	C	1	133
Witmer, Daniel	1834	G	1	144	Woods, Thomas	1817	-	-	-
Witmer, David	1837	H	1	239	Woods, Thomas	1818	-	-	-
Witmer, Elizabeth	1837	H	1	246	Woods, Thomas	1822	A	1	117
Witmer, Esther	1833	G	1	76	Woodworth, Ira	1841	K	1	130
Witmer, Esther	1839	I	1	178	Wooleslagel, Anna	1771	-	-	-
Witmer, Henry	1816	-	-	-	Woolfenton, Mathew	1743	-	-	-
Witmer, Henry	1847	M	1	309	Woolgate, George	1745	-	-	-
Witmer, Jesse	1850	N	1	424	Work, Andrew	1801	-	-	-
Witmer, Joel	1796	-	-	-	Work, James	1816	-	-	-
Witmer, John	1794	-	-	-	Work, James	1823	B	1	51
Witmer, John	1813	-	-	-	Work, Joseph	1743	-	-	-
Witmer, John	1820	-	-	-	Work, Joseph, Esq.	1796	-	-	-
Witmer, John	1824	B	1	192	Workman, Robert	1776	-	-	-
Witmer, John	1826	C	1	234	Workman, Samuel	1759	-	-	-
Witmer, John	1840	I	1	305	Worley, Caleb	1752	-	-	-
Witmer, Joseph	1821	-	-	-	Worrall, Sarah	1753	-	-	-
Witmer, Mary	1804	-	-	-	Worst, George	1842	L	1	11
Witmer, Michael	1820	-	-	-	Worst, George	1843	L	1	47
Witmer, Peter	1785	-	-	-	Worst, Mary	1847	M	1	276
Witmer, Peter	1811	-	-	-	Worst, Mary	1847	M	1	367
Witmore, John	1749	-	-	-	Worst, Peter	1838	I	1	82
Witter, Elizabeth	1830	E	1	200	Wright, Benjamin	1850	O	1	9
Wittmer, Christian	1777	-	-	-	Wright, Ebenezer, Esq.	1829	E	1	73
Wittmer, Peter	1792	-	-	-	Wright, Isaac	1749	-	-	-
Witty, Elizabeth	1790	-	-	-	Wright, James, Esq.	1775	-	-	-
Witwer, Abel	1821	A	1	66	Wright, James	1838	I	1	141
Witwer, Daniel	1819	-	-	-	Wright, John	1749	-	-	-
Witwer, Jonas, Jr	1822	A	1	230	Wright, John	1771	-	-	-
Witwer, Noah	1832	F	1	153	Wright, John	1806	-	-	-
Witz, Frederick	1834	G	1	221	Wright, Joseph	1832	F	1	233
Wohlgemuth, Abraham	1785	-	-	-	Wright, Joseph	1838	I	1	154
Wolf, Abraham	1815	-	-	-	Wright, Joseph	1839	I	1	281
Wolf, Ann	1833	G	1	55	Wright, Robert	1844	L	1	175
Wolf, Anna M.	1802	-	-	-	Wright, Samuel	1811	-	-	-
Wolf, Barbara	1785	-	-	-	Wright, Thomas	1819	-	-	-
Wolf, Barbara	1829	E	1	32	Writs, Solomon	1790	-	-	-
Wolf, Bernard	1792	-	-	-	Wunderly, John	1808	-	-	-
Wolf, Catherine	1847	M	1	251	Wybright, Jacob	1751	-	-	-
Wolf, Conrad	1757	-	-	-	Wyland, Christian	1740	-	-	-

Name	Year	Bk.	Vol	Page
Wyland, Peter	1759	-	-	-
Y				
Yackey, Stephen	1783	-	-	-
Yager, John	1820	-	-	-
Yaiser, Englehart	1762	-	-	-
Yaiser, Frederick	1762	-	-	-
Yaiser, Jacob	1766	-	-	-
Yantz, Mathias	1805	-	-	-
Yarel, Augustus	1822	A	1	213
Yeader, Peter	1754	-	-	-
Yeager, Earhart	1829	E	1	134
Yeakle, Dr. George	1837	H	1	222
Yeates, John	1844	L	1	212
Yeates, Sarah	1829	E	1	141
Yeider, Jacob	1810	-	-	-
Yellotts, Thomas	1812	-	-	-
Yentz, Peter	1821	A	1	40
Yentzer, Jacob, Esq.	1811	-	-	-
Yentzer, Jacob	1816	-	-	-
Yentzer, John, Jr	1835	H	1	13
Yentzer, John	1837	H	1	218
Yentzer, John H.	1835	H	1	42
Yoder, John	1821	A	1	12
Yohn, Catherine B.	1827	D	1	129
Yordy, Daniel	1849	N	1	246
Yordy, Magdalena	1815	-	-	-
Yorter, Jacob	1793	-	-	-
Yorter, Peter, Jr	1784	-	-	-
Yosey, Nicholas	1748	-	-	-
Yost, Adam	1849	N	1	297
Yost, Conrad	1785	-	-	-
Yost, Conrad	1829	E	1	20
Yost, Frederick	1825	C	2	59
Young, Edward	1791	-	-	-
Young, Henry	1836	H	1	150
Young, Jacob	1845	L	1	316
Young, John	1760	-	-	-
Young, John	1795	-	-	-
Young, John	1801	-	-	-
Young, John	1817	-	-	-
Young, John	1821	A	1	2
Young, John	1821	A	1	48
Young, John	1841	K	1	76
Young, John	1846	M	1	144
Young, Lazarus	1771	-	-	-
Young, Marcus	1783	-	-	-
Young, Martha	1818	-	-	-
Young, Peter	1836	H	1	208
Young, Robert	1783	-	-	-
Young, Samuel	1795	-	-	-
Yritz, Anthony	1781	-	-	-
Yuhn, Abraham	1842	K	1	251
Yundt, Andrew	1841	K	1	113
Yundt, Archibald	1838	I	1	146
Yundt, George	1816	-	-	-
Yundt, Rachel	1833	F	1	254
Yundt, Samuel	1839	I	1	173
Z				
Zahm, George	1833	G	1	127
Zahm, John	1823	B	1	99
Zartman, Alexander	1819	-	-	-
Zartman, Catherine	1844	L	1	170
Zartman, Magdalena	1838	I	1	127
Zartman, Michael	1825	C	1	47
Zatzin, Henry	1803	-	-	-
Zehan, John	1763	-	-	-
Zehenheim, Peter	1828	E	1	10
Zehmer, Anthony	1807	-	-	-
Zehring, John	1773	-	-	-
Zeigler, Francis	1800	-	-	-
Zeigler, Frederick	1791	-	-	-
Zeigler, Dr. Frederick	1842	K	1	269
Zeigler, George	1784	-	-	-
Zeigler, John	1836	H	1	158
Zeitstechter, Henry	1765	-	-	-
Zell, Henry	1801	-	-	-
Zell, John	1803	-	-	-
Zell, John	1809	-	-	-
Zell, Nicholas	1794	-	-	-
Zeller, Andrew	1807	-	-	-
Zensinger, Paul	1753	-	-	-
Zenzell, Ann	1794	-	-	-
Zerbe, John	1794	-	-	-
Zercher, Ann	1837	H	1	289
Zercher, Christian	1838	I	1	38
Zercher, Emanuel H.	1849	N	1	290
Zercher, George	1837	H	1	267
Zercher, Henry	1805	-	-	-
Zercher, John	1817	-	-	-
Zercher, Maria H.	1849	N	1	293
Zerfas, Abraham	1787	-	-	-
Zerfass, Samuel	1843	L	1	86
Zetter, Peter	1827	D	1	109
Zimmerman, Andrew	1832	F	1	273
Zimmerman, Christian	1847	M	1	378
Zimmerman, Elizabeth	1764	-	-	-
Zimmerman, Gerhard	1748	-	-	-
Zimmerman, Henry	1760	-	-	-
Zimmerman, John	1771	-	-	-
Zimmerman, John	1814	-	-	-
Zimmerman, John	1839	I	1	291
Zimmerman, Michael	1752	-	-	-
Zimmerman, Woolrich	1738	-	-	-
Zinn, Jacob	1815	-	-	-
Zinn, John	1831	F	1	52
Zinn, Peter	1806	-	-	-
Zook, Abraham	1826	C	1	252
Zook, Ann	1841	K	1	141
Zook, Joseph	1821	A	1	149
Zouk, Ulrich	1747	-	-	-
Zublin, Abraham	1836	H	1	104
Zublin, Daniel	1842	K	1	240
Zuck, Elias H.	1847	M	1	234
Zug, Andrew	1824	B	1	152
Zug, Christian	1838	I	1	55
Zugg, Margaret	1829	E	1	132
Zwally, Christian	1758	-	-	-
Zwebach, George	1836	H	1	160

BIBLIOGRAPHY

———————

I. <u>GENERAL SOURCES</u>

"American Weekly Mercury" - Earliest Newspaper of Penna.
    Pub. in Phila., 1719-1746.
A Bibliography of Lancaster County, Penna., 1745-1912,
    by Lottie M. Bausman.
    Patterson & White Co., Phila., Pa., 1917.
Census of U.S., 1790 - Penna.
    Washington, D.C., Govt. Print. Off. 1908.
Chester County, Around the Boundaries of,
    by W. W. MacElree.
    West Chester, 1934.
Chester County, Pa., History of,
    by Futhey & Cope
    Phila., Everts, 1881.
Church Music and Musical Life in Penna. in the 18th Century.
    Pub. of Pa. Soc. Colonial Dames of America, No.IV.
    Lanc., Wickersham Print Co., 1926, 1927.
Colonial Records of Pennsylvania
    by Samuel Hazard.
    Harrisburg, Printed by T. Fenn & Co., 1851-53.
Daughters of the American Revolution Register, 1930, of
    Penna. Soc.
    Henrietta Dawson Ayres Sheppard
    Phila., 1930
Frontier Forts of Penna.
    Harrisburg, Pa., Wm. Stanley Ray, State Printer, 1916.
German, Swiss, Dutch, French and Other Immigrants from 1727-
    1776, A Collection of Upwards of 30,000 Names of,
    by Daniel I. Rupp.
    Phila., Leary, Stuart & Co., 1875.
Historical Society of Pennsylvania, Original Papers in the,
    1300 Locust Street, Philadelphia, Pa.
Institute of American Genealogy publications.
    Chicago, Ill.
Lancaster County, A Brief History of,
    by Israel Smith Clare and ed. by Anna Lyle.
    Lancaster, Pa., Argus Pub. Co., 1892.
Lancaster County, History of,
    by I. Daniel Rupp.
    Lancaster, Penna., Gilbert Hills, 1844.
Lancaster County, History of,
    by J. I. Mombert, D.D.
    Lancaster, Pa., J. E. Barr & Co., 1869.
Lancaster County, Pageant of Gratitude for 200 years of
    Blessing upon,
    by Percy J. Burrell, presented by people of city and
    county of Lancaster, June 24, 25 and 26, 1929.
    Intelligencer Print. Co., 1929.
Lancaster County, Pennsylvania, A History,
    by H.M.J. Klein, Ph.D.
    New York and Chicago, Lewis Historical Pub.Co.,Inc.1924.
Lancaster County, Penna., The Physical and Industrial Geog-
    raphy of,
    by H. J. Roddy, Ph.D.
    Lanc., Pa., New Era Printing Co., 1916.
Lancaster County, Pennsylvania, with Biographical Sketches,
    History of,
    by Ellis and Evans
    Phila., Everts and Peck, 1883.

Lancaster, England and Lancaster, Pennsylvania, A Comparison,
    (written in Lancaster, England for Phila. Press 1880)
    by W. Wilberforce Nevin.
Lancaster's Golden Century, 1821-1921,
    by H.M.J. Klein.
    Pub. by Hager & Bro., 1921.
Lancaster-York History and Legend Magazine,
    Pub. by V. O. Reichard, Holtwood, Pa.
Map of the Counties, Genealogical,
    Dept. of Internal Affairs, Bureau of Land Records,
    Commonwealth of Penna., 1933.
National Genealogical Society Quarterlies
    Washington, D.C.
Notes and Queries, Historical and Genealogical,
    ed. by William Henry Egle, Harrisburg, Pa.
    Hbg. Pub. Co.
Pennsylvania Archives, 8 Series
Pennsylvania Gazette,
    begun by Benjamin Franklin in 1728.
Pennsylvania Genealogical Society.
    Phila. pub. annually.
Penna. Magazine of History and Biography
    Phila. Historical Soc.
    published annually.
Pennsylvania, The Statutes at Large of
Register of Pennsylvania, Hazard's,
    ed. by Samuel Hazard, Ph.D., Phila., 1828-35,
    16 Vols.
Religious History of Lancaster County,
    (Dr. Klein's History, Vol.II, Section Seven)
Roman Catholics in U.S. as a source for Authentic, Genealog-
    ical and Historical Material, Records of,
    by Cora C. Curry.
    Nat. Gen. Soc., Washington, D.C.
State Library, Harrisburg, Penna., Original Papers in the,

II. INDIANS

Conoy, Indian Town and Peter Bezaillon,
    by D. H. Landis
    L.C.H.S., Vol. XXXVII.
Indian Folk Songs of Penna.,
    by Henry W. Shoemaker
    Ardmore, Pa., Newman F. McGirr, 1927.
Indian Habitations and Ancient Relics Found Near Lanc. City,
    by David Bachman Landis.
    L.C.H.S. Vol. XXXVII.
Indians of Lancaster County, from about 1500-1763,
    by H. F. Eshleman, Esq.
    Lancaster, 1909.
Indian Town of Conestoga, Manor Twp., Lancaster Co., Penna.,
    Record, Title and Description,
    by D. F. Magee.
    L.C.H.S., Vol. XXVIII.
Indian Town of Conestoga in Manor Twp.,
    by D. H. Landis.
    L.C.H.S., Vol. XXVIII.
Indian Town Site at Washington Borough,
    by D. H. Landis
    L.C.H.S., Vol. XXIX.
Indian Tribes of Lancaster County,
    by Dr. F. R. Diffenderffer.
    L.C.H.S., Vol. I.
Iroquois, The Origin of the, As Suggested by their Archaeol-
    ogy,
    by Arthur C. Parker.
    Lanc., Amer. Anthropologist, N.S., Vol.18, pp.479-507,
    1916.

Lancaster's First Court House,   1739-1784,   Great Historical
     Scenes Enacted in,
     by H. F. Eshleman, Esq.
     L.C.H.S., Vol. VII.
Lenape or Delawares, and the   Eastern   Indians in   General,
     Physical Anthropology of the,
     by Aleš Hrdlička.
     Wash., D.C., Bureau of Amer. Ethnology, Bulletin 62, 1916.
Manheim Township and Its Part in the Indian History of the
     County,
     by C. H. Martin.
     L.C.H.S. Pub., Vol.XIX.
Nanticoke Indians in Lancaster County,
     by Dr. H. E. Bender.
     L.C.H.S., Vol. XXXIII.
Nanticoke Indian Village Marked, Site of,
     by W. F. Worner.
     L.C.H.S. Pub., Vol. XXXVI.
Pequehan, Location of,
     by D. H. Landis.
     L.C.H.S., Vol. XXIII.
Petroglyphs in the Susquehanna River near Safe Harbor, Pa.,
     by Donald A. Cadzow.
     Penna. Hist. Com., Vol.III, pub. Harrisburg, 1934.
Photographs of Inscriptions Made by our Aborigines on Rocks
     in the Susquehanna River in Lancaster County, Pa.,
     by D. H. Landis.
     Lancaster, 1907.
Six Nations, Lancaster in 1744, Journal of the Treaty at Lan-
     caster in 1744 with the,
     by Witham Marshe.
     Lancaster, 1884.
Susquehannock Fort, Location of,
     by D. H. Landis.
     L.C.H.S., Vol. XIV.
Susquehannock Indians, Indian Life and Indian Trade of the,
     by D. H. Landis.
     Lanc. reprint of New Era & Intell. Journal, 1929.
Susquehannock Indians of Pennsylvania, Archaeological Studies,
     by Donald A. Cadzow.
     Penna. Hist. Com., Vol.III, pub. Harrisburg, 1936.
Two Delaware Indians Who Lived on Farm of Christian Hershey,
     by C. H. Martin.
     L.C.H.S. Pub., Vol.XXXIV.

III.   EXPLORERS: ADVENTURERS: TRADERS

Brule's Discoveries & Explorations,
     by C. W. Butterfield.
     Cleveland, 1898.
Hazard's Register of Penna., Vols. 4 & 5,
     ed. by Samuel Hazard, Ph.D., Phila., 1828-35, 16 Vols.
Indian Trader, Captain William Trent,
     by Judge C. I. Landis.
     L.C.H.S. Pub., Vol.XXIII.
Indian Traders, Some Early,
     by Samuel Evans.
     L.C.H.S. Pub., Vol.IX.
Indian Trader Troubles,
     by Dr. F. R. Diffenderffer.
     L.C.H.S. Pub., Vol.IX.
Jesuit Relations, Vol.V.
Martin Chartier Tract, Addresses at Unveiling of Tablet Mark-
     ing Site of,
     L.C.H.S. Pub., Vol.XXIX.

New Sweden, History of,
    by Israel Acrelius.
    Phila., Hist. Soc. of Penna., 1874.
Virginia, Generall Historie of,
    by Captaine John Smith.
    Richmond, Va., repub. Franklin Press, 1819.
Watson's Annals of Phila. and Penna., 3 Vols.
    Phila., Stuart, 1884.

IV.   EARLY HISTORY - GENERAL

American Philosophical Soc., Lancaster Co., Members of the,
    by W. F. Worner.
    L.C.H.S. Pub., Vol.XXXI.
Assessment Lists and Other Manuscript Documents of Lanc.Co.
    Prior to 1729,
    by H. F. Eshleman.
    L.C.H.S. Pub., Vol.XX.
Augusta Co., Va., Historical Notes from Records of,
    by C. E. Kemper.
    L.C.H.S. Pub., Vol.XXV.
Cherished Memories of Old Lancaster, Town and Shire,
    by William Riddle.
    Lancaster Intelligencer, 1910.
Conestoga Navigation Company, Organization and Early History of,
    by Prof. Horace R. Barnes.
    L.C.H.S. Pub., Vol.XXXIX.
Early Local History as Revealed by an Old Document,
    by Dr. F. R. Diffenderffer.
    L.C.H.S. Pub., Vol.II.
Early Settlement and Population of Lanc., County and City.
    by Dr. F. R. Diffenderffer.
    L.C.H.S. Pub., Vol.IX.
Federal Revenues of Lancaster County, Penna.,
    by C. H. Martin.
    L.C.H.S. Pub., Vols.XXV, XXVI, XXVII.
Fire Companies of Lancaster City and County, Early,
    by Bertha Cochran Landis.
    L.C.H.S. Pub., Vol.XL.
History of Pennsylvania
    by Robert Proud.
    Phila., Zachariah Poulson, Jr., 1797.
Impress of Early Names and Traits,
    by W. M. Franklin.
    L.C.H.S. Pub., Vol.III.
Influence of Lancaster Co. on the Penna. Frontier,
    by Hon. F. A. Godcharles.
    L.C.H.S. Pub., Vol.XXIV.
Irish Occupation of Lancaster Land,
    by R. M. Reilly.
    L.C.H.S. Pub., Vol.I.
Items of Interest from the Neue Unpartheyische Lancaster
    Zeitung, und AnzeigsNachrichten,
    by Albert Cavin.
    L.C.H.S. Pub., Vols. XXXIV & XXXV.
Lancaster Co. from Hazard's Register, 1613-1835, A Running
    Story of,
    by H. F. Eshleman, Esq.
    L.C.H.S. Pub., Vol. XXVII.
Lancaster County History in the Several Series of the Penna.
    Archives and Other Provincial and State Source Books,
    by H. F. Eshleman, Esq.
    L.C.H.S. Pub., Vol.XXIX.
Lancaster County in Province, State and Nation (A Bicentennial Review),
    by H. F. Eshleman, Esq.
    L.C.H.S. Pub., Vol.XXXIII.

Lancaster - Old and New,
    by James D. Law.
    Lanc. 1902.
Lancaster, Old and New, 1730-1918, The Story of,
    by William Riddle.
    Lanc. 1917.
Lancaster Taxables, Early, 1754,
    by H. F. Eshleman.
    L.C.H.S. Pub., Vol. XIII.
Local History, Odds and Ends of,
    by Dr. F. R. Diffenderffer.
    L.C.H.S. Pub., Vol. X.
Local References from an Early Newspaper (The American Week-
    ly Mercury, Philadelphia, Pa.),
    by H. F. Eshleman.
    L.C.H.S. Pub., Vol. XI.
Maps and Pictures of Old Lancaster,
    by H. F. Eshleman.
    L.C.H.S. Pub., Vol.XXVI.
Mason and Dixon's Line,
    by Dr. J. W. Houston.
    L.C.H.S. Pub., Vol.VIII.
Newspapers of Lancaster County,
    by Dr. F. R. Diffenderffer.
    L.C.H.S. Pub., Vol.VI.
Notables, Some Early Lancaster,
    by Martha B. Clark.
    L.C.H.S. Pub., Vol.VIII.
Penna. Gazette, Items of Interest in, 1734-1781,
    by H. F. Eshleman.
    L.C.H.S. Pub., Vols.XXII to XXVI.
Penna. Packet and General Advertiser from November 29, 1777,
    to June 17, 1778, Notes of Local Interest from the,
    by H. F. Eshleman.
    L.C.H.S. Pub., Vol.XXX.
Penn's City on the Susquehanna,
    by J. F. Sachse.
    L.C.H.S. Pub., Vol.II.
People Who Made Lancaster County,
    by W. M. Franklin.
    L.C.H.S. Pub., Vol.I.
Persons Naturalized in the Province of Penna.
    Penna. Archives, 2nd Series, Vol.II.
Pioneer Notables of Lancaster Co., Some Unknown Early
    by Eleanore J. Fulton.
    L.C.H.S. Pub., Vol.XXVII.
Playbills and Playhouses, Early, Lancaster,
    by Dr. F. R. Diffenderffer.
Provincial Papers; Proprietary and State Tax Lists of the
    County of Lancaster, 1771, '72, '73, '79, '82.
    Penna. Archives, 3rd Series, Vol.XVII.
Provincial Records and Archives, Early Lanc. Co. History in,
    by H. F. Eshleman.
    L.C.H.S. Pub., Vol.XXVII.
Tales and Traditions of Old Lancaster,
    by W. F. Worner.
    Lanc. 1927.
Tax Lists of Lancaster Co., 1751, 1756, 1757, and 1758,
    by Dr. A. H. Gerberich and Dr. G. M. Brumbaugh.
    Washington, D.C., 1933.
Territorial Raids on Lancaster County,
    by G. M. Steinman.
    L.C.H.S. Pub., Vol.VIII.
Titles to the Lands of Lancaster County,
    by H. F. Eshleman.
    L.C.H.S. Pub., Vol.XI.

Warrantees of Land in the County of Lancaster, 1733-1896.
   Penna. Archives, 3rd Series, Vol.XXIV.
Wills, Curiosities of Some Old,
   by Mary N. Robinson.
   L.C.H.S. Pub., Vol.XXII.
Wills, Gleanings From Some Old,
   by Mary N. Robinson.
   L.C.H.S. Pub., Vol.XXIV.

V. QUAKERS

Abolitionists of Lancaster County, The Early
   by Thomas Whitson.
   L.C.H.S. Pub., Vol.XV.
Blunston, Samuel, the Man and the Family,
   by Mrs. H. S. Hiestand.
   L.C.H.S. Pub., XXVI.
Blunston, Samuel, the Public Servant,
   by H. F. Eshleman, Esq.
   L.C.H.S. Pub., Vol.XXVI.
History of Penna., by Robert Proud - Introduction.
   Phila., Zachariah Poulson, Jr., 1797.
Little Britain Township, including Fulton Township, Early
   Settlement and History of,
   by D. F. Magee.
   L.C.H.S. Pub., Vol.XVII.
Penn Hill Meeting House, Fulton Township, Centennial Anni-
   versary of,
   by L. H. Kirk.
   Quarryville, Pa., Sun Print. House, 1924.
Quaker Exiles, The
   by Dr. F. R. Diffenderffer.
   L.C.H.S. Pub., Vol.IX.
Quaker Experiment in Government, A
   by Isaac Sharpless.
   Phila., Ferris, 1898.
Quakers in the American Colonies,
   by Dr. Rufus W. Jones, assisted by Isaac Sharpless and
   Amelia M. Gummere.
   London, MacMillan, 1911.
Underground Railroad,
   by Marianna Gibbons Brubaker.
   L.C.H.S. Pub., Vol.XV.
Wright, John, Pioneer Ferryman, Addresses at Unveiling of
   Tablet to,
   L.C.H.S. Pub., Vol.XXXV.
Wright, John, Esq., Public Career of,
   by H. F. Eshleman, Esq.
   L.C.H.S. Pub., Vol.XIV.

VI. THE MENNONITES

Brechbuhl, Benedict, Hans Burkholder, and the Swiss Menno-
   nite Migration to Lancaster Co., Pa.,
   by J. C. Burkholder.
   L.C.H.S. Pub., Vol.XXXI.
Conestoga Neighbors, 1715-1729,
   by H. F. Eshleman, Esq.
   L.C.H.S. Pub., Vol.XIX.
German and Swiss Settlements of Colonial Penna.,
   by Prof. Oscar Kuhns.
   New York, Henry Holt, 1901.
Herr, Hans, and Martin Kendig, New Light on,
   by Martin H. Brackbill.
   L.C.H.S. Pub., Vol.XXXIX.

Herr Hans, The Emigration of,
    by C. H. Martin.
    L.C.H.S. Pub., Vol.XXIX.
Mennonite Immigration to Pennsylvania in the 18th Century,
    by C. Henry Smith.
    Norristown, Pa. 1929.
    Pub. by Penna. German Soc. Vol.XXXV.
Mennonites of Lancaster Conference,
    by Martin G. Weaver.
    Scottdale, Pa., Mennonite Pub. Co., 1931.
Migration of Lancaster Co. Mennonites to Waterloo County,
    Ontario, Canada, from 1800-1825,
    by Hon. A. G. Seyfert.
    L.C.H.S. Pub., Vol.XXX.
Pioneer of Peace (The): The Mennonite Farmer, 1710-1910,
    by Lloyd Mifflin.
    L.C.H.S. Pub., Vol.XIV.
Plain People of Lancaster County, Pa.,
    by Rev. H. K. Ober.
    Klein's History, pp.360-383.
Swiss and German Pioneer Settlers of Southeastern Penna.,
    Annals of,
    by H. F. Eshleman, Esq.
    Lanc. 1917.
Swiss Emigrants in 18th Century to American Colonies,
    by Dr. G. M. Brumbaugh and A. B. Faust, 2 vols.
    1920 & 1925.
Two Hundredth Anniversary of First Permanent White Settle-
    ment in Lancaster County.
    L.C.H.S. Pub., Vol.XIV.
Weaverland,
    by Martin G. Weaver.
    New Holland, New Holland Clarion, 1933.

VII. HUGUENOTS

Huguenots,
    by Henry M. Baird
    N.Y., Charles Scribner's Sons, 1895.
Huguenots - Their Rise and Their Settlement in America,
    by R. B. Strassburger.
    Huguenot Soc. of Pa., 1927.
Madame Mary Ferree and the Huguenots of Lancaster County,
    by Judge C. I. Landis.
    L.C.H.S. Pub., Vol.XXI.
Memorials of the Huguenots in America,
    by Rev. A. Stapleton, D.D.
    Carlisle, Pa., Huguenot Pub. Co., 1901.
Publications of the Huguenot Society of Pa.
    Norristown, Pa., Norristown Press.
Valley of Pequea, Early Settlement of,
    by Redmond Conyngham.
    Lancaster, 1842.

VIII. THE SCOTCH IRISH

Bellevue Presbyterian Church, Gap, 1823-1912.
    Lancaster, 1912.
Cedar Grove Presbyterian Church in East Earl Twp., History of
    by Hon. A. G. Seyfert
    L.C.H.S. Pub., Vol.XXVIII
Donegal Church; Colin McFarquhar, a Landmark of Presbyterian
    History,
    by Martha B. Clark.
    L.C.H.S. Pub., Vol.XVII, 251.

Donegal Presbyterian Church, History of,
     by Dr. J. L. Ziegler.
     Phila., F. McManus, Jr., 1902.
Leacock, Bellevue and Marietta, with records of marriages,
     by Rev. P. J. Timlow.
     Lancaster, Pa., 1891.
Little Britain Twp., including Fulton Twp., Early Settlement
     and History of,
     by Dr. D. F. Magee.
     L.C.H.S. Pub., Vol.XVII, 138.
Middle Octorara Presbyterian Church, History of,
     by J. E. McElwain
     1917.
Octorara United Presbyterian Church,
     by Thomas C. Evans.
     L.C.H.S. Pub., Vol.XXXIV, 73.
Pequea Presbyterian Church, History of,
     by W. C. Alexander.
     Lancaster, 1878.
Pequea Presbyterian Graveyard,
     by W. F. Worner.
     L.C.H.S. Pub., Vol.XXIV, 39.
Presbyterian Historical Society, Journal of the,
     Witherspoon Building, Phila.
Presbyterianism in Lanc. Co., Early,
     by Dr. J. W. Houston.
     L.C.H.S. Pub., Vol.VIII.
Presbyterianism in the Pequea Valley,
     by W. U. Hensel.
     Lanc. 1912.
Presbytery, Donegal and Carlisle, Origin and History of,
     by West.
Presbytery, Westminster, 1732-1924, History of,
     by Rev. R. L. Clark.
     1924.
Register of Marriages and Baptisms (1751-1791),Performed by
     Rev. John Cuthbertson, Covenanter Minister (1718-1791).
     Prepared by Helen Fields, Washington, D.C., 1934.
     Re - Lanc. Co., pp.132-196.
Scotch-Irish,(2 vols.)
     by Chas. A. Hanna.
     G. P. Putnam Sons, N.Y. & London; Knickerbocker Press,
     1902.
Scotch-Irish: Their Impress on Lancaster County,
     by W. U. Hensel.
     L.C.H.S. Pub., Vol.IX.
Scotch-Irish Pioneers in Ulster & America,
     by Charles Knowles Bolton.
     Boston, Bacon & Brown, 1910.
Scotch-Irish Society, Penna., Publications of,
     Phila., Allen, Lane & Scott.

IX.   GERMANS

Bethany Charge of the Reformed Church, History of,
     by Rev. D. C. Tobias.
     Lititz, Record Print. Off., 1881.
Brickerville Congregation in Lancaster County, History of,
     by Rev. F. J. F. Schantz, D.D.
     Lanc. 1899.
Conrad Weiser, the German Pioneer, Patriot, and Patron of
     Two Races, Life of,
     by C. Z. Weiser.
     Reading, 1899.

Earls, The Three,
    by Dr. F. R. Diffenderffer.
    New Holland, Ranck, 1876.
Folklore of the Penna. Germans,
    by Dr. J. B. Stoudt.
    Phila., Wm. J. Campbell, 1916.
First Reformed Church of Lanc., Pa., Two Hundred Years and
    More of the,
    by Prof. C. N. Heller.
    Lanc. 1936.
German Baptist Brethren in the 18th Century, Literary Activ-
    ity of the,
    by J. S. Flory.
    Elgin, Ill., Brethren Pub. House, 1908.
German Baptist Brethren in Europe and America, History of,
    by Dr. M. G. Brumbaugh.
    Elgin, Ill., Brethren Pub. House, 1899.
German Emigration into Penna. Through the Port of Phila.,
    from 1700 to 1775, Part II, the Redemptioners, prepared
    at request of Penna. German Society,
    by Dr. F. R. Diffenderffer.
    Lancaster, 1900.
German Emigration to America, 1709-1740,
    by Rev. Henry Eyster Jacobs.
    Lancaster, 1899.
German Inhabitants of Penna., An Account of the Manners of
    the, written in 1789
    by Dr. Benjamin Rush.
    Phila., Samuel Town, 1875.
German Reformed Congregations in Penna., 1747-1792, Minutes
    and Letters of the Coetus of the,
    Reformed Church Pub. Bd. Phila., 1903.
German Sectarians of Penna., 1708-1742,
    by Julius F. Sachse
    Phila., 1899.
Germans in Pennsylvania,
    by Dr. R. M. Bolenius.
    L.C.H.S. Pub., Vol.X.
Lancaster County, The Reformed Church in, during the 18th
    Century,
    by Prof. W. J. Hinke.
    L.C.H.S. Pub., Vol.XXXIII.
Maytown, Lancaster Co., St.John's Evangelical Lutheran Church
    1765-1904,
    by Rev. Geo. Philip Goll.
    Lanc., Wickersham Print. Co., 1904.
Muddy Creek Reformed Congregation, History of,
    by Prof. W. J. Hinke, Ph.D., D.D.
    L.C.H.S. Pub., Vol.XXXVI.
New Holland Charge of the Reformed Church, The History of,
    by Rev. D. W. Gerhard, D.D.
    New Holland, Ranck & Sandoe, 1877.
New Holland, Memorial Volume of the Evangelical Lutheran
    Church of,
    by Rev. John W. Hassler.
    New Holland, 1880.
Pennsylvania Dutch and Other Essays,
    by Phoebe Earle Gibbons.
    Phila., Lippincott & Co., 1882.
Pennsylvania Dutch, The
    by Dr. A. B. Hart.
    L.C.H.S. Pub., Vol.XII.
Pennsylvania-German, The (13 vols.)
    pub. Lititz, Pa.

Penna. German and Huguenot Families, Genealogical Research
    among,
    by Charles Rhoads Roberts.
    Washington, D.C., Nat. Gen. Soc.
Pennsylvania-German Land, In
    by Jesse Leonard Rosenberger.
    Chicago, Univ. of Chicago Press, 1929.
Pennsylvania Germans, Ethnical Origin of the
    by Prof. Oscar Kuhns.
    L.C.H.S. Pub., Vol.XIV.
Pennsylvania German in the Field of the Natural Sciences,
    by Thomas Conrad Porter.
    Lancaster, 1896.
Pennsylvania German Pioneers (3 vols.)
    by Ralph Beaver Strassburger, LL.D.,
    ed. by William John Hinke, Ph.D.,D.D.
    pub. Norristown, Pa., Penna. German Soc., 1934.
Pennsylvania Germans, Social Conditions among the
    by J. O. Knauss, Jr.
    Lanc., Westhaeffer, 1872.
Pennsylvania German Society, Publications of
Susquehanna Valley Settlements, as Shown by Official Letters,
    etc., of the time,
    by D. M. Landis.
    L.C.H.S. Pub., Vol.XXV.
The Homeland of the 1st Settlers in Lancaster County,
    by Prof. Oscar Kuhns.
    L.C.H.S. Pub., Vol.XXI.
The True Heroes of Pennsylvania.
    by Julius F. Sachse.
    Lanc. 1892.
Taufers or the German Baptist Brethren,
    by F. R. Diffenderffer.
    Lancaster, 1899.
Trinity Graveyard,
    by J. W. Lippold.
    L.C.H.S. Pub., Vol.XXXII, 109.
Trinity Lutheran Church, Lancaster, 175th Anniversary of
    by Dr. J. E. Whitteker.
    Whitteker, 1905.
United Brethren Church, Landmark History of,
    by Rev. Daniel Eberly, Rev. Isaiah H. Albright,
    Rev. C. I. Brane
    Reading, Pa., Behney & Bright, 1911.

X. EPHRATA COMMUNITY

Chronicon Ephratense, A History of the Community of the Sev-
    enth Day Baptists,
    by "Lamech" and "Agrippa", Jacob Gass and Peter Miller,
    trans. by Dr. J. Max Hark, pub. 1786.
    Lancaster, Pa., S. H. Zahm & Co., 1899.
Ephrata Cloister, Music of the, also Conrad Beissel's Treat-
    ise on Music as set forth in a preface to the   "Turtel
    Taube of 1747"
    by Julius F. Sachse.
    Lancaster, New Era Print., 1903.
Ephrata Community 120 Years Ago, as Described by an English-
    man,
    by Dr. F. R. Diffenderffer.
    L.C.H.S. Pub., Vol.IX.
Ephrata Community 125 Years Ago,
    by Dr. F. R. Diffenderffer.
    L.C.H.S. Pub., Vol.III.

Ephrata Community, Register of
    by Julius F. Sachse.
    Phila. 1891.

XI.   MORAVIANS

Early History of Lititz,
    by A. R. Beck, 1899
Extracts from Moravian Diaries at Bethlehem
Re - to Early Events in Lancaster, Pa.
    by Dr. J. W. Jordan
    L.C.H.S. Pub., Vol.XXVII.
Epitaphs. (Inscriptions in Shreiner's Cemetery,Lancaster,
    and Moravian Churchyard, Lititz,
    by Lydia D. Zell
    L.C.H.S. Pub., Vol.II.
Lititz as an Early Musical Center
    by Dr. H. H. Beck
    L.C.H.S. Pub., Vol.XIX.
Military Hospital at Lititz, 1777-78
    by Dr. H. H. Beck
    L.C.H.S. Pub., Vol.XXIII.
Town Regulations of Lititz, 1759
    by Dr. H. H. Beck
    L.C.H.S. Pub., Vol.XXXIX.
Tanneberger, David, Organ Builder
    by Prof. Paul E. Beck
    L.C.H.S. Pub., Vol.XXX.

XII.   ENGLISH

Church of England in Lancaster County, The
    by W. F. Worner
    L.C.H.S. Pub., Vol.XXXVII.
Churchyard, Old St.John's, Pequea,
    by W. F. Worner
    L.C.H.S. Pub., Vol.XXI,
Churchyard, St.James's, Old,
    by W. F. Worner
    L.C.H.S. Pub., Vol.XX,
Graveyard Adjoining St.James's Church, Inscriptions on
    Tombstones in the
    by W. F. Worner
    L.C.H.S. Pub., Vol.XXXVII,
Mount Hope Church
    by W. F. Worner
    L.C.H.S. Pub., Vol.XXVI,
Pequea, St.John's
    by R. Chester Ross
    Intelligencer Print. Co. 1929.

XIII.   WELSH

Caernarvon, The Story of
    by Dr. J. B. Lincoln
    L.C.H.S. Pub., Vol.XVIII.
Caernarvon History, Two Centuries of
    by H. F. Eshleman, Esq.
    L.C.H.S. Pub., Vol.XXVI.
Welsh Graveyard
    by Benjamin F. Owen
    L.C.H.S. Pub., Vol.I.

XIV.   JEWS

Early Jewish Colony in Lancaster Co.
    by Monroe B. Hirsh
    L.C.H.S. Pub., Vol.V.

Hebrews in America (The)
    by Marken
    pub. 1888.
Jewish Historical Society publications.

XV. POLITICAL

Bench and Bar
    (Ellis and Evans' History of Lancaster County,
      Chapter XXI)
Birth of Lancaster County
    by H. F. Eshleman, Esq.
    L.C.H.S. Pub., Vol.XII.
Boroughs and Townships
    (Ellis and Evans' History of Lancaster County,
      Chapter XXX et seq)
City of Lancaster
    (Ellis and Evans' History of Lancaster County,
      Chapter XXIX.
Civil List
    (Ellis and Evans' History of Lancaster County,
      CHAPTER XX.
Courts, Civil, Our First
    by H. F. Eshleman, Esq.
    L.C.H.S. Pub., Vol.X.
Court, District, of the City and County of Lancaster,
    History of the,
    by Judge C. I. Landis
    L.C.H.S. Pub., Vol.XVIII.
Court Records of Chester Co., Pa., Extracts from Early,
    by Harry Wilson.
    L.C.H.S. Pub., Vol.XXXV.
Flag of Lancaster
    by Dr. J. P. McCaskey
    L.C.H.S. Pub., Vol.XI.
Four Great Surveys in Lancaster County
    by H. F. Eshleman, Esq.
    L.C.H.S. Pub., Vol.XXVIII.
Great Historical Scenes Enacted in Lancaster's First
    Court House, 1739-1784.
    by H. F. Eshleman, Esq.
    L.C.H.S. Pub., Vol.VII.
Hamilton Grant, History of Lot 159 of,
    by Martha B. Clark
    L.C.H.S. Pub., Vol.XX.
Law Library Association, The Lancaster
    by Daniel B. Strickler, Esq.
    L.C.H.S. Pub., Vol.XXXIX.
Political History of Lancaster County
    (Dr. Klein's History, Vol.I, Section Three)
Political History and Development of Lanc. Co's. First
    Twenty Years, 1729-1749,
    by H. F. Eshleman, Esq.
    L.C.H.S. Pub., Vol.XX.
Postlethwaite's and Our First Courts
    by Judge C. I. Landis
    L.C.H.S. Pub., Vol.XIX.
Postlethwaite's Chosen and Then Abandoned as the County
    Seat of Lanc. Co., Why Was,
    by David H. Landis
    L.C.H.S. Pub., Vol.XII,
Postlethwaite's Tavern Where First Courts of Justice in
    Lanc. Co. Were Held, Addresses at Unveiling of Tab-
    let, Oct.8, 1915, Marking Site of,
    L.C.H.S. Pub., Vol.XIX.

Quarter Sessions' Dockets, Local History Contained in the
     Early,
     by Martha M. Bowman
     L.C.H.S. Pub., Vol.XXVI.
Sons of Lancaster County Who Won Congressional Honors   at
     Home and Elsewhere,
     by C. H. Martin.
     L.C.H.S. Pub., Vol.XXXVI.
Titles to the Lands of Lancaster County
     by H. F. Eshleman, Esq.
     L.C.H.S. Pub., Vol.XI.
Townships, The Names of the,
     by Dr. J. H. Dubbs
     L.C.H.S. Pub., Vol.I.
Washington, George, in Lancaster
     by W. F. Worner
     L.C.H.S. Pub., Vol.XXXVII.

XVI. TRANSPORTATION: ROADS AND FERRIES

Anderson's Ferry
     by S. M. Sener
     L.C.H.S. Pub., Vol.XI.
Artificial Roads in Penna., The Beginnings of
     by Judge C. I. Landis
     L.C.H.S. Pub., Vol.XXIII.
Conestoga Six-Horse Bell Teams of Eastern Pa.
     by John Omwake
     Cincinnati, Ebbert & Richardson Co., 1930.
Conestoga Wagon, The
     by H. C. Frey
     L.C.H.S. Pub., Vol.XXXIV.
First Long Turnpike in the United States, The
     by Judge C. I. Landis
     L.C.H.S. Pub., Vol.XX.
Great Conestoga Road, The
     by H. F. Eshleman, Esq.
     L.C.H.S. Pub., Vol.XII.
Highway System from 1714 to 1760, History of Lancaster
     County's, and Map,
     by H. F. Eshleman, Esq.
     L.C.H.S. Pub., Vol.XXVI.
List of the Original Lancaster Subscribers to the Capital
     Stock of the Philadelphia and Lancaster Turnpike,
     by Judge C. I. Landis.
     L.C.H.S. Pub., Vol.XXII.
Philadelphia and Lancaster Turnpike
     by Dr. F. R. Diffenderffer
     L.C.H.S. Pub., Vol.VI.
Post Roads in Eastern Penna., Early
     by H. E. Steinmetz
     L.C.H.S. Pub., Vol.VII.
Rival Ferries Over the Susquehanna in 1787 - Wright's and
     Anderson's
     by George R. Prowell
     L.C.H.S. Pub., Vol.XXVII.
Road Petition, An Early
     by Dr. F. R. Diffenderffer
     L.C.H.S. Pub., Vol.X.
Stage Dispatch, The Lancaster
     by Judge C. I. Landis
     L.C.H.S. Pub., Vol.XIX.
Survey of the Philadelphia and Lancaster Turnpike Road
     by Judge C. I. Landis
     L.C.H.S. Pub., Vol.XX.

Transportation on Newport Road, Pioneers and
    by H. H. Bomberger
    L.C.H.S. Pub., Vol.XXXVI.
Transportation Troubles in Lancaster County during   the
    Revolution
    by Lottie M. Bausman
    L.C.H.S. Pub., Vol.XIX.

XVII.   EDUCATION

Academy, The Lancaster County
    by W. F. Worner
    L.C.H.S. Pub., Vol.XXXVI.
Beck, John, Pioneer Educator of Lancaster County
    by Simon P. Eby
    Lancaster, 1890.
Chestnut Level Academy
    by James Blair Moore
    L.C.H.S. Pub., Vol.XIII.
Education
    (Dr. Klein's History, Section Nine)
Franklin College, Old
    by Dr. J. H. Dubbs
    L.C.H.S. Pub., Vol.II.
Franklin & Marshall College, History of
    by Joseph Henry Dubbs,D.D., LLD.
    Lancaster, Pa., pub. by F. & M. College Alumni
    Association, 1903.
History of Some Old School Houses
    L.C.H.S. Pub., Vol.XL.
Juliana Library Company of Lancaster, The
    by Judge C. I. Landis
    L.C.H.S. Pub., Vol.XXXIII.
Linden Hall Seminary
    by Rev. H. A. Brickenstein
    1895
Nicholas Comenius: or Ye Pennsylvania Schoolmaster of Ye
    Olden Time
    by William Riddle
    Lancaster, 1897.
One Hundred and Fifty Years of School History in
    Lancaster, Pa.
    by William Riddle
    Lancaster, 1890.
Ross, James, Latinist. An Early Lancaster Pedagogue,
    by Dr. J. H. Dubbs
    L.C.H.S. Pub., Vol.IX.
Schools in the Valley of the Octorara, Early
    by Dr. J. W. Houston
    L.C.H.S. Pub., Vol.II.
Scott, John, and the Public Schools
    by B. J. Myers, Esq.
    L.C.H.S. Pub., Vol.XVIII.
School Systems of Lancaster City, The Early
    by William Riddle
    L.C.H.S. Pub., Vol.VIII.
Strasburg Academies
    by W. F. Worner
    L.C.H.S. Pub., Vol.XXXII.
Superintendents of Public Instruction
    by Hon. A. G. Seyfert
    L.C.H.S. Pub., Vol.XXXII.
Theological Seminary of the Reformed Church in the United
    States (Lancaster, Pa.), History of
    by Dr. George W. Richards
    (in preparation)

XVIII. ARCHITECTURE, ART, and EARLY ARTISTS

Architecture of Penna., Early Domestic,
    by Eleanor Raymond
    1931
Architecture of Lancaster County, Early,
    by A. L. Kocher
    L.C.H.S.Pub., XXIV.
Architecture, Typical Old Buildings and,
    by Jacob Hill Byrne, Esq.
    L.C.H.S.Pub., Vol.XXVI.
Artists, Early:
    Arthur Armstrong, by Dr. F. R. Diffenderffer
    Jacob Eichholtz, by Hon. W. U. Hensel
    Aaron Eshleman, by C. B. Demuth
    Jasper Green, by Lillian Evans
    Peter Lehn Grosh, by Dr. H. H. Beck
    Benjamin West Henry, by G. M. Steinman
    John Landis, by Mary N. Robinson
    John Jay Libhart, by A. C. Libhart
    W. Sanford Mason, by Lillian Evans
    Leon von Ossko, by Harry Breneman
    Luigi Persico - An Italian Artist in Lancaster,1820,
    by Hon. W. U. Hensel
    Jacob Eshleman Warfel, by Dr. F. R. Diffenderffer
    Isaac L. Williams, by Adaline Spindler
        (L.C.H.S.Pub., Vol.XVI)
    An Artistic Aftermath, by Hon. W. U. Hensel
    Ferdinand Huck, by Dr. F. R. Diffenderffer
    Adam Mortimer Lightner, by Dr. F. R. Diffenderffer
    Ludwig Reingruber, by Walter C. Hager
        (L.C.H.S.Pub., Vol.XVII)
    Jacob William Deichler, Artist, Shoemaker,
    by Walter C. Hager
    Benjamin West and His Visit to Lancaster,
    by Judge C. I. Landis
        (L.C.H.S.Pub., Vol.XXIX)
    Jacob Eichholtz, Notes Concerning Some Portraits by
    the Distinguished Artist,
    by Prof. H. R. Barnes
    Jacob Eichholtz Points the Way,
    by Cornelius Weygandt
        (L.C.H.S.Pub., Vol.XXXIX)
    Jacob Eichholtz. Notes on Eichholtz Paintings,
    by O. D. Brandenburg
        (L.C.H.S.Pub., Vol.XXVII)
    Robert Fulton's Career as an Artist
    (Robert Fulton and the Clermont)
    by Alice Crary Sutcliffe, Part I
    (List of Paintings by Robert Fulton), Appendix,
    pp.354-356.
        (N.Y., The Century Co., 1909)
Arts and Artists
    by Laetitia H. Malone
    (in Dr. Klein's History, pp.964,965)
In the Time of the Lily: or The Meaning of Penna-German
    Art,
    by Dr. J. B. Stoudt and son. (In preparation)- 2nd
    Year Book of Penna-German Folklore Society.
Loan Exhibition of Historical and Contemporary Portraits
    Illustrating the Evolution of Portraiture in Lanc-
    aster County....under the Auspices of the Iris Club
    and Lancaster County Historical Society....Catalog-
    ue, revised edition.
    Lanc. 1912

Picture of Washington by a Lancaster Artist,
    by Judge C. I. Landis
       L.C.H.S. Pub., Vol.XXII.
Preface to Copy of Memo of Jacob Eichholtz,
    by Ida L. K. Hostetter
       L.C.H.S. Pub., Vol.XXIX.
Rustic Art in Lancaster County
    by Dr. J. H. Dubbs
       L.C.H.S. Pub., Vol.VII.

XIX. ARTS AND CRAFTS AND CUSTOMS

An Amish Wedding
    by Miller Ressler
       L.C.H.S. Pub., Vol.XXXIX.
Antiques, Penna.- German and Huguenot
    by Walter Lewis Stephens
       1925
Arts, Customs and Experiences, Early,
    by David Bachman Landis
       L.C.H.S. Pub., Vol.XXXVII.
Book Plates, Lancaster,
    by Dr. J. H. Dubbs
       L.C.H.S. Pub., Vol.VIII.
Cookery, The Penna.-Dutch and Their,
    by J. George Frederick
       N.Y., The Business Bourse, Publishers, 1935.
Craftsmen, Early American
    by Walter A. Dyer
Customs in Lancaster, Old-Time
    by W. F. Worner
       L.C.H.S. Pub., Vol.XXXVI.
Date Stones, with Examples
    by Dr. F. R. Diffenderffer
       L.C.H.S. Pub., Vol.IX.
Grandfathers' Clocks: Their Making and Their Makers in
    Lancaster County,
    by D. F. Magee
       L.C.H.S. Pub., Vol.XXI.
"I.C.H.", Lancaster Pewterer
    by John J. Evans, Jr.
       L.C.H.S. Pub., Vol.XXV.
Illuminative Writing Among Penna.-Germans, The Survival
    of the Mediaeval Art of,
    by Henry C. Mercer
       1897.
Printers of Lancaster, Early German, and the Issues of
    Their Press,
    by Dr. F. R. Diffenderffer
       L.C.H.S. Pub., Vol.VIII.
Rifles, The Lancaster,
    by Dr. F. R.Diffenderffer
       L.C.H.S. Pub., Vol.IX.
Stiegel Glass
    by Frederick Wm. Hunter
    Boston and N.Y., Houghton-Mifflin Co. Riverside
    Press, Cambridge, 1914.
"The Bible in Iron" and Decorated Stove Plates of the
    Penna.-Germans,
    by Henry C. Mercer
       1906.
The Red Hills, a Record of Good Days with the Penna.-
    Dutch
    by Cornelius Weygandt
    Phila., Univ. of Penna. Press, 1929.

The So-Called "Kentucky Rifle", as Made in Lancaster Co.
by D. F. Magee
L.C.H.S. Pub., Vol.XXX.
Tulip Ware of the Penna.-German Potters
by Edwin Atlee Barber
(printed for the Museum, Memorial Hall, Fairmount
Park, Phila., Pa.)

XX. INDUSTRIES

Aviation in Lancaster County, A History of
by Hugh W. Nevin
L.C.H.S. Pub., Vol.XXXIX.
Cattle and Stock Yards in Lancaster County Prior to 1800
by J. Andrew Frantz
L.C.H.S. Pub., Vol.XXVIII.
Chickies Furnaces. The First Furnace Using Coal.
by H. L. Haldeman
L.C.H.S. Pub., Vol.I.
Elizabeth Farms and Furnaces, Brickerville, Pa.
by Hon. W. U. Hensel
L.C.H.S. Pub., Vol.XVII.
First Commercial Telegraph Line
by W. L. Sullenberger
L.C.H.S. Pub., Vol.XXXVIII.
Forges and Furnaces in the Province of Penna.
by the Penna. Society of Colonial Dames of America.
Lancaster, New Era Print. Co., 1914.
Furnaces and Forges, Provincial
(Dr.Klein's History, Vol.I, Chapter XXXVIII.)
Industries of Lancaster County
(Dr. Klein's History, Vol.II, Section Six)
Industries Located Along the Conowingo Creek, Early,
by Edgar B. Maxwell
L.C.H.S. Pub., Vol.II.
Industries on the Octorara, Early
by Dr. J. W. Houston
L.C.H.S. Pub., Vol.I.
Inns of Lancaster, Historic
(Dr. Klein's History, Vol.I, Chapter XL)
Iron and Iron Manufacture
(Ellis and Evans' History of Lancaster County,
Chapter XXIV)
Lost Industries of the Octorara, Some of the
by Dr. J. W. Houston
L.C.H.S. Pub., Vol.III
Mills of Lancaster County, Early
(Dr. Klein's History, Vol.I, Chapter XXXVII.)
Mills, Some Early County. A Fulling Mill in 1714.
by Samuel Evans
L.C.H.S. Pub., Vol.I.
Mills and County Ordinaries, Old
by Samuel Evans
L.C.H.S. Pub., Vol.I.
Mining Industries of Lancaster County, Two Notable
by H. L. Willig
L.C.H.S. Pub., Vol.XXVIII.
Two Hundred Years of Farming in Lancaster County
by L. B. Huber
L.C.H.S. Pub., Vol.XXXV.

XXI. WAR RECORDS

Lancaster County in the Various Wars
by H. L. Haldeman
L.C.H.S.Pub., Vol.XVIII.

Colonial Wars:

Arsenal of Colonial America, The Lancaster
    (Dr. Klein's History, Vol.I, Chapter XXXIX)
Colonial Wars, The
    Klein, Dr.H.M.J., Lancaster County, Penna., Vol.II,Ch.XLII)
Cresap's "War" - Mason and Dixon's Line
    (Dr. Klein's History, Vol.I, Ch.XLI)
French and Indian War
    (Ellis and Evans' History of Lancaster County, Chapter V)
Officers and Soldiers of the Province of Penna., 1744-1765
    (Penna. Archives, 5th Series, Vol.I)

Lancaster County in the Revolution:

Barracks During the Revolution, The Lancaster
    by S. M. Sener
    1895
Continental Stables in Lancaster
    by Jacob Hill Byrne, Esq.
    L.C.H.S.Pub., Vol.XXXVI)
Donegal in the Revolution - Patriotism and Piety
    by Dr. F. R. Diffenderffer
    L.C.H.S.Pub., Vol.IV.
Graveyard of Revolutionary Soldiers at Lititz
    by Dr. H. H. Beck
    L.C.H.S.Pub., Vol.XXXVII.
Hessians, The
    by Martha B. Clark
    L.C.H.S.Pub., Vol.IV.
Lancaster County in the Revolution
    Ellis and Evans' History of Lancaster County,
    Chapters VI, VII, VIII.
Lancaster Girl in History, A, (Barbara Frietchie)
    L.C.H.S.Pub., Vol.XXIII.
Liberty Bells of Pennsylvania, The
    by Dr. J. B. Stoudt
    Chapter XII re-to Lancaster
    Phila., Wm. J. Campbell, 1930
List of 591 Persons Who Were Paid For Forage
    Furnished for the Magazine at Lancaster, Pa., 1778-1779,
    by F. J. Metcalf
    Wash., D.C., Nat.Gen.Soc., June & Sept. 1928
Location of Revolutionary Soldiers' Graves in Lancaster Co.,Penna
    by Mary Shee Hess
    L.C.H.S.Pub., Vol.XXX.
Loyalists in the Revolution
    by Dr. F. R. Diffenderffer
    L.C.H.S.Pub., Vol.XXIII.
Marshall, Christopher, Extracts from Diary kept in Philadelphia
and Lancaster during the American Revolution, 1774-1781.
    ed. by William Duane
    Albany, Munsell 1877.
Marshall's Diary in its Relation to Lancaster City and County
    by Dr. F. R. Diffenderffer
    L.C.H.S. Pub., Vol.III.
Marshall's (Christopher) Home in which he Lived and Wrote his
Diary from 1777 to 1781.
    by D. F. Magee
    L.C.H.S.Pub., Vol.XXXI.
Morris, Robert, in Manheim
    by George L. Heiges
    L.C.H.S.Pub., Vol.XXXIV.
Muster Rolls re- to Associators and Militia of the County of Lanc.
    Penna. Archives, 5th Series, Vol.VII.

Muster Rolls and Papers re- to Associators and Militia of the
County of Lancaster.
 Penna. Archives, 2nd Series, Vol.XIII, p.269 et seq.
Pageant of Liberty, Commemorating Lancaster, Pa., in the American
Revolution.
 by Percy Jewett Burrell and Laura F. Kready and H. Clifton
 Thorbahn, Presented by the People of Lancaster, July 5,6,7,
 1926.
 Lancaster Press, Inc., 1926.
Peter Miller Did Not Translate The Declaration of Independence In-
to Seven Languages
 by W. F. Worner
 L.C.H.S.Pub., Vol.XXXVIII.
Relief of Boston, 1774, Lancaster County Contributors to
 by H. F. Eshleman, Esq.
 L.C.H.S.Pub., Vol.XXVIII.
Revolution, The
 Klein, Dr.H.M.J., Lancaster County, Penna., Vol.II, Ch.XLIII
 and Appendix.
Revolutionary Soldiers and Patriots of Lancaster County
 by Mary Owen Steinmetz
 L.C.H.S.Pub., Vol.XXXV.
Revolutionary Soldiers at Donegal
 by Samuel Evans
 L.C.H.S.Pub., Vol.XII.
Revolutionary Soldiers and Patriots of Lancaster County
 by W. F. Worner
 L.C.H.S.Pub., Vol.XXXIV.
Revolutionary Soldiers Buried In Reamstown
 by Mrs. Mary Owen Steinmetz
 L.C.H.S.Pub., Vol.XXXVI.
Revolutionary War Pensioners Living In Lancaster County, Pa., in
1840, Notes on
 by H. F. Eshleman
 L.C.H.S.Pub., Vol.XXVII.
Tombstone Inscriptions, Lancaster County
 by W. F. Worner
 L.C.H.S.Pub., Vol.XXXIX.
Valley Forge During the Revolution, Lancaster County and
 by H. F. Eshleman
 L.C.H.S.Pub., Vol.XXXII.

War of 1812-1814:

Military Abstracts, 1792, re- to Lancaster County
 Penna. Archives, 6th Series, Vol.IV, pp.140-154
Military Activities in Lancaster During the War of 1812
 by W. F. Worner
 L.C.H.S.Pub., Vol.XXXV.
Militia Rolls of Lancaster County, 1783-1790
 Penna. Archives, 6th Series, Vol.III.
Muster Rolls of Penna. Volunteers, War of 1812-1814, with Con-
temporary Papers and Documents.
 Penna. Archives, 2nd Series, Vol.XII.
Muster Rolls of Soldiers from Lancaster Co. in the War of 1812
 by Mrs. J.V.R.Hunter and Mrs. Mary Owen Steinmetz
 L.C.H.S.Pub., Vols.XXXVI and XXXVII.
War of 1812, The
 Klein, Dr.H.M.J., Lancaster County, Penna., Vol.II,Ch.XLIV
 and Appendix, p.1141,1142.
War of 1812-15, and Mexican War
 Ellis and Evans' History of Lanc. Co., Chapter X.

The Mexican War, 1846-48
 Klein, Dr.H.M.J., Lancaster Co., Penna., Vol.II, Ch.XLV.

Civil War:

Christiana Riot (The), and the Treason Trials of 1851 -
An Historical Sketch
    by Hon. W. U. Hensel
    Press of New Era Print. Co., Lanc. 1911.
Christiana Riot (The): Its Causes and Effects, from a
Southern Standpoint
    by D. F. Magee
    L.C.H.S.Pub., Vol.XV.
Invasion of Penna. by Confederates under General Robert E.
Lee, and Its Effect Upon Lancaster and York Counties
    by George R. Prowell
    L.C.H.S.Pub., Vol.XXIX.
Lancaster County in the War for the Union
    by Hugh R. Fulton, Esq.,
    (Dr. Klein's History, Vol.II, Chapter XLVI, and App.,
    pp.1142-46)
Lincoln, Abraham, in Lancaster
    by C. H. Martin
    L.C.H.S.Pub., Vol.XXXVIII.
Slavery in Lancaster County
    Ellis and Evans' History of Lanc. Co., Chapter IX.
War of the Rebellion
    Ellis and Evans' History of Lanc. Co., Chapters XI
to XIX.

Spanish-American War, The:

    Dr. Klein's History, Vol.II, Chapter XLVII.

Lancaster County in the World War:

    Dr. Klein's History, Vol.II, Chapter XLVIII and App.

XXII.   BIOGRAPHICAL

Biographical Annals of Lancaster Co., Pa.
    Chicago, J. H. Beers & Co., 1903.
Biographical History of Lancaster County
    Dr. Klein's History, Vols.III and IV.
Biographical History of Lancaster Co., Pa.
    by Alexander Harris
    Lanc., Barr & Co., 1872.
Biographical Record of Lancaster Co., Portrait and
    Chicago, Chapman Pub. Co., 1894.
Biographical Sketches
    Ellis and Evans' History of Lancaster Co.
Biographical Sketches
    by Martha B. Clark
    L.C.H.S.Pub., Vol.IX.
Atlee, Col. Samuel J.
    by J. Watson Ellmaker
    L.C.H.S.Pub., Vol.II.
Barton, The Rev. Thomas
    by F. M. Barton
    L.C.H.S.Pub., Vol.XXX.
Buchanan, James:
    A Pennsylvania Presbyterian President
        by Hon. W. U. Hensel
        Lanc. 1907
    Attitude of James Buchanan Towards Slavery
        by W. U. Hensel
        Lanc. 1911

James Buchanan
 by W. F. Worner
 L.C.H.S.Pub., Vols.XXXV, XXXVI, XXXVII, XXXVIII.
James Buchanan - Diplomat, International Statesman
 by Hon. R. L. Owens
 L.C.H.S.Pub., Vol.XXXII.
Harriet Lane (Later Harriet Lane Johnson)
(James Buchanan's Niece)
 by Ida L. K. Hostetter
 L.C.H.S.Pub., Vol.XXXIII.
Letters of James Buchanan, Unpublished
 by C. H. Martin
 L.C.H.S.Pub., Vol.XXXVI.
Life of James Buchanan, 2 vols.
 by George Ticknor Curtis
Religious Convictions and Character of James Buchanan
 by Hon. W. U. Hensel
 Lanc. 1912
Rev. Edward Young Buchanan, D.D., Brother of the President,
 by Bertha Cochran Landis
 L.C.H.S.Pub., Vol.XXXII.
Story of Wheatland, The
 by Philip Shriver Klein
 Lancaster, Junior League of Lanc., Inc.
 Lancaster Press, Jan. 1936.
Works of James Buchanan, The
 by John Bassett Moore
 12 vols.
 Phila. and London, J.B.Lippincott Co., 1911
Crawford, Colonel James
 by J. W. Schaeffer
 L.C.H.S.Pub., Vol.III.
Fulton, Robert:
Robert Fulton, Addresses at Unveiling of Tablet on
House in which he was born
 L.C.H.S.Pub., Vol.XIII.
Robert Fulton and the Clermont
 by Alice Crary Sutcliff
 N.Y., The Century Co., 1909
Robert Fulton: His Life and Its Results
 by Robert H. Thurston
 N.Y., Dodd, Mead & Co., 1891
Robert Fulton, Life of
 by J. F. Reigart
 Phila., C.G.Henderson & Co., 1856
Journal of American History - Centennial of Steam
Navigation, 1807-1907
General Hand, Addresses at "Rockford", Home of
 L.C.H.S.Pub., Vol.XVI.
Henry, William (1729-1786), of Lancaster, Pa.
 by Francis Jordan, Jr.
 Lanc., New Era Print. Co., 1910
Herrman, Augustine, Lancaster County's First Map Maker
 by Dr. H. H. Beck
 L.C.H.S.Pub., Vol.XXXV.
Iron Masters of Caernarvon
 by T. Roberts Appel, Esq.
 L.C.H.S.Pub., Vol.XXIX.
Leman, Henry E., Rifle Maker,
 by Dr. H. H. Beck
 L.C.H.S.Pub., Vol.XL.
Mifflin, Lloyd - America's Greatest Sonneteer
 by E. Hershey Sneath, Ph.D., LL.D.
 Columbia, Pa., Clover Press, 1928

Mifflin, Thomas
    by Martha Mifflin
    L.C.H.S.Pub., Vol.III.
Muhlenberg, Henry E., Botanist,
    by Dr. H. H. Beck
    L.C.H.S.Pub., Vol.XXXII.
Porter, Colonel Thomas
    by R. B. Risk
    L.C.H.S.Pub., Vol.XXV.
Ramsay, Dr. David - Historian, Surgeon, Statesman
    by H. F. Eshleman
    L.C.H.S.Pub., Vol.XXV.
Ross, George, Addresses at Dedication of Memorial to,
    L.C.H.S.Pub., Vol.I.
Ross, George - A Poem
    by Blanche Nevin
    L.C.H.S.Pub., Vol.I.
Slough, Col. Matthias
    by Dr. F. R. Diffenderffer
    L.C.H.S.Pub., Vol.VI.
Steele, General John - Revolutionary Soldier
    by Susan C. Frazer
    L.C.H.S.Pub., Vol.XXV.
Stevens, Thaddeus:
    A Refutation of the Slanderous Stories Against the Name
    of Thaddeus Stevens Placed Before the Public by Thomas
    Dixon
        by Judge C. I. Landis
        L.C.H.S.Pub., Vol.XXVIII.
    Charity of Thaddeus Stevens, The
        by W. F. Gorrecht
        L.C.H.S.Pub., Vol.XXXVII.
    Life of Thaddeus Stevens
        by J. A. Woodburn
        Indianapolis, Bobbs-Merrill Co., 1913
    Thaddeus Stevens
        by Samuel W. McCall
        Boston & N.Y., Houghton, Mifflin & Co.
        Cambridge, Riverside Press, 1899
    Thaddeus Stevens
        by T. F. Woodley
        Harrisburg, Pa., Telegraph Press, 1934
    Thaddeus Stevens and Slavery
        by Judge B. C. Atlee
        L.C.H.S.Pub., Vol.XV.
    Thaddeus Stevens and the Southern States
        by H. L. Haldeman
        L.C.H.S.Pub., Vol.XVII.
    Thaddeus Stevens as a Country Lawyer
        by Hon, W. U. Hensel
        Address before Penna. State Bar Association, 1906
        Phila., Press of George H. Buchanan Company
    Thaddeus Stevens' Attitude Toward the Omnibus Bill
        by Dr. R. K. Buehrle
        L.C.H.S.Pub., Vol.XV.
    Unpublished Correspondence of Thaddeus Stevens, Some
    Hitherto
        by T. Richard Witmer
        L.C.H.S.Pub., Vol. XXXV.
  Stiegel:
    Baron Stiegel
        by Rev. M. H. Stine, Ph.D.
        Phila., Pa., Lutheran Pub. Soc. 1903
    Baron Henry William Stiegel
        by J. W. Sieling, M.D.
        L.C.H.S.Pub., Vol.I.

Henry William Stiegel's Land Holdings
    by Jacob Hill Byrne, Esq.
    L.C.H.S.Pub., Vol.XXXIX.
Sutter, General John A., The Life and Work of
    by Jacob B. Landis
    L.C.H.S.Pub., Vol.XVII.
Tanneberger, David - Organ Builder
    by Prof. Paul E. Beck
    L.C.H.S.Pub., Vol.XXX.
Wright, John - Pioneer Ferryman
    by Dr. H. H. Beck
    L.C.H.S.Pub., Vol.XXXV.

XXIII. GENEALOGIES

Audenried, with allied families of Musche, Wills, Wallace
and Fulton
    J. C. Audenried
    Phila. 1933
Bachman family
    DeFaust L. Bachman
Baer, Johannes, Genealogy of (1749-1910)
    D.M. & R.B.Bare
    Harrisburg, Central Print., 1910
Bard family
    G. O. Seilhamer, 1908
Barr, Martin
    Hon. W. U. Hensel
    L.C.H.S.Pub., Vol.II.
Becker family, Biographical History of
    Leah B. Becker
    Lititz, Pa., Express Print. Off. 1901
Blickensderfer Family in America
    Jacob Blickensderfer
Bomberger, Christian, Pioneer
    C. M. Hess
    Jeanette, Pa. 1923
Brenneman Genealogy (in preparation)
    Dr. A. H. Gerberich
    Dickinson College, Carlisle, Pa.
Brinkman, Otto Henrich Wilhelm, Descendants of
    I. H. DeLong
    Lancaster, 1905
Buchanan, Genealogy for 695 years. Presented to President
James Buchanan by Edward F. Sise
    Capt. McNeil, 30 pp.
Burkholder Family Reunion, Reports of
    7 pamphlets
Carpenter family
    Edwin Sawyer Walker
    Springfield, Ill., State Journal Co., 1907
Cunningham family from about 1748 to 1930
    Frances C. Harper, Francis A. Cunningham and Fern H.
    Bain
    Williamsport, Cunningham & Co., 1930
Diffenbach, Adam and Fraena (Fronica), Genealogical Chart of
    Milton Hess Diffenbach
    Bare, 1930
Dubendorf, John Michael, Descendants of (1695-1778)
    Dr. F. R. Diffenderffer
    Lancaster, 1910
Eberle, John - A Pennsylvania Dutch Pioneer
    pamphlets, Vol.IV.
Eby family, The Swiss
    Franklin Stanton Eby
    Chicago, 1923 and 1924

Evans family, Reprint from Notes and Queries
    Harrisburg Pub. Co., 1895
Ferree family, Genealogical Chart of
    Mrs. C. I. Landis
Forney family from Lancaster County
    John K. Forney
    Abilene, Kansas, 1926
Fulton family and related families of Ramsey, Kerr,
Hutchison, Watt and Miller
    H. R. Fulton, Esq.
    Lanc. New Era, 1900
Fultons of Lisburn, Memoirs of
    Sir Theodore C. Hope
    London and Bungay, Clay & Sons, Ltd., 1903
Funk family history
    A. J. Fretz
    Elkhart, Ind. Mennonite Pub., 1899
Galt family
    T. A. Galt
    Sterling, Illinois, 1910
Gleim, John Gottleaf Godfrey, Descendants of
    Lily Gleim Mentzer
    Harrisburg, Central Pub. Co.
Graff-Groff-Grove family, 1681-1900
    O. P. Grove
    Denver, Colo., 1900
Groff, Hans, Chart
Grubb family in America (Military Service only)
    G. F. P. Wanger
    Pottstown, 1914
Henderson Genealogical Chart
    Watson Ellmaker
    compiled by Milton Eshleman
Henry, John Joseph, Dr. Stephen Chambers Henry, Daniel Farr-
and Henry, Lineage of
    Wm. Louis Henry
    Detroit, 1909
Herr, Descendants of Rev. Hans, 1639-1908
    Theo. W. Herr
    Lancaster Examiner, 1908
Hershey family History
    Henry Hershey
    Scottdale, Mennonite Pub. Co., 1929
Hershey family, History from 1600
    Scott Funk Hershey
    New Castle, Pa., Petite Book Co.
Hess Genealogy
Hiester family
    V. E. C. Hill
    Lebanon Rept. Pub. 1903
Holliday family
    J. C. Holliday
    1931
Hoffer Genealogy
    Isaac Hoffer
    Mt.Joy, Pa., J.R.Hoffer, 1868
Houston family
    S. R. Houston
    Cincinnati, Elm St.Print. 1882
Huber-Hoover family history
    Harry M. Hoover
    Scottdale, Pa., Mennonite Pub. Co., 1928
Kagy Family, The
    Franklin Keagy
    Harrisburg, Pub. 1899

Keller family, Genealogy of the
  Jacob B. Keller
  Ephrata, 1899
Kuhns family, Notes on
  E. McFall Kuhns (35 pp.)
  Dayton, Ohio, 1934
Landis family of Lancaster County, The
  D. B. Landis
  Lancaster, 1888
Landis family reunion, Reports of
  Publication Com.)
Light family in America, The
  Moses Light
  Lancaster, 1896
Long family of Penna., The
  W. G. Long, Huntington, W.Va.
  Hunt. Pub., 1920
Lowrey family, Genealogy of the
  Samuel Evans
  50 pp. MS.
Ludwig Mohler family, Genealogical Chart of the
Mast, Bishop Jacob, A brief history of, and other Mast
Pioneers
  C. Z. Mast
  Scottdale, Pa., Mennonite Pub. House, 1911
Muhlenberg, H. M., Descendants of, 1783-1903
  Table
Nissley Family Chart
Omwakes, The
  G. L. Omwake and John Omwake
  Cincinnati, 1926
Patterson, James, of Conestoga Manor and his Descendants
  E. H. Bell and Mary H. Colwell
  Lancaster, Wickersham Print., 1925
Pfautz family
  John Eby Pfautz
  Lancaster, 1881
Postlethwaite family, 1750
  C. E. Postlethwaite
  L.C.H.S.Pub., Vol.XIX
Reist family
  H. G. Reist
  Schenectady, N.Y., 1933
Schneder family
  Pub. for the Reunion, Sept.15, 1921
Sehner ancestry, The
  S. M. Sener
  Lanc. 1896
Shank, Descendants of Adam Shank
  John Longenecker
  1908
Shirk family history and genealogy
  Henry Yocom Shirk
  Elkhart, Ind. Mennonite Pub. Co., 1914
Shuman, George, Family of
  Wm. C. Shuman
  Evanston, Ill., 1913
Snively, Genealogical Memoranda, 1659-1882
  W. A. Snively
  Brooklin, 1883
Spengler family, with Local Historical Sketches, 1150-1896
  Edwin W. Spengler
  York, Daily Pub., 1896
Stauffer, Descendants of Jacob Stauffer
  E. N. Stauffer
  1917

Strickler family
    Harry M. Strickler
    1924
Swarr family of Lancaster Co., Pa.
    J. M. Swarr
    Lancaster, 1909
Swope family
    Gilbert E. Swope
    Lanc., Cochran, 1896
Uhler family, from 1735
    G. H. Uhler
    Lebanon Report, 1901
Wenger, Christian, History of Descendants of
    Jonas G. Wenger, Martin D. Wenger, Joseph H. Wenger
    Elkhart, Ind. Mennonite Pub. Co., 1903
Wissler family, Record in U. S. and Canada
    Henry Wissler
    Toronto, Bryant Press, 1904.
Witwer family
    George Witwer and A. C. Witwer
    South Bend, Ind., Hardy, 1909.